The
Wild
Boy
of
Aveyron

The
Wild
Boy
of
Aveyron

Harlan Lane

Harvard University Press
Cambridge, Massachusetts
1976

Library of Congress Cataloging in Publication Data

Lane, Harlan L
    The Wild Boy of Aveyron.

    Includes bibliographical references and index.
    1. Wild Boy of Aveyron.   2. Mentally handicapped children—Education.
3. Deaf—Education. [DNLM: 1. Education of mentally retarded—History.
2. Education, Special—History.   3. Deafness.   LC4601 L265w]
GN372.L36   155.4′5′67   75-34080
ISBN 0-674-95282-0

For Fred, Roger, and Ursi

Acknowledgments

Professors F. S. Keller and Roger Brown first awakened my interest, more than a decade ago, in the wild boy of Aveyron and what we could learn from him about the nature of man and his language. This account of the wild boy and his teacher, Jean-Marc Itard, was written during my tenure at the Institut d'Etudes Linguistiques et Phonétiques, Université de la Sorbonne Nouvelle, and at the Department of Linguistics, University of California, San Diego. My work was aided by a grant from the American Council of Learned Societies. I am particularly indebted to Mme. Duhamel, Chief Librarian, Bibliothèque de la Faculté de Médecine, Université de Paris; to M. Delmas, Director of the Archives Départementales de l'Aveyron; to M. Barnard, Archivist, Institution Nationale des Jeunes Sourds de Paris; and to the Bibliothèque Nationale for placing their resources at my disposal. Ursula Bellugi, Edward Klima, Sanford Schane, Roger Shattuck, and Laurence Wylie all read the manuscript and made many valuable suggestions. I am grateful to them and to Joyce Backman and Franklin Philip, my discerning editors. Finally, I want to acknowledge Debbie Clauson's skilled and indefatigible typing of the manuscript.

Boston   H. L.
May 1975

Contents

DE L'ÉDUCATION

D'UN HOMME SAUVAGE,

OU

DES PREMIERS DÉVELOPPEMENS PHYSIQUES ET MORAUX

DU

JEUNE SAUVAGE DE L'AVEYRON.

Par E. M. ITARD, Médecin de l'Institution Nationale des Sourds-Muets, Membre de la Société Médicale de Paris, etc.

Quand on dit que cet enfant ne donnait aucun signe de raison, ce n'est pas qu'il ne raisonnât suffisamment pour veiller à sa conservation; mais c'est que sa réflexion, jusqu'alors appliquée à ce seul objet, n'avait point eu occasion de se porter sur ceux dont nous nous occupons..........................
.... Le plus grand fonds des idées des hommes est dans leur commerce réciproque.

CONDILLAC.

A PARIS,

Chez GOUJON fils, Imprimeur-Libraire, rue Taranne, Nᵒ. 737.

VENDÉMIAIRE AN X. (1801).

De L'Education
D'un Homme Sauvage
Par E. M. Itard

Jeté sur ce globe sans forces physiques et sans idées innées, hors
d'état d'obéir par lui-même aux lois constitutionnelles de son or-
ganisation, qui l'appellent au premier rang du système des êtres,
l'homme ne peut trouver qu'au sein de la société la place éminente
qui lui fut marquée dans la nature, et serait, sans la civilisation, un
des plus faibles et des moins intelligents des animaux, vérité, sans
doute, bien rebattue, mais qu'on n'a point encore rigoureusement
démontrée . . . Les philosophes qui l'ont émise les premiers, ceux
qui l'ont ensuite soutenue et propagée, en ont donné pour preuve
l'état physique et moral de quelques peuplades errantes, qu'ils ont
regardées comme non civilisées parce qu'elles ne l'étaient point à
notre manière, et chez lesquelles ils ont été puiser les traits de
l'homme dans le pur état de nature. Non, quoi qu'on en dise, ce
n'est point là encore qu'il faut le chercher et l'étudier. Dans la
horde sauvage la plus vagabonde comme dans la nation d'Europe
la plus civilisée, l'homme n'est que ce qu'on le fait être; nécessaire-
ment élevé par ses semblables, il en a contracté les habitudes et
les besoins; ses idées ne sont plus à lui; il a joui de la plus belle pré-
rogative de son espèce, la susceptibilité de développer son entende-
ment par la force de l'imitation et l'influence de la société.

The
Wild
Boy
of
Aveyron

The notes are arranged at the back of the book, keyed to the text by significant words and page number. References for every quotation, as well as for books, experiments, and persons the first time they are mentioned, appear in the notes. When a note gives more than a reference—for example, supplementary remarks or a list of relevant works—this is signaled in the text by an asterisk.

Chapter One

A
Wild
Boy
Is
Found

A search for knowledge—The wild boy is captured—He escapes and returns to society—Constans takes him home— Transfer to the orphanage—Bonnaterre requests the boy—As does the Society of Observers of Man—And the Minister of the Interior—Search for the boy's origins —Transfer to Rodez—Paris agog—What is the nature of man?—Man is an animal, but different in appearance, station, and speech—Man has innate ideas— Man is perfectible—The wild boy to resolve the controversy.

The Luxembourg Gardens are an island of calm, of lawns, gravel paths, fountains, and statues, in the heart of left-bank Paris. On a summer's day in 1800, two young Frenchmen from the provinces met there for the first time and joined together their lives and futures. Although neither could have said so, each was engaged in a search whose success required the other.

The first young man was well but not elegantly dressed in a long coat, drawn in at the waist, with full lapels. His curly hair fell in locks over a slanting forehead; his aquiline nose extended the plane almost as far as his jutting chin. Tightly drawn wide lips and large, dark brown eyes completed the Mediterranean features, set off by a broad white collar that rose funnel-like from his frilly white shirt. Jean-Marc-Gaspard Itard was twenty-six and had just become a doctor. He had left the barren village at the foot of the French Alps where he was raised and had come to Paris in search of a place for himself in the new social order that had emerged from the chaos of the Revolution. Paris at this time was vibrant: painting, theater, music, and literature were flourishing, abetted by the glittering salons of the very rich, the rendezvous of the intellectual and social elite. Medicine was surging ahead; it had become possible to protect people against disease by giving them some of the disease itself, although no one really knew why. One of Itard's teachers, Philippe Pinel, had just written the first book on psychiatric diagnosis, and had dramatically ordered inmates of the city's insane asylums to be unchained. The first anthropological society was formed, while expeditions returned with the flora, fauna, and inhabitants of Africa, Indonesia, and the New World, to the delight and fascination of naturalists, anatomists, and, above all, philosophers. Itard had left the relative isolation of the provinces in search of this excitement of senses and mind, to share in it, even to contribute to it if he could. His alliance with the strange boy rocking back and forth in front of him would surely bring him public attention; it might admit him to the ranks of the great doctors and philosophers of his time, or it might destroy his career right at its beginning.

3

The boy was twelve or thirteen years old, but only four-and-a-half feet tall. Light-complexioned, his face was spotted with traces of smallpox and marked with several small scars, on his eyebrow, on his chin, on both cheeks. Like Itard, he had dark deep-set eyes, long eyelashes, chestnut brown hair, and a long pointed nose; unlike Itard, the boy's hair was straight, his chin receding, his face round and childlike. His head jutted forward on a long graceful neck, which was disfigured by a thick scar slashed across his voice box. He was clothed only in a loose-fitting gray robe resembling a nightshirt, belted with a large leather strap. The boy said nothing; he appeared to be deaf. He gazed distantly across the open spaces of the gardens, without focusing on Itard or, for that matter, on anything else. That same day, he had ended a grueling week-long journey. By order of the Minister of the Interior, Napoleon Bonaparte's brother, Lucien, the boy had come to Paris from a forest region in the province of Aveyron in southern France. This journey was the latest development in his search, which began a year before when he clambered out of the forests, worked his way across an elevated plateau in the bitterest winter in recent memory, and entered a farmhouse on the edge of a hamlet. He exchanged the freedom and isolation of his life in the forests of Aveyron, where he had run wild, for captivity and the company of men in society. He came without a name, so he was called the Wild Boy of Aveyron.

Perhaps Itard knew better than the savants of his time, who expected to see in the boy the incarnation of Rousseau's "noble savage," man in the pure state of nature; perhaps he did not. What he saw, he wrote later, was "a disgustingly dirty child affected with spasmodic movements, and often convulsions, who swayed back and forth ceaselessly like certain animals in a zoo, who bit and scratched those who opposed him, who showed no affection for those who took care of him; and who was, in short, indifferent to everything and attentive to nothing." The society of the eighteenth century had held both young men at bay, depriving the first of the best it had to offer, depriving the second of everything. Itard sought to master the ultimate skills of his culture—trained observation, persuasive language, social grace—the boy, their rudiments. So be it: they would help each other. Educating the boy would be a test of the new science of mental medicine and a proof of philosophy's new empiricist theory of knowledge. It would give still more justification for social reform by showing how utterly man depends on society for all that he is and can be. If the effort succeeded, the nineteenth century would give them their proper place, where the eighteenth had not.

Much more than a century later, nearly two, I sat in the Luxembourg Gardens and wondered about the two young men who had met there. Off to my left, the National Institute for Deaf-Mutes, where Itard had taken the wild boy to live and to learn. There, in his efforts to train him, Itard created a whole new approach to education, centered on the pupil, closely adapted to his developing needs and abilities, seconded by instructional devices—an approach we have accepted so thoroughly as our ideal that we scarcely imagine any other or credit anyone with its discovery. Behind me, the Sorbonne, where Itard had defended the possibility of educating the boy against the judgment of the great philosophers and doctors of the time, who contended that the boy was left in the wild because he was an idiot, not an idiot because he was left in the wild. Behind me, and farther north, the Academy of Medicine, where Itard read his historic reports on methods for teaching the deaf and the retarded to speak—methods he had developed with the wild boy. In front of me and to the south, the Hospital for Incurables, where Itard's student, Edouard Séguin, set out to prove that idiots were educable, contrary to unanimous medical opinion; where George Sumner came to see Itard's methods in action, bringing them back to America to start the education of the retarded there; where, finally, Maria Montessori came, to end by extending Itard's methods to the education of the normal preschool child as well as the handicapped.

Thinking of these places close at hand, where the drama of Dr. Itard and the wild boy took place, shaping the lives of countless children up through my own time, imagining the excitement of another time when men affirmed, "Yes, the deaf *can* speak, the retarded *can* learn," when they believed that the only sure limit

5   A Wild Boy Is Found

to a child's knowledge is his society's ignorance, when they were convinced, as I am, of the perfectibility of man—thinking of these times and places one summer afternoon in the Luxembourg Gardens, I decided to begin my own search, to find Itard and the wild boy. I retraced their steps, gathering copies of letters and documents as I went. The town hall in Rodez and the regional archives for Aveyron, the boiler-room "archives" and library of the National Institute for the Deaf, the dusty attics of the Sorbonne and School of Medicine (with the priceless view of Paris rooftops accorded only to students and cleaning ladies), the opulent quarters of the National Archives and the Academy of Medicine, the corridors of the hospitals Bicêtre and Val-de-Grâce, a dozen other places but especially the cavernous hushed reading rooms of the National Library: these were my joyful haunts in every spare minute for two years.

Here is the outcome—a moving story about how a man and a boy helped each other in the search for knowledge, and how that search changed their lives and ours.

The story begins one day in 1797, in the fifth year of the new French Republic, when peasants in the region of Lacaune, in south central France, spied a naked boy fleeing through the woods called La Bassine. Curiosity aroused, they lay in wait on the following days and finally saw him again searching for acorns and roots. In 1798 he was sighted again by woodsmen and, despite violent resistance, taken to the village of Lacaune, where his arrival created a sensation. He was put on display several times in the public square, but the crowd's curiosity was quickly satisfied by the sight of the filthy mute urchin and, under relaxed surveillance, he was able to escape into the forest.

Over the next fifteen months, the wild boy was seen from time to time in the fields on the edge of the forest, digging up potatoes and turnips, which he ate on the spot or occasionally carried off. Several lairs were found and attributed to him, including one with a bed of leaves and moss. Then, on July 25, 1799, three hunters spotted him in the same woods, gave chase, and succeeded in dislodging him from a tree. Tied up tight, he was led back to Lacaune and entrusted to the care of an old widow. This devoted guardian, one of her contemporaries recounts, dressed him in a sort of gown to hide his nakedness and offered him various foods, including raw and cooked meat, which he always refused. He did accept acorns, chestnuts, walnuts, and potatoes, always sniffing them before putting them in his mouth. When not eating or sleeping, he prowled from door to door and window to window seeking to escape. After eight days, he succeeded.

This time the wild boy did not return to the forest. Climbing the nearby mountains he gained the broad plateau between Lacaune and Roquecézière, in the department of Aveyron. Through the autumn, and into a particularly cold winter, he wandered over this elevated and sparsely populated region, entering occasionally into farmhouses where he was fed. When given potatoes, he threw them into the coals of the hearth, retrieving and eating them only a few minutes later. During the day, he was seen swimming and drinking in streams, climbing trees, running at great speed on all fours, digging for roots and bulbs in the fields; and, when the wind blew from the Midi, turning toward the sky he rendered up deep cries and great bursts of laughter. Finally, working his way down the mountain along the course of the Lavergne and Vernoubre rivers, he arrived on the outskirts of the village of Saint-Sernin.* Encouraged perhaps by the treatment he had received from the farmers on the plateau, urged on perhaps by hunger, he approached the workshop of the dyer Vidal. It was seven o'clock in the morning, January 8, 1800. The boy slipped across the threshold into a new life, and into a new era in the education of man.

"Everyone in the neighborhood soon heard about [his arrival]," wrote Constans-Saint-Estève, the government commissioner for Saint-Sernin,

and everyone came *en masse* to see the child that was said to be a wild beast. I went there directly to evaluate the popular rumor. I found him seated in front of a fire that appeared to give him great pleasure but he was disquieted from time to time, which I attributed to the large gathering of people around him. I looked at him for some time without saying a word; then I spoke to him; and it didn't take long for me to realize that he was mute. When I noticed that he gave no response to the various questions that I put to him, both loudly and softly, I concluded that he was deaf.

I took him affectionately by the hand to lead him to my home; he resisted vigorously; but repeated caresses and particularly two kisses I gave him with a friendly smile decided him on the spot, and he trusted me a good deal from that time on.

Once back at the house, I thought he would be hungry, and I saw to it that he got something to eat. On the way back, people had tried to persuade me that the boy lived off roots and other raw vegetables. In order to confirm this or to learn his tastes, I had a large earthen plate prepared, with raw and cooked meat, rye and wheat bread, apples, pears, grapes, walnuts, chestnuts, acorns, potatoes, parsnip roots, and an orange. He confidently took the potatoes first and threw them in the middle of the fire to cook. He seized each of the other foods in turn, smelled them and rejected them. I told my servant to get more potatoes and he rejoiced in seeing them; he took them in his two hands and threw them into the fire. A moment later he reached his right hand into the coals and took out and ate the potatoes, while they were still burning hot. There was no way to make him wait until they had cooled off a bit; he burned himself, and expressed his pain by loud inarticulate sounds, which were, however, not plaintive. When he became thirsty, he looked left and right; spotting a pitcher, without making the least sign, he took my hand in his and led me to it; then he struck the pitcher with his left hand, thus asking me for something to drink. He was brought wine, which he rejected, showing great impatience with my delay in giving him the water.

This frugal lunch finished, he got up and ran through the door; despite my cries, he continued to flee so that I had a hard time catching him. I led him back without his making any sign of pleasure or displeasure. He had already interested me greatly as a hapless child; I began to have other feelings, those of surprise and curiosity. His refusal of bread and meat, his preference for potatoes, the sort of agreeable sensation he seemed to get from looking at an acorn that had been given to him and that he held in his hand longer than any other object, his air of satisfaction that nothing could trouble—except occasionally, although he was utterly destitute, the realization that he was deprived of the open air—led me to conclude that this boy had lived in the woods since his early childhood, a stranger to social needs and practices.

Constans-Saint-Estève was forty-one at the time. A native of Saint-Sernin, he was trained as a lawyer, then joined the governing board of the department of Aveyron, in the troubled last decade of the eighteenth century. He was sent as a deputy to the Legislative Assembly which convened in October 1791, in the dying days of the constitutional monarchy. Allied with the majority Girondins, he witnessed the growing pitch of violence in Paris. On the night of August 9, 1792, crowds assaulted the king's residence massacring some 600 loyal guards, and the Assembly voted to suspend the monarchy and create a new National Convention based on universal suffrage. Constans-Saint-Estève fled to his native village. Other Girondins, notably Condorcet, were later to flee under growing persecution by the Jacobins, which culminated in the Reign of Terror. When the Robespierrists fell and the Thermidorean reaction set in (1794), Constans-Saint-Estève surfaced and was appointed by the government as commissioner for the canton of Saint-Sernin.*

It was in this role that Constans took charge of the wild boy on January 9, 1800, and, the following day, sent him to the orphanage at Saint-Affrique. The *Journal des débats* published these letters two weeks later:

Variétés

Copy of the letter written [January 10, 1800]* by the government commissioner for the district of Saint-Sernin to the president of the administrative board of the children's home at Saint-Affrique:

I have ordered brought to your orphanage, Citizen, an unidentified child of twelve to fifteen years of age, who appears congenitally deaf and mute. Not only is he interesting because of his sensory losses, there is, moreover, something extraordinary in his behavior, which makes him seem close to the state of wild animals. In every respect, this interesting and unfortunate being invites the care of humanity, perhaps even the attention of a philanthropic observer. I am informing the government, which will probably consider that the child should be placed in the hands of the celebrated and respected Sicard, instructor of deaf-mutes.

Would you see to it that all possible care is provided; have the child watched during the day and bedded for the night in a room from which he cannot escape. Although I was able to win his confidence during the two days and two nights that I kept him under observation in my home, he incessantly sought an opportunity to flee. His usual and preferred nourishment, now that he is somewhat civilized, consists of baked potatoes; at the time of his capture he ate roots and raw potatoes.

I will shortly send you an official report containing in detail the circumstances under which the child was brought into my hands, the information I have acquired concerning his existence, and the grounds for considering him an extraordinary being.

Greetings and regards [signed] Constans-Saint-Estève.*

The following letter, which was addressed to us by one of the administrators of the Saint-Affrique orphanage, contains some details which can serve here in place of the official report promised by the government commissioner:

Saint-Affrique, 21 Nivôse an 8

I believe I should inform you, Citizens, of a phenomenal occurence which has preoccupied all the inhabitants of this community since this morning. Yesterday, a child who had been caught in the Lacaune woods by three hunters was led to our orphanage, of which I am one of the administrators. At the approach of the hunters, the child, who was nude, took flight and scrambled up a tree. He was led to Lacaune, from which he escaped. He was recaptured in some woods near Saint-Sernin and led to the home of Citizen Constans-Saint-Estève, government commissioner. The gendarmes who brought him confirmed that the child had been taken into custody just as I have described. It is certain that he lives only on potatoes and nuts. If given some bread, he smells it, bites it, then spits it out and throws it away. It is the same for all other foods. These facts leave no doubt that the child has lived in the woods for a long time. But how could he have withstood the rigors of the winter in the Lacaune woods? They are on the highest and coldest mountain in our region. The cold was more extreme this year than in [17]95. The child appears to be twelve years of age at most. He is nice-looking. His eyes are dark and full of life. He searches incessantly for a means of escape. We let him out this morning in a field next to the orphanage. He took to running on all fours. It we had not followed him closely and overtaken him, he would soon have reached the mountain and disappeared. He trots when walking. We made him a gown of gray linen. He does not know how to get it off, but this garment annoys him greatly. We have just let him free in the garden. Wanting to escape, he tried to break one of the strips of wood in the gate. He never speaks. When he is given potatoes, he takes as many as his pretty little hands can hold. If the potatoes are cooked (he prefers them thus), he peels them and eats them like a monkey. He has a pleasing laugh. If you take his potatoes away from him, he lets out sharp cries. Constans believes that he is deaf. We have just convinced ourselves to the contrary; at most he is hard of hearing. I leave to scholars the task of explaining this phenomenal being and of drawing conclusions. But I desire very strongly that this interesting child receive the beneficent attention of the government.

The local commissioner* at Saint-Affrique confirmed that the wild boy was completely mute when he arrived at the orphanage. In two weeks time, however, he was uttering various cries. Accustomed to running naked and to the vigorous winter weather on the plateau with an elevation of some 3,800 feet, he did not share his captors' first concern, to clothe his nakedness, and tore off whatever garments he could not slip off. At first he would not sleep in the bed provided, but gradually acquired the habit and even seemed to take pleasure in having the sheets changed. Although his preferred foods remained potatoes and nuts, he gradually came to accept a bowl of soup containing hunks of dark bread. As always, he would put nothing in his mouth without first smelling it. But shelter, food, a bed, warmth, and clothing seemed poor recompense for the loss of personal freedom, and the boy was always on the lookout for opportunities to escape. Twice he found them, and twice he was chased across the fields at full tilt. It was in these frenzied pursuits that he was seen to place his hands on the ground and run on all fours. Twice he was recaptured and led back to Saint-Affrique.

With the publication of the letters from Saint-Sernin and Saint-Affrique, word of the capture of the extraordinary wild boy spread rapidly, not only in the provinces but in Paris where several other newspapers and most of the intelligentsia took up the theme of the "enfant sauvage de l'Aveyron." Never was a name more unsuitable or so much responsible for later confusion. In the first place, the "enfant" was already an adolescent, some twelve to fifteen years of age. In the second place, he was from Tarn, not Aveyron, as we have seen. But most important is the label "sauvage," which could refer equally to wild animals, primitive people, such as Tahitians, and original man such as Rousseau's noble savage; the "enfant sauvage" was later to be identified with each of these in turn and was, of course, none of them.

When word reached Abbé Pierre-Joseph Bonnaterre, professor of natural history at the Central School for Aveyron, located in the department's seat, Rodez, he went to see the government commissioner and offered to leave at once for Saint-Affrique, in order to conduct a detailed examination of the wild boy. This was on January 23. Later in the year Bonnaterre published a learned paper, "Historical Notice on the Sauvage de l'Aveyron and on Several Other Individuals Found in the Forests at Various Times," which leads one to think that he was already quite familiar with the earlier, rather scantily documented cases of wild children and realized the importance of obtaining a precise, first-hand description of this child before his socialization progressed any further. Bonnaterre's career, from birth (in 1751 at Saint-Géniez) to ordainment (in 1779 at Rodez)—classical studies, philosophy, seminary—does not differ from that of the innumerable other priests who flooded France in this period. Soon after taking orders, however, his interest in natural science led him to Paris where he collaborated with other scholars on an *Encyclopédie méthodique,* a successor to Diderot and d'Alembert's *Dictionnaire des sciences;* he was responsible for the section on zoology. With the arrival of the Reign of Terror, Bonnaterre fled to Saint-Géniez where he was pursued with a warrant issued by the infamous Committee of Public Safety, and thus forced into hiding for over a year and a half. When the central schools were created, Bonnaterre was appointed professor at Rodez (May 16, 1796).*

Impressed by Bonnaterre's qualifications and arguments for studying the boy, and visibly annoyed that he had not been properly informed by his subordinate at Saint-Sernin of the wild boy's capture, the government commissioner for the department of Aveyron, J.-P. Randon, immediately sent off a letter to Constans-Saint-Estève:

> For several days now, Citizen, word has been spreading that there was apprehended in your district a child of twelve to thirteen who, by his manner, gestures, and appearance seemed to be a savage. This information, which up to now has had no official sanction, increasingly seems confirmed, leaving aside all the absurdities spun out on the theme. It appears that the reality of the fact cannot now be doubted, once stripped of everything that is contrary to sound reasoning. I am astonished that you have failed to inform me of a fact which under no circumstances

should be unknown to your administration and to me since, in the first place, it is a police matter and, in the second place, it is a matter of potentially greater interest to scientific observers and naturalists. On the assumption that the individual apprehended has remained a stranger to society, the administration considers that, in this case, he should be brought here, so that his first tendencies can be observed before he acquires specific ideas in this respect, either by habit or by instruction. The administration has charged me with communicating to you its wishes in this matter, which are quite distinct from those motivated by healthy curiosity, since its goal is to bring about investigations and useful observations which will be carried out by a professor of natural history.

Would you therefore, Citizen, take the appropriate measures without delay to fulfill the wishes of the district administration, or otherwise inform me of the falsehood of the rumor should it have no factual basis. P.S. Would you also kindly transmit a copy of my letter to the commissioner for the administration of Saint-Affrique, if the individual apprehended is, as I am assured, in that community. You will in this case request your colleague in my name to transfer this young man to Rodez without delay.

Bonnaterre was not the only one anxious to make scientific observations of the boy as soon as possible. Another abbé, Roche-Ambroise Sicard, the celebrated director of the Institute for Deaf-Mutes, was keenly interested, as Constans-Saint-Estève had anticipated in his first letter. Just a month earlier, Sicard had joined six others in founding a society of scholars devoted exclusively to the natural history of man. Under the motto *Connais-toi, toi-même* the society proposed, among other projects, "to unravel the origin and the different migrations of various peoples [and to] clarify the obscure points in our primitive history" by comparing the customs, languages, and activities of uncivilized peoples. L.-F. Jauffret, secretary of the Society of Observers of Man, sent a letter on January 29 to the orphanage at Saint-Affrique:

If it is true that you have currently in your orphanage a young wild boy, twelve years old, who was found in the woods, it would indeed be important for the progress of human knowledge that a zealous and sincere observer take him in charge and, postponing his socialization for a little while, examine the totality of his acquired ideas, study his manner of expressing them, and determine if the state of man in isolation is incompatible with the development of intelligence.

These interesting studies should be conducted in Paris, through the offices of my friend and colleague Sicard, instructor of deaf-mutes, and before the eyes of several other Observers of Man. They will bring public attention to bear on the boy and secure his future. It would thus be a worthy act on your part to take him to Paris. Following your reply, funds will be sent to you on the spot; if, to hasten his arrival, you were to make an advance, it would be reimbursed immediately.

Bonnaterre applied to the government commissioner for Aveyron, J.-P. Randon, to obtain the wild boy. Sicard did him one better, applying to the Minister of the Interior, Lucien Bonaparte, who sent the following curt note off to Randon, three days after Jauffret's request to have the boy brought to Paris:

> I learn from the newspapers that a young man has been found in the woods of your department who only knows how to utter indistinct cries and who does not speak any language. If this is the case, and if you have no hope at all of discovering the parents of this unfortunate boy, I claim him and request that you send him to me forthwith.

The wild boy had meanwhile been taken to Rodez,* in accord with Randon's instruction of January 23. He arrived on the fourth of February, so harassed by an enormous crowd of onlookers that he bit people who came too near. Bonnaterre and Randon launched a campaign to obtain reliable information about the boy's background and, especially, his abandonment. Randon wrote to Constans-Saint-Estève on February 5:

> Yesterday I received, Citizen Colleague, your letter of the 11th.* It arrived at the same time as that written by Citizen Guiraud while sending me the rustic child you had sent him.* This unfortunate being, whose origin it would indeed be interesting to know, is well suited to excite the curiosity of perceptive people and especially that of a naturalist; it appears from your letter that you have overlooked nothing in trying to discover everything about the boy that could serve the ends of an investigation by an enlightened observer, and the details provided by your letter could not be better described. One could wish that the boy's stay at Saint-Affrique had been less extended, since it appears that he has already been made to lose a part of his habits and ways of doing

things. Hardly had I the time to observe him for a moment than the crowd swarmed around him, and it was only with some difficulty that he was led within the confines of the Central School where we handed him over to Citizen Bonnaterre.

This scholarly naturalist will do everything that can contribute to satisfying the curiosity aroused by the young boy, and the care that the boy receives at his hands will compensate in part for the discomfort he is experiencing in his new way of life. I will carefully assemble all the observations concerning him, and it will be my pleasure to transmit to you all the knowledge I acquire. For all you have done for this unfortunate boy, and for the manner in which you have acted in his behalf, you have undeniably earned the right to the public's appreciation and my own.

P.S. I would like to know if the child was indeed found perfectly naked, if he was in this condition when seen in the woods several years before his capture, finally if anyone clipped his nails and cut his hair, and if it is true that someone saw him swimming. Give me the name of the person who can certify the boy's identity.

Now that proper arrangements had been made for the boy and measures taken to obtain further information, Randon prudently informed the minister, on February 10, of the boy's existence, adding:

While waiting for the time when I am able to convey corroborated details, I will simply transmit to you copies of the letters that were written to me on this subject. In a short time I will be in a position to communicate to you all the observations that will have been gathered by Citizen Bonnaterre, professor of natural history at the Central School of this department, to whose care we have confided the boy. This learned naturalist will overlook nothing that might help us to know the origins of this unfortunate boy, his tastes, his behavior, and the progress he makes as a result of the daily care provided. I entreat the concern and benevolence of the government in his behalf.

Two days later Lucien Bonaparte's demand for the boy finally arrived, and the next day yet another request from the minister. Randon, who may well have felt set upon by all this tumult in his normally tranquil province, sent off an appeal for information to his counterpart in the department of Tarn. He could hardly send the boy to Paris, as instructed, with a report containing a mixture of fancy, fact, and superstition. Worse yet, if the boy were subsequently found to be a fraud, as many in the capital were saying, or a recent runaway later reclaimed by his parents, heads would surely roll (even, conceivably, literally).*

With little reliable information yet in hand, and with Bonnaterre's detailed study of the wild boy just begun, the administration of Aveyron decided to resist the minister's decision to transfer the boy to Paris.

Citizen Minister,

We have received your letters of the 12th and 13th demanding the young child found in the Lacaune woods. We would immediately have taken suitable measures to fulfill your request had we not believed that it was necessary to submit certain observations to you.

This child was sent to us about twelve days ago. We entrusted him to Citizen Bonnaterre, professor of natural history, who is responsible for observing him, and to whom we have advanced some funds for clothing and feeding the boy. At the same time, we wrote to the communities where he is said to have been seen, to confirm the facts reported to us and to alert any relatives who might be in a position to claim him.

It appears certain that he is not a true savage; at most, he is an abandoned child, who lived in isolation in the woods or who did not, at least habitually, come into contact with society. The facts reported, those the professor of natural history has observed and those we have seen ourselves, are sufficiently contradictory for doubts to arise concerning the habits and ways of life of the child at the time he was found. The way in which he was found is not certain, and we must separate out the supernatural that exaggeration or ignorance has mixed into the account.

When we have received the information we have requested, when Citizen Bonnaterre has made more extensive and precise observations, it will be possible to make less wild conjectures. But if the child were subsequently to be claimed, the government would probably regret having transferred him to the capital. In any case, whatever his origin and his status, and while awaiting the reports that we will transmit enabling you to judge if he is worthy of the particular attention of the government, he is of great interest to humanity and deserves the full protection of the administration.

If, despite the observations that we have just presented to you, Citizen Minister, you continue to want to summon him at once without waiting for new information, would you kindly so instruct us and specify the method to be followed for his transfer; we will hasten to carry out your orders.

Greetings and respects,
Rogéry, Cambon, Passelac, Daudé, Combes

The minister wisely acceded to this request, giving Bonnaterre time to complete his detailed study of the *enfant sauvage* and the administration time to seek more information on the boy's background. Two fathers did in fact travel to Rodez to see the boy. One man had lost his son during a royalist revolt near Aveyron in the first year of the new republic; the other lost his during the seige of Toulon. Not too surprisingly, neither embraced the wild boy as his own. Rumor also had it that the boy was the illegitimate son of a *notaire* and was abandoned at the age of six because he was mute. But no more credence could be given to this story than to the many fictional accounts that now began to circulate. Five months passed, with little more learned about the boy's origins, when on Bastille Day in 1800 the formal order arrived to transfer him to Paris:

The Prefect of the Department of Aveyron decrees as follows:
Citizen Pierre-Joseph Bonnaterre, professor of natural history at the Central School of the Department of Aveyron, is notified to bring the child known by the name of Sauvage de l'Aveyron, whose description is given below, to the school of Citizen Sicard, instructor of deaf-mutes, by order of the Minister of the Interior.

The sum of 740 francs* is provided to Citizen Bonnaterre for travel expenses, in accord with the letter of the Minister.

Description of the child: Size——; age, approximately 12 years, hair and eyebrows, light brown; eyes, dark and deep-set; face, round; nose pointed; four scars on the face and one on the throat.

The wild boy of Aveyron left for Paris on July 20 accompanied by his guardian Clair Saussol, who was the gardener of the Central School, and by Abbé Bonnaterre. While scholars and laymen awaited their arrival impatiently (this was in the days before Paris emptied in August), the fiacre made its slow progress north, delayed en route at Moulins because the boy contracted smallpox—another milestone in his initiation into society. Eighteen days later, he arrived in Paris, to great acclaim. A sketch of his appearance and a presentiment of the tangled philosophical issues surrounding him may be had from an article published two days after his arrival, in the newspaper *Gazette de France* (and in the *Journal du commerce*).

This child called the "Sauvage de l'Aveyron," about whom the newspapers made such a fuss six months ago, who was awaited in Paris with justifiable impatience, excited by the memory of the wild girl Leblanc and other events of the same kind recorded in the proceedings of various academies—this child, who seemed never to arrive and who faded from conversation, arrived in Paris the day before yesterday, 18 Thermidor, at ten in the evening . . .

As yet we know very little about the child, who will now be the object of observations by true philosophers and who will surely be visited promptly by those who have long desired to raise a child cut off from all of society and all intellectual communication, a child to whom no one had ever spoken and who would be scrutinized down to the slightest movements he might make to express his first sensations, his first ideas, his first thoughts—if indeed one can think without fixed and conventional signs. That child has been found. There is no certainty yet whether he is a deaf-mute. He does not make, nor has he yet made, an articulate sound, not even to express his desires, which could not be more circumscribed. He has only a few cries, and a few manual and facial gestures. What will seem even more astonishing is that, although he spent a month in the hospice at Saint-Affrique, where he was treated like a beggar taken in from the streets, without collecting any of the observations that would have been so precious in those first days, he has not taken a single step toward civilization and is today as far from our customs and habits as he was on the first day he was found in some woods of the Department of Aveyron.

The boy has a nice enough body, reasonably well developed, but he is completely bundled up like a three-year-old child, although he appears to be twelve, since he has never been willing to tolerate any other garment. This sort of body sheath is encircled by a broad belt; he does not wear shoes and stockings and is unwilling to wear any. He normally sits on the ground and lies there as well to sleep, and it was only to oblige his old guardian, whom he appears to love very much, that he sometimes sits on a chair or consents to spend the night in a bed . . . He occasionally seems touched by the care he is tendered, and he offers his hand of his own accord to those who express any interest in him. But nothing can console him for the loss of his former freedom and his earlier way of life, and he seems as desirous as ever of escaping . . .

He is still in an almost purely wild state for, to repeat, he is as far now from the condition of other men as would be the subject of the experiment [in social deprivation] described above. Ample matter for reflection! For the moment, we leave this vast field open to our readers.*

The field was indeed vast: the wild boy was to help answer the central question of the Enlightenment, What is the nature of man?

There were three major issues, epitomized by the names of Linnaeus, Descartes, and Rousseau.* In his *Systema naturae* published in 1735, Linnaeus scandalously placed man and the primates within the same order. Man was at the top of the list, to be sure, in recognition of his privileged position in the animal kingdom, and the Book of Genesis was cited in the same connection, but this did little to appease Enlightenment philosophers who saw a "slippery slope" in the continuity of the species and its affirmation of the animal nature of man.

For example, Louis Daubenton, who edited the *Encyclopedia* to which Bonnaterre contributed, had this acid appraisal of Linnaeus' sixth edition:

> I am always surprised to find Man listed there under the general heading of quadrupeds. What a strange place for Man! What an unjust ordering! What an invalid method that places man at the rank of four-footed beasts! Here is the reasoning on which the order is based: Man has hair on his body and four feet, Women bring living children into the world and not eggs, and they carry milk in their breasts: therefore, Man and Woman are four-footed animals. Men and Women have four incisors in each jaw and nipples on their chests: therefore, Man should be placed in the same order, that is, at the same rank, as the monkeys, etc.

In the latter half of the eighteenth century, man found himself squarely in the company of wild animals, primitive people, and wild children (treated at length in later editions of Linnaeus' taxonomy). The mélange is more striking in French: *l'homme, les bêtes sauvages, les sauvages,* and *les enfants sauvages* were keeping company, and this served to sharpen such questions as, What makes us men? What are our relations with the rest of creation?

What are the criteria for membership in the human species? Is the difference between man and animal one of kind or one of degree? What can be learned from these beings that are at the same time like and unlike man? If men—not only scholars but laymen—found this humanoid diversity disquieting, they also felt that it might hold the key to an understanding of their own humanity. Buffon wrote in his monumental *Histoire naturelle,*

> Since it is only by comparing that we can judge, since our knowledge rests entirely on the relations that things have with others that are similar or different, and since, if there were no animals, the nature of man would be even more incomprehensible, after considering man in and of himself shouldn't we employ the comparative method? Isn't it necessary to examine the nature of animals, compare their structures, study the animal kingdom in general, in order to . . . arrive at the capital science of which man himself is the object?

The search for terms of comparison led out of society and into near and distant wilds. Numerous expeditions returned with samples of alien flora and fauna, including a parade of orangutans, gorillas, and chimps as well as Pygmies and Hottentots, all of whom were subjected to detailed naturalistic and anatomical observation. Orangutans (whose name comes from Malaysian and means *homme sauvage*) were especially prized. The president of the Berlin Academy of Sciences wrote in 1768: "It is in the isles of this sea that voyagers assure us they have seen wild men, hairy men with tails: a species intermediate between the monkeys and us. I would rather one hour of conversation with them than with the finest mind in Europe." Many of the finest minds in Europe were busy dissecting the same orangutans, and even proposed, to the outrage of the clergy, that one be mated with a prostitute. Rousseau wisely pointed out that such indignation took for granted just what the experiment was designed to test. Wild children were studied with equal zeal. Linnaeus reviews the scanty documentation of nine cases, but only a few were recent enough to be illuminating. Rousseau cites five examples: the wolf child of Hesse (discovered in 1344), the wolf child of Lithuania (1694), two children found in the Pyrenees (1719), and the wild child, Peter of Hanover (1724).

The woods rendered up another child who received wide discussion and study in Paris before the wild boy of Aveyron arrived: the girl of Sogny (1731), Mlle. Le Blanc.

Many of these studies in what later would be called physical and cultural anthropology were motivated and carried out by the adherents of a prominent school of philosophy around the turn of the century, called *Idéologie*. These philosophers and doctors, inspired by Condillac's writings, were committed to observing and experimenting with the broadest possible range of natural phenomena; they rejected the tradition in metaphysics which proceeded by abstract reasoning and deduction. They dominated the newly formed Institut de France, which was charged by the Convention with "recording discoveries and perfecting the sciences and the arts." Three "classes" superseded the academies of the old regime: the Class of Physical Science and Mathematics, with ten specialized sections; the Class of Literature and the Arts, with eight sections, including one devoted to linguistics; and the Class of Moral Sciences and Politics, whose very subdivisions reflected the influence of the Idéologues: analysis of sensations and ideas, moral philosophy, social sciences and legislation, political economics, history, and geography. These same scholars also founded the Société des Observateurs de l'Homme, which was to play a large role in the life of the wild boy of Aveyron. One of its major objectives was "to study the causes that differentiate one people from another, and that modify in various countries the original form and color of the human species [in order to] venture a systematic classification of the different races."

The growing body of comparative data and analysis tended to undermine the standing of the traditional criteria for manhood: human appearance, vertical station, and speech. The behavior of wild children was critical in the controversy. Mocking the first criterion, Locke relates the case of the Abbé de Saint-Martin who, when he came into the world, "had so little the figure of a man that it bespake him rather a monster. It was for some time under deliberation whether he should be baptized or not. However, he was baptized and declared a man provisionally, till time should show what he would prove." But savages, primates, and wild children all share with the abbé this lack of resemblance to the man in the street. The status of savages was decided once and for all by papal bull in 1537: the Americans discovered by Columbus were declared human. The status of primates was the subject of many anatomical studies and dissections of the skull, brain, larynx, hand, and foot, but a sharp dividing line was not forthcoming that avoided egregious errors in circumscribing the family of man. In the words of a leading naturalist of the times:

> The Orangs and Man have quite the same skeletons, with a hyoid bone, equal numbers of molars, a true face, and a physiognomy that reflects the slightest results of thought and the effects of sensations; the females in both cases carry one or two children from seven to nine months; the fingernails have the same shape in both cases, flat and rounded; they adorn the upper extremity of fingers that spread, structures that are excellent bases of comparison; there is equally a true foot with a sole extending to the heel.

The difference in appearance between man and animal seemed, therefore, more a matter of degree than of kind, especially when the most humanoid animals (the orangs) and the most animal-like humans (the wild children) were considered. Perhaps apes and wild children should be admitted to humankind provisionally, like the Abbé de Saint-Martin, until time would show what they are able to accomplish with proper training.

Vertical station, one of Aristotle's criteria, was no more satisfactory a dividing line between man and beast. Our naturalist continues:

> The arrangement of the thighs [in man and orang] attached to a large pelvis by powerful muscles that form pronounced cheeks, and the strength of the legs enhanced by more or less marked calves, determine in both cases the upright position of the body, in a word the biped gait believed to be a divine attribute. Thus Man is not the only one who walks upright and who "turning the majesty of his august face toward the heaven, holds to the earth only by his feet." If Plato had known the Orang would he then likewise have called him a heavenly Plant?

Some anatomists argued that man was originally quadruped and that the price for vertical station was susceptibility to many physical ills, including fatigue. Others argued that the upright position is phylogenetically prior to man. Still others, that it was the true frontier separating man from animal, for it liberated his hands for defense, prehension, and toolmaking. But vertical station was apparently natural for orangutans, and wild children were reported to be quadruped. Indeed, for Linnaeus it was one of the defining features of *homo ferus*. It is this controversy that explains why Nougairoles, Bonnaterre, and the *Gazette de France* were at pains to describe the peculiar gait of the wild boy of Aveyron, and especially his running on all fours.

Then there was the criterion of speech, which a philosopher of the era lyricized in these terms: "All that man has ever thought, wanted, done, or will do that is human on this earth depends on the movement of a breath of air, for if this divine breath had not inspired us, and floated like a charm on our lips, we would all still be running wild in the forests. So it is that the entire history of humanity, with all the treasures of tradition and civilization, is merely the result of the solution of this divine problem." Aristotle also considered language a criterion, and Descartes wrote:

> Of all the arguments that persuade us that animals are without thought, the key one is that, although animals have the ability to express their affections, never to this moment have we seen any animal arrive at the point of perfection of using a true language, that is to say, of expressing, either by voice or by gesture, something which can be related to thought only and not to natural impulse. Language is in effect the sole sure sign of latent thought in the body; all men use it, even those who are dull or deranged, who are missing a tongue, or who lack the voice organs, but no animal can use it, and this is why it is permissible to take language as the true difference between man and beast.

Still there seemed at first to be no reason why orangutans could *not* learn to talk if one were to teach them. In 1751 La Mettrie proposed just that, speculating that it would be easier than trying to give education and ideas to a congenitally deaf child. And he suggested that the method to follow was one of those used with these very children, thus presaging current psycholinguistic research in which chimpanzees are learning to communicate with the manual sign language of the deaf.* When later anatomical studies showed differences between the larynges of the orangutan and man, the naturalist J.-J. Virey, who was later to write a lengthy dissertation on the wild boy of Aveyron, had occasion to rejoice: "Observe with what wise foresight nature has distinguished man from the apes that resemble him the most. She did not want a beast joining in human conversations and so she created this artificial obstruction, these membranous sacs in the larynx of the orangutan to swallow up and muffle their voices. Thus, man alone can speak." No obvious impediment could be found, however, to the chimpanzee's acquiring spoken language, so the question remained open. (La Mettrie's experiment was not actually conducted until the twentieth century.*)

The behavior of wild children proved even more troubling for Descartes' most persuasive criterion, language. They were as mute as the apes, and most seemed to be irrevocably mute. Indeed, Linnaeus listed *mutus* as the second attribute of *homo ferus*, after *tetrapus* (quadruped). Had the wild boy of Aveyron turned out to be deaf, as Constans-Saint-Estève originally thought, his case would have been less critical for the issue of defining man. Such people are generally called *sourds-muets* in French, "deaf-mutes." But since he proved to have hearing and could even utter a few cries "on natural impulse," it was hard to see how he could be distinguished from an ape on the sole grounds of possessing language. Of course he might be able to learn it (but then so might an ape), and in any case, as the *Gazette* was at pains to record, he had made no progress in acquiring language during all the time he was at Saint-Affrique and Rodez.

If wild children were of great interest in the search for suitable criteria for defining man, their example was equally relevant to a second major controversy of the times, associated with the name of Descartes, the existence of innate ideas. Some had hoped unreasonably to learn from these wild children, as they had hoped to learn from deaf-mutes who later recovered their hearing, the secret of what man was like before language, what his ideas were like before they were filtered and shaped by convention. Did man have an innate idea of God? Such inquiries were frustrated, of course, by the wild children's mutism. The girl from Sogny, captured in 1731, after spending some years in the wild with a companion, did later acquire language. Her case was certainly the rare exception, which makes the lack of documentation all the more regrettable—the validity of the available descriptions is doubtful. In any event, when asked, she revealed that she did not initially have an idea of the Supreme Being. She rapidly acquired one, however, no doubt abetted by the nuns responsible for her care. Very rapid acquisition seemed a good augur to nativists then as now, and a contemporary philosopher concluded: "As soon as she heard men speak, she quickly learned to express her thought as they did; as soon as she was told about spiritual matters, she conceptualized them. It is because we are able to understand them—*divinorum capaces*, says Juvenal—that our reason comes from Heaven."

La Mettrie emphasized that these wild children and deaf-mutes, when interrogated, revealed that they had had no prior notions, no innate ideas: "Where then is this immortal share of divinity? Where then is this spirit so learned and enlightened which enters into the body, and which with the aid of instruction merely recalls to mind the knowledge that it had formerly instilled?" Since these children could not reason until they acquired language, it seemed that language was the precursor and substratum of thought. Jauffret no doubt wanted to test just such a proposition when he asked the orphanage at Saint-Affrique to delay the wild boy's socialization until an observer could "examine the totality of his acquired ideas [and] study his manner of expressing them." Condillac's prediction was explicit: "Gestures, signs, sounds, numbers, letters; it is with instruments as foreign to our ideas as these that we bring them into play to raise ourselves to the highest levels of knowledge . . . take away the use of all kinds of signs [from a superior mind], so that he cannot make even the least gesture correctly to express ordinary thoughts, and you will have an idiot." Would the wild boy arriving in Paris from Aveyron indeed resemble an idiot? How many of our innumerable discriminations, concepts, tastes, skills, fears, and desires would he lack and which ones would he prove to have natively or, in any event, without social intervention?

According to one view, in the third great controversy of the

Enlightenment that focused attention on wild children, man is nothing without society. Itard himself gave this moving description of man's social nature: "Cast upon this globe without physical strength or innate ideas, incapable by himself of following the fundamental laws of his nature which call him to the first rank of the animal kingdom, it is only in the heart of society that man can attain the preeminent position that nature has reserved for him. Without civilization he would be one of the feeblest and least intelligent of animals." This view could be confirmed empirically by studying a wild child with the most recent methods, to "determine what he is and deduce from what he lacks the hitherto uncalculated sum of knowledge and ideas which man owes to his education."

The opposing view, which Rousseau's name evokes, emphasizes the many ills that man contracts in the process of socialization. A wild child testifies to the extraordinary physical resistance of natural man, able to live naked and without protection in the most rigorous climate, enjoying robust health, free of the many vices of society. The point was not to deny the enormous influence of society on man: man is able to leave the state of nature and in collective life to become educated and to educate himself, but this predisposition may work for good or for evil—"this faculty of perfectibility or of degradation that only he possesses."

It was thus tempting to find in perfectibility the distinguishing characteristic of man. A profound belief in this human potentiality motivated many of the reforms brought about by the Revolution. But wild children proved once again to be an embarassment, since they were so refractory to education (orangutans, incidentally, were more readily trained). Perhaps the wild boy of Aveyron would be a suitable subject for the crucial experiment, which could for the first time be conducted properly, thanks to recent advances in metaphysics, specifically Condillac's insights into the origins of human knowledge.

Most philosophers rejected the concept of man in the state of nature, but for Rousseau and Kant there was an era in which "the state of culture necessary to family life did not exist," where man lived in the wilds and children did not emit the birth cry for fear of detection by predators. Was the wild child an atavism of the noble savage? Louis Racine, son of the playwright, thought so when he wrote about the wild girl from Sogny:

Scattered, fierce, and mute in earlier times,
Men wandered through the forests in all climes;
Clashing only with their fingernails for arms
They filled the woods with death cries and alarms.
The state of these our savage forbears in the wild
We see before our eyes in this young child.

Since he discusses five cases of social isolation, Rousseau had an idea, however poorly documented, of what wild children were like, and it is doubtful that he saw in their traits a throwback to the nature of man before it was uncorrupted or masked by artificial education. In the perspective of man as a social animal, the wild child does not pose a problem. However, if society is not the natural end of man but the fruit of an accident, then why should social isolation have such disastrous consequences? Thus most observers expected to find, with the wild boy of Aveyron, more evidence that man in the state of nature would be an ignoble savage; that, in any event, this state could never have existed because man is so patently disenfranchised of his humanity when outside society. If man is perfectible, it is only as a social animal.

The behavior of the isolated individual, then, promised to resolve this controversy, and nearly every philosopher had his isolated man, as the article from the *Gazette* implies. Rousseau preferred *les hommes sauvages*—members of primitive tribes—but they were hardly a good test case. Montesquieu had his Persian prince; Voltaire, Candide and a Huron indian. Buffon asked his readers to imagine an Adam reborn, a man "whose body and organs were perfectly normal, but who was born anew in all that concerned him and his environment." La Mettrie and Diderot thought something could be learned from the partial isolation of the deaf-mute. Condillac had his famous statue, replete with the structures of the human body but originally insentient, acquiring knowledge as the senses were awakened one at a time. The Society of Observers of Man proposed the normal infant as a proper subject of study to clarify the relation between the development of man and his physical and social environment. A prize of six hundred francs (the equivalent of about six hundred dollars today)* was offered for the best essay on the subject: "determine by daily observation of one or several children in the crib the order in which physical, intellectual, and moral faculties develop and up to what point this development is reinforced or opposed by the influence of the objects surrounding the child and by the influence, greater yet, of the persons who communicate with him." (A tall order—no psychologist has yet merited the award.)

In this large pool of real and imaginary subjects, the wild boy of Aveyron no doubt appeared one of the most promising. With proper observation and training he could clarify what is characteristic about man, his native endowment, and the relative importance of nature and nurture in his development. Apart from his relation to all the philosophical hubbub, the wild boy must have been intriguing in his own right. In his animal impulses, men could recognize, to their horror and fascination, the acting out of their own desires, unbridled by social constraints. The image of his life in union with nature could recall (falsely) moments of their own past, full of freedom and serenity, moments in which they too, perhaps, communicated with the universe. The wild child may have been a reassuring witness that, no matter how utterly a child is rejected by its parents, there is a benign nature that looks after all its children. The ubiquity and timelessness of such speculations cannot be doubted.

How else are we to explain the tales of Romulus and Remus, of the satyrs in Greek and Roman antiquity and up through the Middle Ages, and of the wild children in the Renaissance, when Shakespeare wrote:

> . . . a present death
> Had been more merciful. Come on, poor babe:
> Some powerful spirit instruct the kites and ravens
> To be thy nurses! Wolves and bears, they say,
> Casting their savageness aside, have done
> Like offices of pity.

How else are we to explain the *enfants sauvages* of the eighteenth and nineteenth centuries, Defoe's Robinson Crusoe and Kipling's Mowgli, Tarzan, and for that matter King Kong and the Abominable Snowman?

How else are we to explain the crowds of curious onlookers that beseiged the boy in Saint-Affrique, Rodez, and Paris? Why else indeed was he caught in the first place and put on public display in Lacaune? How else are we to explain all the space devoted to him in the popular press, not only throughout France but throughout Europe? A letter from an Irish peer in 1802 reads: "The Abbé [Sicard] gave us a long impassioned dissertation on the origin of idioms. The Young Savage of Aveyron, is amongst his pupils and begins to articulate. The story of this boy you have read in all the magazines." And laymen continue to read the story of this boy in novels, poems, and plays, to see it in films, and to hear it in song right up to the present.

Chapter Two

The
Savage
Described

*Bonnaterre's report—External appearance
—Gait—Senses—Speech—Instinct—
Nourishment—Intelligence—Character—
Regimen—Comparison with other
wild children.*

Pierre-Joseph Bonnaterre published his "Historical Notice on the Sauvage de l'Aveyron" in 1800, basing it on his study of the boy at Rodez. In its detail, scope, and emphasis it reflects the dominant philosophical trend of the period. This influence is more explicit in "Dissertation on a Young Child Found in the Forests of the Department of Aveyron, Compared with Savages Found in Europe in Diverse Eras, with Some Remarks on the Original State of Man," written by Itard's colleague at the hospital Val-de-Grâce, the distinguished naturalist, J.-J. Virey. Published later in 1800, the report is based on first-hand observation of the boy in Paris, on information related by the boy's caretaker at Rodez, and on Bonnaterre's "Notice." Taken together, these two documents give a fascinating account of the effects of social isolation and of the original repertory of behavior with which Itard would have to work in his later attempt to educate the boy. Much of the description also bears incisively on the philosophical questions we have already encountered.

For these reasons, Bonnaterre's account is worth reproducing here in its entirety, translated into English for the first time, with his own apology for its length: "This series of facts and observations will seem perhaps simple and minute, but vast and brilliant accounts can give only vague and imperfect knowledge; the little details, on the contrary, furnish exact and precise ideas." (Where Virey has something significant to add, it appears in parentheses.)

External appearance. From external appearance, this child is no different from any other. He is 136 centimeters [4½ feet] tall: he appears to be twelve or thirteen years old. He has a light complexion (He was dark-complexioned and well-tanned when captured; but several months of domestic life, repeated baths, and the smallpox he contracted when leaving Lyon for Paris have given him the skin color commonly found with all children of his age somewhat exposed to the sun); a round face; he has dark deep-set eyes; long eyelashes; brown hair; a long, somewhat pointed nose, an average mouth; a round chin; an agreeable visage and a pleasant smile. His tongue moves freely and shows no deformity. The teeth of the lower jaw are exposed and yellowish at the base. (His teeth were reportedly darkish; now they are almost white and a little yellowed at the base; his gums have greatly receded, no doubt because of the hardness of the foods that he ate; his lips and mouth are little and very mobile; the opening is fairly narrow.) His whole body is covered with scars, of which the greater part seem to have been produced by burns. There is one on the right eyebrow; another in the middle of the cheek on the same side; another on the chin; and another on the left cheek.

When he raises his head, there will be seen, at the upper extremity of the trachea and on the middle of the glottis, a horizontal scar of some 41 millimeters in length, which seems to be the scar of a wound made with a cutting instrument. Did some barbaric hand, having led the child into the wilds, strike him with a death-dealing blade to render his loss more certain and more complete? The whole length of his left arm, from the homoplat up to the middle of the forearm, we find six wide scars. Then there are several small ones on the shoulders near the right homoplat; a large one in the region of the groin on the same side; two or three just above the pubis; and several others on the legs and on the left buttock, including one rather round and deep one.

If these numerous scars are not an irrefutable proof of the bad treatment he suffered and of the attempts made to destroy him, they prove at least that he had no garments while he lived in the forest; and that his body must have been that much more vulnerable to scarring since he was not at all protected against the attack of animals, the mordant points of thorns, the cutting edges of rocks, and the density of the undergrowth. (He has no more hair on his body than any other child of the same age and complexion. The latter is rather flaccid and lifeless in our wild boy.)

(His sexual organs are moderately developed, a little less than those of children of the same age living in the city, for social development hastens their growth.)

[Gait.] (When walking, or rather when trotting more or less rapidly—for he does not normally walk steadily—he rocks from one side to the other, which greatly facilitates his progress, as it does with runners. He is never winded. When running rapidly, he leans forward; and when he escapes, he is not readily caught, unless a wall, a river, or the like stops him. He does not know how to swim. The people who caught him saw him take refuge in a tree to evade their pursuit. But he does not seem to climb habitually, as he has not been seen to go up a tree since then. He would not be afraid to jump from the second storey to flee, which he has done more than once; but too great a height frightens him.

I expect that one would like to know if this wild child crawled on all fours as reportedly did those from Bamberg, Hesse, and Ireland, etc. We cannot know what he did in the woods, but it is certain that he was only seen once to walk in this way, when he was exhausted, during an escape. I have examined his knees; they are no harder, more calloused, or more worn than any ordinary child's. It is very likely that he has always walked erect, except in a few rare instances and during infancy. According to Clair, his guardian, he has been seen, when dissatisfied somewhere, to drag along the ground rapidly on his bottom, propelled by his feet and hands.

This opinion that wild men walk on all fours seems to me extremely erroneous and contrary to our structure, although the celebrated anatomist Moscati has maintained it. The rear end would be too high if the knees were not bent, and the sole would not rest squarely on the ground since the feet would press only on the toes; however, on one's knees, the legs would get in the way behind. But that is not all: taking this position our face looks at the ground, and we could not see what is around us, or avoid danger, or find food at a distance. The position of the occipital hole is too far forward. Moreover, since the human head is quite large in proportion to the strength of the neck, it is quite heavy, and there is no cervical ligament, as in quadrupeds, to keep the head erect; supposing we were to walk on our hands and knees, the weight of the head would become overwhelming, as one can readily test. All these considerations are in conflict with Nature's purpose, which was to have us walk erect, no matter what Moscati, Monboddo, and others say. Otherwise, we would be the most poorly arranged of all the animals and we would inevitably become their defenseless prey.

The body of our young boy is reasonably well proportioned; his hands are of medium size and correspond to that of his body; he does not use the right sooner than the left. The skin on the inside of his hand, which I examined, is quite soft and not at all calloused or thick. His fingers are long, slender, well formed, and his fingernails strong and large; they were cut but have grown a lot since. His thumbs are a little larger in proportion to those of other children. The flexibility of his fingers in all directions is astonishing; one would even say they were dislocated, and he uses them with great skill.

He has moderately large legs, always bare; his feet are a little wide, his toes well developed, neither too spaced nor too compressed; the bottom of the foot is fairly hard, without being excessively thick. He turns his left knee a little inward.)

However serious his wounds were, there appears to be no significant external deformity; and if his right knee is turned somewhat inward toward the other and the leg outward, which gives him a vacillating and unstable gait, this should probably be attributed to rheumatism caused by the humidity and the severe cold he has experienced. (When he runs, he does not seem to pay much attention to his path; he does not falter, however, and he avoids obstacles without collision. He prefers shortcuts to the beaten track. When running, he swings his arms alternately, while keeping them half-bent, not hanging down. Whatever he carries in his hands, such as a large vessel containing a stack of walnuts or hazelnuts, etc., nothing falls or spills even though he runs very quickly; he has the skill of making it follow the rhythm of his rapid advance without jolting it. If he sees some woods, he makes every effort to escape into them, uttering cries of joy, desire, and distress.]

When he is seated, and even when he eats, he lets out a guttural sound, a dull murmur; and he rocks his body in an oscillatory movement from right to left or from front to back, holding his head high, his chin forward, his eyes fixed, and his lips closed. In this position, he occasionally undergoes spasms, some kind of convulsive fits, which seems to indicate that the nervous system is affected.

[Sensory process.] Otherwise, his organs seem normal and his senses good. Certain persons had believed that he was deaf, since he neither turns nor responds to shouts and questions addressed to him; but on reflection we can conceive that his ears, although normally formed, are much less useful to him because of his defective speech mechanism, which, in man, is an organ of communication that depends on the sense of hearing, and renders it active; in the individual in question here, this sense is almost entirely passive and without any link whatsoever to language.

It is true in general that those who lose some advantage in one sense recover it in the others; thus we note that the blind have a sense of hearing and touch which is superior to those of persons who see, either because nature has proportioned the discernment of the various senses for the welfare of the animal, or because frequent exercise has perfected these [remaining] senses in the same interest.

The truth of this generalization is confirmed in the present case. Since this child, by his type of life, is more like an animal than a man, the senses of smell and taste, which are the senses of the appetite, have become much more developed and perfected through exercise. It is by smell, which he employs regularly, that he recognizes what is suitable and what is contrary to his nature; it is by sniffing foods presented to him that he distinguishes those that he ought to take and those that he must reject.

Taste being an interior sense of smell and consequently more related to the appetite than any of the other senses, we can expect that this child also has a sense of taste more certain, more fine, and more exquisitely tuned than civilized man's. This conjecture is founded on the unconquerable repugnance that he has for certain foods as well as on the natural appetites he has which lead him unfailingly to choose those foods that suit him.

Keen, clear, and distinct perception of objects depends on the perfection of the organs of sight, and in this respect our wild boy is well endowed since he has quite normal eyes; but since visual judgments concerning his nourishment need to be corrected by the olfactory organ, they cannot be sure, and cannot serve as a guide to knowledge, except with the aid of smell; thus the sense of view, considered as a source of evidence, is more imperfect, or rather has acquired less perfection, in this child than in an individual who lives in society.

(Shiny objects attract his attention; thus he likes anything that glitters; but he does not put any value on it. If shown some coins, he selects the shiniest, the whitest, the silver rather than the gold or copper; but I have seen him readily prefer a walnut to all these metals.)

In a man gifted with great intelligence, the sense of touch is of first importance, because it is this sense which is most closely related to thought and knowledge; but in a severely limited and almost imbecile individual, governed more by appetite than by knowledge, the sense of touch must be considered of secondary importance. (Our wild boy is ticklish, and he likes to be tickled, especially when he has eaten well or when he is in bed. When someone stops tickling him, he grasps their hand to get them to continue. He has a very pleasant laugh.)

Thus we have the order of the senses as nature seems to have established them in the wild boy who is the object of these observations: the sense of smell is first and most perfected; taste is second, or rather these two senses are but one; vision occupies the position of third importance, hearing the fourth, and touch the last. The sensations also follow the same ordering; that is, the child is most moved by impressions of smell and the greater part of his judgments, of his evaluations, depend on these dominant sensations; those of the other senses, less strong and less numerous, are subordinated to the former and have only a secondary influence on the nature of this individual.

Speech deprivation. Among the writers who have tried to sort out the distinctive attributes of the human character and to define the line that separates nature from art, several have represented man in his primitive state as limited to purely animal feelings, without any use of those faculties that make him superior to the beasts, without any means of communicating his feelings, and even entirely deprived of voice and those gestures so appropriate for the expression of ideas: our wild boy justifies a part of these conjectures; he employs, in truth, some signs that he has learned since his entry into society, in order to make known his principal needs and the means that can satisfy them; but he is entirely without the gift of speech and makes himself heard only by cries and inarticulate sounds. Perhaps this is due to a structural flaw in the voice organs; perhaps it is the result of the wound he received on the glottis. But even supposing that he formerly spoke, it is certain that, having remained for some time out of all communication with humans, he would have lost the use of speech. A California boy, twelve years of age, who had lived with his father in the desert, knew so little of his maternal language, which was highly defective itself, that when found some years later, all that he retained was limited to a very small number of words. Selkirk, a Scotsman, forgot his language and even lost the ability to speak, having spent five years alone on the island of Juan Fernández.

(Although the tongue of this young wild boy is normally formed, and does not cleave to the palate, he has no language other than some inarticulate sounds. His expressive sounds, rarely emitted unless he is emotional, are rather noisy, especially those of anger and displeasure; when joyful, he laughs heartily; when content, he makes a murmuring sound, a kind of grunting. He does not utter raucous or frightening cries; almost all of them are guttural and depend only slightly on the movement of the tongue. He makes only a few natural signs, such as those associated with strong emotion; but he has learned other, conventional signs since his capture. The sounds that he makes lead us to suppose he is not mute, even though mutes may utter a few cries. His neck wound, located where several muscles travel from the tongue to the hyoid bone, may be suspected as an obstacle to articulate language.)

Instinct. Consigned by nature to instinct alone, this child performs only purely animal functions: he has no knowledge whatever of those artificial passions or those conventional needs which become as demanding as natural needs: his desires do not exceed his physical needs. The only blessings he knows in the universe are nourishment, rest, and independence. Age has not at all developed that impetuous passion which torments and perpetuates all living beings; he has not yet experienced the sentiment of love. All his sensations then are concerned uniquely with procuring necessary food, with the allure of liberty, or with the sweetness of rest. If he displays a few ideas, these have as their object his means of subsistence; if we recognize in him some element of reason, he applies it only to his own needs; if it seems that he has some traces of memory, he uses memory only in relation to self-preservation. The mind of a man deprived of the commerce of others is so little exercised, so little cultivated, that he thinks only in the measure that he is obliged to by exterior objects. The greatest source of ideas among men is in their human interactions.

(How could he possibly be expected to have known the existence of God? Let him be shown the heavens, the green fields, the vast expanse of the earth, the works of Nature, he does not see anything in all that if there is nothing there to eat; and there you have the sole route by which external objects penetrate into his consciousness. It is astonishing how thoroughly this one idea absorbs him completely; he is always looking for something to eat, and he eats a lot. I am quite surprised that he does not have dozens of attacks of indigestion and that he can digest so many things that are raw, hard, wild, bitter, etc. Habit is truly a kind of nature, and this young man is indeed fat. You might say his mind is in his stomach; it is his life center. The scholar, the philosopher, on the contrary, live entirely in their heads. I am embarrassed to find natural man such an egoist; but I must report matters as they appeared to me.)

His affections are as limited as his knowledge; he loves no one; he is attached to no one; and if he shows some preference for his caretaker, it is an expression of need and not the sentiment of gratitude; he follows the man because the latter is concerned with satisfying his needs and satiating his appetites.

The shrillest cries, the sounds of the most harmonious instruments, make no impression on his ear, or at least he appears to be insensitive to them, and he shows no perception of the noises made next to him; but if a cupboard that contains his favorite foods is opened, if walnuts, to which he is very partial, are cracked behind him, this noise strikes forthwith the organ of hearing and he will turn around to seize them. (Thus a walnut broken behind him, a dog that barks out of sight, a door that is opened in the dark are heard quite well by our young boy; but let someone speak, cry out, sing, play music, talk to him, make a deafening noise in his ears, as I did, and he pays no attention; he shows no indication of surprise, above all, if he is eating; if something does not bring him either pleasure or pain, he does not care about it at all.)

Nourishment. All those who examined the child at the moment of his entry into society are agreed that he had a very pronounced distaste for bread, meat, soup, and that he only ate potatoes, raw chestnuts, and acorns. During his stay at Lacaune, at the end of Messidor an 7 [July 1799] he learned to cook his potatoes, and since that time he does not eat them without having laid them in the fire. At Saint-Affrique he began to eat rye bread, soup, beans, and walnuts.

In the first days he spent at Rodez, he ate only roasted or half-burned potatoes, raw chestnuts, and walnuts; subsequently he went back to eating rye bread and soup. In the month of Prairial [May–June] he had developed such a taste for meat that he ate it raw or cooked indifferently. Finally, the foods he desires the most at present are green peas, broad beans, and green walnuts.*

This ever-present need of nourishment sharpens his connection to the objects around him and cultivates a certain measure of intelligence. He was constantly occupied during his stay at Rodez in shelling green beans; and he fulfilled this task with an expertise appropriate to the most practiced man. Since he knew by experience that these kinds of vegetables were destined for his own subsistence, as soon as he was brought a bunch of dried stalks, he went to get a jug or an earthen pot and laid out the scene of this operation in the middle of the room. There he distributed his materials as conveniently as possible. The pot was placed to the right and the beans to the left: he opened the pods one after the other with an inimitable suppleness of movement. He put the good beans in the pot and rejected those that were moldy or tainted. If by chance a bean got away from him, he kept his eye on it, picked it up, and placed it with the others to be cooked. As he emptied the pods, he piled them up next to him symmetrically: and when his work was through, he took away the pot, added water, and put it next to the fire which he fueled with the pods he had piled up. If the fire was out, he took the shovel and placed it in the hands of Clair, signaling him to go looking for some nearby coals. As soon as the pot began to boil, he showed his impatience to partake of the meal he had prepared himself, and his entreaties were so urgent that it was necessary to serve up the beans less than half cooked—which he ate with avidity.

When he felt like eating hash-browned potatoes, he chose the largest, brought them to the first person he found in the kitchen, tendered a knife to cut them into slices, went to find a frying pan, and pointed out the cupboard where the cooking oil was stored.

In the last few days of Ventôse [March 1800], he was given some sausage, which he sniffed, as was his habit, and which he ate voraciously thereafter. The next day, a captain of the auxiliary battalion of Aveyron, who was dining in the room where the child was, signaled him to approach, by showing him a little piece of sausage he had cut from a larger piece on his plate; the young man approached to accept the offer that had been made. With his left hand he took the morsel that the captain held between his fingers; with the other hand, he adroitly seized the rest of the sausage on the plate.

To observe the impression produced by the sight of the countryside, I led him one day to the home of Citizen Rodat at Olemps, some distance from Rodez. All had been arranged for his welcome; beans, potatoes, chestnuts, and walnuts were prepared. The abundance of food gave him a great deal of pleasure and, without paying any attention to the people around him, he seized the beans, which he placed in a pot, added water, and brought the pot next to the fire. With the shovel, he spread out the embers and threw in the potatoes, and he detained Rodat's sister next to him in order to help him prepare the food. While waiting, he was given some walnuts and chestnuts; next he had to have some potatoes and beans, and when he was quite satiated he took the leftovers in his gown, went into the garden, and with that foresight common to all animals who are exposed to shortages, hid them and buried them in the earth, undoubtedly in order to retrieve them later in case of necessity. (If he has more nourishment that he can consume, he gathers it together and goes off to store it, to hide it, to bury it in the ground, without ever forgetting it the following day; in this respect, his memory is infallible. It must have been in this way that he stored food during his solitary life; he never considers that he has too much, and he seems thus to have some foresight for future needs in making these hidden stockpiles.)

For some time now, when he enters a kitchen, he is in the habit of going at once to the fireplace or the stove and examining all the pots arranged around the fire; he raises each of the pot covers in turn; and if he should find in one of them some bouillon made with meat, he dips some bread into it and immediately puts it to his mouth. But as this act of gluttony was severely reprimanded by the woman responsible for his care, he tried to hide this from her and waited for the moment when she was distracted by other household duties, in order to dip the bread in the pot, which I saw him do one day five or six times in a row without being caught.

During the course of our journey to Paris, we had taken care to put in a knapsack a small provision of rye bread, potatoes, beans, and walnuts—both because we were not certain to find any in the inns along the route; and because, rushed to leave, we never did have the time to cook them. The child thus knew that his sack held his food and he gave it his particular attention; he always kept it next to him when he was seated; and whenever we changed carriages or arrived at an inn, he stopped in front of the door and would not enter the lodgings until preceded by this object of his dearest affection.

The first time we gave him a mirror, he looked immediately behind it, thinking to find there the child whose image he perceived: at the same time, a young man who was alongside and a little behind him offered him a potato. In his impatience to grasp the food that had been offered to him, he moved his hand toward the mirror; but he saw that he was further than ever from his goal; thus, without turning his head, he extended his hand behind him, a little to one side, and placed it just on top of the hand that proffered the potato.

Suspicion of imbecility. All these details and many others that we could add establish that this child is not totally without intelligence, reflection, or reasoning; however, we are obliged to say that in all those cases where it is not a matter of meeting his natural needs or of satisfying his appetite, we find only purely animal function: if he has sensations, they do not give rise to ideas; he does not even have the faculty of comparing them among themselves. One would say that there is no connection between his mind and his body, and that he reflects on nothing; consequently, he has no discernment, no imagination, no memory. This state of imbecility is reflected in his gaze, for he does not fix his attention on any object; in the sounds of his voice, which are discordant, inarticulate, and can be heard night and day; in his gait, for he always walks at a trot or a gallop; in his actions, for they lack purpose and determination.

(The somewhat frightened gaze of the young Aveyronnais does not fix on anything apart from his nourishment or the objects he seeks to avoid or take; in these cases a confident glance, a fast look, suffices, for he seems to have sharp vision. He distinguishes very well from afar between those who give him food and those from whom he expects nothing.)

(I have not, however, detected any clear sign of idiocy in this young man; I have found only the profound shadowy ignorance of a simple soul, who no doubt appears quite stupid next to a Parisian of the same age, well-brought-up and sharp-witted. I believe, moreover, that it may prove impossible, even for the renowned Sicard, to remove completely this inertia in the mind of the boy.)

Character. When he is flattered and caressed, this young man is sweet and complacent; if he is signaled to approach he does so. (He seems insensitive to expressions of affection; he does not know what it is to be caressed. When kissed, he does not notice whether it is a man or a woman and, to put it better, he does not care about it at all. While not wicked, he is not good, for he is unaware of both. He never does a mischievous or spiteful act, like children of his age; his caretaker has never seen him do anything of the sort.) If a hand is extended, he puts out his own, but he withdraws it brusquely, like a monkey; when on the contrary he is made impatient, when he is provoked, he makes movements of frenzy and anger: he moves his arms, legs, and head with agitation. He places his closed fists over his eyes and strikes his head with vigor. At the same time he lets out cries that announce his vexation, and occasionally skillfully bites those who are the cause of his rage. (When, impetuously, he wants to eat, go to bed, or flee, he sets about it vigorously and displays impatience, eagerness, anger. If he is thwarted, he loses his temper, becomes agitated, prances with rage, strikes his head, bites, nips, scratches, weeps, and cries out.)

(He detests children of his own age and runs away from them without fail. This aversion comes originally, perhaps, from his having been pursued when living in the forests, for it appears that the village boys got sight of him more than once, according to the rumors that circulated in the districts where he wandered.)

(The young Aveyronnais is naturally distrustful and on his guard unless he thinks the people around him are indifferent to him; however, he has not been struck at all since he was captured. If he is afraid of something, he throws himself in the arms of his caretaker and pushes him urgently toward his room, where he tries to close himself in and remain alone. He likes solitude a great deal; crowds irritate him and make him uncomfortable and temperamental; he avoids them as much as possible. When he is alone, he is happy to sleep, for he has nothing to do after he has eaten, and he almost never plays by himself; he does not even know what recreation is. He is indifferent to all childish amusements; he finds them alien, strange, insipid. He likes to run bits of straw between his teeth while sucking the lightly sweetened marrow that they contain—that is his favorite amusement.)

(I wanted to know if this child of nature would be content with his share if I put him with another person and gave them each an equal proportion of the same food—if he would respect that of his neighbor as property not belonging to him. But nothing of the sort transpired; he has no idea of property, wants everything for himself alone, because he thinks only of himself. Thus he is much inclined to theft, and quite adroit at stealing; when eating at the table he takes everything that he wants from his neighbors, quickly and stealthily, even though he has those foods already. But he never steals anything other than food; everything else, silver, gold, the most precious jewels, have no value in his eyes... One would think that he shows some gratitude toward the man who feeds him. Not at all; he takes the food from the kindly hand that offers it as he would take it from the ground; it is not that he thinks he is owed what is given to him, but rather that he seems to believe his benefactors do not know how to do otherwise. He accepts gladly when spared the trouble of preparing or peeling his food; but he does not pay attention to the fact that no one is obliged to do it, that he should show at least some appreciation, that he is served by the hand of a pretty girl, etc.)

(Is our young Aveyronnais capable of pity?—he who focuses everything on himself, who never encompasses the objects that surround him in his own existence? It is useless to ask, since he lives only for himself. His caretaker has never seen him show any sign of pity ... However, this question would be of the highest importance to resolve, in order to know the original tendencies of the human heart. Personally, I venture to believe that if this young man could come out of his intense moral lethargy, if he could bring some interest to bear on the things around him, then he would be inclined to commiserate as much as children ordinarily are.)

Regimen. It would probably have been imprudent to reform precipitously the kind of life that the child had taken up in the forests; and too sudden a change could have brought about his destruction or at least could have altered his health, as did happen to the girl from Chalons.* Consequently, since the 15 Pluviôse [February 4, 1800] he has followed his inclinations and his tastes without interference.

Despite the liberty he enjoys and the ease with which he can obtain his preferred foods, he is always looking to escape and takes advantage of every occasion on which he finds the door open to get away. He has already escaped four or five times from Rodez; but happily he was always retaken, sometimes at considerable distance from the town. During our trip, he also made several unsuccessful attempts at escape.

The presence of fire always produces an agreeable sensation for him; he shakes his hands in signs of joy; he roars with laughter; he draws up his gown as far as his belt, the better to feel the heat. When one cries out in a loud voice "For shame!" he drops his robe back over his knees at once; but a moment later he raises it again.

This eagerness to warm up and the pleasure he displays near a fire made me suspect that the child had never lived, as some would have it, in a state of absolute nudity during a winter as severe as the one that we have just experienced; I could not imagine how an individual who had tolerated such severe cold could also be so sensitive to impressions of heat; but some experiments I performed have removed all my doubts and my uncertainty. One evening, with the thermometer at four degrees below zero [25 F.] I undressed him completely and he appeared glad indeed to be rid of these garments. Next I pretended to take him out into the open air; I took him by the hand through the long corridors, up to the main door of the school building; instead of showing any reluctance to follow me, he dragged me out of doors by repeated yanks. From this I conclude that these two facts are not at all incompatible: he can be indifferent to impressions of cold and find pleasure in the gentle effects of heat, since we see dogs and cats with the same habits. (He was made to wear a jacket, but he prefers to be naked, even during the cold of winter . . . He was dressed in breeches, but they bothered him; he could not put up with them and he defecated in them. He seems to be insensitive to extremes of cold and heat; however, I have seen him prefer the shade to the sun, and he likes to warm up.)

During his stay at Rodez he slept in a dry room in which the windows were covered with linen, because he had broken the panes. His bed was made of some bundles of straw, and he had for covering only a linen sheet, with which he enveloped his body. Although this covering was quite light, he never was cold during the winter's rigors—I confirmed this by running my hand over his arms and legs, which I always found comfortably warm. I also noticed that while sleeping he pressed his two closed fists over his eyes and his face against his knees . . .

(This young boy sleeps a lot, but never very deeply, during the day as well as during the night, according to his needs or desires. He never snores. When captured, he went to sleep only late at night, when overcome by drowsiness; but he stayed asleep until ten or eleven in the morning. I suspect that this habit of staying up came only from his boredom in captivity for, before going to sleep, he stood at the window, pressed against the grating, gazing at the countryside. At first he slept anywhere, sleeping just as well on the bare earth as in bed; but now he prefers the straw and huddles up with one sheet, which he has learned to wrap around him. Sometimes he dreams and becomes agitated, as if he were vexed. He usually has these dreams after a lot of people have visited him during the day. He sleeps bareheaded, without a nightshirt, wrapped up in a sheet. At first he rolled into a ball to sleep, but he has learned to stay stretched out in the bed. When he wants to go to sleep, he rocks for a little while. I have these details from his caretaker, who slept with him. In bed, he is calm and well behaved.)

His sleep is very light, and he wakes at the slightest knock on the door. When the wind of the Midi blows, his bursts of laughter can be heard during the night and, from time to time, other vocal sounds that express neither pain nor pleasure.

He normally wakes at dawn: then he takes a sitting position, his head and the rest of his body wrapped in his blanket; he rocks back and forth for a while, lying down at intervals, until it is time for breakfast. During these periods, which could be called recreation times, he wants neither to get up and start the day nor to leave his room.

At nine o'clock at the latest, the door of his room is opened; he goes into the rooms of his caretaker; he is given rye bread, roasted potatoes, walnuts and chestnuts, green peas and uncooked broad beans. If it is cold, he warms himself up for an hour or so, crouching on his knees like a monkey; then he goes back to his room where he remains until lunchtime.

This meal, which he eats around eleven o'clock, consists of soup with bread and sometimes a piece of meat, sometimes potatoes or beans. Water is his usual beverage; up to now he has refused to drink wine.

If he gets his finger or some other part of his body wet, when eating soup or through some other accident, he uses ashes rather than cloth to wipe up. This seems to be sufficient for his instinct of drying off. (When his hands are sweaty, he sprinkles them with dust or ashes; he does likewise to his face, and in general he does not like wetness.)

Sometimes after lunch he is taken for a walk. In the winter he stays by the fire, but every day around two o'clock he eats some bread, chestnuts, potatoes, or vegetables. After this snack, when he has no beans to shell, he retires to his room, stretches out on the straw, wraps himself up in his blanket and rocks back and forth or goes to sleep until six o'clock in the evening.

Then he has supper, sometimes meat, sometimes vegetables; potatoes, kidney beans, and broad beans are served at all meals.

When it is time to go to bed, nothing can stop him; he takes a torch; he points to the key to his room; and he becomes furious if not obeyed.

He eats daily about two pounds of rye bread and a like quantity of roots or vegetables.

His winter garments include a shirt, a jacket, and a little gown that comes to his knees. His head and feet were bare all winter long. When he goes to bed, he sets aside those garments worn during the day and takes those provided for the night.

This sort of life seems favorable to his development and his health. He has grown a lot during his stay in the community of Rodez; his body is stronger (He is putting on a lot of weight, but he was excessively thin when first caught . . . He is fairly big, and his new way of life has caused him to grow several inches rapidly); and he has had only a severe cold or other such slight indisposition. (He is not scarred from smallpox; this illness was benign and passed without incident although he would not eat anything during it. He refused to eat for two days; he was sad and troubled. He was not given any medicine and he recovered very well in a few days, although the journey must have disagreed with him and the movement of the coach displeased him . . . His pulse is fairly strong and has a normal rate.)

When he first came from Saint-Affrique he had the habit of relieving himself wherever he happened to be; but nowadays, when necessity calls, he generally signals to have the door opened; he goes out; and he goes in a courtyard or in some other spot provided for this purpose. (If he feels the need to defecate, everywhere is the same to him, in his room or out of doors, in front of everyone or alone; however, he never soils himself in bed. Animals also keep their sleeping places clean. It is curious that he always squats to urinate and stands erect to defecate; now he has been taught to go outside for that.) He coughs and never spits.

Comparison with other wild children. The facts and observations we have just cited show that there is a close analogy between the customs of this child and those of other children. The first and second time he was captured, he was entirely naked; when he came to take refuge at the home of Citizen Vidal, he had only a few shreds of a shirt, just like the child from Hanover; and like him his body was covered with scars.

He has white skin, an agreeable physiognomy, and a slender body, like the wild children of Lithuania and Ireland and the girl from Châlons.

He has had trouble getting accustomed to taking nourishment from ordinary foods, like the child of Lithuania. He selects by smell those foods that suit him, like the children of Ireland and Hanover and like Jean of Liège.

At the time of his capture and even during our trip, when he found a fountain or a rivulet, he lay down on his stomach and drank, putting his chin into the water right up to his mouth, like the girl from Châlons. Like her, he despises all sorts of clothes, and is always looking to escape.

He has been seen, when tired, to walk on all fours like the wild children of Hesse, Ireland, and Bamberg. He defends himself by biting, like the children of Lithuania and Bamberg. Like the child of Lithuania found in 1694, he shows only feeble signs of reason. He has no articulate language and perhaps will have the same difficulty in speaking as the children found in Ireland, Lithuania, and Hanover. Like the child of Hanover and the girl of Over-Yssel, he is gentle, complacent, and lets himself be caressed.

Finally, like all the wild children of whom we have just spoken, he has lived for some years in the forest far from men; and this is the most curious and most interesting feature of his history. The fact appears to be established by accounts from responsible sources, by the scars that cover his body, by his habit of smelling foods, of biting, of walking on all fours, of refusing bread and meat, of crouching on his knees like a monkey, of running always at a trot or gallop, of hiding excess foods in the earth, of relieving himself wherever he happens to be, and of remaining almost entirely naked.

[Virey cites the following characteristics in common with one or more wild children: dark skin (initially), scars, large thumbs, leanness, sensitive hearing, mutism, guttural sounds, frightened look, eats raw meat, detests children, walks on all fours, climbs trees.]

Such an astonishing phenomenon will furnish philosophy and natural history with important ideas about the essential nature of man and the development of his intellectual faculties, provided that the state of imbecility we have noticed in this child places no obstacle in the way of his instruction. But every success may be hoped for from that philosopher-teacher who has worked such miracles in this kind of education; and we must hope that the child who has just been confided to his care will become perhaps one day the rival of Massieu, Fontaine, and Mathieu.*

(Few children of the same age as our wild boy are as destitute of knowledge; he is in the greatest possible ignorance of everything that has no relation to his life and well-being. If it were not for his human face, what would distinguish him from the apes? Basic drives occupy his entire existence. He is truly and purely an animal, limited to simple physical sensations; he does not yet have anything beyond that. What enormous barriers separate him from us! What a long way he has yet to come!

Go forth, poor youth, on this unhappy earth, go forth and lose in your relations with men your primitiveness and simplicity! You lived in the bosom of ancient forests; you found your nourishment at the foot of oaks and beech trees; you quenched your thirst at crystal springs; content with your meager destiny, limited by your simple desires, satisfied with your way of life beyond which you knew nothing, this usufruct was your sole domain. Now you can have nothing except by the beneficence of man; you are at his mercy, without property, without power, and you exchange freedom for dependence. Thus are poor-born three fourths of the human race: nothing but bitterness was prepared for you in tearing you away from the protective dryads who watched over you. You had only the one need of nourishment. How many others that you will be unable to satisfy will now relentlessly assail you? How many desires will be born in your footsteps, and will grow with the tree of your knowledge and with your social ties? How utterly you will lose your independence, bound with our political shackles, caught in our civil institutions; you should truly weep! The path of your education will be sprinkled with your tears; and when your pristine soul again turns toward the azure vaults of the sky, when you discern the order and the beauty of this vast universe, what new ideas will germinate in your young head! When love at last opens to you the gates to a new way of life, oh how many new and delicious sensations, how many unknown passions will trouble your vulnerable heart! Oh, may you live happily among your countrymen, may you, man without pretension, display the sublime virtues of a generous soul and transmit to future generations this honorable example, as an eternal proof of what can be done by a student of innocent Nature.)

Chapter Three

A
Dispute
over
Diagnosis

*Itard becomes a doctor—Leaves for Paris
—An urgent call to the Institute for
Deaf-Mutes—The Abbé Sicard despairs—
Itard appointed resident physician—Will
train the wild boy—An idiot because left
in the wild or left in the wild because an
idiot!—Pinel, the first psychiatrist—Pinel's
report—His examination of the boy—
Description of children in the asylums—
Comparison with other idiots—Diagnosis:
idiocy—Prognosis: a hopeless case.*

It must have been a curious encounter that day in August 1800, when the two young men from the provinces met in the Luxembourg Gardens. The boy seemed "indifferent to everything." And how did Itard appear to the boy? To judge from Bonnaterre's observations, it is doubtful that he noticed him at all. The meeting was in the first place an instance of pure serendipity.

Itard had been born in Oraison, Provence, only twenty-six years earlier, on April 24, 1774. Were it not for the events leading up to the Revolution, he would have become a successful banker. His father, a merchant and master carpenter, member of the petite bourgeoisie, had the means to provide him with a better education than could be found in a village. At the age of eight, Itard was sent to school at Riez, the district seat, where his paternal uncle was canon of the cathedral. After the boy completed some years of largely classical studies, Abbé Itard recommended his nephew to his colleague, Abbé Isnardy, at the Collège de l'Oratoire in Marseilles. Subsequently he returned to Riez to complement his studies in science.*

Revolutionary France was becoming increasingly embroiled in war. When Edmund Burke denounced "the cannibal philosophers of France," he was expressing not only the hostile sentiments of conservatives in England but of monarchists throughout the Continent. Under the constitutional monarchy in France, Louis XVI declared war on Austria, perhaps in the hope that military victories would restore royal authority. By the end of 1792 France had three republican armies in the field; a few months later the National Convention, the popularly elected legislature, declared war on England and Holland, and called up 300,000 men. The following August found Itard, nineteen, as an apprentice at a Marseilles bank when a *levée en masse* was proclaimed; all unmarried men between the ages of eighteen and twenty-five were liable for immediate military service. If this was the beginning of modern universal conscription, Itard responded in a way that has become equally classic. The French respect a man who knows *le système "D."*—how to operate—and Itard displayed, as he would so often in his career,

51

more than the usual measure of this skill. He knew how to take advantage of good fortune, in this case a fortuitous friendship between his uncle, the canon, and a certain Citizen Arnoux from Riez, who was director of a military hospital, temporarily moved to Soliès when the British occupied Toulon in September. Itard, who had never been in a hospital or opened a medical book, became a health officer overnight. When Toulon was recaptured from the British four months later, Arnoux returned to take charge of the military hospital there and brought with him the young man whom he had been coaching, now raised to the rank of surgeon third-class. Assigned to headquarters of the Armée d'Italie, Itard was responsible over several months for public health on the island of Port Cros, facing Hyères, on the Mediterranean coast.

Eighteen months after Itard's transfer to Toulon, the distinguished surgeon Dominique Larrey arrived from Paris to head up the medical corps of an expedition destined for Corsica to bring this island, which had just declared its independence, back into the fold. Before embarcation, Larrey offered courses in anatomy and pathology, which Itard followed avidly. When the expedition was canceled, Larrey returned to the military hospital in Paris, Val-de-Grâce, and Itard followed soon after, in 1796. He took up duties as surgeon third-class in the former Benedictine abbey, just a few blocks down the Faubourg Saint-Jacques from the former seminary of Saint-Magloire, which the Convention had converted into the National Institute for Deaf-Mutes in 1794.

What were Itard's aims in leaving the provinces for Paris? To emulate his mentor, Larrey, and to pursue his instruction, surely; but more generally to extend the range of his ideas, to integrate himself into the extraordinary social and intellectual life of the capital.

Not long after Itard's arrival at Val-de-Grâce, an examination was held for a post as surgeon second-class: Itard won out over his more conventionally trained competitors. One day early in 1800 a student was hurt at the Institute for Deaf-Mutes. Abbé Sicard sent out urgently for the nearest doctor, and the twenty-five-year-old surgeon arrived. Apparently the student recovered, for a friendship sprang up between the novice physician and the renowned linguist-educator.

A few months later the wild boy was delivered into Sicard's hands. The abbé must have been disappointed. Here was no docile city child with a hearing loss who could be taught the language of signs and initiated into the mysteries of the Supreme Being. This was no Massieu who would one day address a learned society in the language of the deaf. If this was not clear in August, it surely must have become clear by the end of the fall. "Many people otherwise commendable for their insight," wrote Itard, "forgetting that the more a man is separated from society and from his early childhood the more imitation is difficult and his sense organs inflexible, believed that the education of this individual would be a matter of a few months, and that he would soon recount the most interesting stories concerning his earlier life." After the natural philosophers stopped coming to see the *enfant sauvage*; after the boy had shown no progress that would allow some hope for his instruction; after distinguished observers repeatedly cited the signs of congenital idiocy, the abbé finally embraced this diagnosis. Idiocy was well known to be untreatable. Itard's friend, the philosopher-philanthropist Baron Joseph-Marie de Gérando, was undoubtedly referring to Sicard when he wrote in an unpublished manuscript: "Some enlightened men also shared this erroneous belief [in the boy's idiocy]. Certain people, having tried their methods of instruction out on him without success, concluded that he could not be instructed, rather than suspecting inadequacies in the methods themselves, methods that were justified by success in quite different circumstances." Still the Institute and its celebrated director had contracted an obligation—to the boy, says Itard, and, one would add, to the government.

So, Sicard created the post of resident physician at the Institute and appointed Itard on December 31, 1800. As the new year arrived, the young physician took up the training of the *enfant sauvage*. It was just one year earlier that the wild boy had entered the workshop of Citizen Vidal.

Itard was indeed ready to attempt the education of the *enfant sauvage*, even when others were pessimistic or convinced of its futility, because he had already formed opinions on the metaphysical questions of the Enlightenment; in particular, he held to the sensualist philosophy expounded by Etienne Bonnot, Abbé de

Condillac, in his *Essay on the Origin of Human Knowledge.* A man without language, according to Condillac, depends on the sight, sound, and direct sensory experience of objects or events to evoke the corresponding ideas. Since he has no recourse to signs that designate these objects, he cannot imagine them in their absence, cannot recall them, and cannot contemplate their properties and relations, thus creating new and abstract ideas. He cites the case of the deaf-mute boy from Chartres, recorded in the annals of the Academy of Sciences in 1703, who at twenty-three recovered his hearing, acquired speech, and answered questions on the ideas he had been able to form without language. "He led a purely animal life," the report states, "totally concerned with tangible and present objects, and with the few ideas he received visually. He did not even derive from the comparison of these ideas all that he might have. It is not that he lacked intelligence; but the intelligence of a man deprived of the commerce of others is so little exercised and cultivated that he thinks only in the measure that he is forced to by external objects. Most of man's ideas come from his commerce with other men." Itard could find an even closer parallel in the case Condillac cited eight years later in his *Treatise on the Sensations,* the wolf boy of Lithuania: "When I say the child showed no signs of reason, I do not mean that he could not reason sufficiently well to look after his own preservation, but that his thoughts had been necessarily applied to this single object and he had never had the occasion to trouble himself with the things that occupy us."

So the *enfant sauvage* was not necessarily defective; he needed language if he were to perform the higher mental processes, and he needed occasions to trouble himself with the "things that occupy us"—that is, he needed acquired drives. Cut off from society, from social intercourse and from language, having lived in the wilds for nearly half his life, the savage was nothing other than what he had to be. Itard reasoned:

If it were proposed to solve the following problem of metaphysics, to "determine what would be the degree of intelligence and the nature of the ideas of an adolescent who, deprived since infancy of any education, had lived entirely separated from individuals of his own species," then unless I am greatly mistaken, the solution of the problem would be as follows: There should first be assigned to that individual nothing but an intelligence relative to the small number of his needs and one deprived by isolation of all the simple and complex ideas we receive from education, which combine in our mind in so many ways solely by means of our knowledge of signs. Well, the mental status of this adolescent would be that of the wild boy of Aveyron, and the solution of the problem would consist in exhibiting the extent and the cause of his intellectual state.

Itard stood virtually alone in this sanguine analysis of the wild boy's bizarre behavior. He was contradicted by nearly every member of the Society of Observers of Man, most notably by his former teacher, Philippe Pinel, the leading authority on mental disorder, medical director of the Paris asylums for the insane, the man many consider to have been the first psychiatrist. Pinel, twenty-nine years older than Itard, came to Paris in 1778 after medical studies at Montpellier. To make his way in the capital, he became a journalist, hobnobbed with the social and intellectual elite at the salon of Madame Helvétius, taught geometry, and pursued the mechanical analysis of bodily movement.* A distinguished essay in competitive examination on the treatment of the insane led to his appointment as a physician at the Bicêtre Hospital in 1792.

During this period, all the mentally ill in the Paris region were screened at a hospital in the center of the city, Hôtel-Dieu. Its cavernous halls received alike the insane, the epileptics, and the mentally retarded. The treatment consisted of cold baths, bleedings, and purges. If patients showed no improvement in a few weeks, the men were sent to Bicêtre and the women to La Salpêtrière, two asylums located in the outskirts. Here patients were chained in filthy cubicles, without air or light. Many cells were below ground level, humid and rat-infested. Disease was rampant. About a fifth of the patients were naked. At Bicêtre, clothing was made and given to calmer patients, while used clothes were given to the more agitated. The patients slept on the ground on straw. The diet was bread and soup daily; meat on Sunday, Tuesday, and Thursday; a fifth of a liter of peas or beans on Monday and Friday;

an ounce of butter on Wednesday; and an ounce of cheese on Saturday. There was no treatment.*

Pinel introduced a series of reforms at Bicêtre and then at La Salpêtrière, of which the most celebrated was the unchaining of patients (straitjackets were used instead, where necessary). He published a series of articles in the 1790s on the treatment of insanity, but his highly analytical mind was concerned foremost with developing a systematic classification of its various types, much in the spirit of *Idéologie*. In 1798 Pinel published his *Philosophical Nosology*, proposing five great classes of all illnesses and four types of mental illness in particular: mania, melancholia, dementia, and idiocy. Soon after the wild boy's arrival in Paris, Pinel's *Treatise on Insanity* was published, in which he characterized idiots as "destitute of speech or confined to the utterance of some inarticulate sounds. Their looks are without animation; their senses stupefied; and their motions heavy and mechanical." To Pinel it was obvious that the wild child, who shared so many of these traits, was indeed an idiot. As for etiology, the boy was not an idiot because he was abandoned in the woods; he was abandoned in the woods because he was an idiot. Life in the woods cannot itself produce idiocy; after all, the savages of Indonesia and Africa, a popular subject of study at the time, led an uncivilized life in the woods and did not behave as idiots do. Thus Pinel called the wild boy a *prétendu sauvage*—a fake savage—and considered him a true idiot, recognized by heartless parents for what he was. Had not Bonnaterre already voiced his suspicions of the boy's imbecility? But for Itard the wild boy was a *prétendu idiot*: the idiocy was not real because the boy had lived isolated in the wild. Bonnaterre had already given ample examples of the boy's foresight, cunning, and dexterity.

The Society of Observers of Man appointed an impressive commission to study the boy and report its observations: Pinel, unequaled authority on mental disease; Sicard, linguist, educator, and director of the Institute for Deaf-Mutes; Jauffret, secretary of the society and naturalist; De Gérando, philosopher and author of a prize-winning four-volume treatise on language and thought; Cuvier, the most celebrated anatomist of his time and secretary of the Academy of Sciences. Two days before Itard was appointed resident physician at the National Institute for Deaf-Mutes, the society met and Jauffret read the commission's initial report, prepared by Pinel, concerning the "child known by the name of *sauvage de l'Aveyron*." The report was lost, despite insistent searches by scholars who thought it would hold the key to a proper evaluation of the wild boy's original behavior and his later progress—or lack of it—under Itard's tutelage. If the boy was demonstrably retarded from birth, then he could no longer prove the importance of environment for normal development. Itard was accordingly misled, and some of the failures of his treatment become immediately understandable and imputable to the student rather than to the teacher; but some of his successes become all the more remarkable. The dispute concerning the diagnosis of the boy has continued to this day without benefit of Pinel's firsthand observations and evaluation.

I recovered the Pinel report in 1973. It took a few hours' reading of Pinel's biographers to prepare a list of all the societies to which he belonged—on the premise that he would probably address a society of which he was a member. It took a few days' more work to search out the minutes of these societies. Unable to find those of the Society of Observers of Man, I scanned the journals of the Society of Anthropology, which revealed that it was descended from the Observers of Man and that it discovered the Pinel report among its archives in 1911, whereupon it published the report in its journal. I quote it here at length.

> Report to the Société des Observateurs de l' Homme concerning the child known by the name of "Sauvage de l'Aveyron," by Ph. Pinel, Professor of the School of Medicine and Member of the Society.
>
> For some time public attention has been fixed on a child that was found running wild in the woods of one of our departments in the Midi, and who was reduced to the most rustic state possible. The natural interest that children of this age always inspire, combined with the idea of complete abandonment and the extreme dangers that were the consequence, has renewed interest in the history of other children who, in various epochs, were reduced to the same degree of isolation. We congratulated ourselves on witnessing one of these phenomena which normally can be examined only at some distance and concerning which we still have only vague and inaccurate reports. Certain scholars, those who are concerned particularly with the history of human understand-

ing, were delighted at the possibility of studying the rudimentary character of man and of finding out the nexus of ideas and moral sentiments which are independent of socialization. But soon this brilliant perspective disappeared, confronted with the highly circumscribed mental faculties of the child and with his complete inability to speak. A stay of several months in the National Institute for Deaf-Mutes has given no sign of progress or of perfectibility and, however circumspect we should be in prognosis, there seems to be no evidence for a more happy outcome in the future. So it was necessary to abandon the direction taken by our colleague Bonnaterre, who examined the case of this child in relation to that of so-called wild children, concerning whom we have only very incomplete information or exaggerated reactions. Thus we have restricted ourselves here simply to revealing and drawing parallels among facts that are easy to obtain and verify.

It has been noticed that the so-called wild boy of Aveyron had several characteristic traits in common with many children whose sensory functions or intellectual faculties are more or less impaired and who are condemned to vegetate sadly in our asylums, since they are not susceptible to any training. Beginning with this observation, the proper course of analysis is straightforward: we should begin by describing the current intellectual state of the so-called wild boy, and follow this with detailed descriptions of a certain number of children whose sensory functions or intellectual faculties are more or less damaged. The other part of the memoir, which will be kept for another meeting, will have as its object to bring together the facts previously set forth and to report the inferences that follow naturally.

I. Current state of organic functions and of intellectual faculties of the child known under the name of wild boy of Aveyron.

His eyes do not seem to fix with any attention except on the objects of his subsistence, or on the means of escape available when he is in a room; in all other circumstances, he lets his gaze wander vaguely and without showing any direct intention, except for those things that momentarily surprise him. A cameo caught his attention one day and he put his lips to it to kiss it, but a moment later he was shown it repeatedly with no effect. Regarding himself in a mirror, as he has done several times—is this to raise oneself above the level of animal instinct? Does not a cat or a monkey do the same thing? His vision is so untrained that he does not seem to distinguish between an object that is painted and one that is in relief, and he will try as readily to seize one as the other.

Although he does not have speech, he is far from being deaf. If one lets out a cry behind him, or makes an intense noise, he turns around right away, but only the first time, when surprise is combined with the impression made on the organ of hearing; for if the same noise is repeated he no longer pays any attention. A slighter impression is sufficient to make him turn around when it concerns his physical needs, as for example when he hears a walnut cracked; but he is completely insensible to any kind of music, and on this point he is much inferior to many individuals who are locked away in our hospitals. I should not be afraid to say that in this respect even elephants have a marked advantage over him.

The sense of smell is the one he uses most often to judge the good or bad qualities of foods, and here we undoubtedly see the result of the rustic life he led in the woods. If he opens a cupboard and finds some meat or soup roots, cooked or raw, he immediately sniffs them before putting them in his mouth; and if a fire is near, he throws in the food, takes it out forthwith, and sniffs it up again before eating it. But is this gross preparation of food anything other than an automatic habit, acquired since the time he began living in society? One might think that his sense of smell is very delicate and cultivated if it were not for the fact that he is disgustingly filthy and will defecate even in his own bed, which seems to put his faculty of smell beneath the instincts of nearly all animals, whether wild or domestic.

The course of his progress in the choice and preparation of certain foods, as he witnessed various kitchen procedures, reveals less a developed sense of taste than it does an automatic imitation of what he has seen done, an imitation provoked by physical needs.

According to the first accounts that we have on his condition, he ate only raw potatoes, chestnuts, and acorns: subsequently, he saw that potatoes are cooked and since that time he has limited himself to a rough imitation of this procedure, that is to say, he was satisfied to put them for a moment on the fire and to take them off right away. His tastes increased and he learned to eat rye bread, soup, vegetables, walnuts, baked potatoes, and finally raw or cooked meat. We find in the background statement concerning him [Bonnaterre, 1800], the series of advances that his instinct for subsistence has made till now; but its limits are still very narrow, since he does no better than rummage in the kitchen cabinet and, without distinguishing between cooked and raw meat, puts them all on the hearth indiscriminately, takes them off at the same moment, smells them, and puts them in his mouth. His skill has not reached the point of cutting bread with a knife: it seems to be a supreme effort, an unheard of combination of force and dexterity which leaves him at a loss, since he always leaves the task to somebody else.

It has justifiably been said that the sense of touch is the sense of intellect, and it is easy to see how imperfect this sense is in the so-called wild boy of Aveyron. Far from consulting this sensory information to judge the diverse shapes of bodies and from running his fingertips over them to examine them better, he reveals, on the contrary, a great deal of gaucherie in his manner of picking up various articles of food; his fingers remain extended and the sense of touch absolutely inactive. He is consequently far from using this organ to rectify vision, since he does not appear to distinguish a painted object on a plane surface from an object that is tangible and in relief, and since at the same time he puts his hand on an object to grasp it, he looks elsewhere or lets his gaze wander from side to side without any direction. We note in him, then, a sort of dissonance between vision and touch, and here we have a characteristic that I observe in the asylums among children without intelligence.

What other means can we have of judging the nature of the ideas of a member of the human species, if not from gestures of certain types, certain movements of the head and trunk, or the use of speech? Now, the child of whom we speak is deprived of all these outward advantages, since he cannot speak and all his gestures and other bodily movements are meaningless, or otherwise simply tied up with his means of sustenance. In these circumstances, how can one determine whether he has ideas of a certain kind, and is not one justified in assuming that he has only those concerning purely animal instinct? Are we not led to the same hypothesis because of the inadequacy of his sensory impressions? It appears that the child retains no idea whatsoever of things that are unconnected with his subsistence or his means of escape, and that, incapable of attention, he has only fleeting ideas which disappear as soon as they are produced.

For that matter, how narrow are the limits that circumscribe the feeble combinations of ideas relating to his nourishment or his means of living independently! If someone snatches a potato from him he will go up to the person to take the potato back in turn; but if the person gets up on a chair to put the potato out of reach, the so-called wild boy does not even have the intellect to get up on an adjacent chair to reach the object, and he will undertake this only when given a model. That is to say, he only seems to act by automatic imitation. When he is locked in a room with other people, he remembers very well that the key must be turned in the lock in a certain direction in order to open the door, but, during the several months I have been observing him, he has not managed to memorize this slight movement of the key in the lock and, put off by the enormous difficulty of the enterprise, he will lead someone to the door to help him get out.

One might attribute to a vivid memory, or to the impulse of a lively imagination, the outbursts, and the immoderate peals of laughter which suddenly occur from time to time with no known cause, lighting up his face. But I can affirm that these brief transports of vague and ecstatic hilarity are observed most often in children or adults fallen into idiocy and put away in our asylums; these are intense and spontaneous outpourings, which reappear either in the day or in the night, without provocation, and I have long considered them temporary accesses of insanity and wildness and sometimes even the reflection of a total absence of ideas, as I will illustrate by example in the later part of this memoir. There is nothing to lead us to suspect some reminiscence, some expression of an agreeable sensation which soothes the imagination in these momentary accesses. The feelings with which he is apparently endowed are again extremely limited and hardly extend beyond the pleasure he takes in his favorite foods or the movements of anger he displays when these foods are taken away from him, or when he is irritated. Is not his slight smile on receiving some kindly attention merely a weak simulacrum of true sentiment?

The sexual organs are still immature, and he is entirely unfamiliar with the violent desires that might show up in puberty. It would not be wise to presage the details of this tempestuous period, or the influence that it may exert on his intellectual faculties. This time of life undoubtedly will provide provocative material for an attentive observer, but limiting ourselves to the present state, which is much less problematic, all the indications are that the child is scarcely susceptible to feeling affection even for those who do him good turns—and how can one separate these marks of affection from his favorable disposition toward anything connected with his subsistence?

We have just filled the straightforward role of historian and have confined ourselves to an exact accounting of the facts to give a precise idea of the intellectual and affective faculties of the child known by the name of the "Sauvage de l'Aveyron." Before allowing ourselves any final judgment, any sort of inductive generalization, we will report as a basis for comparison the principal characteristics of several children or adults of one or the other sex who are committed to our asylums as a result of a more or less complete state of idiocy or dementia.

II. Account of several children or adults whose affective or intellectual faculties are more or less impaired.

The limits of this memoir allow only some simple accounts of several children, or rather ill-fated persons with defective or damaged constitutions, whose histories have been compiled fully. We will speak first about some male children whose condition offers more or less clear parallels with that of the child of Aveyron.

One of these children is deprived of speech by a physical defect, specifically a very short tongue, which he is absolutely incapable of using to articulate any syllable; he makes only vague guttural sounds. Otherwise he seems full of intelligence, and we have observed no damage to his mental faculties. Next to this child we can cite another who is deaf and dumb and who, without having a teacher, expresses his ideas rather incompletely by gestures; he too is full of discernment and susceptible to training. M. Sicard could well claim him for his domain.

A third child, nine years old, is the very image of idiocy; he laughs or cries by purely automatic imitation, and is sensitive only to physical needs. He slavishly does everything that he is ordered to do, and he responds only with yes or no, and without judgment, to the questions put to him. If he has hunger pangs, he asks for food and will resist any effort to take it away from him; but, without foresight, he keeps nothing in reserve . . .

A fifth child, or adolescent, sixteen years old, also has a very limited understanding that does not go beyond the circle of his physical needs; repeated attacks of epilepsy have completely deadened his mental faculties; he remains isolated from other children and spends his day alone playing with pebbles. He has a weak degree of memory concerning his nourishment or the rigorous treatments that we make him undergo.

A sixth adolescent, nineteen years old and suffering from epilepsy, seems on the contrary completely deprived of memory for certain objects and forgets equally readily the bad treatment and the good offices given him. From another point of view, he has some feeble measure of intelligence and he links the idea of his needs with that of objects suitable for satisfying them; he even knows the value of some coins, and in some circumstances is readily angered. But he receives all provocations blindly; he articulates sounds weakly and if told to sing he endlessly repeats the same couplet like an automatic machine, unless he is obliged to stop; he does not yet distinguish between the sexes.

A seventh adolescent, twenty-one years old and also suffering from epilepsy, but gifted with the use of speech, is noteworthy for his apathetic inertia, his pallor, and a physiognomy without expression. Reduced one day to crying in the corner, he was questioned on the cause of his tears and replied that he had no idea; a moment later, he roared with laughter on seeing another child romping about. He is indifferent to an object unless it has some connection with his feeding and, if not pressed by hunger, he always remains seated or stretched out in an immobile posture. The future simply does not exist for him, and we find no sign of foresight.

I hasten to proceed to other objects of comparison chosen among some young women of the asylum La Salpêtrière. One of these girls, seven years old, gives a first impression of all the attributes of health and in-telligence, ruddy complexion, black hair and eyebrows, an animated and a lively look; she looks at objects with an air of assurance and with a kind of attention; but she is absolutely deprived of speech and occasion-ally utters only dull and guttural sounds. Entirely insensitive to caresses and to threats, and in a kind of stupor, even regarding physical needs, she accepts food without any sign of satisfaction and allows it to be removed with no opposition. She never laughs and, if she is pinched or injured, she cries out and weeps, but without trying to remove the offending object. The only indication she has given of some pleasant emotion occurred when another child sounded a reed pipe in her ear . . .

I should not omit another epileptic, fourteen years old, who cannot pronounce a single syllable although she has retained a sense of hearing; she puts up a lively resistance when we try to take away her food but seems to forget everything as soon as it is out of sight. She often lets out piercing cries without any cause, bursts of intemperate laughter, and sudden explosions of delirious gaiety, but she shows no awareness of the kindnesses shown her. The clearest mark of her stupefaction is that she soils herself in the most disgusting manner and shows no repugnance to wallowing in her own filth.

We can place on a slightly higher level three other young persons whose mental faculties nevertheless show marked impairments.

The first, now twenty years old, presents on first impression all the characteristics of healthy faculties: small size, dark complexion, a lively look, thick dark hair. Her aberration seems to be the result of an un-happy love affair; she often pronounces the name of Debreuil, but her reasoning is so disturbed that she applies this name indiscriminately to everyone, male or female, who comes in view. She switches with light-ning speed from tender and affectionate language to the most gross invectives; she talks night and day, and her emotions, even the most disparate, alternate without order, without consequence, and without known cause.

The process of getting her second teeth produced a profound effect on another woman, now forty years old. During the dentition she was attacked by convulsions, which were followed by an almost total loss of mental faculties. Her outward appearance reflects her mental state: she answers yes and then no to the same question, with a silly smile, and the total sphere of her knowledge seems limited to the satisfaction of her basic needs. She seems indifferent to bad treatment as much as to kindnesses. She was asked one day if she wanted to go out; she an-swered repeatedly that she wanted to be drawn and quartered, a phrase she had just heard from one of her companions.

I will place in final position and at a level above the child of Aveyron someone who is now twenty-eight and whose mother suffered a most extreme fright at the time of giving birth. The girl stays constantly in one place, unable to make a sound, although her speech organs show no physical lesion. She has pronounced the vowel *a* alone and by repeated attempts has managed to produce the vowels *e* and *o*, but it was not possible to achieve as much for the vowels *i* and *u*. A student was assigned the task of trying to make her articulate a few syllables by leading her to examine the position and movements which must be given to the lips and to the tongue, but the only achievement, after repeated efforts, was to make her pronounce the syllables *pa* and *ba*. She carried out every command slavishly without distinguishing whether her actions were appropriate, extravagant, or absurd. A kind of habit, acquired a long time ago through fear, leads her to dispose of any sort of dirt and no one is more extraordinarily clean. In the absence of speech, her voice is endowed with rare precision, although the sounds are formed only by the vowel *a*. She sings when instructed to do so, or when she hears someone else sing, and in the latter case she straightaway adopts the unison or the octave of the voice she is hearing. If the tempo speeds up or the key is changed, or if some notes are held, she does likewise, with almost as much precision as an echo; but if at the same time she hears another person sing a tune that is more lively or that she prefers, then she drops the first and hooks onto the one that makes a more lively impression on her. Her emotional faculties seem to have been destroyed, and all her active movements uniquely concern her subsistence.

I have just set forth the facts and the objects of comparison which can lead us to the solution of the original question. In the second part of the memoir, which will be read in another session, I will examine the truths that follow and I will indicate if the so-called wild boy of Aveyron can be submitted with well-founded hope to instruction and acculturation, or if it is necessary to abandon this agreeable prospect and confine him simply in our asylums with the other unfortunate victims of an incomplete and damaged constitution.

III. Comparison between the use of intellectual and physical faculties by the child of Aveyron and by children reduced to dementia or idiocy.

The lively look of the child of Aveyron is an equivocal indication of some judgmental ability that can be cultivated, since most of the idiots in our asylums give the same outward appearance and very few are reduced to an expressionless physiognomy. A child of seven of whom I have already spoken, and who is reduced to complete idiocy, is noteworthy for the extreme vivacity of his look and for the superficial appearance of a healthy mind: one might even say that he has an advantage over the child of Aveyron since his attention is not only alerted by his means of subsistence but he often looks at his fingers and amuses himself in intertwining them or in varying their position with a meditative air. Another girl of twenty, also reduced to complete insanity, is noteworthy for her dark eyes full of life and a highly animated countenance. Indeed should not the lack of coordination between vision and touch in the child of Aveyron inspire a certain distrust? When he is given a new object, either painted or in relief, he will sometimes place his hand on it but in a very maladroit manner, and in such a way that the line of sight is not at all directed toward the object; on the contrary, his gaze wanders and he generally turns toward the window or the most brightly lit part of the room. This is what I noticed repeatedly during the time his portrait was being sketched. On the other hand, some idiot children or adults know very well how to coordinate sight and touch even in connection with objects that have nothing to do with subsistence. One of these children passes a good part of the day counting pebbles with a kind of attention; another, of whom I have already spoken, saves pins and other little objects in a case that he opens and closes at will, with all the signs of true memory. Another idiot, much more advanced than the child of Aveyron, has come as far as calculating numbers up to sixteen—but she never could comprehend that two fingers from her right hand added to two others from her left hand gave the number four.

The absence of speech, which could be taken to be the result of a lack of exercise of the voice organs through long isolation, is a further point of similarity among several idiots who give no sign of any nervous impairment. One young girl reduced to idiocy is unable to articulate a single syllable, although her sense of hearing seems to be healthy and her tongue freely executes all movements; like the child of Aveyron she makes only inarticulate sounds and from time to time piercing cries. We have the same situation with a child aged seven who has all the earmarks of good health but who is completely mute and who only emits occasionally a dull, guttural sound. Finally, how much more advanced than the child of Aveyron is the girl, twenty-eight years old, who seems to suffer from a partial lesion of the voice organs and who has achieved only after repeated efforts the pronunciation of certain vowels, imitating with great precision, moreover, all of the tunes and cadences that we have her listen to?

When it comes to subsistence, there is a remarkable disparity between the child of Aveyron and the idiots of the asylums. The latter, with no concern for the future and with no efforts on their own, receive prepared food at certain hours and are in this respect in a sort of passive state, without knowing, except to a very slight degree, the pangs of hunger. The child of Aveyron, long condemned to a wandering and vagabond life, either in the woods or in the hamlets, and often motivated by ravenous hunger, must have acquired the habit of nourishment with the crudest sorts of food, first judging its wholesome or harmful qualities by the sense of smell. Led back subsequently into the bosom of society, his sense of taste acquired a sort of development and led him to prefer more carefully prepared food . . . but do not we have here the simple result of imitation rather than the proof of a cultivated taste? Are there not to be found, even among the idiots, differences that place some above and others below the child of Aveyron?

A certain child I have often observed has such a limited degree of instinct concerning basic needs that he does not even know how to pick up food within reach, although he is very hungry; he makes no movement, no effort to reach it, and he only moves his head and lips toward it when it is offered to him at a slight distance from his mouth. Another child reduced to idiocy, but capable of articulating sounds, names the objects of his needs and indicates his desires by external signs. The child of Aveyron has only simple memory, and can indicate the objects of his needs neither by articulate sounds nor by gestures; he simply recognizes them by vision, which is to say that the current sensation only recalls a prior sensation. Another idiot looks at his dinner with satisfaction and he eats it avidly; if we pretend to want to take it away, he makes a piercing cry and a threatening gesture; but as soon as his appetite is sated, he will indifferently look on as his dinner is taken away, showing no concern for the future. This makes him inferior to the child of Aveyron, who puts some food in reserve against the return of his appetite. Finally, one should place at a much higher level than the child of Aveyron an idiot girl who indicates the objects of her basic needs with articulate sounds, who saves the leftovers from her meals carefully, who becomes irritated when someone wants to take them away, who even knows that money provides the means to obtain more, who leads strangers to contribute money and takes these coins to the attendant on her ward, as a mark of appreciation: even so, the whole sphere of her knowledge comes down to objects of basic necessity.

Should not we consider insoluble the problem of the total absence or nonabsence of ideas in the child of Aveyron, since he can express himself neither by articulate sounds nor by gestures and since everything that he does seems to come back to the principle of imitation? Can one even count in his favor his slavish tendency to imitate what he has seen performed when it comes to making choices or to the rough preparation of foods? From this point of view several domestic animals are capable of a sort of education, and in any event we find this imitative capacity more or less developed among hospitalized idiots, even concerning those objects that have nothing to do with subsistence.

This is what we observe with a girl who talks in a disorganized and disorderly way, but who abruptly changes her incoherent comments the moment a new object strikes her; she even has an agreeable singing voice and performs dances with impassioned movement. Another girl reduced to complete idiocy is dominated by a marked and irresistible tendency to imitate, since she immediately simulates everything she sees done, and repeats automatically all that she has just heard without in any way judging the appropriateness, and without distinguishing if she is speaking properly or not; she retains readily a series of couplets that she has heard sung once but without attaching any sense to the words that she is pronouncing. The imitative faculty is so overwhelming, in the case of another girl of whom I have already spoken, that in the middle of a response she will mix in other words she has heard pronounced which have no connection with the original theme that concerned her.

The tendency to imitate is much weaker in the child of Aveyron, since he limits himself to objects of basic necessity and to imperfect attempts at preparing food or finding means of escape. Even for these things his imitation remains very circumscribed, since he has not yet managed to cut bread or to turn a key.

The bursts of laughter, the accesses of intense and mad gaiety manifested by the child of Aveyron at different hours of the day or night, far from being a favorable sign, are simply a further point of similarity that we can establish between him and certain idiots in the asylums. The ten-year-old girl of whom I have spoken previously sometimes spends whole hours uttering inarticulate shouts mixed with bursts of laughter, and it is impossible to assign them any cause other than a sort of nervous and purely automatic excitation. The fourteen-year-old girl reduced to a state of stupefaction, entirely incapable of speech, experiences these abrupt attacks of hollow and delirious hilarity from time to time; both day and night she emits piercing cries that seem to express unhappiness as readily as agreeable situations.

In other persons suffering from idiocy or insanity these passing attacks are more or less extended and even take on the character of psychotic breaks. One twenty-six-year-old woman every morning undergoes a similar nervous excitation of very brief duration during which she performs actions of extreme violence. The tinge of sensitivity that the child of Aveyron shows for kindnesses undoubtedly places him above those idiots in the asylums who seem insensible both to threats and to caresses and who give no evidence of appreciating kindness; but we can also cite others who show a more or less active awareness of what is done in their behalf. And is there not one among them who is superior in this respect to the child of Aveyron since she seems to be attached to the attendant on her service and expresses this appreciation by giving her coins that she collects from hospital visitors?

IV. Inferences based on points of similarity and congruity observed between the child of Aveyron and the children in the asylums suffering from idiocy or insanity.

A distinguished naturalist has sought to draw public attention to the subject of the wild boy of Aveyron by relating the results of observations on this child confided to his care for some time and by referring to antecedent events based on various reports. He thought it pertinent, moreover, to draw parallels between this detailed account and the surviving fragmentary reports concerning other children lost in early youth and found subsequently in places far from society. We will not criticize these studies here, and we restrict ourselves to the sole comment that the subjects of comparison considered by this naturalist have not been communicated with circumstantiated details or sufficient precision for allaying all doubts. They are nothing more than vague reports gathered together in dictionaries, newspapers, or works of literature, and one cannot cite a single one of these so-called savages whose intellectual functioning, customs and habits were studied in depth and analyzed by a careful observer. In these circumstances, what are the advantages of such comparisons?

Or should one take the word *sauvage* in a narrower sense and only according to the authentic accounts of travelers who have described the primitive civilizations of diverse peoples? The objects of comparison are in this case much better defined and more detailed, but no light can thus be shed on the child of Aveyron since there is little similarity between him and the individuals who make up these savage hordes. To be convinced of this, one need only read a recent collection that has appeared under the title "Voyage Among the Savages, or The Man of Nature."

It has been necessary therefore to reconsider the present subject of research from another point of view or, rather, to undertake to verify the suspicions of imbecility that Bonnaterre had already formed concerning the child of Aveyron . . . These suspicions could only be confirmed by attentive study to the customs and habits of this child at different times, and by disallowing any new development in intellectual faculties since his arrival in Paris. His outward actions, limited to a sort of animal instinct, gave us the idea of comparing him with children and adults whose intellectual faculties are more or less damaged and who, incapable of providing for their own subsistence, are confined in the state asylums. The history of several of them has brought out all the points of similarity that can exist. The objects of comparison are here before our very eyes, and each person can come examine, study, observe the facts on which our account is based. Some of the children in our asylums reduced to a state of idiocy or insanity are inferior in intellectual faculties to the child of Aveyron; others are his equal or are even superior to him. Do we not then have every reason to think that the child of Aveyron ought to be considered in the same category with the children or adults fallen into insanity or idiocy?

Now what are the circumstances that have led the child of Aveyron to this state of idiocy? Here we lack authentic details and at first nothing seems able to allay our uncertainty. His parents are unknown; the child is without speech and without the advantage of making himself understood by gestures. The past is for him as if it had never existed and we have no other certain source of information; we can only be guided by analogy in looking for the usual causes that produce insanity or idiocy in childhood. Now, excluding from this category complications from epilepsy and rickets, the possible causes come down to three: (1) an intense fright suffered by the mother during childbirth; (2) a fright or convulsions occuring in infancy as a result of verminous infection; (3) a painful and tempestuous first or second dentition. Nothing permits us to determine which of these causes might have worked on the child of Aveyron so disastrously to undermine his intellectual faculties. But whatever one of the three we adopt, we can conjecture that inhuman or impoverished parents abandoned the child as incapable of education, around nine or ten years old, at some distance from their home, and that pangs of hunger led him to nourish himself on various foods which nature placed within his grasp, with no other means of judging their wholesome or harmful character than impressions first of smell, then of taste. He seems thus to have remained wandering and vagabond in the woods or the hamlets during the following years, always reduced to purely animal instinct and solely concerned with his subsistence and escaping from dangers that threatened him. We know the other details of his life from the time he entered society—his judgment always limited to the objects of his basic needs; his attention captured solely by the sight of food, or by means of living independently, a strongly acquired habit; the total absence of subsequent development of his intellectual faculties with regard to every other object. Do these not assert that the child ought to be categorized among the children suffering from idiocy and insanity, and that there is no hope whatever of obtaining some measure of success through systematic and continued instruction?*

Chapter Four

From
Condillac
to
Itard

Itard's Sources: Condillac, Pinel, Sicard—
Condillac revolutionizes medicine—The
beginnings of psychotherapy—Applied to
education—Abbé de l'Epée forges sign
language—Founds education of the deaf—
Sicard to head new institute—His flirtation
with death—His critique of Epée's methods
—How he taught Massieu—Massieu's own
story—Itard a student of Condillac—A
new conception of education.

Because Itard believed in Condillac's analysis of the origin of human knowledge, he was thoroughly opposed to the prevailing explanation of the wild boy's inabilities, namely that the boy was a congenital idiot. "A very few philosophers protested this rather severe judgment," De Gérando wrote, referring to himself and Itard.

They observed that before it is possible to reach this conclusion based on the resemblances between the condition of the boy from Aveyron and that of idiots produced by organic lesion, it is first necessary to demonstrate that there is not a kind of functional idiocy [idiotisme moral], similar in its effects to organic idiocy, and that certain extra-ordinary circumstances, such as long isolation and an animal existence, cannot produce in a subject who has not yet received any instruction the very habits of inattention and paralysis of the intellectual faculties that have been observed in the young savage. In support of their protest they cited all the observations that prove the influence of society over the development of human faculties, and the reasoning that shows the close relations between our ideas and our needs . . . They concluded that wise men would suspend judgment until real methods were tried out which were suited to developing the child's intelligence . . . At the same time they indicated what these methods were, in their opinion. Locke and Condillac gave an inkling of them. They insisted, following these great teachers, that before trying to make the child associate ideas, it was necessary to make these ideas come to life; that in order to make them come to life, it was necessary to fix his attention; and that the only way to fix his attention was to engage his needs. For them it was inconceivable that he should be expected to understand signs when he still had none of the notions expressed by these signs, when he had no motive at all for noticing the signs, when he had no method at all for comparing them. They saw, therefore, in the art of taking control of his sensory experience, of directing and developing it, the only way of destroying his habitual, ubiquitous inattention, which could only be the result of his indifference to the new world in which he remained so much an outsider.

To the prevailing conviction that the wild boy was ineducable, then, Itard opposed his own more optimistic prognosis. He merely had to teach the boy the distinctions, categories, needs, language,

and mental processes that were normally the unprogrammed result of socialization. Moreover, the time was ripe for this "medico-
pedagogical" treatment. Until recently, he argued, metaphysics
was in its infancy and crippled by the Cartesian belief in innate
ideas; medicine was encumbered by a highly mechanistic doctrine;
and the two were scarcely in a position to come to grips with
mental disorders. But these disciplines had made enormous progress, thanks to the analytical approach to knowledge set forth by
Condillac. "Thus there was reason to hope that if ever another
[isolated child] appeared, these [two sciences] would apply all the
resources of their current knowledge to his physical and intellectual development."

Condillac provided the basis not only for Itard's diagnosis and
prognosis but also for his training strategy. What is not original in
Itard's technique, he either borrowed directly from the first
Idéologue, who died in 1780, or from contemporary leaders in the
fields of medicine and the instruction of deaf-mutes. However,
since Philippe Pinel in the former case and Charles-Michel
de l'Epée in the latter were profoundly influenced by Condillac's
thought, Condillac can be called the patron saint of the whole enterprise, from beginning to end.

Pinel mediated Condillac's influence on Itard not only because
he represented the new era in medicine—indeed was one of the
founders of scientific medicine and, in particular, of psychiatry—
but also because he had been Itard's teacher. At the time of his
arrival in Paris, Itard found medical instruction divided into two
warring camps. The leader of the first school, Jean Corvisart, was
akin in spirit to today's clinician; his single-minded purpose was
healing, his guiding lights were the great practitioners before him,
his field of action was the hospital ward. Pinel viewed medicine as
more a natural science than an art and sought to redress its excesses. On the one hand, he rejected an undisciplined empirical
approach whose diagnostic method was an endless listing of symptoms set down willy-nilly, without order or classification, and
whose therapeutic method was an ad hoc trial-and-error administration of drugs, bleedings, baths, and such. On the other hand,
he rejected equally resolutely—as did all the Idéologues—what

was touted as the deductive approach, abstract arguments from first principles, abstruse discussions of the internal mechanisms underlying organic functions, reciprocal actions of fluids and solids and so on. Itard took up Pinel's banner.

Rejecting both empiricism and apriorism, as Itard would later do, Pinel adopted Condillac's method of analysis. The philosopher describes the method by inviting the reader to imagine arriving at a chateau at night. In the morning, the shutters are opened for just an instant, allowing us to glimpse a magnificent landscape. If we were allowed a second glimpse, or a third, each time we would receive exactly the same sense impressions as the first, as we would if the shutters were left open. Yet the first glimpse alone is not sufficient for us to become familiar with the countryside—we could hardly recount what we had seen—while more time for inspection allows us to sort out the major features of the view, then to distinguish and relate more and more minor features to these, finally to become familiar with the landscape. Thus knowledge, in immediate perception as in thought, requires us to sort out elements and to arrange in some order what occurs simultaneously in the original experience.

> We begin then with the principal objects: we observe them successively and compare them in order to judge their relations. When, by this means, we have their respective positions, we observe in turn all those that fill in the intervals, we compare each one with the nearest major object and we determine its position. Now we sort out all the objects whose form and location we have apprehended and we take them in in a single view. The order among them in our mind is then no longer successive; it is simultaneous. It is the very order in which they exist and we see them distinctly all at the same time.

For Pinel, medical science must first "set aside all hypothetical notions and keep to sensory impressions." In 1801 he wrote: "The habit of analytical investigation, thus adopted, has induced an accuracy of expression and a propriety of classification which have themselves contributed in no small degree to the advancement of natural knowledge. Convinced as I was of the essential importance of using the same means in explicating a subject so new and so difficult as that of the present work, it will be seen that I have availed myself of its application in all or most of the instances of this most calamitous disease that occurred during my practice at Bicêtre." This devotion to concrete details and to the study of the individual case history was already evident from the character of Pinel's report on the wild boy. But analysis only begins here, for its watchword is classification. We must decompose the complex disease entity, beginning by sorting out its major features, proceeding to lesser features and fixing their positions, as it were, in relation to the major features. The principal objects that dominate the medical horizon are the underlying organic structures that are impaired in various classes of disease. Only by following this strategy, modeled after the natural sciences, can we arrive at general and effective therapeutic methods. "Once a type of disease has been determined, and its general course and varieties observed, the principles of treatment are then known, along with the modifications that may be indicated by these varieties in relation to [the patient's] environment, age, sex, and way of life."

Although Pinel favored medical intervention in many kinds of disease (and advocated vaccination, for example), he was more conservative than most of his contemporaries, skeptical of the "pharmaceutical monstrosities" employed in the empiricist approach to therapy, confident of nature's own healing powers in many disorders when combined with the right environmental conditions.

For the treatment of mental disorders, Pinel was hostile to the use of medication and preferred controlling the social and physical environment of the patient, in accord with "age, sex, and way of life," to provide salutory human contacts, work and distraction, good hygiene and proper diet. In this he was allied with Thomas Willis in England, in the movement called *médecine morale*, that is, psychological medicine or, in modern terms, psychotherapy.

Itard's training reflects these currents of thought. He was a painstaking observer of his patient, providing posterity with its first detailed record of a pupil's education and himself with a keen appreciation of the boy's successes and failures. He sorted out the major components of the wild boy's disorder—sensory, motivational, verbal—and classified them into problem areas to be taken up in precise order, beginning with sensory activity and progressing to language and abstract thought. Finally, he envisaged a "medico-pedagogical" treatment styled after *médecine morale* and therefore adapted to the conditions of his particular patient.

This is what Itard had to say about the possibilities of revolutionizing education through the techniques of medical science, only a few months after beginning his training of the wild boy:

It seems likely that if philosophical medicine could contribute to the physical and intellectual education of children, their progress would become more sure and the results more satisfactory . . . It is not among outstanding and gifted individuals [like Rousseau] that we should look for the benefits and disadvantages of our routine education but among those that this same education has barely shaped, among those that it has left far behind ordinary men; among the idiots, for example, or among those individuals whom we generally call slow-witted; further, among those who are noticeable in our societies for their lack of imagination, their faulty judgment, their lack of purpose, or their highly circumscribed ideas. These gaps or these faults of the human mind are much more the result than we realize of the defective management of education, whose principal fault is that it is essentially the same for all children and never adapted to the innumerable variations in the intellectual makeup of individuals. Let us take one hundred children of the same age and subject their intellectual state to an analytical examination. We will become convinced that there are as many points of dissimilarity as of similarity among them . . . Thus psychological man more than physical man has his idiosyncrasies or individual differences; and it is the task of medicine more than any other science to study them and to bring to bear on their correct evaluation and development the resource of knowledge in physiology. Medicine has risen to new heights in our time through the psychological treatment of mental disease; it can acquire even greater luster by shedding light on the path of education. There is less of a gap than is generally thought between restoring the clarity of ideas and straightening out a troubled mind, between calming the delirium of a maniac and cooling the overheated imagination of a young man.

The advantages of education guided by medicine can be expected most dramatically in cases of idiocy. This education could accomplish a great deal with these people, who for the most part are no different from other men save in their reduced sensory capacities, which can certainly be developed. Medicine has in its hands a powerful method of psycho-logical and physical development. Up to a certain point it can blunt or sharpen nervous sensitivity and by this means influence man's intellect. Its techniques are innumerable: they seem negligible in the eyes of those who see in this science only the art of prescribing drugs; they seem very powerful indeed to those who have studied the substantial influence on the human mind of habits, moods, needs, passions, social intercourse, and the particular working of our basic desires and innate tendencies. The progress that the wild boy of Aveyron has made to this day is due to the combined action of all these agents which were brought to bear on his education; and, undoubtedly, continuing with these same means will finally return to society one who seemed destined to live so far from its embrace.

Condillac's influence on Itard was also mediated through the tradition of deaf-mute instruction, which was initiated by Epée and pursued by Sicard, in the very institute where Itard undertook the education of the *enfant sauvage*. Epée was nearly sixty when he took up the calling for which he would be recognized as the founder of education of the deaf as a field of instruction, not merely an occasional philanthropic activity or teaching experi-ment. After a religious career that was stopped at the deaconhood and continually hampered by disputes with the church hierarchy, and after a brief period of legal study and practice, Epée was led by chance, as he tells the story, into a household with two deaf-mute sisters. At first attributing their silence more to an excess of feminine reserve than to any impairment, he was surprised to learn from the mother that her daughters were indeed deaf-mute and had been tutored by a local clergyman, just deceased, so far as to give them some notion of religious history with the aid of en-gravings, but little more. Puzzling over how he would have pro-ceeded in such a case, he was reminded of a precept from his early training in philosophy: ideas and speech sounds have no more natural and immediate relation between them than ideas and written characters. The notion probably came originally from Locke's *Essay on Human Understanding*, published in French in 1700 and again in 1742 when Epée was thirty:

It was necessary that man should find out some external sensible signs, whereof those invisible ideas which his thoughts are made up of, might be made known to others. For this purpose nothing was so fit, either for plenty or quickness, as those articulate sounds with which so much ease and variety he found himself able to make . . . Words . . . came to be made use of by men as the signs of their ideas; not by any natural connexion that there is between particular articulate sounds and certain ideas, for then there would be but one language amongst all men; but by a voluntary imposition, whereby such a word is made arbitrarily the mark of such an idea.

The signs that come with "ease and variety" to the deaf-mute are gestures. "The natural language of the Deaf and Dumb," wrote Epée, "is the language of signs; nature and their different wants are their only tutors in it: and they have no other language as long as they have no other instructors." So the proper course to follow in the education of the deaf was clear: since they lack spoken language and these oral signs are arbitrary, they can be taught a gestural language, which would give them the same advantages as oral communication. Epée set about elaborating such a conventional language, whose rudiments he took from his pupils themselves. His successor, Sicard, tells how he did it: "He saw that the deaf-mute expressed his physical needs without instruction; that one could, with the same signs, communicate to him the expression of the same needs and could indicate the things that one wanted to designate: these were the first words of a new language which this great man has enriched, to the astonishment of all of Europe." Europe was indeed astonished. The speaking world had acquired language through the medium of sound, and culture through the medium of language. Both had been, in the nature of things, beyond the reach of the deaf and dumb, whom Aristotle called irremediably ignorant, whom the Romans deprived of their civil rights, whom Condillac denied the faculty of memory and hence the power of reasoning.

To the core group of signs taken from his pupils, Epée added many others of his own, sometimes based on those employed by pupils, sometimes entirely original, largely designating perceptible objects, qualities, or events. Then he added many other signs corresponding to grammatical functions in French: signs to indicate tense, person, grammatical category, and such. Thus *aimable* (love-able) is signed in the following way: "I make the radical sign [for love], then the sign for an adjective but of one terminating in *able* formed from a verb: to this I must subjoin the sign for possible or necessary."* One observer reports that the sign for masculine gender (to represent the French article *un*) was the same as that for a man's hat; the feminine *(une)* was represented by the sign for a lady's bonnet. Thus a bench *(un banc)* and a table *(une table)* came out rather originally bedecked. Epée taught the meaning of conventional signs that designated concrete objects or events by making the sign and, at the same time, displaying the referent or a picture or sketch of it. Once the sign was learned by pairing with its referent, it was paired with the written French word. Thus the pupils learned the meanings of French words and, addressed in sign, could take dictation. Proceeding to teach the signs for abstract ideas, which he could not pair with their referents, Epée began with the printed French word, then showed the conventional sign that corresponded to it, finally explained by other signs what the meaning was. The comprehension of abstract sign was facilitated, as Sicard points out, by the process of metaphor. Just as in spoken language a word comes to represent an abstract idea by extension from its concrete meaning, so too the sign that also corresponds to this concrete meaning is understood when it is used metaphorically to designate the abstract idea.

Thus, working from the concrete to the abstract, the instructor was able to communicate any idea he chose. "All the words of the French language had their counterpart in that of the deaf," Sicard later wrote.

> Nothing was easier than to get words and signs committed to memory, indeed engraved there, at the same time. All that was required was ordinary attention, since each gesture accompanied the invariable combination of letters that formed the corresponding word, and the sign was to the deaf-mute what the [spoken] word is to us. Once the nomenclature was retained, the deaf-mute proved to have no difficulty in writing words for signs and making signs for words. Entire pages of the most abstract books were copied from simple dictation by signs.

The Abbé de l'Epée presented annual, highly celebrated public demonstrations of this feat, from 1771 to 1774. They took place in two sittings in the chapel he had added to the spacious home built by his father, a member of the Royal Academy of Architecture. The last demonstration drew over eight hundred people, among them the abbé's growing corps of disciples outside France from Vienna, Rome, Groningen, Zurich, Amsterdam, Madrid, Karlsruhe, Tournai, Mainz, and Copenhagen, and from the French cities of Riom, Rouen, Le Mans, Angers, Toulouse, Chartres, Epinal, Bordeaux, and Paris. Most of these cities would soon have schools for the deaf styled after the one in Paris. Many dignitaries also attended the demonstrations, including the German emperor Joseph II, and there were doctors, educators, and philosophers, including Condillac.

That philosopher's analytical method and conception of language underlie Epée's system: a language comprised of gestures representing ideas, a language that builds from the simple to the complex, from concrete sense impressions to abstract categories. "Gestures, facial expression and vocal expression of emotion [are] the first means that men had to communicate their thoughts," Condillac wrote in his *Grammaire*. "All the sentiments of the soul can be expressed by positions of the body . . . We can render all our thoughts with gestures as we render them with words . . . We can distinguish two action-languages: the one natural, with signs determined by the structure of our organs; and the other artificial, with signs determined by analogy. The former is necessarily very limited; the latter can be so enlarged as to express every thought of the human mind." Sicard goes further, arguing that gestural signs are not merely as good as spoken ones, since language is arbitrary, but are actually preferable since they are a more natural action-language, as is shown by their greater universality: a stranger in a foreign land will be understood by gesture but not by speech.

Condillac had this to say about Epée's "language of methodical signs":

M. l'Abbé de l'Epée, who instructs deaf-mutes with singular wisdom, has made of action-language a systematic art, as simple as it is easy, with which he gives ideas of all sorts to his pupils; ideas, I venture to say, that are more exact and more precise than those we acquire ordinarily with the aid of hearing. Since, in infancy, we are reduced to judging the meaning of words from the circumstances in which we hear them pronounced, it often happens that we grasp this meaning only approximately, and we make do with this approximation all our lives. It is not the same with the deaf-mutes instructed by M. l'Abbé de l'Epée. He has only one way to give them ideas that they cannot observe for themselves directly; namely, to analyze and to have them analyze with him. He leads them, then, from perceptible ideas to abstract ideas by simple and systematic analyses; and it is easy to see how many advantages his action-language has over the spoken sounds of our governesses and tutors.

M. l'Abbé de l'Epée teaches his students French, Latin, Italian, and Spanish. And he dictates to them, in these four languages, with the same action-language. Why so many languages? In order to enable foreigners to judge his method, and he flatters himself that he may find someone in authority to found an establishment for the instruction of deaf-mutes. He has created one himself, sacrificing some of his own funds. I believed I ought to take the occasion to give just credit to the talents of this generous citizen to whom I am not known, although I have been at his school, I have seen his pupils, and he has given me full information about his method.

Whether Condillac's testimonial in 1775 or Epée's public demonstrations during the preceding four years were effective we cannot say; in any case, in 1778 and 1785 the city voted some modest funds to supplement the gifts of private benefactors, notably Louis XVI.* Nevertheless, the school that began in the 1760s with a half-dozen pupils in the abbé's home, growing to number seventy-two in 1785, was never far from destitution. It was only two years after Epée's death, in 1789, that the National Assembly extended the new fraternity of man to include deaf-mutes and established their school as a national institution. Abbé Sicard, who had come from Bordeaux to learn Epée's methods and who had returned there in 1786 to direct a school for deaf-mutes, was selected to head the new institute, following a competitive examination in which each candidate was represented by a deaf-mute he had trained. The abbé's most able pupil, Massieu, was judged easily the best.* Sicard's political tribulations in those tumultuous times are less relevant here than his elaborations of his predecessor's methods, later adopted by Itard, but they are symptomatic of the man and the era and have a certain interest.

Soon after the uprisings that caused Constans-Saint-Estève to flee Paris, in August 1792, sixty armed citizens stormed into the Celestine cloister, where the Institute for Deaf-Mutes was temporarily lodged, and seized Sicard as he was preparing his lessons. The Revolutionary Commune had ordered his arrest, like that of many other priests, since he had failed to take the oath of civil allegiance, required by the National Assembly but prohibited by the Pope—both on pain of dismissal from office. Thus began Sicard's week of flirtation with death in which he would be drawn into the bloody vortex of the September massacre, as infamous as any incident in the Reign of Terror.

Led at sabre point through the streets to the city hall, the abbé was arraigned before the Comité d'Exécution, stripped of personal effects including his breviary, which was minutely searched for counterrevolutionary notes, and locked up with a crowd of people of all social classes. Among them Sicard found a few friends, including his associate instructor at the institute and one who offered to share his bed of straw. The following morning Massieu arrived and gave his teacher a copy of the petition he was going to present to the National Assembly:

Mr. President:
The deaf and dumb have had their instructor, their guardian, and their father taken from them. He has been locked in prison like a thief, a criminal. But he has killed no one; he has stolen nothing. He is not a bad citizen. His whole time is spent in instructing us, in teaching us to love virtue and our country. He is good, just, and pure. We ask for his freedom. Restore him to his children, for we are his. He loves us like a father. He has taught us all we know. Without him we would be like animals. Since he has been taken away, we are sad and distressed. Return him to us, and you will make us happy.

The Assembly was greatly moved when its secretary read Massieu's appeal, and it ordered the minister of the interior to show cause for Sicard's arrest.

But the days passed and the order was ignored. The prosecutor of the Revolutionary Commune arrived and told the prisoners that those among them who could prove they belonged to the clergy would be spared and deported. Sicard decided to open an institute for deaf-mutes in a European capital and wrote to a friend there. Soon the clergy were herded off as promised, but Sicard alone was left behind. A day later two dozen more prisoners arrived, and their visitors reported that the priests were not sent home but to the Abbey of Saint-Germain-des-Prés, to await execution. The minister of the interior instructed the mayor of Paris to show cause why Sicard was arrested; he replied that it was not his province but that of the Comité d'Exécution. The Comité replied that, since Sicard's papers were seized for prosecution, their contents cannot be revealed.

On September 2 the signal is given for the bloodbath: with the third firing of the cannons the people are to slaughter the enemies of the state. Soldiers enter the prison to lead Sicard and the others to the abbey. The prisoners plead for carriages to protect them from the crowds, and Sicard and five others are placed in the first. The soldiers refuse to defend them en route. The word spreads that the cannons were announcing the retaking of Verdun by the Prussians, that this procession winding over the Pont Neuf and up the Rue Dauphine contains traitors and foreign agents. The soldiers keep the doors of the carriages open, and by Buci Crossing all of Sicard's companions are bloody from saber strokes. The court of the abbey overflows with an armed mob which surrounds the carriages. One of Sicard's group leaps out and his throat is cut; a second tries to slip out and disappear in the tumult; the cutthroats fall on him and blood flows. A third is seized and swallowed up by the mob as the carriage approaches the main door. The fourth is struck by a sword as he dashes into the building. Somehow Sicard, cowering in the back of the carriage, is overlooked, and the crowd unleashes its wrath on the second wagon. Sicard slips into a room in the abbey where an administrative committee is in session and pleads for their protection. Soon there is loud rapping on the doors and the prisoner is demanded. Sicard gives his watch to one of the commissioners with instructions to give it to the first deaf-mute who inquires after him; that will be Massieu, who treasures watches. The priest kneels and gives his life to God. The doors open and the crowd floods in: "There are the bastards we're after!" "But it's the Abbé Sicard," one of them cries, "the father of the deaf-mutes." The crowd hesitates and Sicard leaps onto a ledge: "I instruct those who are born deaf and mute. Since there are many more of these unfortunate children among the poor than the rich, I belong more to you than to the rich." A voice cries, "We must spare Sicard. He is too useful to kill. He hasn't the time to be a conspirator." "Spare Sicard! Spare Sicard," chants the crowd and the cutthroats waiting behind him rush forward and embrace him, offering to lead him home in triumph. Sicard demurs; he will remain until officially released. The crowd returns to the slaughter in the courtyard. Bodies are everywhere and the cobblestones are red with blood. The main prison has been emptied and its occupants stuck like pigs. As dusk falls, lamps are set out so the public can witness. The abbé is locked in a small prison where he spends the night listening to the pleas and death cries of the victims in the courtyard outside. By dawn more than one thousand corpses filled the prison yards of Paris.

In the morning, Sicard receives word that he will be executed at four o'clock. He writes to a deputy of the National Asssembly and begs him to come in time and lead him, with the protection of his office, to the Assembly. The Assembly was no longer in session, but a secretary in the hall carried the message to the deputy who approached the president, who went before the Committee on Public Instruction, which ordered the Commune to release Sicard. The message was carried to the Commune at six o'clock, two hours past the deadline, but a downpour had temporarily postponed Sicard's execution. At seven o'clock, a municipal officer, wearing the tricolor to fend off the waiting crowd of public executioners, led Sicard from the abbey to the National Assembly where he was received with applause and pleaded to be returned to his family, his deaf-mutes. Within hours, Massieu was in his arms again, weak from hunger and sleeplessness but reunited with his benefactor.

A few weeks later constitutional monarchy officially ended and republican government began: the National Assembly was superseded by the popularly elected National Convention. In the midst

of its herculean legislative tasks, the Convention managed to devote two meetings the following year to a project of reform for the
education of deaf-mutes. A central demonstration and training
school would be founded in Paris. To this effect, the institute
founded in 1791 would be moved from temporary quarters in the
Celestine cloister to the seminary of Saint-Magloire on the Rue
Saint-Jacques (where the Archbishop of Paris formerly trained the
priests of his diocese and where Itard would later teach the wild
boy). A second National Institute would also be created at Bordeaux.
Sicard managed to stay out of trouble during the Terror, and when
the Convention created the normal school for teacher training,
Sicard was named one of the instructors for grammar. His recorded
lectures in 1795 recount his conception of language, which owed
much to Condillac, and the modifications he made in Epée's
methods of instruction. The following year Sicard was appointed
a founding member of the Institut de France and began publishing
a religious-political newspaper. For his troubles, he narrowly missed
deportation and was forced into a sort of exile in the outskirts of
the city. After a year of fruitless efforts by pupils and friends to
restore him to favor, he published a remarkable avowal in a revolutionary newspaper, claiming that he was not in fact the author
of the religious articles for which he had been banished and that
"for me, all authority exercised by the powers that be is, by that
very fact, legitimate. Thus, by the same faith that I was a royalist
in '89, '90, '91 and '92, I am, since the proclamation of the Republic,
a zealous Republican. The monarchy is, as far as I am concerned,
as if it had never existed." Returned to his functions in 1798, Sicard
worked intensely on his book "Course of Instruction for a Deaf-
Mute," which was published as Itard took up his duties at the
institute.

In this book, as in his earlier lectures at the normal school, Sicard
points out the limitations of Epée's method. The students could
and did take dictation of difficult French texts, but they did not
understand what they had written and could not themselves write
even simple sentences. Conversely, a student could read out a letter in sign but could not carry out the instructions in the letter.
"Of course!" Epée had written: "I understand Italian and I cannot

compose in Italian; the deaf-mutes understand French, since they translate it by signs, and that's enough for me." In another letter, the master advised his pupil: "Don't hope that they can ever express their ideas in writing. Our language is not theirs; theirs is sign language. Let it suffice that they know how to translate ours with theirs as we translate foreign languages ourselves, without knowing how to think or express ourselves in that language." And in another letter:

> What are you up to? You insist on training writers when our method can only produce copyists . . . Content yourself modestly with the share of glory that you see me enjoying. Teach your children the declensions and conjugations right away. Teach them the signs from my dictionary of verbs; teach them to do the parts of a sentence following the diagram, · of which you have the original, without deluding yourself that your students will express themselves in French any more than I know how to express myself in Italian, though I translate that language perfectly well.

"The inventor of this method," Sicard complained,

> thought his work was through when he had invented signs to correspond to every word, whereas he ought to have got the signs from his pupils that conveyed the ideas he was trying to communicate to them. As a result, he thought he was giving them the meanings of words when in fact he was only giving them the corresponding signs. He failed to see that nothing was easier than to make them write words for signs, but since they knew as little of the latter as of the former, he led them from the unknown to the unknown. He succeeded therefore, and succeeded easily, in making them copy whole pages of the most abstract books by means of gestures; but these gestures, which were purely mechanical, conveyed no meaning since, in whatever language, words can only be conventional signs; and to agree upon their meaning, there must be some language mutually understood by those who make the agreement.

Since Massieu was able to present a petition to the National Assembly that he himself had written to spare his instructor's life, it is clear that Sicard was able to overcome the limitations of Epée's method. Massieu—whom Bonnaterre cites as a model for the wild boy in the last line of his essay; who came to Sicard at the age of fourteen, a shepherd from a family with six children, all deaf; who was the deaf-mute in question in the "Course of Instruction for a Deaf-Mute"—this same Massieu appeared nine years later before a large assembly of scholars and teachers and demonstrated Sicard's method by using it to teach other deaf-mutes. He also answered abstruse questions from the floor (in writing); to the inevitable question on innate ideas, "I ask Massieu if he knew God, and what is God, and what idea he has thereof," Massieu replied in writing: "I answer that I know him but before entering the Institute of Deaf-Mutes I did not know him; I was like the animals. God is a spiritual being, incorporeal, eternal, creator and preserver of all that exists in nature; I do not have an idea of Him, but I have a belief in Him."

As for acquired ideas, Sicard's first hurdle—or so he thought in the "Course"—was to teach Massieu that strings of letters, which the pupil had previously learned to distinguish and print, could represent objects, just as sketches or signs could. Some twenty sketches of familiar objects were prepared and, in the first lesson, Massieu learned to fetch the object given the sketch, and vice-versa. For the second lesson, Sicard had lettered the names of the objects above their corresponding sketches on a blackboard. When the outlines were erased, Massieu was unable to fetch the various objects, with only the names as a guide. Sicard then redrew the objects with the letters on, not above, them; the letters extended between the borders so that the printed name had roughly the conformation of the object. Next the outlines were erased carefully between the letters, and an observer was used as a model to fetch the objects according to their printed names. Massieu was puzzled.

Sicard repeated the procedure but had Massieu copy the names of the iconographs, lettering each one just below the corresponding letter-design, which was then erased. The observer then fetched the various objects guided only by the names Massieu had written. Massieu was overjoyed, we are told, at his newfound ability to communicate and learned to fetch all that he had transcribed. Quite soon the intermediate steps of sketching and copying could be dropped. Massieu pointed to all manner of things around him, wanting to know their names.

There wasn't a day in which he didn't learn more than fifty names, nor a day in which I didn't learn from him the signs of as many objects, whose names I made him write. Thus by a happy exchange, when I taught him the written signs of our language, Massieu taught me the imitative signs of his . . . thus neither I nor my illustrious teacher is the inventor of the language of the deaf (it must be said). And, as a foreigner cannot teach a Frenchman the French language, so a man who speaks should not get involved in inventing signs, in giving them abstract values.

Where, then, do the deaf get their signs? This is Massieu's story, written in his own hand, after he had learned to express himself in French through Sicard's instruction. He presented the account to the Society of Observers of Man and delivered it in sign language at one of their meetings.

I was born at Semens, in the canton of Saint-Macaire, in the Department of La Gironde. My father died in January 1791. My mother is still alive. There were six deaf-mutes in our family, three boys and three girls. Until the age of thirteen years nine months, I stayed in my region without receiving any sort of instruction. I was in the dark. I expressed my ideas by manual signs or gestures, which I employed to communicate with my parents and brothers and sisters. These signs were quite different from those of educated deaf-mutes. Strangers did not understand me when I expressed my ideas in this way, but the neighbors understood me well enough. I saw cattle, horses, mules, pigs, dogs, cats, vegetables, houses, fields, grapevines, and after having considered all these objects, I remembered them well. Before my education, when I was a child, I did not know how to read or write. I wished to read and write. I often saw young boys and girls going to school; I wanted to follow them and I was very jealous of them. I asked my father, with tears in my eyes, for permission to go to school . . . My father refused the permission that I asked him for, signing to me that I could never learn anything because I was deaf-mute. Then I cried very hard . . . Despairing, I put my fingers in my ears and asked my father impatiently to unclog them so I could hear. He answered that there was no remedy . . . One day I left my father's house and went to school without telling him. I went to the teacher and asked him with gestures to teach me to read and write. He refused sternly and sent me away . . . I was twelve at the time . . . When I was a child, my father made me pray morning and evening with gestures . . . I knew how to count before my education; my fingers taught me. I did not know numbers; I counted on my fingers and when the number passed ten I made notches on a piece of wood ... One day a man who passed while I was tending my flock took a liking to me and invited me to his house to eat and drink. Then, when he went to Bordeaux, he spoke about me to Abbé Sicard, who agreed to take charge of my education ... In a period of three months I knew how to write several words; in six months, I knew how to write several sentences. In one year's time, I wrote fairly well. In a year and some months, I wrote better and I responded well to questions that were put to me. I was with Abbé Sicard* three and a half years when I left with him for Paris. In four years I became like people who hear and speak.

[Mme. V.C.:] "What were your thoughts when M. Sicard had you draw, for the first time, a series of letters making a word?" [Massieu:] "I thought that the words represented the objects that I saw around me. I committed them to memory with great eagerness. When I had read the word God and I had written it in chalk on my slate, I looked at it very often for I believed that God caused death, and I feared death a great deal.'"

Having taught Massieu the names of things in French, Sicard set about teaching him the names of their qualities. Equipped with seven pieces of colored paper, he lettered the word P A P I E R seven times and intercalated among the letters those of the corresponding color names; thus P R A O P U I G E E R (red paper). Massieu advised him to put the second set in a smaller size: P r A o P u I g E e R, so he apparently got the point. The pupil had little difficulty in matching the names to the sheets of paper, which is not surprising since the sheets differed only in one respect, there were only seven of them, and Massieu was already adroit at naming objects. Next the adjective was dropped below the noun, each letter connected to its original position by a line:

P A P I E R
| | | | | |
r o u g e

Then the several vertical lines were reduced to one:

PAPIER and PAPIER–ROUGE
|
ROUGE

Finally, the dash was replaced by three letters (for the verb *to be*):

PAPIER EST ROUGE. Massieu could now complete a matching task of the type:

	IS	
GRASS		RED
SKY		GREEN
SUN		BLUE

and was reading and lettering his first sentences. Other attributes like ROUND, SQUARE, LONG, SHORT were mastered soon after. Simple, active declarative sentences in the present tense were learned on the same model. Thus GRASS IS GREEN and SICARD IS HITTING were treated alike (with some initial violence to the French, which is more similar to *Sicard hits* in the present tense.). From here the lessons proceeded to the passive, SICARD IS HIT, and on to category names, tense markers, pronouns, adverbs, numbers, and articles.

In teaching complex sentences, Sicard made some concessions to the word order of his pupils' native sign language. This is illustrated by some of the written exchanges between Massieu and another pupil at a public demonstration in 1795. To the question "Do you see me?" the student replied "Oui, je vois toi" following the sign order I–SEE–YOU instead of the correct French order "Je te vois." Asked what he saw in particular, the student replied "Je vois corps vivant avec mes yeux dans toi," following the sign I–SEE–BODY LIVING WITH MY–EYES IN YOU instead of the French word order "Avec mes yeux, je vois dans toi un corps vivant."* Sicard's course terminated with discussions of intellectual faculties and the existence, spirituality, and immortality of the soul.

Thus the analytic method of Condillac came to Itard not only through recent developments in medicine but also through this other mainstream of contemporary thought, the education of deafmutes. The orderly progression from the known to the unknown, from simple to complex, from concrete sensory experience to abstract ideas, would be one of the hallmarks of Itard's strategy for training the wild boy. Itard also took from Sicard his technique of teaching the names of objects and attributes using only the visual mode. Finally, Itard proved skillful in using the technique today called *fading*, in which the behavior manipulator gets new cues to evoke a response by placing them alongside old ones and gradually diminishing the old as the new gain control; Itard may well have been inspired by Sicard's use of iconographs and intercalated letters. What Itard did not borrow from these developments in the education of deaf-mutes is as revealing as what he took. He made no use of the characteristic accomplishment of this school, the action-language of sign. Why he failed to do so, despite the wild boy's recalcitrance in speaking, is another story, worth telling separately later.

But there is a direct route that leads from Condillac's thought to Itard's strategy in addition to the detours via Pinel on the one hand and Epée and Sicard on the other. The education of the wild boy was, in fact, to be an experimental verification of Condillac's theory of mind; the boy was to enact the psychological development of human understanding as Condillac had traced it. Itard's student, Edouard Séguin, makes this explicit:

> At the time that the wild boy of Aveyron was brought to Paris, people thought they had found Condillac's statue, an animated machine, that only needed to be touched in the right places for it to produce the operations of the mind. This school was delighted and went to see the prodigy; all the brilliant men of the period visited the savage; but the wonderment soon dissipated when confronted with the reality, digust replaced enthusiasm, and the unhappy boy was abandoned in the attic of the school for deaf-mutes before Doctor Itard laid claim to him. Allied with the philosophers of his time, a philosopher himself as much as anyone, and, moreover, a brilliant theoretician though guided by the accepted psychology of the period, he put all his originality and his devotion in the service of the *sauvage de l'Aveyron* or, to speak more precisely, in the service of the current metaphysics.

In making the decision to follow Condillac's theory of the development of human understanding, Itard implicitly rejected contemporary conceptions of education and ways of structuring course material. The format of instruction at this time was based on the material taught and not on the student.* The formula "from the known to the unknown" had already been used in attempts to overturn the scholastic tradition of teaching abstract material that was thoroughly unfamiliar to the pupil. The educational progression that was to take its place, however, was based on a priori, external principles: in the case of Comenius, religious doctrine dictated an order that followed Genesis, beginning with air and earth and ending with man; for Rousseau, a social doctrine provided that education start with the primitive or natural talents of man; for Pestalozzi, a logical classification led instruction from concern with simple isolated qualities, such as form and number, to increasingly complex entities. Condillac was the first to give psychological meaning to the notion of strict progression. In this sense his principles of instruction were not external; the material did not dictate what was to be taught, a certain conception of the evolution of the pupil's intelligence did. "My sole purpose," he wrote in the *Essay on the Origin of Human Knowledge*,

> is to reduce to a single principle whatever concerns human understanding ... Ideas are linked to signs, and it is only by this means, as I will prove, that they are linked to each other ... In order to explain my principle I have been obliged not only to follow the workings of the mind in all their gradations, but also to investigate how we have contracted the habit of all kinds of signs and what use we ought to make of them ...
>
> On the one hand, I turned to perception, because it is the first operation that we observe in the mind; and I have shown how and in what order it produces every other operation that we can come to exercise [imagination, contemplation, memory, reflection, discrimination, comparison, abstraction, analysis, synthesis, judgment, reasoning]. On the other hand, I have begun with the language of action. The reader will see how it has produced all the arts that are concerned with the expression of our thoughts ...
>
> Finally, having developed the progression of the operations of the mind and of language, I try to indicate by what means we can avoid error and to show the order we ought to follow, either in making discoveries or in teaching others about those that have already been made. And that is in general the plan of this essay.

This is clearly not a plan for teaching students information but rather for teaching them the means to acquire it. Later in the "Essay" he points out:

> Even in playing with children we can make them improve their intellects, as much as they are capable of being improved, provided that everything is suited to this purpose ... When age and circumstances later change the things that interest them, their minds will be perfectly developed and early on they will have acquired a degree of intelligence that, by any other method, they would have acquired much later or even never. Thus children should not be taught Latin, history, geography, etc. What use could they make of these sciences at an age when they do not yet know how to think?

This suited Itard's predicament. The normal child learns many of the means of education before, during, and mainly despite school; his unprogrammed interactions with the natural and social environment provide him with many of these propaedeutic skills. But Itard's pupil never had these experiences—or, more precisely, he had other ones—and thus was not equipped in any respect to pursue traditional schooling.

The traditional way of planning instruction, according to the structure of the material to be learned, was therefore inappropriate. A range of alternatives remained that increasingly focused on the learner himself. The program of training could follow from a general conception of intellectual development; more specifically, it could be tailored to the developing needs and interests of a particular student or set of students; finally, it could be responsive at every moment to each step forward or backward in the individual student's learning. Condillac had the insight of shifting the focus of education to the first and even the second of these alternatives, but it was Condillac's student, Itard, who brought it squarely to bear on the individual student.

Itard had already been prompted to think in terms of tailoring the instruction to his pupil, of adapting the milieu, by the precepts of "mental medicine" that Pinel followed in the treatment of the insane. He would adopt this as his first objective in training the wild boy. Condillac similarly counseled the teacher in his "Essay":

If a teacher who had complete knowledge of the origin and progress of our ideas considered with his pupil only those things that had the closest relation with his needs and age; if he had enough address to put him in the circumstances best suited for teaching him to form precise ideas and to fix them by invariant signs . . . what clarity, what scope would he not give to the mind of his pupil!

Suiting the circumstances to the child meant for Itard, in the first place, creating a generally healthy and reassuring environment that responded to many of the boy's needs. When Itard admits to indulging the wild boy's whimsies—"People may say what they like, but I confess that I lend myself without ceremony to all this childish play"—we hear the echo of Condillac's description of what *his* pupil demanded: "One had to be a child rather than a teacher; I let him play, and I played with him." But, more significantly, suiting the circumstances meant filtering and altering the environment and even expressly fabricating things, sights, and sounds to serve as vehicles for instruction. It was not merely a matter of introducing colorful objects to hold the child's interest; Comenius and Locke proposed that sort of gambit as have educators before and since; in any event, the wild boy was indifferent to toys. It was a matter of selecting or creating tools to teach particular skills. By this accomplishment Itard became the originator of instructional devices in education.

By shifting the focus of instruction from the materials to the learner, Itard founded a new movement in education, which progressed with Séguin, Itard's disciple, then Montessori and Decroly, and came to be called, in the first decades of this century, Education Nouvelle.* But Itard carried the learner's control of instruction one step further than Condillac had envisaged and adaptively restructured the training sequence from one moment to the next, depending on the pupil's behavior. In using this strategy, which he followed more systematically than any of his predecessors though not invariably, and in shaping learning with such means as fading, conditioned avoidance, and generalized imitation, Itard also anticipated by two centuries the modern techniques of behavior modification.

Chapter Five

The
Return
to
Society

Itard's aims in training the wild boy—
Interesting him in social life—A child of
nature—Awakening his senses—Touch,
taste and smell improve—He catches cold
—Creating new needs—Itard uses
rewards—Food and outings—A day in the
salon of Mme. Récamier—The boy's
affections—Leading him to speak—The
wild boy gets a name—Victor remains
mute—Attempt to teach him "water"—His
gestural communication—Teaching simple
concepts—Victor matches sketches with
objects—He distinguishes shapes and
colors—Rage and frustration—Victor learns
the alphabet—Asks for "milk"—Victor's
report card—De Gérando's evaluation—
"He has leapt the barrier"—Itard's
conclusions.

Pinel's report to the Society of Observers of Man, at their meeting on December 29, 1800, concluded that there was no reasonable hope of educating the wild boy. Itard began nonetheless a few days later, and within six months—on June 17, 1801, to be exact—Sicard told his colleagues that Itard was present and could report some progress. After lengthy discussion, the society invited Itard to prepare a detailed report of all his observations so that the Pinel commission could consider them. It was in response to this invitation that Itard prepared the first of two memoirs that have become classics in education. It was entitled "On the Education of a Man of the Wild, or the First Physical and Moral Developments of the Young Sauvage de l'Aveyron." Itard gave a summary account of the report at the society's meeting on August 26 and communicated the published document at the meeting of October 20, 1801. The society agreed that "these observations made by Citizen Itard, who has tried to conduct the education of this child, lead it to conclude that his faculties have been developed up to a certain point and to hope that more substantial development will be seen subsequently. The assembly applauds this effort."

Itard set down five principal aims for his training program, and organized his report accordingly:

> 1st Aim. To interest [the wild boy] in social life by rendering it more pleasant for him than the one he was then leading, and above all more like the life he had just left.
> 2nd Aim. To awaken his nervous sensibility by the most energetic stimulation, and occasionally by intense emotion.
> 3rd Aim. To extend the range of his ideas by giving him new needs and by increasing his social contacts.
> 4th Aim. To lead him to the use of speech by subjecting him to the necessity of imitation.
> 5th Aim. To make him exercise the simplest mental operations, first concerning objects of his physical needs and later the objects of instruction.

In attempting to make the boy's life in society less traumatic than it had been for over a year and more similar, in some ways at least, to the life he originally led, Itard was not only following the precepts of "mental medicine" but also those of good training procedure. Good teachers and animal trainers alike provide for a period of habituation before beginning instruction, no doubt because strong emotional responses interfere with learning. After several pursuits, captures, and escapes; after his confinement at Saint-Sernin, Saint-Affrique, and Rodez; after his public displays in the provinces and in Paris; after his sequestration at the Institute for Deaf-Mutes, no wonder that "his petulant activity had insensibly degenerated into a dull apathy which had produced yet more solitary habits. Thus, except for the occasions when hunger took him to the kitchen, he was always to be found squatting in a corner of the garden or hiding in the attic behind some builder's rubbish." Itard took the boy into his home, a few blocks from the institute, and charged the housekeeper with his daily care. Madame Guérin treated him kindly and gave in to his tastes and inclinations "with all the patience of a mother and the intelligence of an enlightened teacher." The boy was put to bed at dusk, provided with his favorite foods, allowed his indolence, and taken on frequent walks in the adjacent Luxembourg Gardens.

The weather still held great sway over him, as it did when he had wandered the Roquecézière plateau.

Thus, for example, when observed inside his own room he was seen swaying with tiring monotony, turning his eyes constantly toward the window, gazing sadly into space. If a stormy wind then chanced to blow, if the sun suddenly came from behind the clouds brilliantly illuminating the skies, he expressed an almost convulsive joy with clamorous peals of laughter, during which all his movements backward and forward very much resembled a kind of leap he would like to take, in order to break through the window and dash into the garden. Sometimes instead of these joyful emotions, he exhibited a kind of frantic rage, wrung his hands, pressed his closed fists to his eyes, gnashed his teeth audibly, and became dangerous to those who were near him.

One morning when there had been a heavy snowfall while he was in bed, on awakening he uttered a cry of joy, left the bed, ran to the window, then to the door, going and coming impatiently from one to the other, and finally escaped half dressed into the garden. There, giving vent to his delight by the most piercing cries, he ran, rolled in the snow and, gathering it up by the handful, devoured it with incredible eagerness.

When inclement weather drove everybody from the garden, that was the moment he chose to go there. He went round it several times and finished by sitting at the edge of the pond.

I have often stopped for hours with inexpressible delight to consider him in this situation, to note how all these spasmodic movements and continual swaying of his whole body diminished, subsiding by degrees and giving way to a more tranquil attitude; to observe how his face, vacant or grimacing, imperceptibly took on a decidedly sad or melancholy expression, as his eyes clung fixedly to the surface of the water, while from time to time he threw in some debris or dry leaves. When, on a beautiful moonlit night, the rays penetrated into his room, he rarely failed to waken and go stand in front of the window. There he remained, according to his governess, for part of the night, motionless, head high, his eyes fixed upon the moonlit landscape, carried away by a sort of contemplative ecstasy, whose silence and immobility were only interrupted at long intervals by deep breaths nearly always accompanied by a plaintive little sound.

Gradually Itard reduced the time devoted to bed, excursions, and food, and took up the instruction proper. He turned first to the senses of course, the portals of the mind. What he found there must surely have been as heartening to Itard the empiricist as it was disheartening to Itard the pedagogue. The physician had set out not only to apply medicine and metaphysics to the boy's training, but also to "deduce from what he lacks the hitherto uncalculated sum of knowledge and ideas which man owes to his education." Man's debt to nurture proved heavy indeed, even for the most elementary sensory discriminations, reflexes, and drives: the boy was indifferent to temperature and rejected clothing even in the coldest weather; he would put his hand in a fire; his eyes did not fixate; he reached alike for painted objects, objects in relief, and the image of objects reflected in a mirror; he did not sneeze, even with snuff, nor did he weep; he did not respond to loud voices; he did not recognize edible food by sight, but by smell; he preferred uncooked food and had no taste for sweets or hard drink; he had no emotional ties, no sexual expression, no speech; he had a peculiar gait and would occasionally run on all fours.

Condillac provided that the first operation of the mind is perception and the second, attention, from which all other mental processes arise. Thus, confronted with the boy's failure to respond to all manner of stimuli, Itard undertook to "prepare the mind for attention by preparing the senses to receive keener impressions." Actually Condillac thought that "we have the use of our senses at an early age" without the need for specific instruction, but he did allow that the sensory organs are "sometimes poorly suited to relating ideas since they have not been sufficiently exercised." In order to awaken the wild boy's "nervous sensibility by the most energetic stimulation," Itard administered very hot baths daily, lasting two to three hours; he also clothed, bedded, and housed the boy warmly; and he gave him dry rubs of the spine and lumbar region (although he soon discontinued the latter when he found it to be sexually arousing).

Three months of this treatment, which also included provoking joy and anger on occasion, resulted in "a general excitement of all the senses." The boy would test the bath with his finger and refuse to get in if it were cool. He removed potatoes from the fire with a spoon and squeezed them to judge how well cooked they were. He dropped burning paper well before the flame could reach his fingers. He liked to stroke velvet. "The sense of smell had also gained by this improvement. The least irritation of this organ provoked sneezing, and I judged by the fright that seized him the first time this happened that this was a new experience for him. He immediately ran away and threw himself on his bed. The refinement of the sense of taste was even more marked." The boy accepted a wider range of foods, and kept them fastidiously clean. Itard capitalized on this newly acquired sensitivity to train some new habits, by means of avoidance conditioning, as it is now called. The boy was left exposed to the cold each morning within reach of his clothes, and he soon learned to put them on. For much the same reason, he would get up in the night to urinate, rather than sleep in a cold wet bed.

Sight and hearing did not improve, however. "The simultaneous improvement of [touch, taste, and smell] resulting from stimulants applied to the skin, while the former two senses remained unaffected, is an important fact, one that deserves the attention of physiologists." Since the wild boy had to learn to attend to things in each of the sensory modalities separately, with little carryover from the skin senses to hearing or vision, this belies Itard's original notion of a central "faculty of attention." "Attention" seems only a label we use when a person responds to some things and not others: he is not "paying attention" if the cues influencing him at the moment do not interest us.

It may seem hard to believe that isolation could be responsible for such generally reduced sensitivity, even to pain, and that baths and rubs could produce such widespread improvement, but some recent experiments suggest that Itard may not have been so far off the mark as his detractors contend.* In the 1950s psychologists studying pain found that puppies reared in social isolation from one to eight months of age would stand by impassively as flaming matches were placed in their noses and pins in their thighs; they were also quite slow in learning to avoid shock from an electrified floor by jumping to the safe side of the compartment. Turning to therapy, we may ask if it is reasonable to believe that sensitizing a child with certain stimuli would help him later in learning tasks that involved those stimuli. So it would appear, to judge, for example, from some Soviet experiments with the Pavlovian conditioning of premature babies. The response was not salivation but eye blink, elicited by a puff of air, and the "bell" was mint or anise perfume. After a few dozen trials of scent followed by puff, the babies learned to blink when the mint or anise was presented. However, the babies had been exposed previously to mint, by bottle feeding with mint-soaked nipples, and they learned much sooner to blink at the mint than at the anise. The effect of generally stimulating a sense does seem, moreover, to spread to other senses. Children blind from birth were better at distinguishing shapes and textures by hand when they had first spent ten minutes in a room filled with peppermint scent. Generalized stimulation also improved the "development quotient" of six-month-old infants in one experiment, in which the children were handled for twelve minutes and then tested. Probably all these results, including Itard's, are partly due to the general "arousal" that any stimulation produces along with the specific effect of its perception.

Various physiological measures confirm that the aroused brain is more sensitive to messages coming from any of the senses.* Since the results of energetic stimulation of the wild boy were long-lasting, the steps Itard took to follow up on the initial advantage must have been important. This kind of training was sometimes intentional, as when he taught the boy that cold could be avoided with clothes, and probably sometimes unwitting. For example, the child must have often seen people don clothes in the cold, test baths by hand, and sneeze after inserting snuff in the nose.

"Finally, even disease came forth to bear witness to the development of the wild boy's sensitivity; disease, which is the inevitable and troublesome consequence of the peculiar sensitivity of civilized man. Toward the first days of spring, our young savage had a violent cold in the head and some weeks later two catarrhal affections, one following almost directly on the other." Things were no better the following winter. A year later Itard wrote:

> It is an incontestable fact that the frequency and variety of human illnesses are due less to man's particular physical makeup than to the influence of civilization. The first result of the latter is to refine nervous sensitivity; and the enhancement of this sensitivity becomes the source of our illnesses, as well as that of our pleasures. Numerous facts demonstrate this, and above all those obtained from studying the young wild boy of Aveyron. This child, who from the beginning of his stay in society could not tolerate any clothing and who spent the coldest days of the winter of the year 9 half naked in the gardens of the Deaf-Mute Institute, was sensitized by the effects of civilization and especially by taking hot baths; nowadays he can barely tolerate moderate cold and, during the winter of year 10, he suffered severe colds and several sore throats.

In adopting his third aim, to lead the boy to acquire new needs, Itard had the same goals in mind as society does in pursuing this end with the normal child: it provides a means of "reward, punishment, encouragement, and instruction." Itard spurned the primary rewards, or "primary reinforcers" as they are called in technical parlance, such as food, which were means of influence or control par excellence: the boy's "perception was nothing but a computation prompted by gluttony, his pleasure an agreeable sensation of the organ of taste, and his intelligence the ability to produce a few incoherent ideas relative to his wants." Actually the boy could master rather complicated skills if they led, even remotely, to food, as the bean-shelling episode related by Bonnaterre amply testifies. Rejecting such primary reinforcers as food and freedom at the outset, Itard tried toys, sweets, and social approval, but without success.

> I have given him toys of all kinds one after another; more than once I have tried for hours on end to teach him how to use them and I have seen with sorrow that, far from attracting his attention, these various objects always ended by making him so impatient that he came to the point of hiding them or destroying them when the occasion presented itself. Thus, one day when he was alone in his room, he took it upon himself to throw into the fire a game of ninepins with which we had pestered him and which he had put away for a long time in a night commode, and he was found gaily warming himself before his bonfire.

The teacher only slowly came to realize that the way to attach value to an object or event is to associate it with a primary reinforcer. This he did with notable success in a game of "shells."

> I placed before him without any symmetrical order, and upside down, several little silver cups, under one of which I put a chestnut. Quite sure of having attracted his attention, I raised them one after the other except the one that covered the nut. After having thus shown him that they contained nothing, and having replaced them in the same order, I invited him by signs to seek in his turn for the chestnut. The first cup that he chose was precisely the one under which I had hidden the little reward for his attentiveness. Thus far, he showed only a feeble effort of memory. But I made the game imperceptibly more complicated. Thus after having hidden another chestnut by the same procedure I changed the order of all the cups, slowly, however, so that in this general inversion he was able, although with difficulty, to follow with his eyes and with his attention the one that hid the precious object. I did more; I placed nuts under two or three of the cups and his attention, although divided between these three objects, followed them nevertheless in their respective changes, and directed his first searches toward them.

It is hard to believe we are reading about the same boy whose gaze could not fixate, and who had no attention and no memory. The passage illustrates the difference between a game with toys and an instructional device. Picking up the correct cup should now have became reinforcing in its own right: will the boy play on for a while without the chestnuts? "I took away from this amusement everything which had some connection with his appetite, and put under the cups only objects that could not be eaten. The result was almost as satisfactory and this exercise became no more than a simple game of cups, not without advantage in provoking attention, judgment, and steadiness in his gaze." Itard's method resembles one employed, a hundred and fifty years later, to elicit attention, judgment, and steadiness of gaze from radar observers. The way to maintain a vigilant observer is not so much to exhort him or to reduce his watch, but rather to reinforce him intermittently, and unpredictably, for correct detection. The detection itself then becomes a secondary reinforcer.*

Sweets, seasoned dishes, and alcoholic beverages were no more effective with the boy than toys. Itard wisely "cultivated the few to which he was limited by accompanying them with accessories that could increase his pleasure in them."

It was with this intention that I often took him to dine with me in town. On such occasions a complete collection of his favorite dishes was on the table. The first time he found himself at such a feast he had transports of joy amounting almost to frenzy. Doubtless he thought that he would not do so well at supper time as he had just done at dinner, for on leaving the house that evening it was not his fault that he did not carry away a plate of lentils he had pilfered from the kitchen. I congratulated myself on this first outcome. I had just procured him a pleasure; I had only to repeat it several times to make it a necessity. Which is what I actually did. I did more. I was careful to precede our excursions by certain preparations that he would notice; these were to enter his room about four o'clock, my hat on my head, his shirt in my hand. He soon came to recognize these preparations as the signal of departure. I scarcely appeared before I was understood; he dressed himself hurriedly and followed me with much evidence of satisfaction.

It was impossible when I took him with me to lead him through the streets. It would have been necessary for me to run with him or else to use force in order to make him walk in step with me. We were obliged, then, to go out only in a carriage, another new pleasure that he connected more and more with his frequent excursions. In a short time these days ceased to be merely holidays to which he gave himself up with the liveliest pleasure, but became real necessities. When there was too long an interval between them, his privation made him sad, restless, and fretful. How the pleasure was increased when these trips took place in the country!

By associating innumerable "accessories," notably social contacts, with food and the countryside, Itard gradually brought about the boy's socialization. As it happens, we have a detailed record of one of these outings, when the pupil and his teacher mingled with the Tout-Paris at the salon of Madame Récamier, a political and literary gathering animated by a woman whose beauty and culture were as extraordinary as her wealth. The description written by one of the guests, the Baronne de Vaudey, appears in the memoirs of Napoleon's *valet de chambre* and draws a sharp contrast between the social needs of the boy and those of at least a segment of contemporary society.

Madame Récamier's biographer, Edouard Herriot, first sets the scene:

Mme. Récamier went with her mother and La Harpe [poet, and playwright] to Mass during the morning and, on returning, changed her dress. Narbonne [Minister of War under Louis XVI, Napoleon's aide-de-camp], Camille Jordan [political figure, anti-Revolutionary], Junot [general], and Bernadotte [French general, later King of Sweden and Norway] were awaiting her in the drawingroom. Talma [actor] then arrived, and M. de Longchamps [playwright], who was to read the *Séducteur amoureux*, a piece about which he wanted M. de La Harpe's opinion, before giving it to the Committee of the Théâtre Français. Very soon afterwards Lamoignon [nobleman] appeared, and then Adrien and Mathieu de Montmorency [political figures and nobility], General Moreau [commander of French armies, opposed to Napoleon], Fox [British statesman], Lord and Lady Holland [British statesman], Erskine [British barrister], and Adair [British statesman]. Old and new France met before these illustrious foreigners. There was a moment of embarrassment, and then Mme. Récamier entered, introduced her guests to Fox, and started the conversation. At luncheon she was seated between Fox and Moreau, "War and politics were talked," says the Baronne de V . . . and also literature and the fine arts. . . .

Whilst coffee was being served, Eugène de Beauharnais [French nobleman, Napoleon's adopted son] and his friend, Philippe de Ségur [ambassador under the monarchy, Napoleon's chief of protocol], were announced. The company then dispersed for a stroll in the park. The guests met again to hear Talma in a scene from Othello, and in Macbeth's speech, from the text of Ducis. After the departure of Talma, Nadermann [outstanding harpist] and Frédéric [playwright] gave a duet and, finally, Mme. Récamier sang a charming song by Plantade, accompanying herself on the harp.

Fresh guests took the places of those who had gone [to see Napoleon at the Chateau Malmaison]. The Duchess of Gordon arrived, and her daughter, the Lady Georgiana, later on Duchess of Bedford. M. de Longchamps read his piece in their presence. La Harpe had only just complimented him on it when Vestris [leading dancer] appeared. He had come to rehearse with Juliette [Mme. Récamier] to the accompaniment of the harp and the horn, the gavotte that she was to dance the following day.

After the ballet . . . the Duchess of Gordon, Mme. Récamier, and the Baronne de V . . . started for the Bois de Boulogne. At five, dinner was served at the Château. Other guests were brought in by M. Récamier: Lalande, the astronomer, and Degérando, the philanthropist.

"A remarkable individual was expected that day," the Baronne de Vaudey recounts, "the famous Aveyron savage. He arrived finally, accompanied by M. Yzard [sic], who was his teacher, doctor, and benefactor combined."

This savage, whose origins are unknown, was found in the forest of Aveyron, where he had undoubtedly lived for several years on fruits, vegetables, and animals that he could overtake or hit by throwing a pole, which he handled with surprising dexterity. The woodsmen snared him in nets that they wrapped around him. Soon after his capture, he was brought to Paris, and the government placed him in the care of Doctor Yzard. This doctor took all possible pains to socialize the boy and became attached to him like a father to a son. Nevertheless, no amount of effort could overcome his wild habits; and either for lack of attention on his part or because of an organic impairment, he never could learn to use his voice other than to articulate some guttural sounds, imitating the cries of various animals.

Madame Récamier seated him at her side, thinking perhaps that the same beauty that had captivated civilized man would receive similar homage from this child of nature, who seemed not yet fifteen years old.

It was a scene that could bring to mind for a moment the Ingenu next to the pretty Mlle. de Saint-Yves; but less gallant than was the practice among the Huron [Indians] in Voltaire's time, and too occupied with the abundant things to eat, which he devoured with startling greed as soon as his plate was filled, the young savage hardly heeded the beautiful eyes whose attention he had himself attracted. When dessert was served and he had adroitly filled his pockets with all the delicacies that he could filch, he calmly left the table. No one noticed that the young savage had left the dining room, since everyone was absorbed by a heated discussion between La Harpe and the astronomer Lalande, concerning the latter's atheist opinions and his singular taste for spiders. [He began by eating them in front of his beloved to cure her of a phobia for insects.] Suddenly, a noise came from the garden, and M. Yzard was led to suppose that his pupil was the cause. He got up to go verify his suspicions; our curiosity aroused, we all followed him in search of the fugitive whom we soon glimpsed running across the lawn with the speed of a rabbit. To give himself more freedom of movement, he had stripped to his undershirt. Reaching the main avenue of the park, which was bordered by huge chestnut trees, he tore his last garment in two, as if it were simply made of gauze; then, climbing the nearest tree with the ease of a squirrel, he perched in the middle of the branches.

The women, motivated as much by distaste as by respect for decorum, kept to the rear while the men set about recapturing the child of the woods. M. Yzard employed all the means he knew to recall the boy but without any effect; the savage, insensitive to the entreaties of his teacher, or dreading the punishment that he thought his escapade merited, leapt from branch to branch and from tree to tree, until there were neither trees nor branches in front of him and he reached the end of the avenue. The gardener then had the idea of showing him a basket full of peaches and, nature ceding to this argument, the runaway came down from the tree and let himself be captured. He was clothed as best one could with a little robe belonging to the gardener's niece. In this outfit he was bundled into the carriage that had brought him and he left, leaving the guests at Clichy-la-Garenne to draw a sweeping and useful comparison between the perfection of civilized life and the distressing picture of nature untamed, which this scene had so strikingly contrasted. M. de La Harpe, especially, was fired with enthusiasm: "I would really like to see J.-J. Rousseau here," he cried, "with all his rantings against the social state!" And with this challenge addressed to the spirit of the eloquent sophist from Geneva, the classical orator seemed to express, in the same moment and by an easily explained contradiction, both the anger of a pupil of Voltaire and that of a converted philosopher determined to eradicate the least hint of philosophy and irreligion. In the absence of Jean-Jacques, La Harpe renewed his discussion with the atheist astronomer. They were both wrought up, and it would be too long an affair to recount their dispute.

Although Itard probably felt humiliated by the fiasco that ended the day, he may have taken comfort in the evidence of the boy's progress, since he knew what he was like at the start of the treatment; for example, the boy would now sit at a table, wait for his food to be served, and could eat with utensils. Wanting to indulge and profit by the boy's love of the outdoors without evoking wild flights across the fields and into the trees, Itard proscribed country outings but encouraged those in the city parks, with the boy accompanied by his governess. As part of his increasing socialization, the boy began to show deep affection.

Thus Madame Guérin took him sometimes to the Luxembourg and almost daily to the Observatory gardens where, thanks to the generosity of Citizen Lemeri, he has acquired the habit of going every day for a drink of milk. As a result of these new habits, of certain recreations of his own choosing and, finally, of all the kind treatment that surrounded his new existence he ended up liking it all. This was the beginning of the rather intense affection he has acquired for his governess, which he sometimes expresses to her in a most touching manner. He never leaves her without reluctance nor does he rejoin her without signs of satisfaction.

Once when he had escaped from her in the streets, he shed many tears on seeing her again. Some hours after, he still had a high and broken respiration and a feverish pulse. When Madame Guérin reproached him, he interpreted her tone so well that he began to weep again. The friendship he has for me is much less strong, and justifiably so. The care Madame Guérin takes of him is of a kind which is immediately appreciated, and what I give him is of no obvious use to him. This difference in his affections is unquestionably due to the cause I have indicated, since there are times when he welcomes me, times that I have never used for his instruction. For example, when I go to his room in the evening just after he has gone to bed, his first movement is to sit up for me to embrace him, then to draw me to him by seizing my arm and making me sit upon his bed. Usually he then takes my hand, draws it over his eyes, his forehead, the back of his head, and holds it with his upon these parts for a very long time. At other times he gets up with bursts of laughter and comes beside me to caress my knees in his own way which consists of feeling them, rubbing them firmly in all directions for some minutes, and then sometimes in putting his lips to them two or three times. People may say what they like, but I confess that I lend myself without ceremony to all this childish play.

In order to lead the boy to speak by imitating what he heard, Itard's fourth aim, the teacher realized that his pupil would first have to detect and distinguish speech sounds. Pinel considered the wild boy practically incapable of auditory attention and took this as one more symptom of the boy's hopeless idiocy. Itard knew better.

> When a chestnut or a walnut was cracked without his knowledge and as gently as possible; if the key of the door that held him captive was merely touched, he never failed to turn quickly and run toward the place whence the sound came. If the organ of hearing did not show the same susceptibility to the sounds of the voice, even to the explosion of firearms, it was because he was not very sensitive or attentive to impressions other than those to which he had been long and exclusively accustomed . . . If then, after the early days of childhood, attention is given naturally only to such things that have recognized or suspected connection with our tastes, it is understood why our young savage, having only a small number of wants, would exert his senses only on a small number of objects. Unless I am mistaken, that is the cause of this absolute inattention which struck everybody at the time of his arrival at Paris, and which at present has almost completely disappeared because he has been made to feel the relevance of all the new things that surround him.

Itard thought at first that with the widening circle of the boy's needs and increasing socialization, he might be able to bypass any explicit training of hearing or imitation and, indeed, some progress was made. Whereas originally the boy responded only to sounds associated with food and release from confinement, he increasingly came to react to voices: once he locked his door when there was loud conversation in an adjacent corridor. On other occasions he showed directional hearing of voices: if he heard the cries of the deaf-mute children of the institute at play coming from below as he descended the stairs, he would go back up; if from above, he would hasten his descent. A third example of this growing sensitivity finally earned the wild boy a name:

> One day when he was in the kitchen occupied with cooking potatoes two people had a sharp dispute behind him, without his appearing to pay the least attention. A third arrived to join the discussion who began

all his replies with these words, "Oh, that's different!" I noticed that every time that this person let his favorite "Oh!" escape, the Savage of Aveyron quickly turned his head. That evening when he went to bed I experimented with this sound and obtained almost the same results. I went over all the other simple sounds known as vowels, but without any success. The preference for "o" obliged me to give him a name which ended with this vowel. I chose Victor. This name stuck, and when it is spoken aloud he rarely fails to turn his head or to come running.

It is perhaps for the same reason that he has since understood the meaning of the negative *non*, which I often use to correct him when he makes mistakes in his little exercises.

Probably Victor learned to respond to his name and to *non* because it was in his interest to do so, not because they contained the vowel sound in "oh": all three French vowels are quite different.

Despite these gradual improvements in hearing, the boy remained mute. Itard rejected the hypothesis that the boy's voice organs were impaired because he found no evidence for it, even in the large scar across the larynx which he felt stemmed from a relatively superficial wound; a deeper incision would not have healed so well without medical attention. Itard does argue that it takes some eighteen months for an infant to develop speech, and Victor had been in society perhaps half as long, not counting the time he spent among the deaf-mutes or in isolation; so it was too soon to expect much progress. However, it is hard to see the relevance of this argument since, if Victor was a normal child, he already knew how to speak when he was abandoned in the wild at the age of five or even older. Itard's third hypothesis turned on this isolation. "Complete absence of exercise renders our organs unfit for their functions"—the more so, he argued, when they are still in the stage of development, as they were in Victor's case. Finally, he contended that a young child has a greater capacity for learning to speak than an adult, which translates roughly into the modern hypothesis that there is a critical period for language acquisition.* This hypothesis lacks firm evidence and the "period" lacks clear demarcation, but there are suggestive observations: damage to the language area of the brain leaves much more permanent disability if it occurs after five years of age; the mentally retarded seem to make more progress in language in early childhood; children with hearing impairments have a better chance to acquire speech the earlier they receive training and prosthetic aids.

Despite the obstacles to Victor's acquiring speech by normal means, Itard hoped that substitute means could bring it about, specifically, inducements to imitation. He chose the word for water as his first target—*eau*—since Victor could both hear and produce this simple vowel (as in the first syllable of the English *oboe*), and since water was the boy's preferred drink. But "even when his thirst was most intense, it was in vain that I held a glass of water in front of him, repeatedly crying *eau, eau*. When I gave the glass to someone next to him who pronounced the same word, and when I asked for it back in the same way, the poor child, tormented on all sides, waved his arms around the glass almost convulsively, producing a kind of hiss but not articulating any sound." Apparently Itard thought that he would not have to inculcate imitation as a skill since, as he put it, a child possesses "an innate propensity to imitation." Some psychologists in recent work on the behavior modification of retarded children encountered similar difficulties: "Subject 1, for example, would sit down when told to, but did not imitate the experimenter when he said 'Do this,' sat down, and then offered her the chair. Hence, the initial imitative training for all subjects was [undertaken]."

Switching to milk and the word *lait* (the vowel as in upset), Itard heard his efforts rewarded after four days when Victor pronounced the word *lait*, "distinctly, though rather crudely, it is true; and he repeated it almost immediately." Perhaps Victor did have some vocal imitation skills to begin with—what B. F. Skinner calls echoic behavior*—or perhaps Itard unwittingly shaped the response *lait* by reinforcing successive approximations: giving Victor milk at first for any sound that he made, but only in the end for those that were similar to *lait*. The modern teacher or parent would probably be overjoyed by this breakthrough, and would reward this word at first whenever it occurred, in the hope of making the learner more vocal, later withholding a reward unless the word followed the model. Not Itard—he let it drop. He had set out to train requesting but found he had trained naming; Victor would say *lait* only after he had been given the milk, never before. To use the technical terms, Itard had trained *tacting*—that is, verbal behavior controlled primarily by its antecedents: in this case, the sight of the milk. He trained the tact *lait* by presenting the appropriate object, modeling its name, and rewarding the correct utterance. However, what Itard wanted at this point was *manding* —that is, verbal behavior controlled primarily by its consequences: in this case, receiving the milk. In a modern program of teaching speech to mute emotionally disturbed children, O. Ivor Lovaas similarly found that his pupils, although they had acquired a rather large repertory of names over a period of several months of training, would never use them to make demands or requests; they had to be trained to do this.

Victor also articulated a few related sounds that Itard let go by, not yet realizing that he would need whatever raw materials he could get to build up the boy's vocal skills. Thus Victor said *la* and *li* (pronounced *lee*) on occasion and also a palatal *l* before *i* (as in mil*l*ion), which Itard associates with the visits of Madame Guérin's twelve-year-old-daughter Julie. And he picked up his governess' exclamation *O Dieu!* which he pronounced O-D-uh. To summarize the status of Victor's vocal skills at this point, Itard's report gives evidence of five vowels and four consonants. The vowels are reasonably well spread out over the articulatory positions used in French, with the notable abscence of those produced in the front of the mouth with the lips rounded (for example, the vowel in *une*); nor are there any nasal vowels (neither category occurs in English). The consonants present a more peculiar picture. Linguists would have us believe that sounds made with the lips, like *papa* and *baba*, are more fundamental and precede sounds made with a constriction at the teeth like *d* and *l*;* however, Victor displays the latter and not the former. In fact, all of Victor's consonants share more or less the same place of articulation—the teeth. They do represent four different "manners of articulation"—that is, ways of producing different sounds in the same place in the mouth—and that augurs well. Another good omen for further speech development is that many of the missing speech sounds are among the easiest to detect, and hence to train, by sight and touch —*p* and *m*, for example.

The Wild Boy of Aveyron   114

Despite these good signs, Itard expected the full development of Victor's speech to prove long and difficult, for the reasons already mentioned and one more that is crucial, his skill in using and understanding gestural communication, which supplanted his need to speak on most occasions. Itard cites Condillac's speculations on the origins of spoken language, that it must have been a slow process for the first men to give up their natural action-language for more difficult spoken language, whose advantages could hardly have been foreseen at first. The examples of Victor's gestural communication range from simple, direct mands, as in the first two of the following sketches, to subtle communications of concepts.

> If he is in town dining with me, he addresses all his requests to the person who does the honors of the table; it is always to her that he turns to be served. If she pretends not to hear him, he puts his plate next to the particular dish he wants and devours it with his eyes. If that produces no result, he takes a fork and strikes the edge of his plate two or three times. If she still neglects him, then he knows no bounds; he plunges a spoon or even his hand into the dish and in the twinkling of an eye empties it all onto his own plate. He is scarcely less expressive in his way of showing his emotions, above all impatience and boredom. A number of people visiting him out of curiosity know how, with more natural frankness than politeness, he dismisses them when fatigued by the length of their visits; he offers to each of them, quite deliberately, their cane, gloves, and hat, and pushes them gently toward the door, which he slams shut behind them.
>
> If the time for his walk has come, he appears several times before the window and the door of his room. If he then sees that his governess is not ready, he places before her all the objects necessary for her toilet and, in his impatience, even goes as far as helping her dress. That done, he goes downstairs and opens the door latch himself. Arriving at the observatory, his first concern is to ask for some milk, which he does by presenting a wooden bowl that he never forgets to put in his pocket on leaving; this bowl he appropriated after he had broken a china cup that had been used for the same purpose in the same house.
>
> Again, to make the pleasure of his excursions complete, he has, for some time now, been given rides in a wheelbarrow. As a result, as soon as the inclination arises, if nobody is around to satisfy it, he returns to the house, takes someone by the arm, leads him to the garden and puts the handles of the wheelbarrow in his hands, and then climbs in. If this first invitation is resisted, he leaves his seat, takes the handles of the

wheelbarrow, wheels it around a bit, and gets in again; imagining, doubtless, that if his wishes are not granted after all this, it is not for want of clearly expressing them . . .

Once we wanted him to take a bath that was only lukewarm, and our insisting made him violently angry. Seeing that the frequent tests he made with his fingertips did not convince his governess that the water was too cool, he turned toward her quickly, seized her hand, and plunged it into the bath.

Let me relate another act of the same nature. One day when he was in my study sitting on a sofa, I came and sat at his side, placing a lightly charged Leyden jar between us. He was familiar with its effect because of a slight shock he had received from it the day before. Seeing the uneasiness that the approach of the instrument caused him, I thought he would move it farther away by taking hold of the handle. He took a more prudent course, which was to put his hands in the opening of his waistcoat and to draw back some inches so that his leg would no longer touch the covering of the bottle. I drew near him a second time and again placed the jar between us. Another movement on his part, another adjustment on mine. This little maneuver continued until, driven into a corner at the end of the sofa, he found himself bounded by the wall behind, by a table in front, and on my side by the annoying device. He could no longer make another move. It was then that, seizing the moment when I advanced my arm in order to guide his, he very adroitly lowered my wrist upon the knob of the bottle. I received the charge.

Victor also understood this gestural language, so most people, Madame Guérin included, did not speak to him. If his governess wanted him to go for water, she held the pitcher upside down. When Itard wanted a comb, he pointed to his tousled hair. On the one hand, this gestural skill suggests that Victor might have been adept at learning sign language, which would have been valuable in its own right as well as facilitating the acquisition of speech and higher mental process (the fifth aim). On the other hand, Victor's gestural language was always tied to objects; there was no miming and no indication that he could learn signs that had a purely, or largely, conventional value.

Itard now undertook his fifth and final aim in the initial period of instruction, training at least some of the essential higher mental operations, with a view to preparing Victor to acquire more formal education in various "subject matters," as we like to call them. In all that had preceded this stage, the teacher judged his student at least somewhat prepared in the functions of his senses and in the exercise of his attention, memory, and judgment. At this point, Itard would have preferred to teach various concepts orally, by dialogues with his student, just as Condillac had done with Louis XV's grandson, the Prince of Parma. But Victor was, for the present at least, a deaf-mute, indistinguishable in this respect from Sicard's pupils. Had not the abbé shown, nevertheless, that these unfortunates could be led to the highest degree of intellectual development by his means of instruction? So it was these means that Itard adopted, beginning as Sicard did by teaching the names of familiar objects.

> Thus I began then with the procedure ordinarily used first in that famous school and drew on a blackboard line drawings of some objects that could best be represented by simple sketches, such as a key, scissors, and a hammer. When I saw that I was being observed, I repeatedly placed each of these objects upon its respective drawing; and when I was sure that in this way he had been made to feel the connection, I tried to get him to bring me the objects in succession by pointing to their sketches. Nothing came of this. I repeated the experiment several times and always with little success; he either stubbornly refused to bring whichever of the three things I indicated, or else brought the two others with it and gave them all to me at the same time.

An impasse—Itard had begun just like Sicard, but with two notable differences. First, Sicard started out with twenty-one sketches and objects; it would have been unlikely indeed for his pupil to hit upon the right one by fetching several at a time. Second, and more important, these objects, these response-alternatives in the matching task, were probably even more familiar to Massieu than their sketches: he had often used most of them, such as keys and locks, knives, tables and chairs, hammer, pen and ink, and so on. In contrast, Pinel is sarcastic in assuring us of Victor's difficulties in using keys, and there is no record of his using scissors and hammers.

Itard revised his strategy, drawing on his keen observation of Victor's behavior.

> I had noticed that, for some months past, he had a most decided taste for order; so much so that he would sometimes get up from his bed to

put back into its usual place a piece of furniture or a utensil that had accidentally been moved. He was even more particular about things hanging on the wall: each had its particular nail and hook, and if any of these objects had been interchanged he was not happy until he had replaced it himself. All I had to do then was to make a similar arrangement of the things on which I wanted him to exercise his attention. I suspended each of the objects from a nail below its drawing and left them there for some time. When afterwards I took them away and gave them to Victor, they were immediately replaced in their proper order. I repeated this several times and always with the same result.

Victory? Not necessarily, and it is symptomatic of Itard's genius as a trainer that he realized it. Itard knew that a correct performance was one that occurred for the right reasons—that is, signaled by the right cues and motivated by the right consequences. To check if the sketches were indeed the cues for Victor's orderly replacement of the objects, if he were truly matching the one to the other,

I changed the respective positions of the drawings, and this time I saw him follow the original order in the arrangement of the objects without any allowance for the transposition. As a matter of fact, nothing was easier than teaching him the new ordering entailed by this change in the drawings, but nothing more difficult than to make him reason it out. His memory alone bore the burden of each new arrangement of the objects. I turned then to the task of neutralizing, so to say, his reliance on memory. I succeeded in fatiguing it by increasing the number of drawings and the frequency of their transpositions.

His memory now became an insufficient guide for the systematic arrangement of the numerous articles, so his mind was obliged to compare the drawings with the things. What a difficult step I had taken! I was convinced of this when I saw our young Victor fasten his gaze upon each object in turn, choose one, and next look for the drawing to which he wanted to match it, and I soon had material proof by trying the transposition of the drawings, which was followed on his part by the systematic transposition of the objects. This result inspired me with the brightest hope.

Itard now proceeded to the second stage of Sicard's method, or so he thought: the letter-names are written above the sketches, the sketches are erased, and the pupil fetches the corresponding objects guided only by the names. This procedure did not work with Victor, despite frequent repetition and prolonged pairings of the objects and their names. Itard had not read the *Cours d'instruction*, or consulted with its author, carefully enough and bypassed several intervening steps. Massieu would almost surely have failed a similar program of instruction. First, Sicard recounts that he consolidated his original gains by exchanging roles with his pupil: Massieu drew sketches of various objects and Sicard went to fetch them. Second, the names usurped the role of the sketches gradually: Sicard lettered them on the sketches in a way that preserved the configuration of the object, even after the outline was erased. The fading of the sketch itself as a cue was then completed as Massieu copied the name below the iconograph and the latter was erased. There were yet three more differences between the linguist's methods and the physician's. Sicard had an assistant who first performed the read-and-fetch at each step. Also, Massieu was made to study the names by examining and counting the letters in each of them. And, most important, he had previously been taught to distinguish, match, and write letters, the elements of names. Itard had failed once again to give his pupil preliminary training in a necessary discrimination.

So Itard backed up and set out to teach Victor the preliminary alphabetical skills, which proved to be all the progress toward his fifth aim that he could accomplish in this initial period of instruction. In the first step, he taught matching-to-sample with redundant cues.

> I pasted three pieces of paper of very distinct shapes and colors on a board two feet square. One form was circular and red; another, triangular and blue; the third, square and black. Nails were driven into the board and three pieces of cardboard of the same shapes and colors, with holes pierced in their centers, were placed on their respective models and left there for some days. Then I lifted them off and gave them to Victor, who replaced them without any difficulty. By inverting the board and thus changing the order of the figures, I made sure that this first result was not purely a matter of routine but the fruit of comparison.

In the second step, he selected one from the complex of two cues and obliged Victor to attend to that dimension to solve the matching problem.

> After some days I substituted another board for the first. I had pasted the same figures on it, but this time they all had the same color. Originally the pupil had the twofold cue of shape and color to aid him in recognition; now he had only one guide, comparison of the shapes. At almost the same time, I showed him a third board where all the forms were the same but the colors different. The same test always had the same results, not counting mistakes owing to lack of attention.

Next Itard led Victor to progressively finer discriminations along each dimension.

> To the board with various forms, I added some new shapes that were much less distinct and, to the board with various colors, some new hues that differed only in tint. There was, for example, a rather long parallelogram next to a square in the first case and, in the second, a pattern in sky-blue beside one of gray-blue. This gave rise to some mistakes and some hesitation, which disappeared, however, after some days' practice.

This rapid progress in increasing the boy's resolving power emboldened the teacher to go too far too fast:

> Each day I added, curtailed, and modified, provoking new comparisons and new judgments. At length, the multiplicity and the complications of these little exercises exhausted his attention and his docility. Then those emotions of impatience and rage which exploded so violently at the beginning of his stay in Paris, especially when he was locked in his room, reappeared in all their intensity.

Pavlov had the same unhappy experience at the turn of the following century while teaching a child of six to distinguish the beats of a metronome. To distinguish the difference between 92 and 144 beats per minute was easy enough, but when Pavlov narrowed the difference to 144 versus 120 beats per minute, the child became surly, disobedient, and uncooperative. Itard persisted in inducing this experimental neurosis, and what might have been a minor detour on the route to letter mastery became a major preoccupation.

> My persistence lasted only for a few days and was finally overcome by his independence of character. His fits of anger became more frequent,

more violent, and were like the fits of rage of which I spoke earlier but with the striking difference that their effect was less directed toward persons than toward things. In this destructive mood he ran off and bit the sheets, the blankets, and the mantlepiece, scattered the andirons, ashes, and blazing embers, and ended by falling into convulsions which, like those of epilepsy, involved a complete suspension of sensory function. I was obliged to yield when things reached this frightful pitch; but my acquiescence only increased the evil. The paroxysms became more frequent, and apt to be renewed at the slightest opposition, often without any clear cause.

The teacher realized that, by acquiescing to the disruptive behavior, he was strengthening it. He decided to try a shock treatment, recalling Victor's terror when they had once walked along the parapet of the Paris observatory.

> I soon found the occasion of a most violent fit, which was, I believe, caused by resumption of our lessons. Seizing the moment when his sensory functions were not yet suspended, I violently threw open the window of his room, which was on the fifth floor overlooking some boulders directly below. I approached him with every appearance of anger and grabbing him forcibly by the hips I held him out of the window, his head facing directly down toward the bottom of the chasm. After some seconds I drew him in again. He was pale, covered with a cold sweat, his eyes were wet with tears, and he still trembled a little, which I believed was the effect of his fear. I led him to the form boards, I made him gather up all the cards and replace them all. This was done, very slowly to be sure, and badly rather than well, but at least without impatience. Afterwards he went and threw himself on his bed and wept copiously.
>
> This was the first time, at least to my knowledge, that he shed tears.

The method resembles one that has been employed in recent decades with schizophrenic children and may have worked for the same reasons. The child is placed barefoot on an electrified floor and pushed by one adult toward a second at the periphery. He learns that the shock is terminated when he has sought the safety of the receiving adult. Associated with escape from aversive stimulation (so-called negative reinforcement), these adults took on reinforcing properties themselves, and children formerly indifferent to all social intercourse would now seek out their contact and affection; side effects such as "social-smiling" and enhanced re-sponsiveness also appeared.

In any event, these episodes of hysteria did not recur and Itard resumed the march toward mastery of letter discrimination. He replaced the completely colored forms with linear outlines of these forms and reduced the colored fields to small patches, without im-pairing Victor's matching to sample. Now he was ready for the letters and, to this end, Itard adapted a kind of compositor's bench that Deschamps had used in teaching the deaf-mutes of Orléans.

> I ordered each of the twenty-four letters of the alphabet printed in upper case on a piece of cardboard two inches square. I had an equal number of spaces cut in a plank a foot-and-a-half square. The pieces of cardboard could be inserted into these spaces without paste, so that their places could be changed as required. I had an equal number of letters of the same dimensions made in metal. These were meant to be compared by the pupil with the printed letters, and were to be arranged in their cor-responding places. The first trial was made, in my absence, by Madame Guérin. I was very much surprised on my return to learn from her that Victor distinguished all the characters and arranged them properly. He was immediately put to the test and performed his task without any mistake.

As usual, Itard was not satisfied with the behavior alone but wanted to confirm that it was under appropriate stimulus control.

> Though delighted with such an early success I was still far from being able to explain its cause, which I discovered only some days later by observing the way in which our pupil proceeded to arrange the letters. In order to make the work easier he devised on his own a little trick that allowed him to dispense with memory, comparison, and judgment in performing the task. When we put the board in his hands, he did not wait for us to take the metal letters out of their places but took them himself and piled them on his hand, following the order of their arrangement, so that the last letter, after all were taken from the board, was topmost on the pile. Then he began the task with this letter and finished with the last of the pile, starting the board at the end and pro-ceeding always from right to left. That is not all: he was able to improve upon this procedure; for rather often the pile collapsed, the characters fell out, and he had straighten them all up and put them in order, rely-ing entirely on attention. So the twenty-four letters were arranged in

four rows of six each, making it easier to lift them up by rows only, and even to replace them in the same way by taking letters from the second row only when the first was replaced.

I do not know whether he reasoned as I suppose, but at least it is certain that he executed the performance in the manner described. It was then a true routine, but a routine of his own invention, which did honor to his intelligence just as his mastery of the classification soon thereafter did honor to his discernment. It was not difficult to put him on the right track by giving him the characters pell-mell whenever he was given the board. At last, in spite of the frequent transpositions to which I submitted the printed characters by changing their slots, in spite of insidious arrangements, such as the O beside the C, the E beside the F, and so on, his discrimination became infallible.

Thus did the compositor's board become the prototype of the reading-readiness workbooks of today. And Victor was ready to form words, albeit meaningless ones at first.

Rather than resume Sicard's method of instruction at this point, Itard decided to try a little experiment. He had never forgiven Victor for failing to mand the milk proffered, as it were, at his breast, and so he persisted, hoping to retrieve this loss by substituting written for spoken language.

One morning when he was waiting impatiently for the milk he always had for breakfast, I took the four letters L A I T from his letter board and placed them on a panel I had specially prepared. Madame Guérin, whom I have instructed, comes over, looks at the letters, and immediately gives me a cup of milk which I pretend is for me. A moment later I go over to Victor, give him the four letters I have just taken off the board, and point to it with one hand while with the other I show him the jug of milk. The letters were immediately replaced but in inverted order, so that they formed T I A L instead of L A I T. I indicated the appropriate corrections by pointing to the letters to be transposed and the proper place of each. When these changes reproduced the sign, he was allowed to have his milk. It is difficult to believe that five or six similar attempts were sufficient not only to make him arrange the four letters of the word *lait* but also to give him the idea of the connection between the word and the thing.

So Itard got his tact again, this time more easily and less ambiguously than the first; indeed, he had even been tempted to write off the vocal *lait* as a sort of exclamation. Itard, who usually could not be tricked in such matters, was led by the following incident to think that he got the mand for free once he had trained the tact (they are, after all, the same word):

> One afternoon when [Victor] was ready to set out for the observatory, we saw him take the four letters in question on his own initiative and put them in his pocket; no sooner did he arrive at Citizen Lemeri's house, where as I previously said he goes every day for some milk, than he took them out and placed them on a table in such a way as to form the word *lait.*

Victor may have been asking for milk or, on the other hand, the response may have been evoked by the many cues that accompany milk as presented in this setting. Itard realized in the long run that the latter was true, that the response was an "extended" or generalized tact, and that the problem was the old one he was so good at detecting, namely, misplaced stimulus control. In his second report he wrote:

> I noticed that instead of repeating the words I had taught him in order to ask for the objects they designated, or to express a wish or a need, Victor resorted to these words only at certain moments and always when the desired object came into view. Thus, for example, much as he wanted his milk, it was only at the moment when he was accustomed to drink it and at the precise instant when he saw that it was going to be given to him that the word for this favorite food was expressed or rather formed in the proper way . . . I tried delaying his breakfast time but waited in vain for the written expression of my pupil's needs, although they had become very urgent. It was not until the cup appeared that the word *lait* was formed . . . I took away his cup of milk and shut it up in a cupboard. If the word *lait* had been for Victor the distinct sign of the thing and the expression of his desire for it, there is no doubt that after this sudden privation . . . the word would have been immediately produced. It was not, and I concluded that when my pupil formed this sign, rather than expressing his desires, he was merely engaging in a sort of preliminary exercise with which he mechanically preceded the satisfaction of his appetite.
>
> It was then necessary to retrace our steps and begin again. I resigned myself courageously to do this, believing that if I had not been understood by my pupil it was my fault rather than his. Indeed, in reflecting

on the possible causes of this faulty comprehension of the written signs, I recognized that in these first examples of the expression of ideas I had not employed the extreme simplicity I had introduced at the beginning of my other methods of instruction and which had ensured their success. Thus, although the word *lait* is for us only a simple sign, for Victor it might be a confused expression for the drink, the vessel that contained it, and the desire of which it was the object.

Itard's first report ends with Victor slapping his letters L A I T down on Citizen Lemeri's table. "I state it, naked and stripped of all reflections, so to speak, so that it may mark more strikingly the stage we have reached, and serve as a guarantee of future achievement." It is time to fill in a report card on Victor's progress, present standing, and prospects. In addition to an evaluation by the teacher, we have three newspaper reports by independent observers, and two very brief recorded comments. The teacher speaks first:

[Victor is now] endowed with the free use of all his senses; he repeatedly demonstrates attention, reflection, and memory; he can compare, discern, and judge, and, finally, apply all his intellectual faculties to the objects related to his instruction. It is essential to note that these happy changes have come about during the short space of nine months in a subject believed to be incapable of attention . . . Those who did not see him [originally] and who could see him now would find an almost normal child who does not speak. They would not be able to appreciate the distance that separates this almost ordinary creature from the *sauvage de l'Aveyron*, as he was when first brought back into society; a distance apparently very slight but really immense when we properly reflect on it and calculate how many new ideas and ways of reasoning the boy had to acquire to arrive at these last results . . . The conclusion will follow that his education is possible, if it is not already guaranteed, by this early success, quite apart from the results we can expect with more time.

The two brief remarks on record are these. Sicard stated to the Society of Observers of Man on November 10, 1801: "I always knew he was an idiot." And Virey, in the 1803 edition of the *Dictionary of Natural History*: "Nowadays he begins to understand several things and even to talk a little."

Soon after Itard gave his progress report to the Society of Observers of Man, Joseph-Marie de Gérando,* a member of that society's commission to study the wild boy, was invited to give his own evaluation to the Second Class of the French Institute (Social and Political Sciences) of which he was a member. A few years earlier, this contemporary of Itard's had won the institute's prize for the best essay on "The Influence of Signs on the Formation of Ideas." This early distinction was to launch his career as a political figure and author on metaphysics, education of the handicapped, jurisprudence, and social science.

De Gérando's moral and political support of Itard was probably crucial to the young physician's continuing efforts. Reciprocally, Itard led one of the finest minds of the time to reflect on the conditions of the handicapped. The philosopher's monumental study of the education of the deaf is still authoritative.* He became an administrator of the National Institute and originated several reforms in deaf education, at the same time that he was secretary-general in the Ministry of the Interior. In later years, De Gérando held many senior government posts and published a widely translated history of philosophy, a treatise on moral education that enjoyed acclaim in Europe and America throughout much of the nineteenth century, and a four-volume treatment of French administrative law—some say the best such code ever written. At the time of his report to the institute, he was appointed secretary of the Bureau of Arts and Sciences by Lucien Bonaparte.

The secretary of the institute's Second Class summarizes De Gérando's report on the wild boy of Aveyron:

At first he gave hardly any indication of memory: if he retained a few ideas, he did not know how to compare them. Finding everything around him foreign, he was unable to pay it any attention. His senses were inactive, as was his intelligence; or rather, he was lacking in intelligence because his senses were lacking in activity. His gaze wandered as in a stupor; he appeared not to hear anything, and his senses of touch and smell seemed paralyzed. He was equally insensitive to hot and cold; fetid odors had no disagreeable effect on him. Thus appears what must be nearly the ultimate savage; but the child of Aveyron was considered an imbecile. All hope was abandoned for his education, when C. Ytard [Citizen Itard] offered to see to it: he himself has given an account of his method in an interesting work which C. de Gérando analyzed. Three months sufficed for C. Ytard to revolutionize the condition of his pupil. By resourceful treatment, he has made the organs of the young savage acquire their natural sensitivity, although they are still sluggish. He knew how to get the boy interested in a large number of objects, inspire in him the beginnings of industry, awaken his intellectual faculties, and lead him to make a few comparisons, and to institute a few signs.

What was his method? That of a learned observer of our intellectual faculties, of a philosopher who has delimited the starting and stopping points of human intelligence, to avoid losing his way in the unbounded world of illusion; that of Locke, who has cleared away the errors of so many centuries and anticipated those of centuries to come. The wise instructor has multiplied the needs of his pupils, and he is quite hopeful for a happy outcome. C. de Gérando shares these hopes: but he does not yet dare to assert that the organs of the young savage were not damaged or ill-formed. If it is discovered that he is an imbecile then one can suspect that he did not live for long in the forests; he would thus be an idiot who had escaped from the hands that deigned to take care of him. Those who had sustained his useless existence would not have tried to lay claim to him once they had learned that he was otherwise cared for.

In a letter published posthumously, De Gérando wrote:

In a very short time, Citizen Itard has obtained extraordinary success. . . . Each day the child acquires some new expression; they are, it is true, only those that have some immediate relation to his needs, but such are the only terms that it is permissible for a philosopher to teach him. At last, here he is not only able to communicate with us, here he is in possession of our conventional signs . . . He has broken through the barriers that separated him from our society; we are now on common ground . . . Each of us wonders what the child's past progress augurs for his future . . . It is allowable to extrapolate from the success already obtained, and to expect a great deal of a method that has already produced so much.

The remaining two reports appear toward the end of 1801 as a letter to the editors and their reply in one of the more important periodicals of the era, and the first literary review to appear after the Revolution, the *Décade philosophique*.

Citizens, this young unfortunate boy from Aveyron, who excited such keen curiosity last year, is now utterly forgotten. His was the lot of everything that is a matter of vogue, he inspired interest only by virtue of his novelty. Several people have tried to justify the current indifference by claiming that he was an imbecile and that the impairment of his organs is opposed to his ever acquiring the use of reason. This severe sentence, which deprived him forever of the great endowment of our species, was dictated above all by the need of certain intellectuals to suppose I don't know what manner of *natural man*, living isolated in the middle of the woods, as the true model of our destiny and the most perfect expression of our humanity. This poor child from Aveyron barely escaped dying in the depths of an orphanage and in an asylum for imbeciles, misfortune having apparently usurped for a moment the rightful place of this man of nature and withheld the honors that are his due. C. Pinel, who is deservedly well known for his studies and treatment of mania, gave new force to this opinion by the parallels that he had drawn. He compared the outward characteristics of the child of Aveyron with those of idiot children of the same age that he had had occasion to observe, and he found roughly similar appearances. He even found some signs of idiocy more marked in the former than the latter. It was generally concluded that the similarity of effects reflected a similarity of causes. And it was promptly published that the child of Aveyron had been recognized as an idiot, without taking the trouble to wonder if there could not be a kind of apparent imbecility produced by social causes.

Wiser minds postponed judgment until the young savage would be subjected to more systematic and thought-out treatment. Today they are rewarded for their impartiality by the pleasure of nourishing certain hopes. Ever since this young man has stopped being tormented by the aggressive curiosity of a crowd of people, and has been confided to the care of C. Ytard, an enlightened physician and philosopher, he has made definite progress, albeit quite slowly. His senses have acquired more fixity, more refinement, his attention has begun to apprehend certain objects, he has established certain comparisons, and he has made them accurately; he has acquired a certain skillfulness. C. Ytard, convinced that he is not deaf, trusts that he is in no way condemned to idiocy. Perhaps the ingrained habits that he had acquired, perhaps our present ignorance of the means to begin his education, will postpone his development for a long time, but at least this development remains possible; the initial successes make it virtually probable. The tireless devotion of a philanthropist guarantee us that all means will be tried, and the solution of a great philosophical problem could well turn out to be the ending of this singular adventure.

Editors' note—We had the opportunity to see this child a few days ago. His eyes are still expressionless; he does not fix them on any object.

His gestures are always very intense but meaningless, as are his inarticulate little cries. Nevertheless, he recognizes his habitual companions. He even shows a certain preference for a young lady, the daughter of one of our leading astronomers, whom he finds occasionally in the observatory's public gardens where he is taken for walks. He obeys her almost the way a dog obeys his master, a matter of attachment mixed with fear. If she signals him to come sit down next to her, he comes running. But soon distracted by another object, he gets up and it requires a struggle to keep him there. We must await more observations to form any opinion whatever on the results of the education he is being given.

In ending his first report, Itard returns to the broader philosophical issues of his time that this metaphysical experiment undertook to clarify.

—In behalf of socialization he concludes "That man is inferior to a large number of animals in the pure state of nature, a state of nullity and barbarism that has been falsely painted in the most seductive colors; a state in which the individual, deprived of the characteristic faculties of his kind, pitifully hangs on without intelligence and without feelings, a precarious life reduced to bare animal functions."

—In behalf of acquired ideas, "That the moral superiority said to be *natural* to man is only the result of civilization, which raises him above other animals by a great and powerful force. This force is the preeminent sensibility of his species, an essential characteristic from which proceed the imitative faculties and that continual urge which drives him to seek new sensations in new needs."

—In behalf of a critical period for language acquisition, "That this imitative force, whose purpose is the education of his organs and especially the apprenticeship of speech, and which is very energetic and active during the first years of his life, wanes rapidly with age, with isolation, and with all the causes which tend to blunt nervous sensitivity. We may conclude that the articulation of sounds, indisputably the most unimaginable and useful result of imitation, must encounter innumerable obstacles at any age later than early childhood."

—In behalf of social reinforcers, "That in the most isolated savage as in the most highly civilized man, there exists a constant relation between ideas and needs; that the increasing multiplicity of the latter in the most civilized peoples should be considered as a great means of developing the human mind; so that a general proposition may be established, namely, that all causes, accidental, local or political, which tend to augment or diminish the number of our desires, necessarily contribute to extending or to narrowing the sphere of our knowledge and the domain of science, fine arts, and social industry."

—In behalf of individualized instruction, "That in the present state of our knowledge of physiology, the progress of education can and ought to be illumined by the light of modern medicine which, of all the natural sciences, can help most powerfully toward the perfection of the human species by detecting the organic and intellectual peculiarities of each individual and determining therefrom what education ought to do for him and what society can expect from him."

Chapter Six

A
Report
to
His
Excellency

*The next four years—Itard's second report
on Victor—Developing his senses—
Training hearing, vision, touch, smell—
Developing his intellect—Victor learns
names and remembers them—He thinks
they are proper names—He learns
categories—His categories are too inclusive
—He learns by practical manipulation—
Victor invents a chalkholder—He learns
the names of parts of things—He learns
adjectives, verbs, sentences—Itard teaches
Victor to write—He tries again to teach
him to speak—Pereire's method—Victor
fails—Developing his emotions—Victor
knows gratitude, remorse, the desire to
please, unjust punishment—Troubled
sexuality—Itard baffled—Taking stock.*

Itard and Victor continued their labors uninterrupted for another four-and-a-half years. France was passing through a period of relative peace abroad and progress at home, while its government became increasingly centralized in Napoleon's hands, initially as first consul and then, without pretense, as emperor, beginning in 1804. Itard pursued numerous other duties. He cared for the sick at the National—then Imperial—Institute for Deaf-Mutes. He prepared and defended his thesis on the pneumothorax (a condition in which air or other gas enters the pleural cavity, generally through diseased lung tissue). He treated soldiers at Val-de-Grâce and was promoted to surgeon-major in 1804; but assigned to the line infantry at Bar-le-Duc, he resigned his commission to avoid leaving the deaf-mutes of Paris—and Victor. In this same year, as his fame spread and his private practice increased, the Russian ambassador brought him a ring in the name of his sovereign and tried to induce him to carry on his work in Saint Petersburg. Itard refused the tsar as the abbé de l'Epée had refused the emperor of Germany, some three decades earlier.

June 1806 and the Minister of the Interior under the French emperor wrote to Itard:

> I know, sir, that your care of the young Victor who was entrusted to you five years ago has been as generous as it has been diligent. It is essential for humanity and for science to know the results. I invite you therefore to send me a detailed account, which will allow me to compare his original condition with his current one, and to judge what hopes we may still entertain concerning this child and the type of vocation he could be assigned. I will ask the third class of the French Institute to name a commission to take cognizance of the report that you will be sending me and to follow the methods you have originated in their application to your pupil. You should see in these measures only the desire to do justice to your zeal.
>
> I am yours very truly,
>
> Champagny

Itard replied three months later, enclosing his 1801 report on Victor and presenting a sequel, entitled "On the New Developments and Current State of the Sauvage de l'Aveyron." In a second letter, Champagny acknowledges receipt of the documents and then, at the end of November, he wrote to Itard to communicate their evaluation by the French Institute's Class of History and Ancient Literature, "which recognizes that you could not have put more intelligence, patience, wisdom, and courage in your lessons, in your exercises, and in your experiments." The minister will have the report printed at government expense (with a large number of free copies for the author), and "I ask you to continue, in behalf of the full development of young Victor's faculties, all the efforts that have already produced such happy results, and to consider if the moment has not come for teaching him profitably some mechanical trade."

Itard organized the 1806 report in three sections that corresponded roughly to the ordering of Victor's second phase of instruction: development of the senses; development of the intellectual faculties; development of the affective functions. The teacher realized of course that training and progress in the three areas were interrelated.

> Thus while I was limiting my efforts to exercising the senses of our savage, the mind took its share of the attention given exclusively to the education of these organs, and followed the same order of development. It is readily understandable that in instructing his senses to perceive and to distinguish new objects, I forced his attention to fix on them, his judgment to compare them, and his memory to retain them. Thus nothing was immaterial in these exercises. Everything engaged his mind. Everything put the faculties of his intelligence into play and prepared them for the great work of communicating ideas.

Itard's disciple, Edouard Séguin, contends that the original plan of instruction was designed to create an environment that would call forth the normal self from a boy merely uncivilized, whereas by 1802 Itard came to recognize that there were other impediments besides lack of socialization in his pupil. The new plan of instruction reflects this awareness, suited as it is "more for an idiot than a savage." This is biased speculation, but it is interesting to compare the verbs of the first set of aims with those of the second:

to *endear* (him to social life); to *awaken* (his senses); to *extend* (his ideas); to *lead* (him to speech); and to *exercise* (his mind); compared with, to *develop* (his senses); to *develop* (his intellect); and to *develop* (his emotions).

Itard had previously been content merely to observe the first increases in broadened sensitivity and discrimination that the sense of hearing enjoyed as part of Victor's general rehabilitation. Now he undertook to train hearing explicitly by inducing increasingly fine discriminations, much as he had done to arrive at visual distinctions among the letters of the alphabet. He began by providing student and teacher alike with a drum, a bell, and a stick. Itard struck his drum; Victor did likewise. Now the boy was blindfolded. Boom, Ding! went the teacher. Boom, Ding! went the pupil. The procedure of matching to sample was as familiar to Victor by now as it is to the reader, even if it had been transposed from sight to sound. If the teacher hit the hoop, the rim, or the body of the drum, the pupil followed suit. When the teacher struck a clock's bell or a fire shovel, the echo soon returned.

Edging his way toward the discrimination of vowel sounds, Itard next took up the tones of a wind instrument and then the different voice intonations that very young children are so quick to master. He no longer required imitation, but only that Victor raise his hand when the sound occurred, however softly. The pupil learned this readily, as much to his teacher's delight as to his own. He came to love these games and, of course, his blindfold. Itard took up next "the five vowels"; there are actually some sixteen in French, so it is hard to know just which ones he uttered and required Victor to distinguish, but he labels four of them, *A, E, I, O* (the fifth was probably *U*) which gives us some idea, if we suppose they were pronounced as when reciting the French alphabet. A smaller and more contrastive set could have been chosen to begin with. *A* was assigned to the thumb, *E* to the index finger, and so on, and Victor was to raise the finger corresponding to the vowel uttered by his teacher. Itard reports that the first vowel Victor distinguished clearly was *O*, although it is hard to imagine how he managed to raise just his ring finger. Next *A* seems to have come into focus, reliably distinguished from the others. The remaining three vowels were more refractory. This is not surprising; as every student of French knows, the way to pronounce the alphabet letter *U* is to make the *I* (as in the English *see*) and then round the lips; the two sounds are correspondingly close and hard to distinguish. Moreover, the front rounded vowels were missing from Victor's spoken repertory which Itard had described previously. The *E* (pronounced as in the English so*da*, when reciting the French alphabet) is midway between *A* and *O* on the one hand and *I* and *U* on the other; a kind of "neutral" vowel, it is in a nice position to be confused with all of them. Itard was nothing if not persistent and when Victor was obliged, nevertheless, to make these finer discriminations on repeated trials, lessons, and days, he began showing the signs of experimental neurosis, as he had in the experiment with discriminating visual forms, and as had Pavlov's girl with the metronome. Removing the blindfold, putting it back on, striking his fingers when he made a mistake, persisting doggedly or, on the contrary, spacing out the lessons, none of these availed. The pupil became increasingly rowdy and the teacher lost heart. "How thoroughly did I regret ever having known this child, and fully condemn the sterile and inhuman curiosity of the men who first snatched him away from his innocent and happy life!"

> Nevertheless this series of experiments on the sense of hearing was not altogether useless. Victor owes to it the fact that he can hear several one-syllable words distinctly and, above all, can distinguish quite precisely those intonations of language that express reproach, anger, sadness, contempt, and friendship, even when these various emotions are not accompanied by facial expression or by the natural pantomime that is their outward expression.

Turning now to vision, Itard had previously led Victor by carefully graded exercises to match letter cutouts. The boy had even learned to assemble the word for milk, *lait*. Itard found it easy to enlarge this repertory of reading and lettering words (without meaning or pronunciation), in preparation for the later development of language. He wrote all the words on his blackboard and on Victor's, but in different orders. He then pointed to a sample, and Victor pointed to its match. When his pupil made a mistake,

Itard cleverly used the matching-to-sample within the word itself. Thus he pointed to the first letter and Victor pointed to the first letter of the match he had erroneously chosen; and so on through the word, letter by letter, until Victor discovered that one of the letters in his word did not match. As you would expect, this letter-by-letter analysis speeded up and faded by stages into the mind of the pupil, much as lip movements do when one learns to read. Itard was now ready to resume Sicard's procedure for endowing these words with meaning, but first he paused for some training addressed to the remaining senses.

"I turned my attention to the sense of touch. Although far from sharing the opinion of Buffon and Condillac, who assign this sense an important role, I did not consider wasted any care I might give to it." In this respect, Itard was at variance not only with his master's teachings and with the dominant philosophical position of the times, but also with the procedures advocated by many modern psychologists. Condillac had specified: "No sooner is touch trained than it becomes the teacher of the other senses. It is from touch that the eyes, which by themselves would only have sensations of light and color, learn to estimate sizes, forms, and distances; and they are trained so quickly that they seem to see without having learned." And Buffon wrote in the same vein thirty years before: "It is by touch alone that we can acquire real and complete knowledge; it is this sense that corrects all the other senses whose impressions would only be illusions and would only produce errors in our minds if touch did not teach us to judge." Although he was Itard's student and intellectual heir, Séguin would later assign a fundamental role to touch in sensory education as Montessori and Kephart did after him. Would Itard have had faster and greater success in teaching Victor to read had he begun his sensory training with touch?

Some evidence that touch has a hand in what appears in the eye of the beholder comes from Soviet experiments with preschool children. One group was allowed only to look at a set of irregular wooden cutouts that they would later have to identify; another group, only to touch the forms; a third, only to look and touch; and a fourth to pick them up and replace them in the original board from which they had been cut. Next these cutouts were shuffled together with new ones, and the children were asked which ones they had seen before. Youngsters of all ages who had been allowed to replace the cutouts remembered them very well; the look and touch group was also quite good at recognizing the familiar forms. Sight alone and touch alone apparently gave the youngest children (three to four years old) only a rough 'idea of the forms and they had great trouble recognizing them later; by school age, however, they were able to get a nearly correct image from sight alone. As the Russians see it, the observer makes a model of what he sees by exploratory movements of the hands and the eyes. Visible manipulation is the most effective guide, as Condillac maintained. Apparently, Victor lacked many tactile discriminations, and this sense could hardly come to the aid of his sight. When Itard put chestnuts, acorns, and Victor's hand in an opaque vase and placed a sample acorn in the free hand, Victor often withdrew a chestnut only to realize by sight that it did not match. As usual, Itard retraced his steps and began with more gross discriminations: a stone and a chestnut; a penny and a key; then a nut and some pebbles. Now back to the chestnuts versus the acorns; no difficulty this time, and on to the metal letters, dissimilar ones at first, then Bs and Rs, Is and Js, Cs and Gs. The earlier experiences with hot and cold—bathwater, for example—seem to have been sufficient to enable Victor, without further training, to distinguish hot and cold nuts by touch in the vase, and to draw out the correct match unseen.

Itard believed that "civilization could add nothing to the delicacy of [Victor's] sense of smell." He recalls how the boy sniffed foods, also objects that we consider odorless, like pebbles and bits of dried wood, and even recognized Madame Guérin in this way:

> One evening he got lost in the Rue d'Enfer and his governess could not find him until after dark. It was only after sniffing at her hands and arms two or three times that he made up his mind to follow her, bustling with joy at having found her again ... Moreover, since the sense of smell is much more closely bound up with the exercise of digestive functions than with the development of intellectual faculties, it did not enter into my plan of instruction.

With regard to taste, Itard hoped only to widen the spectrum of foods and drinks in which Victor could take pleasure, and he reports that he was able to do this in short order. Not without some mishaps:

> Victor was dining with me in town. At the end of the meal, on his own initiative, he picked up a decanter containing one of the strongest cordials. Since it was colorless and odorless, the cordial resembled water exactly. Our savage took it for such, poured out half a glassful and, no doubt because he was very thirsty, drank nearly half of it at a gulp before the burning it caused in his stomach alerted him to his mistake. He threw the glass and spirits down, suddenly sprang up furious, made a single leap from his place to the door of his room, and ran howling through the hallways and up and down the staircase of the house over and over again; he was like an animal that has been badly wounded and that in racing off is not, as the poets say, trying to flee the shaft that rends it, but rather trying to mask the pain by intense activity since it cannot, like man, ask a kindly hand to alleviate it.

With all the senses but hearing now in reasonable repair, Itard resumed the language instruction that Sicard had designed for deaf pupils. Since, according to Condillac's metaphysics, language is a prerequisite to all the higher intellectual functions, Itard attached the greatest importance to this instruction, as all his efforts to prepare Victor for it testify. Some years earlier, the teacher had presented objects along with their printed names, but had no success whatever in establishing a bond between the two. But now Victor had been prepared through a graded series of exercises in matching colors, then forms, then letters, and finally words, and he had no difficulty in learning to associate these familiar words with a handful of corresponding familiar objects: if the labels or the objects were shuffled, he restored the appropriate pairings at once. Now, rather than remove all the objects (or pictures of them) and have the pupil fetch them according to the names indicated—Sicard's procedure that had failed with Victor before—Itard hit upon the ingenious strategy of gradually building up to this by introducing increasing delays between seeing the name and seeing the object. When this procedure was reinvented in the twentieth century, it was called delayed matching-to-sample. At first, there was zero delay.

Thus, when I left all the things in one corner of the room and took all the labels to another, showing them successively to Victor who was to fetch each thing for which I showed him the written word, he was able to bring the object requested only if he did not for an instant take his eyes off the letters that designated it. If he was too far away to be able to read the label, or if after showing it to him thoroughly I covered it with my hand, he looked uneasy and anxious from the moment the sight of the word escaped him and he randomly seized the first object at hand.

Then the tolerable delay increased from perhaps half a minute to some two minutes.

Soon he merely needed to glance quickly at the word I showed him, in order to fetch the thing I asked for, without haste or error. After some time I was able to extend the experiment by sending him from my apartment into his own room to look in the same way for whatever object I designated by name. At first his perception of the name did not last nearly so long as the trip, but by an act of intelligence worthy of record, Victor sought and found in the agility of his legs a sure means of making the impressions persist longer than the time required for the journey. As soon as he had thoroughly read the word he set out like an arrow, coming back an instant later with the thing in his hand. More than once, nevertheless, the name escaped him on the way. Then I heard him stop in his tracks and return to my apartment, where he arrived looking timid and confused. Sometimes it was enough for him to glance at the complete collection of names in order to recognize and retain the one that had escaped him. At other times the image of the word was so effaced from his memory that I had to show it to him afresh. When that was what he wanted, he took my hand and made me pass my index finger over the whole series of names until I had shown him the forgotten one.

If the tolerable delay was to become much longer, Victor obviously needed some way of bridging the interval. His problem was not unlike ours in getting from the telephone book to the telephone without losing the number. Itard increased the time available for inspecting the labels and gradually increased the number of items requested at the same time. In this way he led Victor to encode the labels and to bridge indefinitely long delays, as the following passage reveals:

Until then I had limited myself to asking for only one thing at a time. Then I asked for two, then three, and then four by showing an equal number of the labels to the pupil. Sensing the difficulty of retaining them all, he did not stop scanning them with eager attention until I had entirely screened them from his view. Then there was no more delay or uncertainty. He set off hurriedly to his room and brought the things requested. His first concern before giving them to me on his return was to look hastily over the list, comparing it with the things he was bearing. He gave them to me only after he had reassured himself in this way that he had neither forgotten nor taken anything by mistake. This last experiment had variable results at first, but finally the difficulties were surmounted. The pupil, now sure of his memory, no longer bothered to take advantage of his agile legs and applied himself calmly to this exercise. He often stopped in the corridor, put his face to the window at one end of it, hailed with a few sharp cries the sight of the countryside unfolding magnificently into the distance, and then set off again for his room, got his little cargo, renewed his homage to the ever-regretted beauty of nature, and returned to me quite sure of the correctness of his errand.

Just what kind of encoding Victor used we will never know; he could not have rehearsed the words as we might, since he could neither pronounce nor write them. Perhaps he imagined himself using the corresponding objects; Itard only lists four of them: a key, a knife, a box, and a pen.

Victor had no difficulty in using these words, and others he soon added to his repertory, to get other people to fetch the corresponding things; he also would respond to their mands by fetching the desired object. Itard had reason to be content, but a rude surprise awaited him. By invariably associating the identical object with the same name, he had effectively taught Victor a set of proper names. As Roger Brown puts it in *Words and Things*, "What Victor learned about reference was at first too specific. Words do not name particular things, as Victor thought; they name classes or categories."

One day when I had taken Victor with me and was sending him to his room as usual to fetch several objects that I indicated on his list of words, I decided to double-lock my door and take out the key without his seeing. That done, I returned to my study, where he was waiting and, unrolling his list, I asked him for some of the things on it, taking care to indicate none that were not also to be found in my suite of rooms. He set out immediately, but finding the door locked and having searched on all sides for the key, he came back to me, *took my hand and led me to the outer door as if to make me see that it would not open. I feigned surprise, looked for the key everywhere* and even pretended to try opening the door by force. Finally, giving up these efforts, I took Victor back into my study and showed him the same words again, *inviting him by signs to look around* and see if there were not similar objects to be found there. The words designated were stick, bellows, brush, glass, knife. All these things were to be found scattered about my study in plain view. Victor saw them but touched none. I had no better success in making him recognize them when I brought them together on a table, and it was quite useless to ask for them one after the other by showing him their names in succession.

Since Itard believed that action-language preempted communication with words, it is ironic to notice in the italicized phrases how easily he was drawn into nonverbal communication with Victor, even in the very lessons aimed at developing the use of written language. What a strange game this must have seemed to the boy! If the teacher needs a knife, and he does not seem to need one at all, he has only to go get it or to signal for it; instead, he draws it by a set of strange shapes that have no likeness, then locks it away, and then asks for it. With Victor in tears, Itard goes melodramatic: "Since my labors are wasted and your efforts fruitless, go back to your forests and to enjoying a primitive life. Or if your new needs make you dependent on a society in which you have no place, go pay the penalty for your misfortune, die of misery and boredom at Bicêtre." But then he decides to profit by the disruption to enhance his status as a social reinforcer, much as he had done with the emotional interlude in shape discrimination.

[Victor's] tears redoubled, accompanied by gasps and sobs, while I redoubled the caresses, raising his emotion to the highest intensity . . . When all this excitement had entirely passed, I placed the same objects in front of him again, and made him point them out one after the other as I showed him each of the names in turn. I began by asking him for the book. He first looked at it for rather a long time, made a movement towards it with his hand while trying to detect some sign of approval or disapproval in my eyes which would resolve his uncertainty. I was on my guard and my expression was blank. Reduced then to his own judgment he concluded that it was not the thing asked for, and his eyes surveyed all sides of the room pausing, however, only at the books scattered on the table and mantelpiece.

This survey gave me a ray of light. I immediately opened a cupboard full of books and took out a dozen among which I was careful to include one exactly like that Victor had left in his room. Victor only took a moment to spot it, to seize it, and to give it to me with a glowing look.

Itard identifies the source of Victor's difficulty with the use of words: he is overdiscriminating.

What could account for this strange difference [between Victor and normal children learning language who, on the contrary, employ names too broadly]? If I am not mistaken it grew out of his unusually acute visual observation, which resulted inevitably from the special education I gave to his sense of sight. I had trained this sense organ so thoroughly in recognizing by analytical comparison the visible qualities of objects and their differences in dimension, color, and conformation, that Victor could always detect enough dissimilarity in two identical things to make him believe there was an essential difference between them. With the source of the error thus located, the remedy became easy. It was to establish the identity of the objects by demonstrating to the pupil the identity of their uses or properties. It was to make him see which qualities apparently different things had in common that earned them the same name. In a word, it was a question of teaching him to consider things no longer with reference to their differences but according to their similarities.

This last way of stating the problem is probably the best. Surely Victor was able to generalize among different instances of knives, glasses, sticks, and so on; he must have done that every day in Madame Guérin's household. Rather than failing to see the similarities among objects that in fact he daily put to similar uses, he probably had learned that success requires responding differently to similar things, whether they be forms, letters, sticks, or cooking utensils. Indeed, this had been a measure of Victor's progress in education; at the outset of training, when Itard had pointed to the drawing of a scissors, a hammer, or a key, Victor merely fetched all of them, or none of them. Itard now decided—at his own risk and peril, as the French say—to reward indiscriminate responding.

> This new study was a kind of introduction to the art of comparison. At first the pupil gave himself up to it so completely that he was inclined to go astray again by attaching the same idea and giving the same name to things which had no other relation than the similarity of their shapes or uses. Thus under the name of book he indicated indiscriminately a handful of paper, a notebook, a newspaper, a register, a pamphlet. All straight and long pieces of wood were sticks. He gave the name *brush* to the broom, and *broom* to the brush, and soon, if I had not restrained this excessive analogizing, I should have seen Victor restricted to the use of a small number of signs he would have applied indiscriminately to a large number of entirely different things which had only certain general qualities or properties in common.

One of the brakes on overgeneralization is practical manipulation: all bolts seem pretty much the same until it comes to screwing them in. When objects are used, cues that otherwise are simply not there arise to differentiate them. Itard profited by this fact, guided again, perhaps, by Condillac who explains in his *Logic* how a child's activities, when related to his needs, can lead him to discriminate:

> A child will call *tree*, as we tell him, the first tree that we show him, and this name will be for him the name of an individual thing. However, if he is shown another tree, he will not think of asking for its name; he will call it *tree* and will give this common name to two individual things. He will give it in the same way to three or four and finally to all the plants which seem to bear some resemblance to the first tree he saw. This name will even become so general that he will call *tree* everything that we call *plant*. He is naturally inclined to generalize because it is more convenient for him to use a word he knows than to learn a new one. He generalizes, then, without intending to generalize and without even noticing that he is generalizing. In this way an individual idea suddenly becomes general; often it even becomes too much so, and this happens whenever we confuse things it would have been useful to distinguish.
> This child will soon realize it himself. He will not say, "I have generalized too much; I must distinguish different species of trees." He will form subordinate classes unintentionally and without being aware of it, just as he formed general classes unintentionally and without being

aware of it. He will do no more than follow his needs . . . In fact, if he is taken into a garden, and is made to pick and eat different sorts of fruit, we shall see that he will soon learn the names *cherry tree, peach tree, pear tree,* and *apple tree* and that he will distinguish the different species of trees.

So Itard set Victor a practical task which would lead him to distinguish two different kinds of objects that he formerly classed alike.

> I remember that one day when I asked him in writing for a knife, he looked for one for some time and was finally satisfied to offer me a razor, which he fetched from a neighboring room. I pretended it would do, and when his lesson was finished I gave him a snack as usual and made him cut his bread instead of tearing it with his fingers as was his custom. To this end, I gave him the razor he had given me under the name of knife. His behavior was consistent, he tried to use it as such, but the flexibility of the blade prevented this. I did not consider the lesson complete. I took the razor and made it serve its proper use, right in front of Victor. From then on the instrument was no longer a knife and should not seem to him to be one. I was anxious to make certain.
>
> I took up his book again and showed him the word *couteau* [knife] and my pupil immediately showed me the knife he held in his hand, which I had given him a moment earlier when he could not use the razor. To make the result complete, the test had to be reversed. If the book were put in Victor's hands while I touched the razor, he should fail to pick out any of the words, as he did not yet know the name of this instrument. And that is what happened.

At the same time, the person who makes one thing serve for another, when everyone else thought the two were quite distinct, is considered creative: "I remember one day when [Victor] was dining in town and wanted to accept a spoonful of beans offered him at a moment when there were no more plates and dishes on the table. He had the idea of going to the mantelpiece, taking a little circular picture under glass and holding it out as if it were a plate. The picture was set in a frame, whose smooth projecting edge was not unlike that of a plate." If the creative person modifies the object to serve its new function, he is an inventor.

> Only once in my study had I made [Victor] use a [chalkholder] to

grasp a small piece of chalk too short to hold with his fingertips. A few days afterwards the same difficulty occurred again, but Victor was in his room and had no chalkholder handy to hold his chalk. I put it to the most industrious or the most inventive man to say, or rather do, what he did in order to procure one. He took an implement used in roasting, found in well-equipped kitchens but quite superfluous in one belonging to a poor creature such as he, and which for that reason had remained forgotten and corroded with rust at the bottom of a little cupboard—namely, a larding needle. [This instrument resembles a short tube cut lengthwise exposing a concave channel normally filled with fatback that is forced into a piece of meat with a slider.] Such was the instrument which he took to replace the one he lacked and which, by a further inspiration of really creative imagination, he was clever enough to convert into a real chalkholder by replacing the slide with a few turns of thread.

Pardon, my lord, the importance I attach to this act. One must have experienced all the anguish of a course of instruction as arduous as this had been; one must have followed and directed this man-plant in his laborious developments from the first act of attention up to this first spark of imagination before one can have any idea of the joy that I felt, and can pardon me for introducing at this moment, and with something of a flourish, so ordinary and so simple a fact. What also added to the importance of this result when considered as a proof of current achievement and as a guarantee of future improvement is that, instead of occurring as an isolated incident which might have made it appear accidental, it was one among many incidents, doubtless less striking, but which, coming in the same period and evidently emanating from the same source, would appear to an attentive observer to be diverse results of a general tendency. It is, indeed, worthy of notice that from this moment many routine habits the pupil had contracted when applying himself to the little occupations prescribed for him spontaneously disappeared. While rigidly refraining from making forced comparisons or drawing remote conclusions, one may, I think, at least suspect that this new way of looking at familiar things, which gave birth to the idea of using them in new ways, should necessarily force the pupil out of the unvarying round of rather automatic habits.

The next step in Victor's language instruction expanded his repertory of names. Itard introduced more household items and then those in the world at large, pointing to the object with one hand and the word with the other. Teaching the names of the parts that constitute a whole proved a little more difficult. Itard succeeded with this expedient: he tore up a book into several parts, taught the name of each part quite separately (cover, page, binding) and, once the part names were mastered, reassembled the book and had Victor name each of the parts in turn. Finally, when the book was indicated with a vague gesture, Victor pointed to the word *livre*. Thereafter he had no difficulty in learning, for example, the names of the parts of the body.

The lessons advanced to the names of the "qualities of bodies" —that is, adjectives, beginning with big and little books. At first, Victor unhesitatingly designated by *livre* both a small and a large book. When his teacher had him lay his hand over each of the books in turn, however, and he found he could only cover the smaller one, he hesitated to use the same name. Itard then placed the labels *petit* and *livre* on the one book and *grand* and *livre* on the other. After this pairing, he shuffled the four cards and gave them to Victor, who replaced them correctly. Had he understood? To be sure his instruction had succeeded, and the adjectives would be generalized to other big and little things, Itard once again made a diagnostic check. He gave Victor two nails and two cards bearing the word *clou*. Victor at once took the label *petit* and placed it on the smaller nail, *grand* on the larger. In much the same way, Victor soon learned adjectives for color, weight, resistance, and so on.

To teach verbs, Itard took familiar objects and did things with them while writing the name of the object and the actions on the board. Thus he proceeded to touch a key, to pick it up, to throw it, and so on, each time writing the French infinitives *toucher*, *ramasser*, *jeter*, next to *clef* (he was careful to use only transitive verbs ending in -er). Then he repeated these actions with some other object, pointing to the appropriate written verb. Once a small set of verbs had been built up, Itard and Victor had established a miniature language that either of them could understand or produce. The grammar of this language had the following three rules: a sentence consists of a verb followed by a noun; verbs are actions such as *to throw, to kiss, to touch,* and so forth; nouns are things such as *a key, a cup, a knife,* and so forth. The grammar has a rule that the noun comes after the verb, but no rule that restricts which noun may be selected once the verb has been selected. Itard probably did not think of that because French has such rules, which led him naturally to avoid ungrammatical sequences or "strings" as they are called. Oversimplified grammars generate ungrammatical strings, and indeed that would provide a good test of Victor's mastery of the grammar. It turned out to be more a test of his ingenuity:

> When I found myself one day, after successive changes of the objects of the verbs, with such associations of words as *to tear stone, to cut cup, to eat broom,* he evaded the difficulty very well by changing the two actions indicated by the first two verbs into others less incompatible with the nature of their objects. Thus he took a hammer to break the stone and dropped the cup to break it. Coming to the third verb [eat] and not being able to find any other to replace it, he looked for something else to serve as the object of the verb. He took a piece of bread and ate it.

As Victor came to understand and construct more and more sentences, his means of producing them by assembling metal letters or printed cards became increasingly unwieldy. Itard decided to teach him to write. Several methods were open to him and, in retrospect, we can appreciate how clever his solution was. He might have demonstrated a few strokes in the hope that Victor would do likewise. Since a similar strategy had left him high and dry when trying to induce Victor to say *water,* he only made a halfhearted stab at inducing him to draw a line in this way; of course it did not work. He might have tried to shape writing, beginning by rewarding Victor simply for holding the chalk, then for movements toward the board, and so on, perhaps guiding his hand at certain points. What he did instead was to establish a generalized tendency to imitate his behavior by reinforcing Victor for duplicating his actions until duplication became its own reward.

> I proceeded . . . by giving Victor practice in imitating large-scale movements, such as lifting his arms, putting his foot forward, sitting down and getting up the same time as I did; then opening his hand, closing it, and repeating many finger movements—first simple, then combined—that I performed in front of him. I next put a long pointed rod in his hand and another in my own, and made him hold it as if it were a quill for writing, with the double intention of giving more

strength and poise to his fingers through the difficulty of holding this imitation pen in equilibrium and of making visible, and consequently capable of imitation, even the slightest movement of the rod.

Thus prepared by preliminary exercises, we placed ourselves in front of the blackboard, each furnished with a piece of chalk, and placing our two hands at the same height I began by making a slow vertical movement toward the bottom of the board. The pupil did just the same, following exactly the same direction and dividing his attention between his line and mine, looking without intermission from the one to the other as if he wished to compare them successively at all points. The result of our actions was two lines exactly parallel.

A modern experiment is highly reminiscent of Itard's technique for teaching writing and throws light on why it works. A young child is engaged in conversation by a puppet, who encourages him to imitate his nodding, mouthing, and strange verbalizations, and says "good" when he does. Puppet and child are each equipped with a lever, which the puppet presses from time to time; the child soon takes up pressing the lever as well, although he is never reinforced for doing so. If the puppet desists in providing models to imitate or in rewarding imitation (saying "good" at appropriate points in the conversation instead), the child increasingly desists in lever pressing. With retarded or schizophrenic children an extra step must be added when inducing new behavior through generalized imitation because they usually will not imitate the supporting behaviors in the first place—head nodding and mouthing in this example. Itard apparently did not have this problem with Victor, who imitated gross bodily movements right off. Had the problem arisen, Itard could have shaped such a movement, rewarding Victor for raising his arm, for example, while raising it for him less and less on successive trials.

In the subsequent experiment, Itard put Victor's generalized imitation to a rather subtle test. He drew a circle on a blackboard, wrote a half dozen letters around the circumference, and copied the same letters helter-skelter within the circle. He gave a similar array to Victor but with the letters arranged in a different order. Now he drew a line between each letter within the circle and its counterpart on the circumference. If Victor imitated the movements or the lines, he would pair off noncorresponding letters. If he imitated the product, he would have to draw lines differently from his model. Aided perhaps by all his training in matching comparable letters, he did the latter. From these beginnings with generalized imitation, Victor's progress in learning to write was so rapid that Itard spares us the details. Within a few months the boy could copy the words that he knew; soon after, he could reproduce them from memory. Finally, Victor attained a signal milestone in his education; he could communicate using language in the written mode "to express his wants, to solicit the means to satisfy them, and by the same method of expression, to grasp the needs or the will of others."

Despite his earlier failure to teach Victor to discriminate among vowels, Itard had not abandoned his pupil to mutism. If he could not teach him to speak by imitation of an auditory model, then perhaps he could be taught to speak by imitation of a visual model. Having decided to try to teach Victor spoken language rather than sign language, Itard could draw little guidance from the opposing tradition of Epée and Sicard that had made his institute famous as the bastion of "the natural language of signs." In adopting the goals of the oralist school of deaf-mute education, Itard could draw on, most notably, the work of Jacob Rodriguez Pereire, Epée's rival, who had founded this method of instruction in France in the middle of the eighteenth century. Pereire was born in Spain; he came to France when he was eighteen, in 1733, and fell in love with a deaf-mute girl. He had been raised with a deaf-mute sister, and the two women inspired him to devote his life to teaching the deaf to speak. He took a special medical course, read what was available at that time on the education of the deaf, and began to instruct some young pupils with singular success. In 1749 he presented one of his pupils, Azy d'Etavigny, and in 1751 another, Saboureux de Fontenai, to the Academy of Sciences and won its commendations, including those of Buffon, who devotes a page to Pereire in his *Natural History*. According to Itard's student, Séguin, who wrote a book on Pereire's life and work and had spoken with his last surviving pupil, this teacher managed to instill in the deaf "not only a natural voice and a correct pronunciation, but even his Gascony accent." Louis XV conferred a pension on him, and in 1753 Pereire opened a school in Paris which drew about a dozen students from all over Europe.

To establish initial communication with his pupils, Pereire adopted Bonet's manual alphabet, used pantomime, and invented his own syllabic signs. Believing that the latter had been stolen by Epée, and hoping to secure some income from the sale of his method or to leave it as a legacy to his children, Pereire expressly forbade his pupils to reveal his methods and never did so himself in any detail. Nevertheless, Séguin managed to reconstruct the main features:

> Speech was taught by imitation with vision as a guide to the internal positions in the mouth and the external muscles of the face and neck; and, for the first known time, with touch the conductor and monitor of the innermost positions and of the organic vibrations that together produce the emission of articulated sounds. By this method, the deaf-mute of ordinary capacity could learn to speak in twelve to fifteen months.

The pupil with whom Séguin had spoken in her declining years, Marie Marois, affirmed that touch was the principal means by which Pereire taught his pupils to speak.* In his address to the Academy of Sciences, Pereire seems to confirm this:

> Deaf-mute children perceive speech by touch. This sensation occurs when, speaking to a deaf person, one places his mouth against the ear, the face, or another sensitive part of the body, such as the hand. Then the air which forms speech communicates impressions to these parts of the body which are as frequent and distinct as the syllables themselves, vibrations that are sufficient without other means to give a clear perception of several articulations. Thus it is shown, as by the example of young Etavigny [before the academy], that . . . the profoundly deaf are capable of distinguishing some words by this process.

Pereire seems to have anticipated Condillac and Buffon's position on the roles of touch when he stated in this address: "All the senses accomplish their functions by virtue of a more or less modified sense of touch."

In learning a new sound, the student first learned one of Pereire's manual signs which were designed to recall to mind both the shape of the articulators in making the sound and the shape of the letter that generally denotes it. Thus the signs were useful prompts for correcting pronunciation and spelling. The pupil was not allowed to communicate in sign language, however. Once he knew how to write and sign the sound, the student learned to pronounce it, in a series of exaggerations, approximations, and repetitions like those Molière parodied in his *Bourgeois gentilhomme*. Thus the student grasps his teacher's throat, observes his throat, jaws, tongue, teeth, and lips, and follows his articulatory instructions, until the teacher's ear is satisfied. Special training was also given in the way of breathing peculiar to speech.

Beyond pronunciation training, the prospectus of his school (inserted in the academy records) states that Pereire taught his pupils "to understand the force of different parts of speech, to use them correctly whether in speaking or in writing, according to the grammar and the particular genius of the language"—which he evidently succeeded in doing: Marie Marois remained highly intelligent and intelligible in old age; Saboureux de Fontenai became a teacher and essayist. Jean-Jacques Rousseau often visited Pereire's school; the two were good friends, and when Rousseau worked out his scheme for natural education in *Emile*, he found a place for several of his neighbor's ideas and experiments.

Itard had certainly heard of Pereire and his methods of teaching speech; they were roundly criticized in "Instruction of Deaf-Mutes by Methodical Signs," which contains a series of anonymous letters, by Abbé de l'Epée, addressed to an unnamed teacher of the deaf (Pereire). Perhaps he was unable to learn that the technique had involved touch, because of Pereire's secrecy; or perhaps he continued to think the importance of this sense much overrated, as he stated earlier. In any event, it appears that Itard used only vision to supplant hearing in his attempts to teach Victor to speak by imitation.

> In order to follow the method of imperceptible steps once again, I preceded the study of the visible articulation of sound by the slightly easier imitation of movements of the face muscles, beginning with those that were most easily seen. Thus we have instructor and pupil facing each other and grimacing their hardest; that is to say, putting the muscles of

their eyes, forehead, mouth, and jaw into all sorts of motion, little by little concentrating upon the muscles of the lips. Then, after persisting for a long time with movements of this fleshy part of the organ of speech, we subjected the tongue to the same exercises, but varied them much more and continued them for a longer time . . .

All that I could obtain from this long series of exercises was a few unformed monosyllables sometimes shrill, sometimes deep, and far less clear than those I had obtained in my first experiments.

Itard struggled for a long time "against the obstinacy of the organ" but, seeing no progress, he finally abandoned Victor to incurable mutism.

There is no clear evidence that Victor's hearing was abnormal; he could discriminate some vowels and produce some vowels and consonants. Moreover he could read and write simple sentences, both as a formal exercise and in manding and tacting; he may well have had normal use of language as a child before entering the wilds. We are tempted to think he could have learned to speak with the proper conditioning technique. With one hundred and fifty years of hindsight, here is one procedure Itard might comfortably have used; it has much in common with his own and yet the differences are probably crucial. Lovaas used it successfully to teach schizophrenic children to speak in daily two-hour lessons lasting about two weeks. In step one, Lovaas gives his pupil a spoonful of his meal for every vocalization; he is also rewarded for visually fixating on the teacher's mouth. When the child vocalizes every five seconds or more frequently and spends at least half his time looking at the teacher's mouth, step two begins. Lovaas says a word, for example *baby*, every ten seconds or so. If the child makes any vocal response within six seconds of the adult's, he is reinforced. When the teacher's voice frequently evokes his pupil's, he proceeds to step three, which adds the further requirement for reinforcement—the additional "contingency"—that the pupil's reply actually match the teacher's. Lovaas chooses the model carefully. It should be a syllable that the child uttered initially; it should have an obvious visual component; it should be easy to prompt. For example, the teacher says *ba* and prompts by holding the child's lips closed with his fingers, then releases them abruptly when the child exhales; then reinforces. On successive trials the prompt is faded, the teacher moving his fingers away from the child's mouth, then to his cheek, finally touching his jaw. In step four, a second sound is introduced, quite different from the first and randomly interspersed with it as a model. In this way a large repertory of imitative syllables and words builds up at an accelerating pace.

Under the heading "Development of Emotional Faculties," the third section of his report, Itard actually takes up Victor's moral growth and shortcomings during the five years of his acculturation. According to a rather conventional view of morality, something in between Epée's and Rousseau's, Victor has made considerable progress: he has learned gratitude, remorse, the desire to please others, even a sense of justice and injustice. It must be said that Itard had no systematic plan for his pupil's moral education comparable to that for his training of the senses and the intellect. He found no guidance in Condillac, nor did he look to any other philosopher. Itard did attempt to make social contacts more reinforcing; he rewarded Victor in their lessons, interacted with him through gestural and written language, consoled him when he was grief-stricken or frightened. Yet Madame Guérin was probably the source of much of the progress; it was she who fed Victor, who cleaned and caressed him, who was his companion during most of his waking hours. It is a pity that she has not left us an account of her observations and actions, or that Itard, drawing less of a demarcation between lessons and life, did not record more than a few revealing incidents.

Concerning Victor's gratitude, Itard writes:

As the ever-increasing number of his desires made his contacts with us and our attentions to him more and more frequent, his unyielding heart at last opened to unequivocal feelings of gratitude and affection . . . The last time when his memories and his passion for the freedom of the fields led our savage to escape from the house, he headed in the direction of Senlis and reached the forest. He soon came out, however, doubtless driven by hunger and the impossibility of providing for himself any longer. Drawing near to the neighboring fields, he fell into the hands of the police who arrested him as a vagabond and kept him as such for a fortnight. Recognized at the end of this time and brought back to Paris, he was taken to the Temple [an ancient fortified monastery] where Madame Guérin, his guardian, came to claim him. A number of onlookers had assembled to witness this interview, which was truly touching. Scarcely had Victor caught sight of his governess when he turned pale and lost consciousness for a moment but, as he felt himself embraced and fondled by Madame Guérin, he suddenly revived and showed his delight by sharp cries, convulsive hand clenching, and a radiant facial expression. In the eyes of all the spectators he appeared less like a fugitive obliged to return to the supervision of his keeper than like an affectionate son who, of his own free will, comes and throws himself in the arms of the one who has given him life.

The boy also knew remorse:

At about the same time, Madame Guérin's husband fell ill and was nursed away from the house without Victor's being told of it. Having among his little domestic duties that of setting the table at dinner time, he continued to lay a place for Monsieur Guérin, and although he was made to remove it every day, he never failed to set it again the next day. The illness had a sad end. Monsieur Guérin succumbed, and on the day he died his place was again laid for him. One can guess what an effect such a distressing attention had upon Madame Guérin. Witnessing this scene of grief, Victor understood that he caused it; and, whether he only thought he had done wrong, or whether he had penetrated the real reason of his governess's despair and felt how useless and misplaced were the pains he had been taking, he removed the place of his own accord, sadly put the things back in the cupboard, and never set them again.

Here was a sad emotion, belonging exclusively to the sphere of civilized man. Equally so is the profound state of moroseness into which my young pupil always falls when, in the course of our lessons, after struggling in vain with the whole power of his attention against some new difficulty, he realizes the impossibility of overcoming it. It is on such occasions, when he is imbued with the feeling of his impotence and touched perhaps by the uselessness of my efforts, that I have seen the letters which are so unintelligible to him moistened with his tears, although he has not been provoked by any word of reproach, threat, or punishment.

Victor liked to please others:

I will cite such evidences as the zeal he employs, and the pleasure he derives, in helping the people he is fond of, even anticipating their wishes, by little services that it is within his ability to render. This is to be noticed above all in his relations with Madame Guérin. I will also single out, as an emotion of a civilized person, the satisfaction that spreads over his whole face and is even expressed in bursts of laughter when some difficulty stops him in our lessons and he finally succeeds in surmounting it by his own efforts; or when I am pleased with some slight progress and show my satisfaction with praise and encouragement. There is evidence of his pleasure in doing well not only in his exercises but also in the most trivial domestic occupations with which he is entrusted, especially if these occupations are of a nature to require great muscular strength.

In general, Victor was not socialized enough to commit anti-social acts; yet these would seem to be necessary if he were to acquire notions of justice and injustice in the absence of language. Like most parents, Itard used punishment to this end. Originally Victor would help himself to food in the kitchen whenever he was hungry. Itard chastised him whenever he was caught in the act, and so Victor learned to steal with cunning what he had formerly taken openly. This gave Itard the opportunity to steal back; he would expropriate a coveted apple that the boy had earned and eat it in front of him; or he would surreptitiously empty Victor's pockets of provisions the boy had hidden there. Gradually Victor learned to take only what was explicitly his—but Itard was unsure of the cause. He drew a distinction between fear of punishment and disinterested moral motives.

In order to clear up this doubt and to obtain a less ambiguous result, I thought I ought to test my pupil's moral reactions by submitting him to another kind of injustice which, because it had no connection with the nature of the fault, did not appear to be the punishment that was merited and was consequently as hateful as it was shocking. I chose a day for this truly painful experience when, after keeping Victor occupied for over two hours with our instructional procedures, I was satisfied both with his obedience and his intelligence, and had only praises and rewards to lavish on him. He doubtless expected them, to judge from the look of self-satisfaction that was on his face and in his stance. But what was his astonishment when, instead of receiving the accustomed rewards, instead of the treatment he had so much right to expect and which he had never received without the liveliest demonstration of joy, he saw me suddenly assume a severe and menacing expression, rub out with all the outward signs of displeasure what I had just praised and applauded, scattered his books and cards into all corners of the room, and finally seize him by the arm and drag him violently toward a dark closet that had sometimes been used as his prison at the beginning of his stay in Paris. He allowed himself to be taken along quietly until he reached the threshold of the door. There, suddenly abandoning his usual attitude of obedience, he wedged himself with his feet and hands between the door posts, and resisted me vigorously, which delighted me so much the more because it was entirely new to him, and because he had always been ready to submit to similar punishments when merited and had never before refused to submit for a single moment, even with the slightest hesitation. I insisted, nevertheless, in order to see how far he would carry his resistance, and I tried to lift him from the ground with all my force in order to drag him into the closet. This last attempt excited all his fury. Outraged with indignation and red with anger, he struggled in my arms so violently that my efforts were fruitless for some moments; but finally, feeling himself giving in to the rule of force, he fell back upon the last resource of the weak and flew at my hand, leaving deep toothmarks there. How sweet it would have been at that moment to have spoken to my pupil, to make him understand how the pain of his bite filled my heart with satisfaction and repaid all my labor. How could I be other than delighted? It was a very legitimate act of vengeance; it was incontestable proof that the feeling of justice and injustice, that eternal basis of the social order, was no longer foreign to the heart of my pupil. In giving him this feeling, or rather in provoking its development, I had succeeded in raising the wild man to the full stature of moral man by means of the most pronounced of his characteristics and the most noble of his attributes.

In taking stock of Victor's moral development, Itard had to list on the debit side Victor's unattenuated egoism and his failure to show any evidence of pity. What troubled the teacher most, however, was his pupil's explosive and unsocialized sexuality. With young women, Victor seemed caught in a conflict between approach and avoidance. Had not the editors of the *Décade philosophique* described his conduct four years earlier as "attachment mixed with fear"? Itard recounts a similar incident:

I have seen him in the company of women trying to relieve his uneasiness by sitting beside one of them and gently pinching her hand, her arms, and her knees until, feeling his restless desires increased instead of calmed by these odd caresses, and seeing no relief from his painful emotions in sight, he suddenly changed his attitude and petulantly pushed away the woman whom he had sought with some eagerness. Then he turned without interruption to another woman, with whom he behaved in the same way. One day, nevertheless, he became a little more enterprising. After first employing the same caresses, he took the lady by her hands and drew her, without violence however, into the depths of an alcove. There, very much at a loss for bearings, showing in his gestures and in his extraordinary facial expression an indescribable mixture of gaiety and sadness, of boldness and uncertainty, he solicited the lady's caresses several times by offering her his cheeks, and walked slowly round her with a meditative air, finally flinging his arms about her shoulders and holding her closely by the neck. This was all, and these amorous demonstrations ended, as did all the others, with a feeling of annoyance which made him repulse the object of his passing fancy.

Increasingly, Victor had hysterical episodes, which Itard attributes to his unchanneled sexuality.

> Passing suddenly from sadness to anxiety, and from anxiety to fury, he takes a dislike to all his keenest enjoyments; he sighs, sheds tears, utters shrill cries, tears his clothes, and sometimes goes as far as to scratch or bite his governess. But even when he yields to a blind fury he is unable to control, he gives evidence of real repentance and asks to kiss the arm or hand he has just bitten. In this state his pulse is raised and his face apoplectic. Sometimes blood flows from his nose and ears. This puts an end to the transport, and postpones a recurrence of the outburst, especially if the hemorrhage is abundant.

Itard's treatment consists of cool baths, violent exercise, and bleedings, although he recognizes that Victor's education has failed to provide him with the required "agreement between need and inclination." In this domain, not only did Itard lack a training strategy, he himself had the most singular reactions, a sense of foreboding mixed with deep prudery and intense adolescent curiosity. All of this is apparent between the closing lines of his first report, where he writes cryptically:

> [The need to await more facts] has prevented me, when speaking of

young Victor's varied development, from dwelling on the period of his puberty, which erupted some weeks ago, and whose first expressions cast doubt on the origin of certain tender emotions which we regard as very "natural." Here, too, I have found it advisable to reserve judgment and conclusions; I am convinced that any consideration that tends to destroy our beliefs, perhaps worthy ones, as well as the sweetest and most consoling illusions of social life, must be seasoned by the passage of time and confirmed by further observations.

The teacher's conflicting emotions are clearer at the end of the final report:

> I did not doubt that if I had dared to reveal to this young man the secret of his restlessness and the aim of his desires, he would have reaped incalculable benefits. But, on the other hand, supposing I had been permitted to try such an experiment, should I not have been afraid to reveal a need to our savage which he would have sought to satisfy as publicly as his other wants and which would have led him to acts of revolting indecency? Intimidated by the possibility of such a result, I was obliged to stop at this point and once more to resign myself to seeing my hopes fade away, like so many other ones, before an unforeseen obstacle.

Significantly, Itard's report and, so far as we know, his program of education end on this note.

Itard summarizes first what he has been unable to accomplish:

> First, as a result of the almost complete incapacity of the organs of hearing and speech, the education of this young man is still incomplete and must always remain so; second, by reason of their long inaction, the intellectual faculties are developing slowly and painfully, and this development, which in children growing up in civilized surroundings is the natural fruit of time and circumstances, is here the slow and laborious result of an intense training in which the most powerful methods are used to obtain the smallest effects; third, the emotional affections of his heart, then this sympathetic agreement is, like the manated to a profound egoism, and puberty, instead of turning these emotions outward, seems to have expressed itself strongly only to prove that if there exists a relation between the needs of man's senses and the affections of his heart, then this sympathetic agreement is, like the majority of great and generous notions, the happy fruit of education.

Finally, Itard summarizes what his program of education was able to achieve with Victor:

First, the improvement of his sight and touch and the new gratifications of his sense of taste have, by multiplying the sensations and ideas of our savage, contributed powerfully to the development of his intellectual faculties; second, when we consider the full extent of this development, we find, among other real improvements, that he has both a knowledge of the conventional value of the symbols of thought and the power of applying this knowledge by naming objects, their qualities, and their actions. This has led to an extension of the pupil's relations with the people around him, to his ability to express his wants to them, to receive orders from them, and to effect a free and continual exchange of thoughts with them; third, in spite of his immoderate taste for the freedom of the open country and his indifference to most of the pleasures of social life, Victor is aware of the care taken of him, susceptible to fondling and affection, sensitive to the pleasure of doing things well, ashamed of his mistakes, and repentant of his outbursts.

Leaving aside the aim of my self-imposed task, [the education of the savage of Aveyron], considering the undertaking from a more general point of view, it will not be, my lord, without a certain satisfaction that you will see in the diverse experiments I have attempted and the numerous observations I have gathered, a collection of facts suited to throw light on the history of medical philosophy, on the study of uncivilized man, and on the direction of certain systems of private education.

Chapter Seven

Interpreting
the
Legend

The legend of the wild boy—Conflicting interpretations—Why didn't Victor become normal?—Itard's technique—Introduced behavior modification and instructional devices—But overemphasis on sensation— An attempt at total pedagogy—Flaws in his method—Victor born retarded— Authorities endorse Pinel—Flaws in Pinel's report—All wild children are idiots— Victor claimed autistic—Flaws in the argument—Refractory habits—Irreversible mutism—A critical period for imitation.

From the encounter between Itard and the wild boy has come a legend, a tale of epic proportions in which the protagonists play highly stylized roles. There is the ignorant child, not merely ignorant of the intellectual, social, and moral traditions of his society, like any child, but ignorant even of the means by which these might be communicated to him, written and spoken language. More ignorant yet: an incarnation of Condillac's statue, which becomes a man by acquiring knowledge through the senses, the child must be taught to see, to hear, to touch, to attend, to remember, to judge. All these tasks the hero embraces gladly. The ultimate pupil shall be clothed in the mantle of society, both literally and figuratively, by the ultimate pedagogue: an unflagging observer of his pupil, tireless and ingenious in devising techniques of instruction, stern but just in the allocation of rewards, tolerant of innocent childhood enjoyment when the day's profitable education is over, devoted but not loving, leaving that to a kind and uneducated governess—thus did the young Dr. Itard struggle for five years against unreasonable odds. This legend of the wild boy captures a certain conception—or one should rather say, misconception—of the pupil and the teacher, the child and the pedagogue, that has had enormous appeal and impact, and continues to characterize much modern educational practice. The conception has so much appeal, indeed, that we must surely ask if, like most legends, this one does not fulfill certain needs on our part as adults, parents, and perpetuators of the social order. But there are other interpretations that history may ultimately favor. Here is the definitive résumé according to J.-E. Esquirol, Itard's contemporary:

> A reprehensible mother, a poverty-stricken family abandon their idiot or imbecile child; the imbecile escapes from his home and gets lost in the woods, not knowing how to find his way home; favorable circumstances protect him; he becomes fleet-footed to avoid danger; he climbs trees to escape the pursuit of some animal that threatens him; compelled by hunger, he takes nourishment from whatever comes to hand; he is easily frightened, because he has been terrified; he is obstinate, because his intelligence is weak. This unhappy child is encountered by

some hunters, brought to town, taken to the capital, placed in a vocational school, confided to the care of the most renowned instructors; the government, the city take an interest in his future and his education; scholars write books to prove that he is a savage, that he will become a Leibniz, a Buffon; the modest and observant doctor maintains that he is an idiot; the judgment is contested; new essays are written; the issue is debated; the best methods, the most enlightened care are brought to bear for the education of the so-called savage; but from all these claims, from all these efforts, from all these assurances, from all these hopes, what is the result? That the doctor-scientist had judged rightly; the alleged savage was nothing other than an idiot. Such was Pinel's opinion on the Savage of Aveyron. Let us conclude from all this that men utterly without intelligence found isolated in the mountains, in the forests, are imbeciles, idiots lost or abandoned.

Or, yet again, should we conclude that a gross misconception of child psychology combined with poor training led to negligible progress in proportion to the enormous investment of time and effort? Or have we here a tale not so much about good and bad technique or about good and bad constitution but about critical ages for learning, or about a kind of psychosis produced by isolation? Literally dozens of psychologists, educators, and anthropologists have debated these alternatives over the last century and a half. The pivotal question seems to be, why didn't Victor progress further in his intellectual development and, in particular, why didn't he acquire spoken language? The answer you receive to this question tells a lot about your respondent's conception of man. If he is impressed by the plasticity of human behavior, by the ability of the environment to determine the human condition, as Itard was, he is liable to answer "Itard's technique left much to be desired"; or, if he has a higher opinion of Itard's methods, "the asocial habits Victor acquired in the wild were practically irreversible"; Itard himself cited this possibility. Besides the "poor technique" and "refractory habits" explanations, there is a third, allied interpretation, namely childhood autism: "early and prolonged mistreatment left Victor with a profound emotional disorder." If your respondent is more impressed, on the other hand, with givens in the human condition, if he sees human growth in terms of biological unfolding, he is liable to answer that Victor had passed the critical period for language learning; Itard considered this a possibility. Or, he may answer, agreeing with Esquirol, "apparently Victor did not learn language by the time he was five; there is a simple explanation for this and for his sluggish intellectual development; he was born brain-damaged." Choosing a position, an interpretation, begins by deciding the merits and demerits of Itard's technique and, in particular, of his instruction in language.

It is to Itard's great credit that he did not view the pupil as a little adult but as a developing child. The format of the instruction is not determined then by some logical progression in the subject matter to be taught but rather by a genetic progression tailored to the individual—his history, physiology, affective needs, intellectual and social maturity. Not only did Itard arrange a milieu especially suited for the student, he often put that milieu under his pupil's control, as part of his instruction. Itard was astute in analyzing and controlling the immediate antecedents of behavior: he made frequent checks to ascertain just what cues were attended in apparently correct performance (as in letter-matching and form-matching); he did not assume that the desired cues were the ones in control (as in his analysis of the response *lait*), and he was careful not to read his own meanings into Victor's actions. He had enormous patience in proceeding by gradual approximations and was always ready to retrace his steps, to analyze a complex performance and to synthesize it from its components, as in teaching Victor to read lettered words; indeed, Itard is credited with originating the analytico-synthetic method of teaching reading. Itard knew how to fade out the supports or prompts for correct responding (as when he introduced delays in the fetching task), and in his armamentarium, which anticipated that of modern behavioral modification by nearly two centuries, he also counted the method of generalized imitation, which he used for teaching writing and speech. No doubt thanks to his medical training in an era when observation was the watchword of science, Itard was an astute observer of his pupil's behavior.

Turning from his manipulation of the antecedents of behavior to his arrangement of its consequences, Itard should be credited for his skill in leading Victor gradually into social life and rendering that life reinforcing. He appreciated the necessity of creating new needs, for the most part social. Finally, Itard was the originator of instructional devices to instrument all phases of learning. Here is a list of those he constructed or adapted for training: a plank painted black on which everyday objects were placed and their outlines chalked; the same objects suspended underneath their designs; letter cutouts to form names; a vertical board displaying a red disk, blue triangle, and black square, and the corresponding cardboard cutouts hung from nails; similar boards with the same forms in one color, or circles of contrasting colors, or kindred geo- metric forms, or circles of similar hues, or irregular patches of color; a board with twenty-four slots containing two-inch letters printed on cardboard; the corresponding letters in metal; a board with two equal circles, each having six points on the circumfer- ence for placing letter cutouts; drum, bells, shovel, drumstick; various sweets, drinks, snuff; a narrow-neck vase containing hot and cold nuts, acorns, stones, a penny and a die, metal letters; a blindfold; goblets, books, nails, a skewer, chalk, various household objects.

The official evaluation of the merits of Itard's program of in- struction, solicited from the French Institute by the Minister of the Interior, has this to say:

[This class of the Institute] acknowledges that it was impossible for the instructor to put in his lessons, exercises, and experiments more in- telligence, sagacity, patience, and courage; and that if he has not achieved greater success, it must be attributed not to any lack of zeal or talent but to the imperfection of the organs of the subject upon which he worked. Moreover, [the Institute] cannot see without astonishment how he could succeed as far as he did; and thinks that to be just toward M. Itard and to appreciate the real worth of his labors, the pupil ought to be compared only with himself; we should remember what he was when placed in the hands of this physician, see what he is now, and consider the distance separating his starting point from the one he has reached; and by how many new and ingenious teaching methods this lapse has been filled. The pamphlet of M. Itard also contains the ex- position of a series of extremely singular and interesting phenomena and of astute and judicious observations; and contains a combination of instructive procedures capable of furnishing science with new data, the knowledge of which can only be extremely useful to all persons engaged in the teaching of youth. In view of the foregoing, the class believes it desirable for your excellency to order the publication of M. Itard's memoir; and for the education of Victor, begun and pursued so profitably to this day, not to be abandoned but for the government to continue its beneficence in behalf of this unfortunate young man.

Nevertheless, Victor's education was abandoned. The ministry allocated 150 francs a year to Madame Guérin for her efforts and care, and the young man went to live with her in a nearby house belonging to the institute, at number 4, impasse des Feuillantines. When the naturalist Virey visited him there nearly a decade later, he found him "fearful, half-wild, and unable to learn to speak, despite all the efforts that were made." Victor of Aveyron died in that house, in his forties, in the year 1828.

Séguin, who knew Victor, characterizes Itard's endeavor as "a sublime attempt":

> This expression captures the nobility of the goal that he set for himself, his manifold efforts to attain it, and the point where he left the enterprise; all his originality, all his inventiveness, all his courage, amounted only to the most complete and well-founded critique of the sensualist philosophy that he had accepted . . .
>
> His errors were these: he obstinately saw in the idiot, the savage untamed. Relying in his studies, as well as in his faith, on the materialism of Locke and Condillac, his teaching sometimes reached the senses of his pupil but never penetrated to his mind and soul; he gave to his senses certain notions of things, he even excited some physical sensibility to the caresses bestowed upon him; but the boy remained destitute of ideas and of social or moral feelings, incapable of labor and, consequently, of independence.

It is true that Itard devoted much of Victor's instruction to sense training but false to say he never got beyond notions. For Séguin, ideas are notions of objects determined by their relationships: the pupil has a notion of a key when he distinguishes it from other objects, an idea of it when he learns its relation to a lock. From this outlook, Itard slighted the sensorimotor basis of learning and should have arranged more practical manipulation, through games, work, gymnastics, rhythmic and musical skills, and so on. In fact, however, all the educators who voice this criticism* have worked with severely retarded children and, unlike the latter, Victor was adroit at practical manipulation from the outset, as his tree climbing and bean shelling—to name just two examples—illustrate. Moreover, Itard was struck initially by the "prodigious muscular activity of the child compared to his sensory capacities, which were barely developed at all," and he expressly set out "as a basic and general strategy, to establish a kind of balance between sensory and motor activity, by diminishing muscular activity and concurrently developing his nervous sensitivity and intellectual faculties." Once Victor achieved this balance, Itard did arrange for learning through practical manipulation: Victor received this kind of instruction from his everyday household tasks, like setting the table, and from Itard, when the teacher thought it appropriate as in the episode with the razor and the bread. The boy's behavior in acting out anomalous sentences such as "tear cup" also show his mastery of relational concepts. It is simply untrue to say that Victor was "destitute of ideas." Also it is true that Itard failed to train conventional sexual expression; he isolated the boy from physical and social contact with his peers of both sexes, hearing or deaf. But it is false to say that Victor had no social or moral feelings; there are many counter-examples in Itard's report.

Those who look at human development and notice chiefly what the child brings to his education will see in Itard's strategy, and in its contemporary descendants, a misguided attempt at total pedagogy, an insufficient appreciation of what the child does and learns on his own, "spontaneously" as it were, outside organized instruction. Much like Pinel, Itard wrote off the many skills that Victor brought with him: his ability to scamper up trees and to leap from one to the next, with all that that implies in eye-hand coordination; his skill in preparing his own food, whether plucking and eviscerating a bird, shelling beans, or selecting foods by smell and by sound as well as sight. Not only did Itard fail to profit by his pupil's original performances and reinforcers (these were the products of "base animal appetites"), he continued to do so as their collaboration progressed; thus, for example, he saw no arm for his battle against Victor's mutism in the boy's "lli, lli" when he was with Julie in the Luxembourg Gardens; nor did he see an avenue of attack in Victor's own action-language. Beyond this, he actually drew Victor back into a cocoon in which life alternated between the household and the classroom, nearly abolishing all Victor's opportunities for unstructured contact with the natural and social environment; instruction became the predominant means of learning. Even within the cocoon there was an inner barrier, between lessons and life; if Itard occasionally took note of Victor's behavior in the household, he never led his instruction across that threshold, integrating it with the childish recreations in which he occasionally took part.

More narrowly, within Itard's own framework, his conditioning technique had enough flaws so that we cannot know if Victor might not have been able to recover speech, and to go on to greater development in language, thought, and social life. For these failings we share Victor's suffering, even if our protest is more articulate. Victor finally stands mute on charges of retardation and autism; had he become a Leibniz or even a Massieu, they would be dropped; had he failed to develop further despite impeccable technique, they would be supported. In attempting to teach Victor to discriminate speech sounds, Itard began with too many vowels, including some that Victor did not pronounce; he made his selection based on the alphabet, rather than on audible differences, and failed to use his own principle of dwindling contrasts; he chose an awkward mode of responding; ideally, he might have been able, using generalized imitation, to lead Victor to identify which one of a pair of vowels was presented by reproducing it vocally. Finally, Itard failed to consider that Victor's native language, since he came from south central France, may have been *langue d'oc*, and the selection of beginning vowels should have been based on that language or on those it has in common with French.

In attempting to teach Victor to speak, Itard erred at the outset in failing to raise the frequency of vocalizing—the "operant level" —by immediately reinforcing each utterance. He tried to use generalized imitation to induce vocalizing, and yet he apparently did not reinforce Victor's imitations of his facial movements. He did not report what vowels and consonants he tried to elicit first, but these should have been chosen from Victor's repertory and may not have been; in any event, it apparently did not occur to him to prompt the correct vocal imitation by manipulating Victor's articulations himself, then gradually fading these prompts as Victor increasingly executed the full movement on his own. In general, Itard was good at arranging gradual progressions of stimuli, but not of responses; that is, he did not shape behavior. Itard failed to build vocal imitation on Victor's existing utterances, such as "lait," by rewarding the response only if it occurred soon after the teacher's model (as Lovaas did), or by embedding the model in a chain of actions that Victor would already imitate. Finally, Itard did not capitalize on Victor's sense of touch to aid him in making distinctions like voiced versus voiceless consonants (for example, d/t) or nasal versus nonnasal sounds (õ/o).

In teaching Victor to understand and produce written language, Itard inexplicably left off once Victor had mastered strings of verb plus noun. Small steps indeed lay between this performance and the control of elementary French sentences, and Sicard's technique was a handy, if imperfect, guide for this and further progress. If Itard had been less committed to oral language, Victor might have realized Bonnaterre's ambition for him and gone on to master the written language and to become a Massieu after all. Perhaps because of this same commitment to spoken language, Itard never even attempted to teach Victor sign language; a questionable omission before he had abandoned Victor to mutism, it was inexcusable thereafter.

Granted that Itard's program of education was inadequate in some respects, this cannot in itself explain Victor's limitations in speech, language, and socialization. The obvious explanation for the differences between Victor and almost any other rural French adolescent of the same era lies in Victor's experiences during his years of isolation in the wild. Still other explanations have been given, beginning with Pinel's warning to Itard that the boy was simply a born idiot or, as one says today, congenitally retarded. Itard's classmate under Pinel, Esquirol, who would later pioneer in psychiatry as Itard did in otology, agreed with this grim diagnosis and felt that the outcome of Victor's education amply justified it. A leading naturalist of the day, Bory de Saint-Vincent, judged the teacher as harshly as the pupil, calling Victor "this savage of Aveyron, a true idiot, filthy and disgusting, whom some people these days tormented by a mania for publication would turn into a celebrity so they could become one too." In their classic work on neuroanatomy, which would prove to have such profound impact on psychology, Gall and Spurzheim cite Victor's case among others to show that "these savages, found in the forests are ordinarily miserable creatures with a faulty constitution ... they are true idiots that can receive no education, no training ... As they are a burden to their families ... it often happens that they are abandoned or left to wander off at their will." Franz Gall had examined Victor:

> He is an imbecile to a high degree, his forehead is very little extended on the sides and highly compressed on top, his eyes are small and quite sunken, his cerebellum is little developed. We have not been able to convince ourselves that he can hear; no one could get his attention in our presence either by calling him or by striking a glass behind his ears. He has a tranquil manner; his posture and way of sitting down are correct; one notices only that he rocks his trunk and head back and forth incessantly; he greets people who arrive by bowing slightly and is visibly pleased when they depart. An interest in sex does not yet seem to have developed. He knows a few written characters and he can even indicate the objects that these characters designate. Moreover, his favorite occupation is to restore objects to their proper places when they have been disarranged. And there we have the outcome of all the hopes that were engendered, of all the effort that was expended, and of all the patience and kindness that his governess expresses in her conduct toward him. We can affirm with certainty that no better outcome will ever be obtained.

The man who inspired Itard to pursue a medical career and who later became surgeon general of the French army, Jean-Dominique Larrey, saw Victor while visiting his former pupil and, like Gall and Spurzheim, thought the skull of the wild boy congenitally deformed. During the Napoleonic invasion of Russia he wrote in his military diary,

> [I also saw] the skeleton of a dwarf whose origins remain unknown,

and who was encountered several times in the forest of Lithuania, dressed in untanned animal skins. His body was covered with hair. He rarely came near houses; he nourished himself with the meat of animals and with wild fruits, of which he doubtless made provision in the favorable seasons. These are the only details which we have been able to collect from the life of this man, whose skull seemed to have much likeness to the skull of the wild boy of Aveyron whom I saw at Dr. Itard's on my return from Egypt. The skeleton of the wild man of Lithuania shows a close analogy to that of an orangutan. The skull is very small, compared with one of persons of the same size and age. The forehead is almost nonexistent, the occiput is very much developed, and forms a very strong projection at the occipital protuberance. The two jawbones are very projecting at the dental arcades; the incisors and canines of a remarkable whiteness are almost conical, sharp and longer than in ordinary cases. The upper members are longer than with a well-built man; the lower limbs are very short in proportion and the calcaneums are elongated backwards.*

In our times the father of structuralism, Claude Lévi-Strauss, holds to this view, curiously enough, that "most of these [abandoned] children were congenitally abnormal and it is imbecility, which they nearly all seem to have suffered, that is the original cause of their abandonment and not, as some contend, its result." Maria Montessori and psychologists Arnold Gesell and Wayne Dennis have expressed much the same opinion as Lévi-Strauss. Returning to nineteenth-century France, Destutt de Tracy, Condillac's disciple and author of "Elements of Ideology," also believed that children such as Victor were born retarded, and Séguin writes, "Itard, contrary to the misgivings of Bonnaterre and to the all but convincing demonstrations of Pinel, undertook [Victor's] education. He did not believe idiocy curable . . . but he was the first to educate an idiot with a philosophical object and by physiological means."

Were the parallels that Pinel drew between Victor and the "children sadly condemned to vegetate in our asylums" convincing proof that Victor was retarded from the outset? There are so many flaws in Pinel's argument, it is hard to understand why it has had so much weight. The first objection must be that the children with whom Victor was compared were not themselves proven congenital retardates, so that however similar his behavior was to theirs, the diagnosis would remain unsupported. This is one of the pitfalls of diagnosis by comparison, which the founder of mental medicine had designed according to Condillac's analytical method. If today it is often difficult to distinguish between organic and functional retardation (while the child is alive), and between functional retardation and childhood psychosis, how much more difficult was it in the feeble light of the dawn of psychiatry, when all these varieties of human misfortune were cast together to deteriorate alike in the cells of Bicêtre and La Salpêtrière. Moreover, was Victor's behavior in fact similar to that of these inmates? The second objection must be that the distinguished doctor examined the boy under the most unfavorable conditions, precisely those that could not evoke the panoply of discriminations, concepts, and skills he had acquired adaptively for life in the wild.

The *Décade philosophique* described the proper examination procedure in 1800:

> In the first place, to observe properly the current state of such an individual, it is not sufficient to spend a few hours with him on occasion; it is necessary to live at his side, so to say, for several days. The observer should follow him in the different phases of his existence, witness the birth of the development of his needs, compare the impressions that he receives, and not allow a single facet of his character and actions to escape attention. That is not all. He must be observed when he is at liberty, where he is completely himself. But how can this be accomplished when he lives in continual constraint, always tempted to flee, and always so restrained that he is led about like a prisoner, with a leash attached to his belt, and when he is endlessly surrounded by a thousand curious persons, as importunate as they are indiscreet, who tire him out with various ordeals that he does not understand.

Nevertheless, Pinel had word of Victor's skills from other observers but—and this must be the third objection—he systematically belittled every example of Victor's intelligence. Does he choose and prepare his foods? It is merely automatic imitation. Does he show nuances of sensitivity for the kindnesses extended to him? These are a weak imitation of true sentiment. Does he stock away food for later consumption? Hardly more than animal instinct. The same boy who clambered up trees and leapt from one to the next in Aveyron has "a sort of dissonance between the sense of vision and the use of touch" in Paris. The very boy who "put the good beans in the pot and rejected those that were mouldy or tainted," and who "if by chance a bean got away from him, kept his eye on it, picked it up, and placed it with the others" in Rodez, is "disgustingly filthy," "does not fixate," and leaves "his fingers extended and the sense of touch absolutely inactive . . . in picking out various foods that he uses" in Paris. The boy who "if the fire was out, took the shovel and placed it in Clair's hands signaling him to go looking for some nearby coals" cannot "express himself either by articulate sounds or by gestures." If Pinel's gaze should have fixed on these episodes, among others, in Bonnaterre's report, we cannot say the same of course for the many more examples of Victor's sensitivity, skill, cunning, and originality cited in Itard's report. But Itard, like Pinel, provided an environment that must largely have stifled the boy's intelligent expression and, like Pinel, he belittled the domain of skills in which Victor was the master. If Victor could have led these two physicians by hand into the forests, and could have examined their gaze, their hearing, their use of smell, their motor skills, would he not have been forced by the method of comparison to put them in a class of wounded or constitutionally defective animals, and how much might they then have learned from the boy?

In drawing parallels between Victor's conduct and that of presumed idiots, Pinel does not seem to consider that the same effects can be produced by different causes. This must be the fourth objection. Perhaps Pinel took the behavior of savages as his measure of the effects of life in the wild and, finding "no similarity beween Victor and these individuals," concluded that Victor's behavior must have some other cause, namely idiocy. But the salient fact about Victor is not that he lived in the wild, but that he lived there alone, left to his own devices, and without human companionship, for years on end. Will this fact alone suffice to explain his mutism, his sexual inhibitions, his indifference to extremes of temperature and other sensory anomalies? It appears to. Zingg has tabulated some three dozen cases of children who have lived in extreme isolation or possibly with animal companions in the wild.

Victor's is probably the best documented case, despite the many questions it leaves unanswered. If the cumulated evidence has lapses and fantasy, it nevertheless has a certain weight. In every case, the child is mute when captured. And in every case of demonstrably prolonged isolation, there is little or no recovery from mutism. Zingg also finds that the children's sexual impulses are inhibited, which is surprising "considering the gross animal behavior of feral man in other urges, like hunger." Vision, hearing, and smell are generally acute when judged in relation to getting food. Many of the children are insensitive to heat and cold. Laughing and smiling are rarely recorded, but anger is frequent. Most of these children initially shun human society and seek every opportunity to escape again into the wild. In virtually all cases they walk occasionally on their hands and feet or hands and knees. Now if Pinel insists that Victor was congenitally retarded—but all the children abandoned as he was suffer from symptoms like his—what must Pinel or his modern counterparts say about these other children? (This is the fifth objection to Pinel's argument.) Surely all thirty-five of them were not born idiots. Yes, they were, Dennis contends. And then in a tour de force he tries to show that each of the symptoms listed above is characteristic of institutionalized idiots.

> Feral man is ordinarily mute ... Deficiency in language is an outstanding trait of the lower-grade defective also ... Feral man upon capture, if not entirely mute, may make animal sounds. Tredgold says of mute idiots: "Their utterances mostly consist of inarticulate grunts, screeches, and discordant yells ... " Feral man is untidy ... "the majority of mentally defective children are late in acquiring control over the bladder and rectum ... " Feral man will eat things which civilized man considers disgusting ... "Some idiots will eat and drink anything which comes within their reach ... " Feral man frequently is grossly insensitive to heat and cold ... "In the lower grades [of deficiency, the temperature sense] seems to be wanting" ... A feral child commonly shows little or no attachment to human beings ... Idiots rank low in scores for affection ... Feral man is said to walk on all fours ... It would probably be most correct to state that many wild children cannot walk upright. Neither can many idiots.

Yet Victor, like many other wild children, could certainly walk upright, as well as climb, run, and leap; he showed none of the spasticity of severely retarded children. Nor would he eat and drink anything within reach; on the contrary, his food preferences were more exclusive—and generally more salubrious—than civilized man's. Finally, if we are to believe that Victor was mute because of congenital retardation before he entered the forests, he must have had a mental age less than three, since that is all that is associated with learning some speech. How could such a severely retarded child survive in the wild left to his own devices, to secure food, prepare shelter, and evade predators? This is the sixth objection to Pinel's argument. Neither Delasiauve's rebuttal, "Hunger has its own genius," nor Dennis' "We do not know how long the individual really shifted for himself" is satisfactory.*

In the light of all these objections to Pinel's argument, several contemporary authorities on child psychiatry* have proposed that Victor suffered originally not from mental retardation but from a personality disorder unidentified in Pinel's day, childhood psychosis or autism. Victor's initial abandonment, his condition when examined in Paris, and his limited progress in education are explained, according to this view, once we compare him with autistic children and recognize all the symptoms they have in common. Characteristically, an autistic child is profoundly withdrawn from contact with people, is obsessively concerned with preserving order and sameness, shows some measure of intelligence and motor skill, is either mute or engages in language that does not seem to serve interpersonal communication, and often presents some sensory anomalies. Victor, we are told,* gave all of the following signs of autism. He sniffed everything, even things we think are odorless; his hearing was acute for some things and not others; he was indifferent to extremes of cold and heat; on outings, he had to be held back from trotting, galloping, and fleeing. Autism is, however, an emotional and character disorder, and the following symptoms should receive more weight. Victor had his moments of joy which rapidly gave way to frenzied rage; yet bad treatment did not make him cry; he could spend long hours doing nothing, in a state of apathy, utterly indifferent to human contact. This emotional lability is an earmark of autism. When Victor was frustrated in a lesson he became enraged. Significantly, this rage was directed toward objects, not people: "On such occasions, he ran off and, in this destructive mood, bit the sheets, the blankets, and the mantlepiece, scattered the andirons, ashes, and blazing embers." Victor was obsessively concerned with order, illustrated in shelling beans and in pairing hanging objects with their outlines. The boy used other peoples' hands as tools: "He took my hand and made me pass my index finger over the whole series of names until I had shown him the forgotten one." The autistic child lacks the desire to communicate with others, and so he does not use or develop such language as he may possess; this can explain Victor's recalcitrant mutism.

Yet it is not more likely that Victor was originally autistic than it is that he was originally retarded. The same kinds of objections that applied to Pinel's hypotheses are equally cogent here. In the first place, the similarities between Victor and autistic children seem to be exaggerated. His rapid changes from laughs to tears, from calm to fury, are unlike the psychotic child's in that they were provoked by specific events that were easily identified, indeed, usually by his transactions with people. Victor wept when reunited with Itard, when reproached by him, or after struggling in vain in the course of their lessons. It is simply impossible to describe Victor as profoundly withdrawn from people; many passages in Itard's report testify to his affection toward those who were kind to him, his desire to please, his sensitivity to reproach. It is true that there were two major crises when Victor became enraged; but Itard specifically precipitated this rage when he pushed discrimination training too fast and evoked a sort of experimental neurosis. Originally Victor directed his aggressive rage against people—in Saint-Sernin, for example, when hounded by the mob of onlookers. If he later addressed it to objects and not Itard, this seems more a sign of Itard's significance than insignificance for the boy. Victor's practical and intelligent arrangements for shelling beans should hardly be stigmatized as a maniacal concern for order. We do not know how much time Madame Guérin or Abbé Bonnaterre spent teaching him that every utensil and every stitch of clothing has its place, but we do know that he did not insist on this "sameness" and was, in fact, infinitely patient in the games

of rearrangement, unlike psychotic children. Victor had no particular difficulty in practical manipulation; it is wrong to say that
he used the adult hand as a tool, when he obliged Madame Guérin
to sample the water temperature or Itard to take the shock from
the Leyden jar or to point out to him the name he had forgotten.
These are, rather, acts of communication; like his abundant gestural language, they are surrogates for speech. Unlike the autistic
child, Victor was, within his limits, highly communicative.

And then there are the other objections. Could an abandoned
five-year-old psychotic survive in the wild? People who work with
these children think not; yet it is certain in Victor's case at least
that he spent a long time in the forest. What of the thirty-five
other feral children who share many of Victor's key symptoms—
were they all also psychotic? Finally, this diagnosis makes no more
allowance than its predecessor for similar effects produced by dissimilar causes. What is there about Victor's deviant behavior in
society that cannot be explained by his adaptive behavior in the
forest?

It appears that Itard's original analysis in 1800 was the correct
one: "If it were proposed to solve the following problem of metaphysics, to determine what would be the degree of intelligence and
the nature of the ideas of an adolescent who, deprived since infancy of all education, had lived entirely separated from individuals of his own species, then unless I am grossly mistaken . . . the
profile of this adolescent would be that of the wild boy of Aveyron." Prolonged isolation in the wild modifies gait, tunes the
senses selectively, inhibits sexual and social behavior, and produces mutism—these are Victor's "symptoms." If Victor was
neither retarded nor psychotic, then he must have spoken French.
Perhaps the children of woodsmen are not voluble, especially in
families that are inclined to cut their throats, and perhaps they
live in any event in semi-isolation and soon learn to fend for themselves; nevertheless they learn to speak. When Victor came out of
the forest at Saint-Sernin, he was mute. Can such a fundamental
habit, acquired so early, be extinguished through disuse? There are
at least three cases on record that suggest that it can. The first was
reported in the eighteenth century by a naval engineer responsible

for forestry studies in the Pyrenees, in connection with the construction of masts. He relates the capture of a girl of about sixteen who had been lost eight years earlier when a snowstorm took her camping group by surprise. She was identified and institutionalized, never to recover speech. More widely known and documented is the case of the Scottish sailor, Selkirk, who inspired Defoe's *Robinson Crusoe.* When Captain Woodes Rogers put in at the island of Juan Fernández in 1709, according to his diary, he found a sailor "as wild as the animals, perhaps more so," who had been put off ship as a punishment, four years and four months earlier, by Captain Stradling. Selkirk had been left with clothing, a bed, a gun and ammunition, a Bible and some other books. By the time he was discovered, he had "almost entirely forgotten the secret of articulating intelligible sounds . . . If he had not had books, or if his exile had lasted two or three years more," he would have lost all ability to speak. The third case is reported by Malson in his introduction to the recent reprinting of Itard's two reports: "Yves Cheneau [was] discovered in 1963 at Saint-Brévin, in Loire-Atlantique, by his uncle and some gendarmes; he had been living in a cellar for eighteen months, imprisoned there by his wicked stepmother. 'When he came out,' his uncle recounts, 'he took a long time to get accustomed to the light. He was shown a cat and a cow and asked what they were. He no longer knew.' Didier Leroux—sent to cover the story by a major Paris newspaper—and who saw the child at the Nantes hospital, states 'His gaze wanders apathetically over things and people. He does not speak; he no longer knows how to speak.' "

Victor's symptoms, then, including his mutism, may overlap with those of congenital retardation or autism, but are explained by neither; instead they are the result of his isolation in the wild, as Itard maintained all along. This is the view that prevails among diverse environmentalists,* but it meets with the following challenge. If Victor merely confirmed the adaptiveness and plasticity of human behavior, why didn't he readapt to society once he returned and, indeed, received intensive rehabilitation. Itard was scarcely in his grave when Bousquet put this argument to him in his eulogy: "If Victor was not born defective; if endowing him with the needs of his species, nature gave him all the faculties; if really, he needed only the power of example to break the bonds that enchained his reason; it is clear that nothing can prevent him from springing back into life now that he breathes the air of civilization." Gall and Spurzheim argued likewise in 1812: "As soon as such [a normal isolated] individual finds himself again in the midst of society we would see him reveal normal human tendencies, not only by prompt imitation of social practices but also by his capacity for instruction ... The development of his reason will soon change his way of life, or else there is no change and thus we are dealing with an imbecile, since education and circumstances can have an effect on man only to the extent that he has the necessary capacities and physical endowment."

Why didn't Victor recover language and progress much further in his intellectual development and socialization? It is not helpful to answer, as Rauber does, that he suffered from a disorder we can call *dementia ex separatione*. Asked why sleeping draughts were effective, Molière's doctor also answered "because of their soporific virtues." Hardly more instructive is the answer of several social scientists that Victor's prolonged isolation in the wild "fixed" his asocial habits. Itard gives one reply that contemporary authors have echoed when they cite a critical period for language learning: "Before arriving at the important point in [Victor's] education [which is fluent speech] much more time and much more trouble will be necessary than would be required for the least gifted of infants."* It certanily does appear that children have some advantage over adults in learning languages, as any family that has moved to another country with its offspring will testify. This advantage may lie precisely in a greater tendency to imitate speech and other social behavior and to learn from imitation. That, in any event, is what Itard believed:

> If we stop for a moment to think about the remarkable role that imitation plays in man's earliest education, we are struck by the fact that speech, which is the very first undertaking of this nascent ability, is at the same time its most difficult and most splendid accomplishment. To realize fully how marvelous this is, is to imagine a country dweller who enters an artist's studio and sees some paintings, a palette, and some

brushes for the first time in his life; who discovers at a glance the relation between painting and brushes; and who uses the brushes right off to copy the paintings that have struck him most favorably.

As Itard's analogy suggests, saying that the child learning his language depends on imitation does not necessarily mean that he passively absorbs what he hears or sees and then produces a replica, like a tape recorder or a printing press. On the contrary, the generalizations the child has already learned about his language play a powerful role in shaping what he takes away from adult speech. This is especially clear when he extends his rules too far: the child who says *buyed* or *foots* is engaged in a sort of creative imitation. Curiously enough, this ability seems to wane rather than improve with age. "What is even more astonishing," Itard wrote, "is that this innate tendency . . . is the more active and the more discerning, so to say, the closer the person is to his early childhood. In this period of life, all the imitative abilities are concentrated in the organs of voice and speech, so that it is incomparably easier for a child than an adolescent to grasp the mechanism of speech by imitation." Nevertheless, adults can imitate and they learn many things, including foreign language, in part by imitation, so if there is a difference between adults and children on this score, it is probably one of degree.

Itard believed that imitation was crucial to language learning; describing the methods he had developed over two decades for teaching the mute to speak, he asserts that the potential pupil must show some aptitude for understanding and imitation: "Having been mistaken on this count once before, I make note of it here." He thought that Victor's native ability to imitate had not only waned with age but whatever remnants there might have been were destroyed by prolonged social isolation. "Similar to congenital idiocy is the accidental state of dullness and brutishness which would characterize an individual who had lived in the woods, given over to a purely animal life . . . [Such] individuals have no other manner to exist and to feel than that of the beasts, and the foremost faculty of human intelligence, that of imitation, is annihilated in their case."* A California girl who was isolated

181   Interpreting the Legend

until recently in a small closed room, tied to a potty chair, from twenty months until nearly fourteen years of age provides in some respects a modern counterpart to Victor. During the four years since her release, Genie has made some progress in learning her first language after the critical period. There is no doubt, however, that this progress is abnormally slow and the prognosis is poor, because of the combined effects of isolation and late acquisition.

Victor did make enormous progress under Itard's tutelage.* Were it possible for the first experiment in behavior modification to benefit from the latest ones, that progress would have been greater, and Victor might have gone on to make a more banal contribution to society. If he failed to do so, whatever the limitations of his education, it may be because prolonged isolation deprived him of the crucial skill by which children and adults profit from social experiences that are not explicitly designed for their instruction, namely, the skill of imitation.

Chapter Eight

Victor's Legacy to the Deaf

*Itard founds oral education of the deaf—
His inspiration—Training hearing as with
Victor—Categories of deafness—Itard's
technique—Taps, notes, and vowels—
Teaching consonant discrimination—
Hearing with an inner ear—Hearing does
not lead to speech—A critical period for
imitation—Teaching articulation—Itard's
predecessors in oralism—His vowel
progression—His consonant progression—
Breathing and imitation exercises—
Students handicapped by native sign
language.*

When I unearthed some of Itard's papers, rotting in the boiler room of the National Institute for Deaf Children in Paris, among them was a memorandum, dated 1825, in which he gives a summary of his early career. After recounting his largely fruitless efforts to find a treatment for congenital hearing loss by medication, surgery, and post-mortem dissections, Itard tells how these experiments and his duties as resident physician at the institute "did not take up all the time I wanted to devote to my work when an extraordinary opportunity presented itself to conduct related studies of a completely novel interest."

> It was the opportunity to observe in a mute child, not deaf but raised far from all human society, the late development of the instinct of imitation, the influence of speech on the formation and association of ideas. Most of my days for six years were given over to this detailed experiment. The child, who was called the wild boy of Aveyron, did not receive from my intensive care all the advantages that I had hoped. But the many observations that I could make and the techniques of instruction inspired by the inflexibility of his organs were not entirely fruitless, and I later found a more suitable application for them with some of our children whose mutism is the result of obstacles that are more easily overcome.

Initiating the education of the mentally handicapped through his experiments with Victor of Aveyron from 1801 to 1806, Itard went on to found oral education of the hearing-handicapped through experiments with six other children from 1805 to 1808.

Pereire was the first to devise reliable methods for teaching the deaf to speak, more than half a century earlier. Although the guiding notions of those methods have been reconstructed, their author carried the secret of his detailed method to his grave, leaving only some astonishingly fluent students to bear witness to its efficacy during their lifetime. To Itard must go the credit for developing, largely independently, a systematic, principled program of oral training which would later be instituted in France and elaborated and modified by other teachers of the deaf throughout Europe and America. Just a little over a year after writing his final report on the boy of Aveyron, Itard presented two memoirs, "On the Means of Providing Hearing to Deaf-Mutes" and "On the Means of Providing Speech to Deaf-Mutes," to the Society of the Faculty of Medicine, and he read the first of these to the society on November 26, 1807.*

Itard's two memoirs created something of a sensation among the members of the faculty as two of their number recount:

> M. Itard has as his particular purpose in the first report that he communicated to the society to present the steps that he had taken and the results that he obtained using a medico-philosophical treatment of hearing loss with deaf-mutes whose hearing suffered an initial impairment opposed to its development. His resourceful methods in all his experiments, the authentic quality of his observations, the important results to which he was led, and above all his analytical way of proceeding, the wisdom and circumspection of his conclusions attracted the keen attention of the society and inspired an interest which it is our duty to relate and which obliges us to set forth in some detail the report that the society has requested us to present.

The report was read to the society in February 1808, and in April Itard himself read his second memoir, concerned with methods of teaching speech. At the May meeting, he presented the six deaf-mute children, "to whom he succeeded in giving the faculties of speech comprehension and production. The society took great satisfaction in seeing the pupils carry out their various exercises."

It soon became widely accepted that Itard's methods of "physiological training of the ear" could improve the lot of the deaf. This fact saved the life of an outspoken literary figure of the times, Fabre d'Olivet, whom Napoleon had been wanting to crush underfoot. When the philologist claimed to have discovered a cure for deafness while preparing a new translation of the cosmogony of Moses, the emperor entrapped him into practicing this cure and then had him arrested for false healing. Itard and Sicard were appointed commissioners to evaluate D'Olivet's cure, a jealously guarded secret that included liquids poured into the ear and a prolonged period of daily lessons as hearing gradually recovered. The commissioners found that D'Olivet was not a charlatan; he simply did not realize that his pupil had some residual hearing in the first place and that it is possible "by graduated exercises to convert congenital deafness into simple hardness of hearing" and even to induce speaking.

This is Itard's own account of how he got the idea that poor hearing could often be improved by discrimination training— which he calls "physiological training of the ear"—thus assisting the partially deaf child in mastering spoken language.

In the winter of 1802 I was invited by Abbé Sicard to witness some acoustical experiments that were to be performed on his pupils. A physicist brought several noise- and sound-making instruments of his own invention and he generated sounds so piercing that many of these children seemed to hear them. But since, in these sorts of experiments, deaf-mutes make it a point of honor to give the impression of hearing, even resorting to deceit to do so, I suggested that they be blindfolded and required to raise their hands for each sound that they could hear. The experiment was performed and it turned out that, of twenty children who had originally claimed they heard the sounds, four had been quite thoroughly deaf and, embarrassed by the public discovery of their little lie, they withdrew from the experiment of their own accord and retook their places among their companions in misfortune. As the ears of the remaining sixteen were repeatedly tested with the same sounds, I noticed to my amazement that some of them, who a moment before had raised their hands slowly and uncertainly, the inevitable result of their weak or vague perception of the sounds, now made the same gesture with much more assurance. To clarify and confirm this result, I asked that this device which emitted excessively shrill sounds be replaced by one less loud. With the first blow struck on the new instrument, eight of the deaf-mutes gave no sign of hearing; after a few minutes, two of these eight raised their hands; soon after, two others joined them and little by little the four remaining began to show in turn, by the signal agreed upon, that they had become sensitive to the new sounds.

The spectators saw nothing other than a very curious phenomenon in this result of the experiments; but as for me, they struck me like a brilliant flash of light that showed me the route I must follow to bring to life a sense born paralyzed. It would not be too difficult for me to develop such a plan. The procedure was not new to me: four successive years of looking after and experimenting with a child found in the woods had taught me the means of awakening the sensitivity of the sense organs and the benefits that can be derived from a kind of training given separately to each of them.

In an unpublished memorandum in 1825 Itard wrote:

> I had noticed that the hearing of several of our pupils who were not
> completely deaf improved rather rapidly when regularly stimulated with
> sources of sound. This chance observation provided the basis for a
> method of physiological training applied to the organs of hearing and
> speech; allowing for a few modifications, the method resembled the one
> I had undertaken with the wild boy. Two hours a day for three years
> were devoted to this new experiment; this time, at last, my efforts were
> successful. Six of our deaf-mutes—and especially three among them—
> were returned to their families with the ability to speak and understand,
> and they were presented as such to the Faculty of Medicine which re-
> corded this result in one of its bulletins.

Obviously, there was no question of training the hearing of most
of the children at the institute. Somewhere between half and two
thirds of them were profoundly deaf.* Initially, Itard saw only
vaguely how to characterize those who would benefit from this
instruction. After some years of experimenting with oral education, however, he arrived at a classification of hearing losses into
five broad diagnostic categories based on the pupil's residual ability
to understand speech. These categories are described in his classic
"Treatise on Diseases of the Ear and Hearing," which for many
medical historians marks the beginning of otology, and they are
also the subject of an unpublished memorandum dated 1824. In
the first category are those more fortunate children who can understand speech if it is addressed to them directly, loudly, and slowly.
They generally acquire speech later in life than their peers with
normal hearing, but they can be educated by the same means, if
somewhat more slowly. In the second category are those children
who fail to distinguish voiced consonants from their voiceless
counterparts. Thus, *beau* sounds like *peau*, *don* like *ton*, and so on.
They can, however, distinguish all the vowels.* They find speech
difficult to learn and conversation impossible. In general, they
cannot go to school with their peers. Itard believed, however, that
his method of instruction would allow these children to enter
normal hearing society, as it would those in the third category.
Here are grouped the hearing-handicapped who fail to distinguish
among nearly all the consonants but can discriminate among the

vowels, which are intrinsically louder. They have difficulty in perceiving and producing intonation. The ordinary means of educating them are useless unless they first receive "physiological training" of hearing and speech. Pupils in the fourth and fifth categories are invariably mute. The former confuse all speech sounds but distinguish them from bursts of noise; the latter are profoundly deaf, and if they detect some intense sounds, it is through the sense of touch and not hearing.

Itard undertook his experiments in 1805 with six children whose hearing loss placed them in the second and third categories. He began by improving their ability to detect sound rapidly and reliably. Originally, he had a church bell installed in their classroom, and he taught his pupils to respond to successively softer notes which he obtained either by striking the bell with different objects or by seating the pupils farther away. Itard neglects to mention that his pupils were blindfolded, until he comes to the later exercises, but it seems likely that their eyes were covered right from the beginning, as were Victor's in his hearing training. Itard next employed the vibrating bell of a clock and, placing his students in a row in a long corridor, he gradually withdrew the source of sound, marking on the wall the point at which it became inaudible for each child. In this way he recorded the relative standing of each of his pupils and the day-to-day progress. One pupil's record began with a threshold of detection at ten paces but increased, by diminishing returns, to twenty-five. Itard sometimes gives the impression that he thought this progress was due to exercising the ear, much like a partially paralyzed limb. Modern psychologists who have obtained the same results talk more in terms of decision processes and training listening. In any case, when the marks on the wall had slowed their advance to only an inch or so a day, Itard left off work on absolute sensitivity, and began training differential sensitivity, starting with a broad contrast between loud and soft sounds, which at first the pupils could not reliably distinguish. Once again, in these days before amplifiers and attenuators, the teacher varied the spacing between the two sound levels by varying the spacing between the two positions in the corridor from which he presented them.*

His third series of exercises engaged his pupils' sense of the timing of sounds as well as of their relative intensities, although it is improbable that Itard knew that when we judge the direction of a source of sound we are guided in part by its earlier arrival at the closer ear. Taking up different positions around his blindfolded students as he sounded a little bell, the teacher had them point to his location, which at first they did hesitatingly and often erroneously, but with assurance and accuracy after a few days' practice. (He presumably let them peek after making their guesses.) The fourth series of exercises concerned the perception of rhythm: Itard dragged out Victor's old drum and tapped out a few simple marches for his pupils—"as often poorly as well," he adds modestly. His selections were apparently good ones, since he reports that his six pupils took to beating them out together in the classroom while awaiting his arrival. Edging his way toward speech discriminations, Itard next taught his pupils to distinguish high and low notes on the flute. This exercise provided no special difficulty, but as Itard himself points out, there is quite a distance between discriminating notes or half-notes, on the one hand, and discriminating the differences in timbre that constitute the various vowels on the other. Thus his pupils reached a point where they perfectly distinguished the *re* and *la* of the musical scale but not the vowels *o* and *a*. To overcome this last difficulty, the teacher placed himself behind the children and pronounced "the five vowels" while writing each in turn on a blackboard. Then the teacher uttered various vowels and the children were to point to the corresponding transcription. This may have been a more practical mode of responding than the five-finger exercise that Itard had imposed on Victor, but it had the disadvantage that the pupils' numerous errors at first probably resulted as much from ignorance of the written letters as from confusion of the spoken vowels. By correcting their mistakes, however, Itard had his pupils correctly transcribing the vowels within a few days.

Consonant discriminations proved much more difficult, and Itard says frankly that he had to use a thousand and one different devices, tailoring his instruction to each individual student. This necessity led him to give an hour's lesson daily to each of the pupils and to reduce the group from six to three. One of the principles he discovered empirically was that some consonants are more readily recognized when followed by one vowel, some by another. A second principle was that these syllables are more readily perceived when they themselves follow an invariant "carrier syllable," for example *ra*. "If it was the consonant *t* that I wanted to be understood, I coupled it with the vowel *a* and, preceding it with the syllable *ra*, I said *rata*, stressing the first syllable." It was not until the middle of the twentieth century that experiments at the Bell Telephone laboratories brought to light the acoustical basis of these perceptual phenomena. Modern investigators, seeking electronic means of making speech visible for the deaf so that, among other things, they could use the telephone, developed a device called the sound spectrograph, which was the forerunner of the contemporary "voiceprint" machine. By studying sound spectrograms and by testing their hypotheses with artificial synthesized speech, phoneticians have learned what cues we use in identifying speech sounds. When Itard sandwiched the target consonant between two vowels, he was wisely providing his pupils with a maximum of cues: in addition to the pitch and duration of the explosion that is the *t*, the student could hear the change in vowel quality as the tongue moved into position against the teeth and then withdrew from that position. This audible track of the tongue's movements during the vowels testifies that one of a small class of consonants occurred between them, just as visible tracks in the snow leading up to and away from some point testify that a certain species paused there.

These findings also explain a third principle that Itard came upon, much to his dismay, in teaching consonant identification: once the pupil succeeded in hearing the *t*, for example, in the word *rata*, he had not "mastered the *t*" in the sense that he could now hear it in any other speech environment; on the contrary, the surrounding vowels had to be varied repeatedly until the child learned the invariant cue for *t*. That is not surprising, since the tongue's audible track will depend on what vowel position it starts from and arrives at. But no matter what the vowels, all the tracks that include *t* will pass through a certain point, one that is different from, say, that for *k*, and it is these audible "loci" that the student finally learns inductively. It took Itard about a year to bring his pupils to the point where they could reliably recognize all the vowels and consonants as they occurred in various simple words. And even then, certain confusions persisted, notably between consonants that share the same locus, such as *f* and *v*, *p* and *b*. Thus his students confused something *frais* (fresh) and something *vrai* (true); also a *poulet* (chicken) and a *boulet* (ball).

Yet Itard recognized that these remaining difficulties need not be too serious, and for an interesting reason with profound implications for the training of the deaf. The young physician had understood what must be the central fact about spoken language, namely that it is highly redundant. The young man who has suffered a hearing loss because of an accident, the old man whose hearing has grown weak with age, and those of Itard's pupils who were born with impaired hearing but who learned sign-language from their peers at the institute all share with us this crucial ability to anticipate what comes next in the message from what has gone before. Truly, we do much of our listening to speech with an inner ear. Only rarely does a listener require every cue he can hear, every last vowel and consonant, to make sense of what a speaker is saying. But deprive the listener of the guide that the structure of the sentence provides, introduce some words whose meaning is unknown, so he cannot deduce from his own experience what follows next, let the message be unrelated to what has been said a moment before and to what is happening before his eyes, then you have created a listener who hangs onto every syllable and whose comprehension will be throttled by feeble hearing or a burst of noise. Introduced at a noisy party to a Mr. Paul (or was it Ball?) we can glimpse from our momentary predicament the daily fare of the child born with hearing loss who has not yet acquired language either by sound or by sign.

> These children, as long as their education is not complete, have only a few ideas, which are disconnected and without orderly progression. The normal chaining of words, which leads us to guess what will follow from what has preceded, the natural linkage of ideas which establishes what is called the gist of the sentence, all that is null for them...

At some other age, the sense of hearing can be weakened without losing the ability to understand conversation; but then habit and intelligence make up for the impairment of hearing; half of a word, half of a sentence, clearly understood, lead the listener to guess the part of the word or the sentence which has left a blurred impression. In the very young child, on the contrary, what he has not understood undermines what he has, and the whole sentence is lost for him.

A recent experiment shows rather well how the normal chaining of words and the natural linkage of ideas lead us to anticipate —indeed to hear—what follows from what has gone before. A group of grammatical sentences are assembled: *A witness signed the official legal document. A jeweler appraised the glittering diamond earrings. A magazine exposed the shocking political corruption.* We can disrupt the normal chaining of words if we make the sentences into anagrams: *Document a witness signed legal official the.* Or we can decouple the natural linkage of ideas if we take successive words from successive sentences: *A witness appraised the shocking company dragon.* We can disable both guides to comprehension if we scramble these semantically anomalous sentences: *Company shocking dragon a witness the appraised.* Listeners have tremendous difficulty, when the altered sentences are read to them, in merely reproducing what they just heard. If a little background noise is added, the grammatical sentences still remain highly intelligible. The anagrams are very difficult to reproduce since the listener tends to hear the words restored to their correct grammatical order. Next, the "poetic" sentences prove a little more intelligible. Finally, the "word salad," stripped both of grammatical structure and of coherent meaning, goes in one ear and comes out the other—tossed a bit more. It is not only hard to remember arbitrary lists of words, proper names, or telephone numbers, it is hard to hear them correctly in the first place.

After a year of physiological training—what would now be called sensory education—Itard's six pupils could detect and distinguish the sounds of speech, and the educationally more advanced could understand sentences addressed to them directly and slowly. Would it be reasonable to expect that, now that they could hear speech better, they would spontaneously begin to speak, to utter some simple words and phrases, much like very young children will pick up and repeat what they hear around them, thus building up a repertory of spoken language? Itard performed the following experiment.

I took the precaution of first confirming the ease with which very young children repeated the vocal sounds that struck their ears. And I noticed above all that, although they normally looked at the person who was speaking to them, this arrangement was not strictly necessary for imitation; exactly the same result occurred if I pronounced the test words standing behind them. Having used these simple tests to demonstrate the ultimate in vocal imitation, I had only to see if my six mutes would achieve this level or to what degree they could approximate it. I placed myself behind them, taking care not to let them understand my purpose; I let them hear those simple voice sounds that they perceived most distinctly even at substantial distances. Not a single one of them repeated the sounds, or even tried to repeat them. I began again two or three times but always without effect. Convinced by this experiment that for these subjects imitation would come into play only if it was demanded, I let them know my goal and, resuming my station behind them, I began anew to utter the same sounds. If I had not more or less expected the result of this new attempt, I would have been astonished to obtain only some poorly articulated sounds that had no relation to those whose imitation I had requested. It was thus necessary for me to stand before their very eyes, and finally to let them see the mechanism of the sounds that I wanted them to repeat, which they then proceeded to do fairly exactly.

Thus we see clearly the superiority of the young child over the adolescent in vocal imitation; a superiority founded on two marked differences well established by my own experiments: first, the child imitates on his own initiative whereas with the adolescent imitation must be incited; second, the child needs only to hear in order to speak, whereas the adolescent must both listen and observe.

With these conclusions, Itard could explain why his adolescent pupils remained largely mute, although they could now understand speech.

Reasoning from the generally recognized fact that deaf-mutes do not speak solely because they have never heard speech, I might have expected from the restoration of hearing the spontaneous development of speech. I had no illusions, however, about the obstacles to this result provided both by the waning of the imitative faculty and by the sluggishness of organs that had long remained inactive during their development.

Itard had given these reasons, among others, for Victor's remaining speechless. It may indeed be true that a child's ability to imitate speech sounds wanes with age, but for Itard's pupils there were additional obstacles that he glosses over: they still had a hearing impairment and they still lived in a silent community, exposed to spoken language only an hour or so each day. Since his students had to be taught to speak, Itard proceeded to develop the second half of his program of oral education, speech training, which was described in his second memoir to the Society of Medicine. If this program had much more success with the children of the institute than did his first efforts with Victor, we must attribute it not only to the difference in the intelligence of the pupils but also to improvements in Itard's technique. With somewhat more phonetic sophistication, he developed a careful progression of sounds to be taught, from the highly contrastive to the very similar, from the easily articulated to the more difficult, from the simple to the complex. Moreover, he brought vision and touch into play; he cites Pereire's pioneering work, as well as that of his predecessors, Bonet, Wallis, and Amman.

Juan Pablo Bonet was a priest, and a secretary to the constable of Castile, three of whose forebears had been born deaf and taught to speak, nearly a century earlier, by Pedro de Ponce. In 1620, without ever mentioning the name of this Benedictine monk from whom he took the main features of his system, Bonet published the first manual for teachers of the deaf and dumb, "Simplification of the Letters of the Alphabet and Method of Teaching Deaf-Mutes to Speak." The first part of the book described the various sounds represented by each of the letters while the second gave teaching methods: the one-handed manual alphabet was to be taught in association with each of the letters. Then the student would learn to pronounce each letter, beginning with the vowels, by observing the teacher who enunciated and gave articulatory instructions with the aid of a leather tongue. Next, the student learned syllables and then words. His first words were the names of objects at hand; after he built up a basic vocabulary by associating words with objects, he studied in turn all of the various grammatical classes of words. Bonet was perhaps the first to record the importance of lipreading, which he claimed could not be taught but only acquired by the student through concentrated attention. The publication grew out of the priest's efforts to train the deaf–mute brother of the current constable, with what success we may judge from this description by Sir Kenelm Digby, who visited Spain with the Prince of Wales in 1623.

> There was a nobleman of great quality that I knew in Spain, the younger brother of the Constable of Castile . . . The Spanish lord was born deaf; so deaf that if a gun were shot off close by his ear he could not hear it, and consequently he was dumb; for not being able to hear the sound of words, he could never imitate nor understand them. The loveliness of his face, and especially the exceeding life and spiritfulness of his eyes, and the comeliness of his person, and whole composure of his body throughout, were pregnant signs of a well tempered mind within, and therefore all that knew him lamented much the want of means to cultivate it, and to imbue it with the motions which it seemed capable of, in regard of itself, had it not been so crossed by this unhappy accident. Which to remedy physicians and chyrurgions had long employed their skill, but all in vain. At last there was a priest who undertook the teaching him to understand others when they spoke, and to speak himself that others might understand him. What at first he was laughed at for made him after some years be looked on as if he had wrought a miracle. In a word, after strange patience, constancy, and pains, he brought the young lord to speak as distinctly as any man whoever; and to understand so perfectly what others said, that he would not lose a word in a whole day's conversation.

John Wallis, whom Itard cited next, was a professor of geometry at Oxford; he published an English grammar in 1653 to which he prefaced a method for teaching the formation of speech sounds—useful for foreigners and the deaf. Finally J. C. Amman, Itard's third source, was a Swiss physician resident at Haarlem; like Wallis, he used articulatory instructions to which he added touch and lipreading, according to his *Surdus Loquens*, published in 1692. The publications of Wallis and Amman, the best known of several seventeenth–century educators of the deaf including

Holder and Dalgarno in England and Van Helmont in Holland, led Defoe to write his "History of the Life and Adventures of Mr. Duncan Campbell, A Gentleman, Who, tho' Deaf and Dumb, Writes Down Any Stranger's Name at First Sight; with Their Future Contingencies of Fortune," an entertaining tale into which he wove much of Wallis' method.

Itard also mentions that Abbé de l'Epée relied on vision in early attempts to teach spoken language, as did Sicard to a limited extent. The crucial difference between the earlier educators of the deaf and these contemporaries of Itard is that the former taught only one or two exceptional pupils at a time, often children of wealthy families that could afford a master tutor in residence. In contrast, Epée and Sicard brought the deaf together in a community where numerous children of all classes received instruction. This accomplishment was intimately tied up with these educators' advocacy of manual communication; a strictly oral gathering of the deaf could not be a community at all, and oral instruction places such demands on the teacher that he could educate only a handful of pupils if speaking was one of the essential goals. Although Epée was above all the great propagator of sign and believed that sign was the sole effective medium for the intellectual development of the deaf, he tutored several pupils in spoken language as an adjunct to their skills; one of them was able to read a five-and-a-half page essay in Latin in a loud and clear voice and to engage in formal debate on the definition of philosophy, while another recited all twenty-eight chapters of the biblical book of Matthew. "To teach the mute how to dispose his organs to emit voice and to form distinct speech is neither a long nor a painful operation," Epée wrote.

Three or four lessons advance this business quite a lot, if they do not thoroughly accomplish it, following the method of M. Bonnet, printed about one hundred and fifty years ago. Then the children need only acquire the usage, and this does not concern me; it is the business of the persons who live with the pupil, or of an ordinary reading teacher . . . When it pleases me, I dictate my lessons *viva voce* without making any sign. I speak with my hands crossed behind my back. The persons near me do not understand what I say because in their presence

I purposely whisper, suppressing all sounds of my speech. However, my deaf pupils . . . understand what I say with their eyes, and write or repeat it at will. This is the more remarkable because the children come only on [Tuesdays and Fridays] at hours set apart for their lessons. Moreover, I seldom repeat this experiment because the language of methodic signs is the shortest and easiest to understand. If teachers were to devote time to making their students speak daily, the deaf-mute children would soon get into the habit of speaking and would be unable to converse only in darkness . . . Once in a while we dictate our lessons orally, without any sign. This operation takes a little longer, and this prevents me from making use of it ordinarily, for which I am ready to acknowledge that I may be wrong.*

Abbé Sicard was, above all, the man who gave the deaf access to written language but, like his predecessor, he had an ancillary interest in teaching them spoken language. "I am not without hope for deaf-mutes when it comes to the speech mechanism," he told his lecture course at the normal school. "I have not abandoned the worthy goal of teaching them to speak. I have some basis for my hopes, as you will agree after seeing what I have accomplished with one of my students, who is going to speak to you." The stenographic record of the lecture continues: "At this point the professor introduces a pupil who loudly and clearly pronounces the words corresponding to signs that are made to him . . . At this juncture, [the deaf–mute] Peyre reads loudly and intelligibly the written questions and answers of Massieu [and his pupil] Thouron." Sicard even claimed that Peyre was more accomplished than any of Pereire's pupils. Although Itard knew and used the techniques employed by his predecessors, notably lipreading, articulatory instructions, and touch, he preferred to minimize these hearing-surrogates with his pupils who had undergone physiological training of the ear. By using hearing as the medium of speech instruction he could concurrently reinforce his pupils' newly acquired auditory skills.

Itard's progression for teaching speech began with eight simple vowels, then proceeded to the nasal vowels (uttered through the nose as well as the mouth).* Next in turn came training in articulating the simple consonants. Not letting himself be misled by the writing system, Itard based his choices purely on articulation.

He excluded the "consonant x," for example, since it corresponds in fact to two articulations (k followed by s, as in *extra*), whereas he included *ch* since in French it corresponds only to one (the initial sound in *château*).* He then coupled sixteen of the consonants into eight pairs, including six pairs contrasting a hard and soft version of the same consonant, as Itard puts it; it is this contrast between voiceless and voiced (as in *pa/ba* and *sa/za*) that his pupils found difficult to hear and to reproduce. With sixteen simple consonants and eight vowels to teach, Itard exercised his pupils on the 148 consonant-vowel (CV) syllables that they comprise. Once they had practiced the CV syllables, Itard had them work on the VC syllables (*or, il* and so on), and then on CV syllables with a nasalized vowel (as in *ton* and *tin*). Next came CCV (*pré*), then CCV with a nasal vowel (*flan*), then CVC (*par*) and CCVC (*bloc*). Now it came time to tackle the semivowels, which are more constricted than vowels but less so than consonants (the initial sounds in *oui* and *hier*, like those beginning the English *we* and *yacht*, respectively).* In the remaining three series, Itard treated three special problems "as difficult for hearing as for speech": first, consonant clusters containing *s*, where there was no vowel to assist in detecting the fricative noise (*stade*); second, the sound "formed by the junction of g and n" as in *peigne*; and third, the sole glide that occurs in the middle of words and is usually written *ll* as in *mouiller*.

Itard invented or marshaled a half-dozen special techniques for helping his pupils make their way through this carefully constructed progression of exercises. He noticed, for example, that their voices were weak and muffled, which gave them difficulty not only in communicating with other people but also in comparing their own sounds with Itard's, in order to imitate their teacher accurately. Itard traced one source of the problem to his pupils' ignorance of how to breathe when speaking. Imagine supplying a fire with a steady stream of air from a bellows whose two handles are connected by a light spring. If a prolonged flow is the goal, the handles must be pulled far apart and the chest will swell with air. The spring draws the handles back to the starting point but to maintain the outward flow of air thereafter the handles must be increasingly pushed together, compressing the chest. As the air leaves the bellows, the opening must be kept fairly small or all the air will escape at once.

> If I asked [my pupils] to prolong and strengthen a sound, instead of inhaling deeply to have a sufficient provision of air, they began randomly at the end or the middle of an ordinary expiration. If I bared my chest and showed them that it swelled up in order to produce these kinds of [reinforced] sounds, they too immediately puffed up with air but, not knowing how to control it, they let it all escape in a rush, yielding nothing more than a brief sound rather like a noisy hiccup. Thus it was necessary, before going on, to exercise the lungs in the role they had to play [in speech breathing], and to teach the deaf-mute to control this organ, to take deep breaths quickly, to let out air slowly and sparingly, and to modify the flow of air in different ways to produce sounds that come out strong or weak, somewhat speeded up or in a headlong rush.

As the students learned better breath and voice control, and spoke more loudly and distinctly, they were better able to compare their own speech sounds with the model's. Even a normal hearing student, however, is at a disadvantage in making such comparisons. In part, his voice makes its way to his ear traveling through tissue and bone and losing some of the treble along the way. (This is the main reason why people are surprised to hear the sound of their voice when it is played back from a tape). In part, the speaker's voice gets to his ear by traveling from his lips around his head but then, Itard noticed, a good portion of the loudness of his voice dissipated; Georg von Békésy showed that it comes to about half. In order to suit nature more to his purpose of facilitating comparison and imitation, Itard invented a device which was reinvented after World War II and then named the "audio active language laboratory." The modern student learning a spoken language, say French, hears the sound he is to imitate amplified through his headphones. When the student imitates the sound, a microphone suspended in front of his lips picks up his voice and feeds it back to his headphones, amplified and largely masking his "inner voice." Thus he hears himself as others hear him and, more important, the model and his imitation are directly comparable, which should make it easier for him to get on target—to imitate exactly. (Sometimes the model and imitation are recorded and he can play them back.) In the days before electrical apparatus, Itard devised a double ear-trumpet that served the same purpose and also met his students' need for a hearing aid. The flared end of the trumpet surrounded the student's mouth and the narrow end entered his ear canal, giving him total amplified feedback of his own voice. From this trumpet branched a second, into whose mouth Itard could enunciate the models to be imitated. With the aid of this device, "all the sounds that could be heard were, from here on in, repeated, and when the first attempts of a voice that had so long been mute were not exactly right, I did not rush to call attention to it; almost always the student's ear noticed the error of his tongue and set about correcting it."

Prepared by auditory training, breathing exercises, and imitation training with the feedback device, the pupils made good progress through the sequence of pronunciation tasks that Itard had so carefully ordered. They learned to pronounce the oral vowels first; the three nasal vowels were not mastered until considerably later, once they had finally learned to distinguish them by ear. In teaching articulation of the consonants and consonant clusters, Itard found it useful to introduce a dummy vowel at first, then fading it out. Thus, *el* was pronounced in two syllables *el-le*, *clou* was pronounced *que-lou*, *bloc*, *be-lo-que*. However, there was a complication, which became especially clear when distinguishing and producing the semivowels. The student had no difficulty in finally dropping out the extraneous sound when speaking, but then he had difficulty in recognizing the original syllable when listening. The semivowels seemed easier to discriminate when preceded by a consonant. Both observations are probably explained by the tendency of speech sounds to leave cues to their identity in the immediately preceding and following sounds. The last two classes of syllables in Itard's progression proved especially difficult. Just as English has three nasal consonants, the sounds in *ram, ran, rang,* so does French: *pâme, panne, pagne.* The latter nasal consonant is produced with the middle of the tongue against the palate. Itard practiced his pupils in pronouncing *ni-a* which, speeded up, became *nya.* Americans learning French usually stop at this approximation, that is, *n* plus a semivowel *y*. But Itard reports that, by speeding his pupils' articulation even more, he finally elicited the single consonant sound he sought. As for the last category, the semivowel in, for example, *billard*, he never could make them produce the desired result.

There remained one more crucial class of sounds which Itard's pupils had never learned to distinguish clearly or, therefore, to produce properly; these were the voiced consonants as opposed to their voiceless counterparts: Ba/Pa, Da/Ta, Va/Fa, Za/Sa, Ja/Cha, Ga/Ca. For their mastery, Itard brought sight, touch, and articulatory instructions into play along with hearing. "The first of these was already involved in our exercises, not yet as a guide to articulation but as a stand–in for hearing to aid the deaf–mute in distinguishing by eye the sounds that he confused by ear." Thus according to Itard, the pupils already discriminated *Fa* and *Cha* from their voiced counterparts *Va* and *Ja* by the obvious differences in the lip movements that they entailed; he now asked them to imitate these movements. Moreover, he had the student place a hand in front of his mouth to detect the greater flow of air in *Fa*, *Cha*, and *Pa* than in *Va*, *Ja*, and *Ba*. *Da* is indistinguishable from *Ta* by both methods, however, so the teacher had recourse to a third device, well known to teachers of foreign languages: he had the student articulate some already familiar sound and then instructed him to introduce a crucial modification. In this case, the instruction was to produce *Ta* but with the underside of the tongue. At the very first try, the students produced the desired *Da* and with practice, as Itard had anticipated, they came to articulate it less awkwardly and more rapidly. Similarily, *Ka* and *Ga* were first elicited by rather elaborate articulatory instructions. Many an American schoolboy has likewise been led to master the French vowels in *tu* and *eux* by rounding his lips and saying *E* or *A*, respectively, or to pronounce the final consonant in the German *reich* by devoicing the *E* vowel. There is even some reason to think that articulatory instructions, which lead the adult student in small steps from a known posture to a new one, are a more effective way of teaching than training in auditory discrimination and imitation. College students in a recent experiment who learned foreign sounds by the former method, without a spoken model, were better in both pronouncing and discriminating these sounds than were their aural counterparts. Itard did not originate the technique of artificial articulation; it was employed by most seventeenth-century teachers of the deaf and by Pereire.

During the lessons in which Itard's pupils imitated the vowels and consonants of French and their combinations in various kinds of syllables, they also learned how to transcribe these syllables and how to read the transcriptions. Soon they were able to write and to read words and simple sentences "more or less intelligibly," but Itard found to his great disappointment that they would never speak of their own accord nor could they respond fluently to questions he was sure they understood.

> What was the nature of this new difficulty which arriving thus at the end of my labors threatened to steal all of its fruits? I noticed first that as soon as my question was put and understood, the deaf-mute began to move his fingers as if he wanted to respond in sign; that, furthermore, before articulating the first sound of his response, the movements of his fingers began anew three or four times; and that, finally, even after beginning his response, if he came upon a word that was a bit long and difficult to pronounce, I could see this awkward word worked over several times on his fingers before being articulated by his lips. It seemed evident to me that the deaf-mute was doing here what everyone does who has learned a foreign language from a teacher and tries to speak it for the first time. He thinks in his own language, constructs sentences with the words of that language, and translates them slowly into those of the foreign tongue.

Itard's pupils had an analogous problem in comprehension. Like students of a foreign language, they tended to follow a sentence sound by sound and word by word, postponing as it were its abstract interpretation. If the sentence proved long or complicated there was more than this low order of memory could retain, and "the deaf-mute ended up by asking me to start my question over again while allowing him to take it down in writing." By extensive exercises with carefully graded materials, Itard was able, nevertheless, to overcome these difficulties of encoding and decoding sentences, at least to a large extent. He believed he would have surmounted them entirely had he been able to separate his pupils from the signing community in which they lived, not just for an hour or two each day but entirely, so as to oblige them to use speech in expressing their needs and thoughts. Just one year after arriving at the institute, Itard wrote:

> [We must] allow no means of communication other than spoken language between the hard-of-hearing child and the people who take care of him; failing this, the first means of training [by speaking loudly and slowly to the child] becomes ineffective; and the child, discouraged by the effort of attention he is obliged to put into speaking or listening, ends up by creating an action language or manual signs, with which he expresses all his needs. Once this modality is discovered and tolerated, the ear loses its sensitivity, the larynx its mobility, and the child remains deaf-mute forever.

Among the pupils whom Itard presented to the Faculty of Medicine, the most accomplished speaker was in fact the most deaf, and the least able to sign. This boy had been given to a governess who worked on training his residual hearing and did not teach him sign. Itard recognized, however, that the deaf-mute who is deprived of sign must be taught language in some other mode—for example, the written mode of instruction worked out by Sicard. This education must precede training in spoken language, at least in part, or the pupil will know nothing of the redundancy of language which is the major guide in understanding a sentence. The Society of the Faculty of Medicine warmly acclaimed the performance of Itard's pupils at its meeting of May 12, 1808, and the two memoirs that explained his method of oral education. The faculty concluded "that those deaf-mutes who have retained a certain measure of hearing or who have recovered it by sustained treatment, can acquire speech; that in this case, speaking is a prompt and necessary consequence of the functioning of hearing; that once a deaf-mute has been taught to hear, he must be aided and taught to listen to himself; that the development of speech will be the more prompt and more complete the less the subject is able to use manual sign language."

Chapter Nine

The
Great
Sign
Controversy

*Itard advocates sign language—Evolution
of the signing society—Massieu versus
Clerc—Beginning of deaf education in
America—Gallaudet locked out in
England—Joins Sicard in Paris—Returns
to Hartford with Clerc—Origins of
American Sign Language—Advantages
of signs in educating the deaf—
Criticisms of sign language—Language in
the visual mode different—Economy of
sign language—Speech, sign, and
pantomime—Academy of Medicine
endorses use of signs—Itard's method
of teaching retardates language—His
bequest for higher education of the deaf, in
which he proscribes sign—His heirs
contest the will as impractical—Oralism
gains ground in France and America—
Advocates of sign resist, and are
overwhelmed.*

The momentous dispute begun by the Spanish Jew, Pereire, and the French priest, Abbé de l'Epée, on the relative merits of teaching the deaf spoken language or sign, has survived to this very day, two centuries later. Jean-Marc Itard, the physician who never learned a sign during forty years among the deaf at the institute founded by Epée; Itard, who had made no attempt to teach sign language to the mutely gesticulating wild boy from 1801 to 1805; Itard, who founded oral education of the deaf, training six pupils in hearing and speech from 1805 to 1808 without ever employing signs; Itard, who lamented that he could not perfect these pupils' speech because he lacked the authority to isolate them from their peers and thus oblige them to do without sign "like children whom we wish to teach a foreign language"; Itard surely seems at first look a four-star general in the oralist camp. But in the remaining score of years before his death, Itard came to believe profoundly that sign language was "the natural language of the deaf," whatever their degree of hearing loss. Moreover, he contended that oral education of the partially deaf must be preceded and accompanied by the use of signs. Itard first expounded these views at length in his "Treatise on Diseases of the Ear and Hearing," in 1821. He tried to put them into practice at the institute, in a program of mixed education in sign and speech, by writing a series of four reports to the administration from 1820 to 1826. Three of these reports* were transmitted to the Ministry of the Interior with a request for funds to institute special classes of combined sign and oral instruction. The ministry, in turn, asked the Academy of Medicine to evaluate Itard's methods of oral education. By the time the special commission published its opinion, the academy had managed to lose Itard's original reports.* I found them in 1974 in the cellars of the institute, amid letters from the king's government and that of Mendès-France. So now it is possible to reconstruct Itard's view, and to see why and how this student of Condillac proposed to combine two systems of communication evolved from action-language—speech and sign—in the education of the hearing-handicapped.

What does it mean to say, as Itard did, that sign, like speech, is a "natural language"? Today there are some who dispute that Ameslan—the American Sign Language used by some half-million deaf children and adults in the United States and Canada—is truly a natural language, like English, say, or Chinese. The issues they raise challenge us to be explicit about our criteria for what constitutes a language—no easy matter. But for Itard, in the first half of the nineteenth century, witnessing the expanding deaf community that used sign, the issue was not linguistic but psychological. In any case, Itard barely knew the language that was evolving under the influence of Epée and Sicard's strictures, to be sure, but also under the influence, greater still, of the deaf themselves. Instead he made his decision in favor of sign, as he did so many others, by asking the psychological question Condillac would have asked: Can gestural language serve as a medium of communication, and therefore as a vehicle for the intellectual development of the deaf child? Itard concluded that it could, and history proved him right. This was his argument:

If, instead of using the covert movements of his larynx and tongue to express his ideas and emotions, man had expressed them by overt movements of his limbs and physiognomy, then vision would have been the most informative sense and the vehicle for intellectual development. It is a mistake to think that the deaf-mute [in our speaking society] gives an accurate picture of what men would be like were mankind created without the sense of hearing. With the aid of the language of signs, this gestural society would not have advanced less rapidly toward civilization. Written language, which has so greatly aided this progress, would in all likelihood have been invented sooner: for it takes less effort to imagine representing signs than drawing sounds. With this accomplishment, man could have embarked just as rapidly on the vast career that this discovery opened to his intelligence; and, apart from lacking a few ideas concerning sounds, he would have become all that the twofold gift of hearing and speech has made possible. Thus he can do without this gift; far from owing his perfectibility to the perfection of his organs, he can, with senses that function only weakly or incompletely, establish relations with his peers, create signs expressing his thoughts, and convert these fleeting signs into permanent ones. Rising above the limitations of his organs, to realize his full potentialities by dint of his genius alone, man can prove, in accomplishing much with few resources, that he has issued from the intelligence that created everything from nothing.

The Wild Boy of Aveyron   208

Yet if sign language can provide the same intellectual advantages as spoken language, why is the deaf child clearly at such a disadvantage?

> How can we explain the incomplete intellectual development to which the deaf-mute is condemned by the privation of one of his senses? We can explain it by the resulting isolation which deprives the deaf-mute of the first and the most powerful means of perfecting the human species, the commerce of his equals. Destined by his constitution to understand the speech of the hands, he lives in solitude in the society of speaking and hearing men. If you want to know how much our equal he really can be, make everything equal, let him be born and live among his own kind, and you will presently have the hypothetical society that I just described.

In fact, Epée created the nucleus of such a society when he opened the school on the Rue des Moulins which soon became the National Institute for Deaf-Mutes.

> A large and seasoned institution of deaf-mutes, bringing together individuals of diverse ages and degrees of education, represents a genuine society with its own language, a language endowed with its own acquired ideas and traditions, and which is capable, like spoken language, of communicating directly or indirectly all its intended meanings. In fact, the deaf-mute raised in the midst of such a gesturing society sees not only the signs that are made to communicate with him but also those that are exchanged in conversations among the deaf that are within his view. [The impact of this indirect communication] explains how these children who have only been taught the names of objects, after several months in a large institution, can conduct sustained animated little conversations with their peers that require a knowledge of [how to sign] adjectives, verbs, and tenses.

By bringing formerly isolated deaf-mutes together into a signing community, the institute unwittingly created the conditions under which a new language of wider communication could develop and evolve, and with it the intellect of those who employed that language and the society they comprised.

> Comparing our current deaf-mutes with those first pupils trained in the same institute, by the same methods under the same director, we are

led to recognize their superiority which can only be due to their having come later, at a more advanced stage of the signing society. There they found two sources of instruction that could not exist in its earliest days: the [signed] lessons given by the teachers, and their conversations with pupils already educated. Thus it is that instruction is easier and more widely effective than it was twenty years ago. At that time, Massieu was a dazzling phenomenon in the midst of his unfortunate companions, who remained well behind him, still at the first stages of their education; nowadays, he is nothing more than a highly distinguished student. Instruction, powerfully assisted by tradition, has more rapidly developed and civilized his companions; one among them has equaled him, and several have come close and would have surpassed him had they not so promptly left the institute . . .

Let us contrast Massieu . . . with [Laurent] Clerc, this student whom I said was his equal in instruction but who, having come quite recently to the institute, ought to have profited by all the advantages that a more advanced civilization can offer. Massieu, a profound thinker, gifted with a genius for observation and a prodigious memory, favored by the particular attention of his celebrated teacher, benefiting from an extensive education, seems nevertheless to have developed incompletely: his ways, habits, and expressions have a certain strangeness that leaves a considerable gap between him and society. Uninterested in all that motivates that society, inept at conducting its affairs, he lives alone, without desires and ambition. When he writes, we can judge even better what is lacking in his mentality: his style fits him to a tee, it is choppy, unconventional, disorderly, without transition but swarming with apt thought and flashes of brilliance.

A glimpse of the contrast between Massieu and Clerc that Itard is pursuing may be had from this eyewitness report of one of Sicard's public demonstrations. It was much the fashion of the times to judge a person's intelligence by his *bons mots,* as it is ours to judge it by his I.Q. Most French intellectuals knew Massieu's definition of gratitude: *la mémoire du coeur.* On this particular Saturday, the visitor waited patiently with the Tout-Paris through Sicard's disquisition on grammar and then asked Massieu and Clerc: "What is the distinction between desire and hope?" Massieu: "Desire is a tree in leaf, hope is a tree in bloom, enjoyment is a tree with fruit." Clerc: "Desire is a tendency of the heart, hope is a trust of the mind."

"Clerc," Itard continues, "with a less encompassing and towering intelligence, trained as much by the institute as by any teacher, presents a picture of much more uniform development":

> Clerc is entirely a man of the world. He likes social life, and often seeks it out, and he is singled out for his polite manners and his perfect understanding of social custom and interests. He likes to be well groomed, appreciates luxury and all our contrived needs, and is not insensitive to the goads of ambition. It is ambition that snatched him from the Paris institute, where he had a worthy and comfortable existence [as a teacher], and led him across the seas to seek his fortune.*

Although Itard does not seem entirely to approve of this zeal, humanity profited by it, for Clerc brought his native sign language to America, where it spread and evolved into today's American Sign Language.

The circumstances were these. In the same year that Itard gave up on Victor's instruction and began the oral education of his six deaf-mute pupils, Thomas Hopkins Gallaudet, an American of French Huguenot descent, was graduated from Yale College at the age of eighteen. In the following decade, history seemed to repeat itself by having Gallaudet reenact on this side of the Atlantic some of the major scenes in the Abbé de l'Epée's early career with the deaf. Gallaudet takes up studies for the ministry; he encounters a neighbor's young deaf-mute daughter and is moved to try teaching her to read and write a few words; his initial efforts meet with some success, and her father and friends press him to exchange one calling for another. The girl's name was Alice Cogswell. Two years after her birth, in 1805, she contracted "spotted fever" and by age four no longer spoke. Her father, a prominent doctor in Hartford, Connecticut, was vaguely aware of efforts to educate the deaf in Europe. Encouraged by the progress his daughter had made with occasional instruction from Gallaudet, he considered sending her overseas to Edinburgh or London but decided instead to establish a school for the deaf in America after he learned from the state's clergyman's association that nearly a hundred children in his state and, therefore, perhaps two thousand in the country suffered the same plight as his daughter. Cogswell organized a committee of several philanthropists who raised funds to send Gallaudet to

Europe, in 1815, to learn methods for instructing the deaf. They also secured an act of incorporation from the legislature establishing "the Connecticut Asylum for the education of deaf and dumb persons."

In Europe, Gallaudet tried first to get into the original Braidwood School, then relocated near London, and also into the London Asylum for the Deaf and Dumb. Both schools could be traced back to Thomas Braidwood who had begun the oral instruction of the deaf in Edinburgh five years after Epée had opened his school in Paris. When Samuel Johnson visited the Braidwood School in 1772, he wrote in his *Journey to the Western Islands:*

> There is one subject of philosophical curiosity to be found in Edinburgh, which no other city has to shew: a college of the deaf and dumb, who are taught to speak, to read, to write, and to practice arithmetick, by a gentleman, whose name is Braidwood. The number which attends him is, I think, about twelve, which he brings together into a little school, and instructs according to their several degrees of proficiency.
>
> I do not mean to mention the instruction of the deaf as new. Having been first practiced upon the son of a constable of Spain, it was afterwards cultivated with much emulation in England, by Wallis and Holder, and was lately professed by Mr. Baker, who once flattered me with hopes of seeing his method published. How far any former teachers have succeeded, it is not easy to know; the improvement of Mr. Braidwood's pupils is wonderful. They not only speak, write, and understand what is written, but if he that speaks looks towards them, and modifies his organs by distinct and full utterance, they know so well what is spoken, that it is an expression scarcely figurative to say, they hear with the eye.

The Braidwood family maintained a monopoly on deaf-mute instruction in Great Britain and had wanted one in America ever since 1783 when a Massachusetts parent who had sent his deaf son to Braidwood's in Edinburgh published a volume entitled "Vox Oculis Subjecta"; this was Braidwood's device, "the voice suborned to the eyes," and the volume extolled Braidwood's methods. The author, Francis Green, also wrote numerous articles in New England newspapers calling for deaf education in the United States and even published a translation of Epée's "Instruction of Deaf-Mutes"—but all to no material effect. Just a few years after Green's death, Thomas Braidwood's grandson undertook a similar mission in America. John Braidwood fled to the States in 1812, Alexander

Graham Bell recounts, to escape financial and other difficulties while head of the institution in Edinburgh. (The Braidwood School had reopened there.) On arriving in America, he advertised that he would open a school in Baltimore but he took the $600 advanced him by a southern colonel, whose deaf brother and sister had been trained at Edinburgh, and launched a drinking spree that landed him in jail. The colonel bailed him out, and in repayment Braidwood moved into his sponsor's Virginia home to tutor his two deaf children. All went well, except when the colonel was off to war with England, and in 1815 Braidwood opened an institute in one of the family's mansions. Within a year, however, he relapsed into his former ways and, under the renewed threat of debtors' prison, slipped off into the night. Some time later he turned up in New York and attempted to start a school, but his binges soon put an end to that. He disappeared again only to surface in Richmond where he successfully threw himself on the mercy of the good colonel. A new Braidwood institution was opened in connection with a nearby classical school, but the alliance lasted only a year. Braidwood then took a job as a bartender, and he died two years later of alcoholism.

Gallaudet traveled to the newly reopened Braidwood School in Scotland, where John Braidwood's successor refused to discuss their methods. He then applied to John's brother, Thomas, to release the principal from his seven-year, thousand-pound bond not to reveal the Braidwood art of instruction; he was refused. He applied to the London Asylum whose director was a nephew of the first Thomas Braidwood. Here his avowed plan to combine the best of the oral and manual methods met with an equally cold reception. Sign was anathema. He was not allowed to inspect the teaching but he was invited to accept a three-year contract as a teacher, or to co-found his school in America with an asylum teacher or, indeed, with John Braidwood. "On this last," Gallaudet wrote to Dr. Cogswell from Europe, "I need make no comment."

In one of those ironies of history, Dr. Cogswell had, in fact, written to John Braidwood in Virginia three years earlier, inviting him to visit Hartford and to consider starting a school there. Fortunately for the American deaf, his letter received no reply. Since Gallaudet was profoundly disappointed by his poor reception in Great Britain, he turned to his last remaining resource, France. While training Alice Cogswell he had procured a copy of Sicard's account of how he trained Massieu, the *Cours d'instruction*. Originally Gallaudet thought, "Could I get all the necessary instruction in Scotland or England, and have a complete set of the Abbé Sicard's works, I should think it of less importance to visit Paris. But time alone can determine this." Now he reread *Cours d'instruction* and arranged forthwith to attend one of the abbé's lectures: Sicard was now in London.

Sicard had fled Paris, taking Massieu and Clerc with him. Even if he had not been a royalist all along, his days of peril in the abbey of Saint-Germain would surely have strengthened his allegiance to the monarchy, and during the Empire he secretly corresponded with the Bourbons in exile. When Napoleon was banished to Elba and the monarchy restored in the person of Louis XVIII, Sicard was safe. Indeed, the king awarded him the Legion of Honor. But when Napoleon sailed for France, just a little before Gallaudet, Sicard decided it was time to spread abroad the French method of educating the deaf. He exhibited Massieu and Clerc before the Duchess of Wellington, the Duke of Orleans, and the members of both Houses of Parliament as well as the public. The format included a lecture by Sicard followed by requests from the floor for definitions designed to probe the scope and abstractness of the pupils' knowledge. They responded with *bons mots* to such questions as: What is the difference between mind and matter; mind and intellect; reason and judgment; envy and jealousy; idea, thought, and imagination; authority and power?

The good abbé offered to instruct Gallaudet without pay. With Napoleon's defeat at Waterloo, Sicard felt it safe to return to Paris, and the American joined him there, to spend several months observing his methods and learning sign from Massieu and Clerc, both instructors at the royal institute. Gallaudet wrote to Alice Cogswell from Paris:

My Dear Alice,
    When I was in Edinburgh I wrote some letters to you. And I sent you a letter from Helen Hall. I hope you have got her letter. You must remember to answer it.

You have said in the letter which you have written to me, that you want me to come back in one year. I want very much to go back to Hartford, and to begin to instruct you and the other deaf and dumb children. But I shall stay here some time. I do not know how long. I must learn all that Abbé Sicard can teach me. Then I shall be able to teach you in the best way.

I have seen the Abbé Sicard and Massieu and Clerc, two of his scholars. In the little book which I send you, you will see their pictures. When you write again, tell me what you think of them.

Do you think you can learn the French alphabet on the fingers? Try. Perhaps it will be the one that I shall use.

The school for the Deaf and Dumb here is a very large building of stone. In front of it is a large yard, and behind it a fine garden. There are nearly ninety scholars, boys and girls. I have seen the lowest class several times. There are fifteen boys in it. The master is a Romish clergyman. He is more than fifty years old.

In the room are a number of large blackboards, on which the scholars write with chalk. I wrote on these boards and talked with the boys. They understood me very well. One told me he was from the same country as I. But he was mistaken. He was from Guadeloupe, an island in the West Indies. Another said he was from the United States, from Georgia. They are taught about God and Jesus Christ, and some of them can read the Bible very well.

Do you learn now any verses in the Bible and any hymns or psalms? And do you often think about God? Do you pray to him to make you good, and to make you ready to go to Heaven when you die? Do not forget to do this every morning and evening.

I hope God will preserve my life. Then I shall be so glad to see you and to have a deaf and dumb school in Hartford.

You must write me long letters. I put your last letter into French and showed it to Clerc. He loved to read it. Do not be afraid to write. You write very well and you will improve by writing.

Give my love to your Mama and Papa and all the family. I shall remember what you wished me in your last letter to give the deaf and dumb scholars—your love.

From your true friend,
T. H. Gallaudet

P.S. All the streets in Paris are paved with round stone. It is not easy to walk fast. And when it rains the streets are very muddy. And there are no sidewalks. Everybody must take great care that the chaises and coaches do not run over them. I had rather live in Hartford than Paris.— You would be sorry to see the Sabbath kept so badly in Paris. Most of the shops are open, and people buy and sell goods. And the theatres are all open, and but few people go to church, particularly in the afternoon. How much we ought to be sorry for such a people, and to thank God that it is not so in Connecticut.

Alice's education continued in Gallaudet's absence. Her teacher, Lydia Howard Sigourney, a New England writer, later recounted that neither sign language nor fingerspelling were known in New England and "the few signs we were able to invent founded principally on visible resemblance . . . were our only means of communication." Mrs. Sigourney enlarged their repertory of signs by consulting Alice's schoolmates, and then taught her pupil to read and write each of the signs. One of Alice's earliest literary efforts was written soon after receiving Gallaudet's letter, on the return of peace in the winter of 1815:

The world—all peace—now I am glad—many candles in windows—shine bright on snow—Houses most beautiful—Mr. G—gone to Paris—Come back with Mr. Clerc—teach deaf and dumb new words—new signs—oh, beautiful—I very afraid wind blow hard on Ocean—turn over ship—Alice very afraid for Mr. G—will pray God to keep, not drown—Wind blow right way Alice trust.

Clerc asked Gallaudet if he might return to America with him; the young Frenchman, seven years a pupil and eight years a teacher at the institute, dared to give up his friends, family, beloved teacher, language, familiar haunts, and the pleasures of Paris to go live across the sea. What he would receive in return was spelled out in a French contract:

Article 1. Mr. Clerc engages to take up his residence during the space of three years, to date from the day of his arrival at Hartford, in the Institution for Deaf-Mutes which Mr. Gallaudet proposes to establish in the United States of America.

Article 2. Under the direction of the head of the Institution, Mr. Clerc shall be employed in the instruction of deaf-mutes for six hours of each day except Saturday, on which day the time shall be but for three hours. He shall be entirely at liberty on Sundays and on holidays, and he shall have, moreover, six weeks of vacation annually. All these exceptions shall be made without any deduction in the pecuniary compensation below specified.

Article 3. He shall be present and assist at all the public lectures, as well at Hartford as in other cities of the United States, always being under the direction of the head of the Institution . . .

Article 6. Mr. Gallaudet pledges himself to defray all Mr. Clerc's traveling expenses from Paris to Hartford, viz., for food, lodging, washing, and transportation for himself and his effects, by land and water; and this to the same extent and in the same manner, as Mr. Gallaudet's own expenses . . .

Article 8. In consideration of the engagements above stipulated, Mr. Gallaudet promises and binds himself to pay to Mr. Clerc at Hartford, as his annual salary, two thousand five hundred francs (argent de France) in quarterly installments; the first quarter to date from the day of his arrival in Hartford.

Article 11. Mr. Clerc shall endeavor to give his pupils a knowledge of grammar, language, arithmetic, the globe, geography, history; of the Old Testament as contained in the Bible, and the New Testament, including the life of Jesus Christ, the Acts of the Apostles, the Epistles of St. Paul, St. John, St. Peter, and St. Jude. He is not to be called upon to teach anything contrary to the Roman Catholic religion which he professes, and in which faith he desires to live and die. Mr. Gallaudet, as head of the Institution, will take charge of all matters of religious teaching which may not be in accordance with this faith . . .

Thus contracted, finished, and signed at Paris, the thirteenth day of June, one thousand eight hundred and sixteen.

[Signed and sealed]   Thomas H. Gallaudet,
                                             Laurent Clerc,
                                             S.V.S. Wilder,
                                             J. C. Hottinguer.

During the voyage to America, which lasted fifty-two days, Gallaudet taught Clerc his third language and Clerc taught the American to communicate in sign. During the fall and winter of that year the pair visited many cities and state legislatures in the eastern United States to demonstrate that education of the deaf was feasible and to secure public support for their project. The collection of funds went quickly. The state of Connecticut gave $5,000—the first legislative act of this kind in America. With $17,000 in all, the first permanent school for the deaf in America opened a year later, April 15, 1817, with seven pupils, including Alice Cogswell. Within a year there were thirty-three students and in 1819 Congress granted 23,000 acres, which were sold for operating funds, to the renamed American Asylum at Hartford for the Education and Instruction of the Deaf and Dumb. Clerc remained as an instructor at the Hartford school for more than forty years while its enrollment grew to over two hundred. In addition, every teacher at the asylum learned sign under Clerc's tutelage; each paid him fifty dollars for this instruction. During Clerc's tenure a score of new schools for the deaf were created in the United States, and those who were to take charge of them went to Hartford to observe the methods practiced at the asylum and to learn sign language from Clerc. From this modest beginning have come over 200 schools for the deaf in the United States with more than 20,000 pupils enrolled.

Thus it seems possible to trace the origins of American Sign Language. It probably began with the signs brought to Epée by his handful of pupils beginning in the 1760s.* Since deaf children tended to be isolated at this period, it seems likely that the signs were relatively few in number and admixed with expressive gestures or iconic pantomime. Nevertheless, the pupils with deaf parents or deaf brothers and sisters may have contributed relatively codified systems of signs to the emerging community. For example, Massieu said about his childhood:

> Until the age of thirteen years, nine months, I remained in my native region where I had not received any instruction; I was in the dark about reading and writing. I expressed my ideas by natural signs or gestures. The signs that I then employed to express my ideas to my parents and to my brothers and sisters were quite different from those of educated deaf-mutes. Outsiders never understood us when we expressed our ideas to them in sign, but the neighbors understood us.

De Gérando remarks that the signs that usually differed among the pupils denoted various material objects, whereas those that expressed feelings, needs, ordinary activities, and objects of immediate use were often similar or identical.

The abbé and his pupils added many new signs to their common repertory, including a rather particular subset corresponding to word endings in spoken language. With the development of the institute and a signing community in Paris, the language evolved, enriched by various additions brought by children coming in from throughout France. The creation of a similar institute at Bordeaux with its own signing community, provided another source of accretion.

By the time Laurent Clerc had entered the Paris institute at the age of twelve, nearly thirty years after Epée opened the doors of his school, it seems likely that there were two reasonably distinct sign languages in general use: on the one hand, the language the deaf used among themselves—let us call it Franslan; on the other hand, that espoused by Epée and Sicard and taught at the institute —let us call it Signed French. The latter language, or more exactly pidgin, was a translation of French into Franslan which preserved French word order, represented French grammatical words and endings with Epée's methodical signs, and conveyed French words with signs in Franslan.

Clerc was fluent in Franslan and in Signed French. Born of hearing parents near Lyon, it seems he was deafened in an accident at the age of one. He studied first under Massieu but soon became a favorite pupil of Sicard and then a member of his teaching staff. Clerc brought with him to America not only his command of sign language but also Epée's unpublished "Dictionary of Signs," which Sicard was still compiling, as well as the latter's "Theory of Signs." Originally, Epée spurred the evolution of sign language by bringing together isolated deaf children and by serving as a repository and teacher of the signs that took on conventional meaning in their little community. "In all my lessons I am a living dictionary," he wrote, "which explains everything necessary for the understanding of the words that occur in the subject treated of . . . That this kind of dictionary does suffice is abundantly proved by the operations of my students, since upon signs which express neither letters nor words but only ideas, they write whatever I please to dictate."

Half a century later, Clerc played a similar role, and the language underwent a second stage of evolution with accretions from the American deaf. This is confirmed by Gallaudet's early annual reports on the asylum:

The instructors, by a constant familiar intercourse with the deaf and dumb, and still more by means of the daily lectures on the language of signs which have been given by their ingenious and experienced associate, Mr. Clerc, have made such attainments in the acquisition of the principles of this science that they hope very soon to become masters of their profession, and thus to secure its advantages beyond the danger of loss.*

Initially Clerc and Gallaudet espoused a pidgin of Franslan and English—Signed English. But it soon became evident that this was unwieldy. "Instead of presenting the idea vividly in brief natural signs, and then turning at once to written language, the idea was first given in free, natural signs, next in word sign in the order of the words, and lastly, by signs in the order of the words, with each word accompanied by other signs indicating the part of speech and giving its grammatical construction. After all this preparation came the written language for the idea." At about the same time, R. A. Bébian, director of the Paris institute, had reached the same conclusion. Signed English and Signed French—with "signs in the order of the words and each word accompanied by other signs indicating its part of speech and giving its grammatical construction"—were falling out of favor, to be supplanted by the "free natural signs" of Ameslan and Franslan, respectively. By midcentury, the director of the New York Institution for the Deaf could report on a visit from Paris that "the laboriously developed system of methodical signs (so far as those signs represent words and not ideas, or were arbitrarily devised to dictate grammatical particles and terminations), and the pompous and imposing metaphysical processes of Sicard [have gradually gone into] total disuse and oblivion."

Clerc also brought a manual alphabet to America, used for spelling words in written language, whose origins can be traced to two centuries before Epée. In 1593 a Franciscan monk, Melchor Yebra, published a book entitled "A Refuge for the Infirm," which contained prayers for sick people to recite. Each prayer was accompanied by a sketch of a hand configuration corresponding to a letter of a manual alphabet, which the author attributes to Saint Bonaventura; the patient could indicate by gesture what he lacked the strength to recite. Pereire adopted this manual alphabet, which he found in Bonet's book, and it was communicated to Epée when Pereire's accomplished pupil Saboureux de Fontenai attended

Epée's public demonstrations and pressed Bonet's book on him. Sicard got the alphabet from Epée, of course, and Clerc learned it from Sicard, taught it in Paris, and then in America. He remained as an instructor at the asylum until retirement at the age of seventy-three and was a moving force in deaf education until his death eleven years later in 1869.

If we object that the contrast between Clerc and Massieu may be more a matter of different personalities than of different degrees of development of the signing society, Itard has other evidence that, as the institute matured, its society and language evolved and its instruction became generally more effective. Comparing his medical files from his first years as resident physician at the institute with those from a period two decades later, he finds that the earlier pupils were unable to respond properly to written questions such as "Are you completely deaf? Can you hear a little? Were you born deaf?" Similarly, their handwritten explanations of the illnesses for which they came to see Itard were often unintelligible or, worse, misleading. But by the time Itard wrote his *Traité*, the level of general education was much higher; the knowledge of French, acquired through the mediation of Signed French following Sicard's methods, was much greater; and these problems of communication had practically disappeared.

From all this evidence that sign language was an effective vehicle for the intellectual development of the child, Itard concluded that he had been wrong in opposing it and that indeed it would be foolish to attempt the education of the deaf without its aid. Of the five categories of hearing loss that Itard distinguished, ranging from failure to follow conversation to profound deafness, only pupils in the first category could be educated by purely oral means, he believed. Those in the second category could conceivably manage without sign in those rare cases where a wealthy family could afford a gifted private tutor. But of the largest number of the partially deaf, who could not distinguish among the consonants and thus belonged to the third category, Itard writes in his unpublished report:

I can affirm even more positively, after numerous attempts, that it is absolutely impossible to educate them exclusively by means of speech.

These children can, in truth, grasp a few very simple sentences guiding themselves by the theme and the movements [of the speaker's] lips and eyes, but if these props are lacking, if the sentence is complicated by pronouns, tenses, abstract adjectives, then it becomes unintelligible for them . . . It is not with a means of communication as imperfect as partial hearing that the student can learn the names of objects, the use of verb tenses, and above all the meaning of pronouns. A child who is not born with complete—not to say perfect—hearing cannot grasp this important part of discourse. How can he learn that something belonging to him, a hat for example, is called, depending on whether he is speaking, is spoken to, or is spoken about, *my hat, your hat, his hat* [*mon, ton, son chapeau*]? Same difficulties, equally insurmountable, to grasp the sense of nouns and adverbs that express intellectual or abstract qualities. Certainly to recognize the sense of [spoken] words like *think, suffer, lie, hate, mind* [*esprit*], *wisdom, gratitude, space, time,* the intellect must be served by ears that are suited for speech perception in allowing distinct hearing not only of what people say to the listener, but also of what they say to each other. I am therefore justified in concluding that, even though they are only partially deaf, children suffering from the second and third degrees of hearing loss must be grouped with those in the fourth and fifth categories in this respect: they cannot receive any instruction except through the medium of signs.

Itard did not mean to exclude the possibility that such children could profit by oral training; he had devoted many years to perfecting methods of teaching them to discriminate and produce speech. But he believed that sign language was the means by which these children could communicate with society, acquire ideas, and develop and exchange those ideas. This kind of knowledge is necessary if children with a partial hearing loss are to understand spoken language despite their handicap. It is crucial for understanding a sentence to be able to anticipate the linkage of ideas, to be able to profit by its redundancy. The Academy of Medicine's evaluation of Itard's three reports states:

It is not rare to encounter people partially deafened by some accident who, once they have grasped the topic of some conversation, end up by following the issue completely, treating it themselves, and participating easily in the discussion. They hear little, see much, and infer the rest. We can readily imagine that they are able, by and large, to infer infinitely more than the congenitally deaf person since, before the accident that deprived them of hearing, they enjoyed the unimpaired and complete use of this sense and as a result they are, thanks to this prior experience, better versed than he in what we should call expectancy [*devinement*].

Itard drew the same lesson from the contrast between traumatically and congenitally deaf students. In the footnotes to a book on medicine and the law, he wrote:

> In experiments with [the traumatically deaf] that are easy to imagine, I decided to separate out the roles of the ears, the eyes, and finally the intelligence in their hearing [of speech]. I found proof that the latter, or to put it better the comprehension of the gist [*l'entente*] of the sentence, carried almost the entire burden, whereas the congenitally deaf were limited almost exclusively to the guidance provided by their eyes and ears. It was precisely this experiment that gave me the idea, when teaching the partially deaf, to make speech hinge on education and not education hinge on speech, as I had first planned; for I had been shown that, when hearing is impaired, it is no great accomplishment to train the ear to hear the sounds of speech or the eyes to judge its visible mechanism; there remains above all the task of cultivating the mind, of enriching it with the substance of conversation, familiarizing it with the combinations of ideas, with the signs that represent them, and finally with the grammatical sequences of these signs and with their reciprocal agreement.

After making this discovery, Itard gave oral instruction only to students who had acquired a general education through the medium of sign. A teacher at the institute in those days described Itard's method:

> Never giving his lessons to more than one student at a time, and always to a student who already had a basic education in the classes of the institution, he explained the language to him with the aid of the language itself, questioned him on his readings, gave him practice in analyzing and summarizing particular texts, in translating poetry into prose, in expressing the same thoughts in various forms, employing synonymy, contrast, and periphrasis to familiarize him with the forms and the spirit of our language. The effectiveness of this method was proven several times over by successful results.

In his first experiment in oral education, which culminated in 1808, Itard had believed that the use of signs was an impediment to perfecting his students' speech. He realized even then that it was an enormous task to educate them without the aid of signs and that they could not master spoken language without this general education. Nevertheless, were it not impracticable, he would have isolated them from the signing community. In the ensuing decades, Itard became convinced that sign language was the proper vehicle for the general education of the deaf; that it facilitated teaching spoken language to the partially deaf not only because it brought about their general intellectual development but also because it gave them habits of communication and spontaneous speech and established contact between the teacher and the student. Thus he concluded in his unpublished report in 1826:

> What we have said earlier about the advantages that our speaking students would gain from the knowledge and use of sign language in initially developing their ideas and in forming many relationships with children of their own age disposes of the question that came up at the last meeting of the administration concerning the merits and disadvantages of isolating these pupils from the rest of the deaf–mutes. All the advantages I have cited and others would be lost while nothing would be gained, for we cannot delude ourselves that, left on their own with speech as the sole means of communication, they would be able to employ it for their mutual relations ... Rather, they would create their own sign language ... [Thus] it is not necessary to isolate them, since sign language is as profitable for them as it is indispensable.

In teaching deaf-mutes to speak, Pereire also used the manual alphabet, sign language, and pantomime as adjuncts to oral instruction. Sicard undertook speech training but with only a few students, one of whom, he claims, was better than any Pereire could ever produce. Again, the medium of instruction was largely sign language, and when this student "was looking at a text or was addressed in sign, he spoke somewhat more fluently."

Even with the aid of signs, oral instruction is an arduous task for teacher and student. Epée made light of it, but Sicard was more realistic. Asked by a member of the audience at the normal school why the intelligent Massieu did not speak, Sicard answered, "It is possible that Massieu would learn to speak, if I had the time to teach him; but that demands long and painful efforts whose success is limited in such cases and it is appropriate only for a few mutes who would in any event use speech rarely; thus I thought it better to develop intelligence by means of sign rather than by voice." Itard also believed that sign language was the proper means for the deaf-mute's intellectual growth, and he uses the same words as Sicard to describe oral education, "longue et pénible," in his 1825 report. Speaking of the children to whom he has given physiological training of the ear and voice, he writes:

> Since [they] only recover their hearing quite incompletely, it follows that the consonants are only incompletely heard, and spoken signs . . . create difficulties, blockages, and misunderstandings from which sign language is exempt. [It is], I repeat, the natural language of deaf–mutes, and has the great advantage of putting them in communication with each other . . . Education that employs hearing and speech as the means of instruction is slower and less complete.

Although reading is an important means of education which can stand in for hearing and complement sign, this skill must also be taught to the deaf through sign language: "This powerful auxiliary can be put within his reach either by oral and written instruction, which is very rare and very difficult, or by the method of signs, which is the natural language of the congenitally deaf, whatever his degree of deafness."

Thus Itard believed that sign language was a natural language because it would serve for intellectual development, and he believed that it was the natural language of the deaf because it would serve their intellectual development better than any other language. Itard, was, in fact, correct in this belief, according to two reports recently published in the *American Annals of the Deaf*. Both studies compared two groups of congenitally deaf children: One group was born of deaf parents, and thus had learned American Sign Language at an early age; the other group was born of hearing parents and had not learned to sign. All of the children, whose ages ranged from twelve to twenty, were enrolled in a school for the deaf that, like many such schools in America, employs oral instruction exclusively and prohibits overt manual communication until the highest grades. "Identical twins" were created by matching each child who knew sign with one who did not; both were of the same sex and nearly the same age and I.Q. Itard would have predicted that the children who knew sign would get higher scores in reading achievement and in written expression than their counterparts, and so they did, with the advantage increasing with age. Moreover, the teachers and counselors in the residence halls gave the children who used signs higher ratings in psychological adjustment. The children who had not learned to sign did no better than their signing twins in understanding speech or in speaking intelligibly. This was true even when they had received three years of intensive oral training in preschool before attending the oral public school. Finally, although these children of hearing parents came from homes where the linguistic and educational level was generally higher, their academic achievement was lower than their signing counterparts: fewer of them completed school and, of those who did and took the college entrance exams, fewer passed them.* Itard conducted a similar study in 1827. The Academy of Medicine Commission describes the results:

> Two deaf–mutes who had recovered the faculties of hearing and speech by this process [physiological training] gave us a basis for comparison which proved the importance of combined [oral and sign] education. One was raised in a hearing family and the other among the deaf–mutes. The former did not benefit in any way from all the advantages that can be attributed to his environment. One might have thought that the nurture provided by this family, its interest in and influence over this adopted child, so to say, would have yielded a better result than the education by signs in the institution for deaf–mutes. The contrary happened: his spoken conversation seemed to us more limited, more narrow than that of the other child.

The moral seems clear enough, but there is no longer any need to take Itard's word for it—or that of Gallaudet, Sicard, or Epée. Quite a few later comparative studies lead to the same conclusion.

Much as Itard was convinced that sign language was the only feasible mode of communication among the deaf, and the proper vehicle for their intellectual development and their learning to read and write, he was equally convinced that they should learn, whenever possible, to understand and produce spoken language. His first reason was that children who have residual hearing and can profit from physiological training can then be returned to speaking society and the full spectrum of communication. His second reason, rather more disputable, was that sign language is by nature clumsy and imprecise, and that the deaf-mute who supersedes it with spoken language can make his ideas more precise and express them more fluently. This argument first appears in Itard's handwritten proposal, addressed to the administration of the institute, for creating a class of mixed instruction for the partially deaf where oral language would supplement sign:

We must put manual signs and oral signs into use concurrently and in this combination make the language of the deaf–mutes play the larger role, for however slight the hearing loss, the ear has only to shut out a few sounds of the human voice for the words to be perceived truncated and distorted and for the simplest sentence to be unintelligible. Sign language, on the contrary, is distinctly perceived, and leaves no part of the ideas it represents in a haze, and this language is the natural language of the deaf–mute. We will allow him therefore to speak and to use it in communication with his teachers and fellow students, demanding at first from the vocal organs only that they translate the things represented in sign, and from the sense of hearing only that it grasp the name spoken and guide its vocal repetition. During eighteen months this kind of translation will yield only an arid catalogue of objects and their qualities such as is taught to deaf–mutes. But once they have likewise learned the verbs and their tenses, the student will come to formulate a few sentences and to describe actions, and from this moment he will begin to differ from other deaf–mutes in expressing his ideas more precisely.

This is the result, gentlemen, of a cause which is not beneath your interest in the education of the deaf and mute. The greatest drawback attached to their language [here Itard refers to Signed French] is the large number of signs required to construct a completely grammatical sentence. The tense of verbs, for example, is simply conveyed by the voice in adding, retracting, or slightly modifying a few sounds, by this means expressing an action in the present, past, future, conditional, or infinitive. These verb tenses make the maneuver of signs designed to express modifications of verbs highly complicated. The same disadvantage of manual language arises in the expression of abstract ideas which can only be conveyed by an overload of signs tacked on to that of the physical idea, whereas in spoken language there is hardly any difference between the words that serve to express the two sorts of ideas, as can be seen from such words as *good* and *goodness, pious* and *piety.* The same problem appears in the signs for collective ideas such as *army, troop, realm, province,* which oblige the speaker to represent the thing and then the collection of things gathered together. (To be convinced of the deplorable complication of sign language one need only take a few words at random from M. l'abbé Sicard's dictionary of signs.)

The result of all this [here Itard refers to Franslan] is that to abbreviate his speech, and also probably as a result of the confusion of ideas, the deaf–mute only produces incomplete sentences without verb tense, without pronouns, without articles indicating case. For example, instead of the sentence "Would you like us to water your garden this evening?" the signs say only this: "We, this evening to water garden you."* So far the sentence remains intelligible, but that does not last as soon as it is slightly more complicated. Such is the inevitable effect that follows from the very nature of sign language, which our speaking students necessarily avoid since they are forced to state precisely in speech the ideas that are rendered only vaguely in sign.

In his notes to a book on the law and the deaf written the following year, Itard repeats many of the same criticisms of sign and adds another:

Manual sign language [is] inherently and inevitably prolix; it is incapable, in most cases, of translating a word by a sign and is compelled typically to join two, three, or four signs together to represent the value of a single word. The word *house* [*la maison*] for example, even when stripped of its article, demands rather complicated signs that portray walls, a roof, a bed to sleep in; the word *coat,* the sign of a garment falling down to the knees; *countryside,* the sign of expanse, of wheat, and of reapers, and so forth. It follows that most nouns which are simple conventional signs in oral language are represented in sign language by images or definitions of the object ... Such an imperfect language engenders imperfect ideas and these, in turn, confused and poorly elaborated, tend to degrade and impoverish the system of signs that should represent them. And there you have the principal and inevitable reason why, if I am not mistaken, the education of the deaf-mute is generally incomplete and why he acquires the ability so rarely or so late to educate himself by reading.

Many of these criticisms, repeated by other scholars and laymen to the present day, reflect grave misunderstandings, of which the most fundamental is misunderstanding what language must be like in the visual mode. Every language constructs utterances from building blocks. But spoken or auditory language lays these blocks out in a row, whereas signed or visual language superimposes them one on top of the other. Contrast English and Ameslan in this light. First, how are the smallest meaningful units constructed? The English speaker strings vowels and consonants out sequentially in order to make a word. In the process of articulating the sounds, he often blurs the boundaries between successive elements so that they overlap in the stream of speech, but this does not detract from their successiveness. The Ameslan signer, on the contrary, chooses a handshape, a hand orientation, a location on his body, and a movement and combines these simultaneously to construct an individual sign. The errors hearing and deaf people make in perception, memory, and production neatly confirm that the basic building blocks for the speaker are vowels and consonants while those of the signer are handshape, orientation, location, and movement. In a recent experiment, English and Ameslan speakers transmitted lists of words to hearing and deaf subjects who then had to recall the lists. The English speakers erroneously recalled *father* as *bother, fox* as *box, gum* as *dumb,* and so on. The Ameslan speakers erroneously recalled *roll* as *who, pepper* as *priest, vote* as *tea,* and so on. These English errors came about by substituting consonants whereas these Ameslan errors resulted from substituting a hand configuration, location, or movement. When the deaf subjects misrecalled *father* it was not as *bother* but as *deer.* This is not surprising since *father* and *deer* differ only in that the latter involves both hands and the former just one.

We find the same difference between auditory and visual language if we ask a second question contrasting English and Ameslan: How are the words of the language modified by the grammar? Here again English prefers to string things out where Ameslan tends to superimpose them. In English we tack on suffixes like *-s* to indicate plurality and *-ed* to indicate past tense, or we tack on prefixes like *in-* and *pre-.* Ameslan, on the contrary, gets the same kind of work done in an unexpected way: it systematically varies

A sign in American Sign Language; English translation, *inform*
(Photo G. Schrader)

 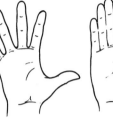 

Twenty handshapes in the signs of American Sign Language*
(Photo G. Schrader)

231

the orientation, handshape, movement, or location of the sign
while it is being carried out. For example, two fingers of one hand
are used to sign *climb*. If two people are climbing, two hands are
used concurrently, with two fingers on each hand. And if many
people are climbing, four fingers on each hand are used.

Motion may also distinguish singular from plural: for example,
the sign for *forest* in Ameslan is identical to that for *tree*, but the
wrist motion is repeated several times. Tense in Ameslan is also
signaled by movement. Signs for the future move forward from
the signer, usually at the level of the face: signs for the past generally move toward the signer, directed over the shoulder. The sign
for *look* when it is made in a forward arc means *prophecy*; the
same sign made in an arc that moves back across the ear means
reminiscing. Other such pairs are *will/past; tomorrow/yesterday;
next year/last year*. Movement may also add negation to a sign: a
downward movement converts *know*, *like*, *want* and *good* into
don't know, dislike, don't want, and *bad*.

If Ameslan combines elements concurrently rather than sequentially, both in constructing words and in modifying them gram-
matically, it is probably for the very good reason that it saves time.
We may ask a third and final question contrasting English and
Ameslan: How are phrases related to each other and modified in
sentences? Once again Ameslan's central concern with economizing time is the key to the difference. Ameslan's greater concern
with economy may well arise because, as Itard correctly states, a
sign takes longer to execute than its English (or French) translation. "All methods of sign are equally obliged to replace sounds
by gestures, that is, weak vibrations of the larynx and almost im-
perceptible displacements of the tongue and lips, by the slow and
clumsy physical interplay of long levers whose movements must
be the more complicated since they cannot, by forming various
combinations like those of the tongue and the lips, produce innumerable composites that are as simple and as brief as their
components."

In order to compare the speeds of speaking and signing, a group
of linguists and psychologists studying sign at the Salk Institute in
La Jolla, California, recruited three young hearing adults who

had learned sign as a native language from deaf parents and asked them to tell a story both in Ameslan and in English. On the average, they produced about two-and-a-half signs per second and nearly twice as many words in the same time (excluding pauses). When the speakers told the story in both languages simultaneously, the picture was basically the same, although the word rate was a little lower. The mere fact that they could tell both versions simultaneously and have them come out at the same time suggests that sign is no less efficient than speech. In fact, the subjects were communicating a simple sentence (or its equivalent) about every second and a half, whether signing or speaking, whether independently or together.

Thus signed *words* take longer to produce than spoken words, despite the economy achieved by combining elements simultaneously rather than successively to form and modify those words. Yet signed *messages* do not take longer to produce than spoken messages. Consequently, the signer must have additional ways to economize that the speaker does not. Predictably, he pauses somewhat less. But investigators Ursula Bellugi and Susan Fischer found that signers use three broad categories of linguistic devices for economizing on time. First, the signer can do without many of the redundant elements that must appear in a grammatical English (or French) sentence. *It's against the law to drive on the left side of the road* is conveyed by three signs: *illegal drive left-side.* Furthermore, pronouns can often be dropped and shorter, specific verbs can be used in place of longer, general ones: *I went back into the kitchen* is signed *return to kitchen.* The signer may not only delete elements, he may incorporate them. The sentence, *then they looked at each other*, for example, requires only two signs, since there is a single sign for *two-people-look-at-each-other.* In addition to shortening the signed message by deleting and incorporating elements, the speaker can economize by simultaneously providing information with facial expressions and bodily movements that are part of the grammar of sign language. Negation, for example, can be conveyed by a shake of the head or, in reduced form, a frown.

It is easy to understand why so many people who were not

familiar with sign language, Itard along with many educators of the deaf, were misled into believing that sign language is impoverished. Since the guiding principle of the language is to superimpose elements and to modify them concurrently, to incorporate and not to addend number, manner, location, size, shape, and so on, it is easy to overlook these regular processes when translating sign language into language in another mode with a different guiding principle. Word-for-sign translations are indeed usually impoverished, the more so as sign language does without many of the redundant "grammar words" in English or French. No wonder Napoleon exclaimed to Sicard that sign language contained only two kinds of words, nouns and adjectives. No wonder Itard thought "the deaf-mute produces only incomplete sentences without verb tense, without pronouns, without articles indicating tenses." Had a deaf person read the translations above that ignore the grammar of his native language, he would have reached the same conclusions as Itard, but concerning French, not sign language: that spoken language is impoverished, that it takes many words to say what sign can say in one, that it is often imprecise or ambiguous. If it is difficult to translate one spoken language into another, how much more difficult it must be to translate a visual language into an auditory one.

What a misguided enterprise it is, then, to attempt to force sign language into the mold of spoken language, to encumber it with affixes and grammar words and French or English syntax, to want to make it into a redundant sequential language when it is, in fact, an economical integrative language, to try to transform its patterns in space into patterns in time—in short, to seek to convert a visual language into an auditory one. Perhaps we should excuse Epée and Sicard: we cannot be sure if the grammatical complexity and richness we find in Ameslan today existed in its Franslan precursor. Their attempts to remedy the "impoverishment" of Franslan explain Itard's impression that the sign language was prolix. Surely when his pupils used Epée's Signed French with all its inflections and grammar words, the signed messages became quite long. In the years after Itard's death, however, the French scaffolding on Franslan began to fall away, and Sicard's successor, Bébian, tore down the remnants that were left, just as Gallaudet and Clerc did with the English grammatical apparatus originally imposed on Ameslan. What can be the merit and the prospects, then, of modern-day attempts to force Ameslan into correspondence with English?

Sign language has not only been confused, on the one hand, with the spoken language that surrounds it, but also, on the other, with the nonverbal communication from which it originally evolved. Fingerspelling is a means of replacing sign's way of forming words with that of spoken language. This writing in the air, as it were, helps the minority language to borrow words from the majority language. Epée's Signed French and the modern system called Signed English, are both means of replacing sign's way of forming sentences with that of spoken language. Both devices, for borrowing spelling and for borrowing syntax, are just that—devices, attached to the surface of sign language. The distinction between sign and pantomime, on the other hand, is deeper, for it touches the underlying nature of the language itself. To appreciate the difference between pantomime and sign, it is only necessary to observe someone skilled at both. When he pantomimes, he will take much longer, but you will understand his message; in sign, you will not understand a word, no matter how slowly he articulates. This is precisely because the sign language he is using is a code. American Sign Language, British Sign Language, and Chinese Sign Language, for example, are all radically different codes. The sign for *secret* in Ameslan means *father* in Chinese Sign Language, that for *false* means *one week,* and that for *cook, explain.* So Itard was quite wrong when he said that "most nouns which are simple conventional signs in oral language are represented in sign language by images or definitions of the objects." If signs were as iconic as Itard claims, he would have understood the language.

Perhaps, however, Franslan was originally more iconic than Ameslan. There are two reasons for thinking this. First, as signs are handed down from generation to generation, as the primary language of the family, from parent to child who becomes a parent in turn, they become simpler, more regular; they are shaped by the general rules for sign formation and thus become more encoded. Second, Franslan built originally on family signs brought to it by children like Massieu and his predecessors under Epée. De Gérando tells us that these children from isolated parts of France often brought similar signs for the same things. Hence we can imagine that some of their signs were relatively iconic. Only some, however—recall that Massieu said, "outsiders never understood us when we expressed our ideas to them in sign."

After studying Itard's three reports on speech and sign, advocating a class of mixed instruction for the partially deaf at the institute, after observing physiological training of hearing and speech in action with a new group of ten deaf-mutes, the commission of the Academy of Medicine reached the following conclusions in 1828:

(1) That the education which consists in the combination of manual signs with speech is possible in the case of one tenth of the children admitted into the Institute for Deaf-Mutes; (2) That this education has the advantage of improving the sense of hearing to the point of enabling the student to hear a part of the word, to make out with his eyes that part that is not heard, and to complete by means of intelligence and judgment the part which can neither be perceived by ear nor judged by sight; (3) That in consequence of the various improvements resulting from this special education, the deaf-mute can ... converse orally, and receive orders as well as give account of his actions; (4) That the execution of this education does not present any serious difficulties, since it can be carried out concurrently with sign education, which is the only type that has been employed up until now and is still employed nowadays for deaf-mutes; (5) That far from being hindered by the latter, oral instruction is accelerated and facilitated thanks to the intellectual gains that will not fail to accrue to a hard-of-hearing child in the midst of a community of children speaking sign language; (6) That this method modifies, and ought necessarily to modify in a desirable way, the elliptical, crude, and prolix language of signs, a language which because of these imperfections generally makes the ideas of the deaf-mute incomplete and truncated; (7) That the commission considers it a demonstrated medical truth, which cannot be too widely disseminated to the public, to families, and to doctors, that sign education is indispensable in all cases of early or congenital deafness, however slight their degree ... (8) That the final result of this education would be to return a tenth or a twelfth of the [institute's] children to their families, able to speak a language which would be understood and by means of which there

would consequently be established free, easy, and reciprocal communication, a thing which is impossible when only gesture language is used; (9) Finally, that the academy ought to support and recommend to the Minister of the Interior M. Itard's proposal, made a long time ago and frequently reiterated to the administration of the Royal Institute of Deaf-Mutes, to create a class in this Institute to teach deaf-mutes to speak.

Soon after the academy issued this favorable report, the ministry provided funds to sustain the class of combined sign and oral instruction that had been instituted at Itard's insistence a year before in 1827. The class was suspended in 1831 but renewed in 1843 by ministerial decree. Léon Vaïsse, who had served as adviser to Clerc in establishing the New York institute from 1830 to 1836, took charge of the new "articulation class."

One wonders whether another *enfant sauvage* arriving at the institute in 1830 would not have fared much better in acquiring language than Victor did in 1800; it seems very likely. Not only had Itard developed techniques for training the mentally handicapped and the hearing-handicapped, he had also synthesized from these a treatment specifically designed for mutism caused by intellectual impairment. This was the title of his address to the Royal Academy of Medicine at its first meeting in 1824.* At the outset of this report, which describes the results of experiments made over a period of twenty years with as many children, Itard states that the acquisition of speech requires four preconditions: "Man needs commerce with other men, so they can communicate this art to him; the assistance of another organ, the auditory mechanism, so he can hear his first lessons; the faculty of imitation to facilitate his repeating them; and the degree of intelligence accorded to his species, to furnish him with ideas which are the materials for comprehension." Children who are mute because the faculty for comprehension is impaired usually display infantile behavior, hyperactivity, extensive gesturing, aversion to manual skills and instruction, fluctuating attention, preoccupation with physical needs, preference for childish games, highly selective memory, and emotional disorders. Intellectual impairment brings with it impairment of another faculty required for speech, imitation. When screening mute children to identify those who would profit from this particular training program, Itard first confirmed that the third required faculty, hearing, was in good order. Moreover, he required that the child could give and respond to simple commands, communicated by either gesture or speech; that he could also answer yes or no, to accept or refuse, confirm or deny; finally, that he could respond appropriately when corrected in tasks involving simple imitation. If all the signs are auspicious, the child receives the treatment whose main principle is "to demonstrate speech as an art of imitation which, like all the others, one must decompose into its elements to teach them first separately, then taken one at a time, two at a time, three at a time, finally in those combinations that represent the complete sentence."

Itard restricts his report to the essential part of the treatment, the procedures "to awaken the need and the faculty for speech." Here is his description of the first step:

> In a room set aside for these exercises, we place all the portable objects whose spoken names or manual signs our young mute pupil already knows. In the latter case, we make the sign while pronouncing the name of each of these objects. Designating them in this way, we have the child bring them to us one after the other, but we abstain from employing any verbs in our requests. Only those objects should be cited at first whose names are very short and made up of loud vowels, such as *o* and *a*, and syllables whose consonants are quite visible, such as the labials and the dentals. After a few days we suppress the manual sign using only the verbal one which is now taken to be retained in memory.

The size of the repertory of names is then gradually increased. In the second step, the ensemble includes pairs of similar objects which can only be distinguished by adjectives, such as *big* and *little*, *red* and *yellow*. Adjectives like *broken* and *fixed* prepare the transition to verbs. First the child is instructed to *walk* or *run* (for example), then the verbs are followed by familiar nouns, *give cup*, and noun phrases, *give red cup (donner tasse rouge)*. Only the infinitive form of verbs is used since it is the least marked for person and tense, and hence the easiest to understand "as can be seen from its preferential and almost exclusive use in the language of poorly civilized peoples, especially the negroes in our colonies."

The Wild Boy of Aveyron   238

The next step adds a few adverbs and prepositions to the commands. Once these elements are practiced, they can all be combined into a very large number of possible sentences the child understands, for example, "place the clock gently on the little table behind the desk." Leaving aside conjunctions and interjections, the teacher next introduces possessive pronouns; the problem is enormously difficult, as we have heard Itard explain, since several pronouns designate the same thing (*my hat, your hat, his hat* can all refer to the same hat depending on who is speaking) and the same pronoun designates different things (so the child may not be correct if he imitates the model "this is my hat"). The rest of Itard's basic training program is concerned with developing imitation; this follows from his original premise that spoken language is normally acquired when the child imitates the utterances that he is exposed to and can distinguish among by ear. Since his pupil is now able to understand a large number of sentences, combinations of the words he has mastered, it only remains to induce the tendency to imitate them. Itard begins with any action that the child already imitates, and he gradually complicates and extends it. Next he teaches imitation of finer movements, for example, letter drawing or simple sketches. Then he proceeds to visible movements of the lips, the tongue, and the chest while breathing. Finally he provides the child with a whistle and they exchange whistle calls, shouts, and various kinds of cries. When those steps proved difficult, Itard found that blindfolding the child was a useful expedient that made him concentrate on auditory cues: the child tended to gesture less, to move about less, to engage in more vocalizing. Four to six months of these blindfolded sessions overcame particularly recalcitrant mutism in two out of three cases; the third was severely retarded.

Itard monitored the progress of his pupils in later years, in some cases over two decades, so he was able to affirm at the end of his report that once these retarded children were launched on a career of hearing, imitation, and speech, they continued to show progress not only in language but in general intellectual development.

Itard was concerned with improving the language skills of the handicapped right up through the last days of his life. He even managed to innovate another class of instruction posthumously, which contributed both to the education of the deaf and to the controversy between advocates of oral and sign education. The pertinent section of his will reads:

> I bequeath to the Royal Institute for Deaf-Mutes of Paris an annuity of 8000 francs . . . to be disbursed by its administrative council under the authorization and responsibility of the government: To create in the aforementioned institute a new class of supplementary instruction and six triennial tuition scholarships for six deaf-mutes chosen by competitive examination among those pupils of the institute who have completed the ordinary period of instruction . . .
>
> The administrative council, in consultation with all the professors, will have to decide what studies will be pursued in the class of supplementary instruction. Nevertheless, if all the observations and experiments I have performed in this connection during forty years may have some weight in this decision, it must be based on the remarkable fact, which I consider to have all the characteristics of a proven truth, that after the six years devoted to their instruction nearly all our deaf-mutes are unable to read most of the works of our language with full understanding. Consequently, the deaf-mute who has been graduated from the institute, unable to draw freely from this vast repository of the mind's and the heart's creations, remains for the rest of his life at the level of education at which he was left by his teachers; it follows that the most fruitful instruction for him would indisputably be one that enabled him to read all of the important works of our language with comprehension and without fatigue. Such would be the result of the class of supplementary instruction. But in order to achieve this goal, an absolute requirement for its implementation ought ·to be to exclude the use of sign language and to oblige the students and the professor to communicate among themselves only by speaking or by the intermediary of writing. It is of the greatest importance that, at this final stage of instruction, the deaf-mute should cease thinking in his inherently defective and abbreviated language in order to translate his ideas into our own, as he is in the habit of doing; instead he should think and express himself directly in the language of speaking society at large, either by voice or by writing. Without this requirement, I repeat, we will have another class of instruction but not a class of special instruction. The experiments to which I devoted an hour daily for ten years allow me, although an outsider to the educational program of the institute, to assert the advantages of this [oral] method which will be confirmed by a detailed examination of the intellectual capacities of young [Eugène] Allibert,

who was a subject in one of these experiments. It is superfluous to add that a special teacher ought to be assigned to this class of higher education and, if its founder could hope that one of his last wishes would be accorded by the administrative council, he would ask that Allibert be named assistant to this speaking teacher.

In founding the class of supplementary instruction, Itard acted on his final conclusions about the language skills of the deaf as well as on a general dissatisfaction at the institute with the product of its education through the vehicle of sign. The emphasis on reading reflects Itard's conviction that it is the only way to complete the deaf-mute's basic instruction and to provide him with a satisfactory education.

> I have already noted that after long education through the medium of sign, reinforced moreover by an unwavering taste for studies and above ordinary intelligence, the deaf-mute can break out of the circle to which he is confined by manual sign language in order to communicate with educated men at any time or place by means of written signs or reading. Once this inexhaustible source of instruction and knowledge has been opened to him, he can draw there all the information that he lacks to complete his education.

Since Itard believed that the limitations of sign as a language were the principal reason for the deaf-mute's achieving "so late or so rarely the ability to educate himself through reading," it is not surprising that he excludes sign in favor of speech in a class devoted to developing reading skills. By imposing this requirement he also helped to entrench the class of oral education that the institute had created on his initiative with the support of the Academy of Medicine. The verbal instruction in the supplementary class could perfect the French skills of the eighteen-to-twenty-year-old students, but they would have to have learned to speak and understand spoken language many years before. Itard also sought to exclude the use of sign because he believed that it came between the student and both his understanding and his direct communication in French, much as a speaker in a foreign land may rehearse what he is going to say in his native language, then translate it into the foreign tongue and, conversely, translate what he hears into his native language before appreciating its meaning. This is clear from the terms of Itard's will, but he held the same opinion nearly twenty years before when he wrote in his *Traité* that deaf-mutes, like second-language learners, "think in their language, construct sentences with the words of that same language, and translate them slowly into those of the foreign language."

In supplementing the normal six-year program of education, beginning around age twelve, with an additional three years, Itard also expressed the belief then current among the teachers that in six years they could not prepare their students for occupations other than manual trades. Eight months before Itard drew up his will, in October 1837, a committee of teachers issued the following report:

> The commission felt that the deaf-mutes would be incapable, after a six-year course of instruction, of taking the apprentice teacher's examination provided for in article 5; nevertheless, it would be unjust to exclude a student from a teaching career of which he might be worthy if he had the freedom to complete his education. On the other hand, since speaking and deaf-mute teachers give the same instruction, both ought to have the same knowledge, and serious difficulties would arise if the same guarantees of ability were not required of deaf-mute and speaking candidates alike. Therefore, a way should be found to provide the deaf-mutes with the knowledge they lack. All these considerations taken together make clear the need for creating a temporary status for deaf-mutes intermediate between pupil and aspirant. The commission thinks that the students who had distinguished themselves by their comportment and progress and who had shown evidence of unusual promise could, at the end of their course of instruction, be kept on for three years in the institute, with the status of monitors . . . After three years, they would take an aspirant's examination if they desired the career of instructing their fellow deaf-mutes . . . An advanced class for perfecting the training of the monitors and students who remain in the institute beyond six years would motivate competition; it would provide a reserve of distinguished students and would serve as a training ground for the aspirants at the end of their apprenticeship.

The creation of the class of supplementary instruction under the terms of Itard's will met with vigorous resistance. When the administrative council sought to consult all the teachers on its implementation, as the will provided, the deaf-mute teachers declined to express an opinion. The dean of teachers, Ferdinand Berthier, a deaf-mute himself, a prolific author, and one of Clerc's former pupils, presented a long and impassioned disquisition to the Academy of Medicine and the Second Class of the French Institute:

> In truth, I do not understand M. Itard, anathematizing the being brought on his own by the abbé de l'Epée and enjoining him to cease thinking in the natural language which he has always employed, in that universal language perfected by the able teacher of the deaf which the learned doctor has acknowledged he does not know and which now he ruthlessly calls "a language inherently defective and abbreviated"—all this to oblige [the deaf-mute] "to express himself directly in the language of speaking society at large."

Berthier rejects, in the first place, Itard's premise that thought depends utterly on language: "It is of the greatest importance that . . . the deaf-mute should cease thinking in his inherently defective and abbreviated language in order to translate his ideas into our own, as he is in the habit of doing." No doubt this premise is part of his heritage from Condillac, who had written that "ideas are linked to signs and it is only in this way that they are linked to each other." According to Berthier, Itard's favorite pupil Allibert was asked at a dinner if he had had ideas before receiving instruction at the institute; to general amazement he said that he had, and proceeded to describe a few of the ideas of his childhood. Whereupon Itard commented, "If you had ideas such as those you have told us about, all of Condillac's theory would be destroyed." For Berthier it was "an uncontestable and uncontested fact that thought exists before language." Since the deaf-mute's thought processes are quite independent of sign, he is in no way obliged to sign in order to formulate his ideas for written or spoken communication; nor need he respond first in sign in order to understand the written or spoken communications of other people. The translation problem that motivated Itard to exclude sign from the advanced class does not exist, except for the less educated students and then only as a consequence of their unfamiliarity with French.

Ordinarily, the first- and even third-year students will, when studying alone, unfailingly read out the words in their notebooks or texts one after the other, with the aid of sign language. Why? For the simplest reason in the world. They are concerned with remembering them. But, when it comes to the more advanced students, their imagination is such a powerful aid that the help of signs becomes quite superfluous. For them, to read or to write is to feel, to feel intensely: they even have the impression they are seeing [what the text describes] . . . It is a mistake to think that the deaf-mute who has been taught speech pronounces words while thinking . . . As for the deaf-mute who has learned language only by writing or sign . . . his mind operates on the written letters. It is superfluous to add images [of signs].

Thus sign would not be an impediment in the advanced class, which is devoted mainly to reading, and habits of oral communication would be of little assistance.

Because of the conflict between the views of the teachers in the citadel of sign and the oralist stipulations of Itard's will, the class he endowed could not begin until four years later, in 1842. Allibert was indeed named adjunct to the teacher, Edouard Morel, who later became director of the Bordeaux institute. Written language seems to have been the sole medium of communication and the students were rather fluent in it, to gather from Laurent Clerc's report of his visit to the class in 1847, while on leave from the American asylum. However, another visitor reports that sign was used extensively; in any event, speech was minimal. Morel's successor Vaïsse, also employed sign, as he explained a decade later:

With the aid of gestural language, the abbé de l'Epée undertook to introduce his students to all our ideas by explaining the significance of our written words . . . His adopted children were no longer mute, having learned to write, nor deaf, having learned to read. The abbé wanted, moreover, to teach his students to articulate speech to a reasonable degree, whenever it seemed possible to accomplish something more than a mere curiosity . . . Such were the goals that guided his instruction; such are still the goals that guide our own. Gestures are for us only what they were for him, a means. Several teachers of deaf-mutes claim to have banished sign systematically from their method. They have acted like the teacher of a blind man who would not allow himself to speak or, again, like the wet-nurse or mother who, when talking to her infant, took it in her head to keep her arms crossed or to cover the child's eyes.

Since the "absolute requirement" set down by Itard was not, and seemingly could not be respected, the government had created "another class of instruction but not a class of special instruction." Itard's express conditions had been betrayed, the will not executed. This, at least, was the argument advanced by his nephew, Joseph Petit, in petitioning Napoleon III for a homestead in Algeria. "Joseph Petit," he wrote, "was born of a very old family from Forcalquier [Department of Alpes de Haute-Provence], and has for many years been established in the town of Digne."

> He would have been the heir of M. Itard, his maternal uncle, who had no children, or paternal nephews, or maternal nephews other than his brother, Honoré Petit, and his sister, Annette Petit, were it not for the will which bequeaths his considerable fortune to public institutions and which leaves, proportionately, only a very small inheritance to [Joseph Petit], 15,000 francs, and a like sum to his sister and nothing to his brother, and a few other bequests to the descendants of Dr. Itard's half-sister, named Breissan . . . [The petitioner] finds that tilling a small plot of land by hand [in the French Alps] does not yield a sufficient return. Head of a family, and experienced after years of practicing farming, he would like to advance himself, to have more land so as to develop farming on a large scale with teams of horses and machines, to set up an agricultural business that would give him a return and be useful to his countrymen, in that regard following his uncle's example . . .
>
> Nothing more need be said concerning the departments of the French Alps, the worst region in France and perhaps in Europe . . . Since 1789, these two departments have lost 120,000 out of 400,000 souls. We will not paint the picture of this Sahara all over again; it has been done by M. Blanqui of the French Institute . . . The migration is directed, characteristically, either to foreign lands, where there are points of concentration as in the Valley of Barcelonette in Mexico, or to our major cities. Wouldn't it be more useful to keep these industrious people, hard-working and temperate, engaged in farming in France, to send them to Algeria where vast and fertile plains await them, generously repaying their labor and providing the bread that their native region refuses them. Let us say it outright, the idea of calling on Chinese coolies to cultivate Algeria is hardly fair when we have Frenchmen in this condition readily available in large numbers. It is only a matter of getting them to understand, of putting oneself at their level, of offering them a new country wherein they will find their old one.
>
> What is the basis of the favor that we are soliciting? . . . Petit bases his

request on the terms of the will of M. Itard, his uncle and physician to the deaf-mutes at Paris. Following its provisions, imperial institutions have received from this inheritance the sum of 260,000 francs. If Joseph Petit had this amount in property perhaps he would not dream of going to Algeria to live among the Arabs. He would prefer perhaps to relocate in Paris to live in the midst of the most refined society. If one stops to think about it carefully, he could and ought to have this sum in his possession, he or his brother and sister, as his uncle's rightful heirs. Indeed, has it not been well established, if not as a general rule at least by innumerable precedents, that the government takes only the smallest fraction of bequests made to public institutions at the expense of relatives? This decision is extremely wise: what good is it to look for poor people elsewhere when they can be found in the [deceased's] family?

Now, it is positively established by the documents he presents, it is indeed a matter of widespread public knowledge, that the resources and standard of living of Joseph Petit are not at all in keeping with the considerable inheritance that his uncle left to public institutions. He is obliged to work to protect the honor of his name. Certainly he would have preferred that the government had renounced succession the better to divide the estate of M. Itard, his uncle, but he refused all right to contest the will, he did not think he ought to appeal to the courts, he did not want to come out directly against the wishes of this uncle, his benefactor.

What Petit did not do in the past, he is far from wanting to do today. If he is correctly informed, the provisions of his uncle's will include a bequest to the deaf-mutes which amounts to not less than 200,000 francs (8000 francs annual income at 4 percent). These explicit provisions have not been carried out, the class of advanced studies has never been established. In recounting these circumstances, he does not wish for the world to hinder these humanitarian institutions in the enjoyment of the bequests made in their favor. It is only a means to emphasize the merits of his request. He appeals to the government which authorized the institutions under its charge to receive the sum of 260,000 francs which it could have redirected to the family, which it could restitute even today, for reason of nonexecution of explicit clauses of the testament.

Well! Petit limits himself to asking, if not something of equivalent value, at least a compensation and indemnity. He earnestly solicits a part of the land that the state possesses by the millions of hectares in Algeria. Doesn't the government have this land to dispose of? Doesn't it sell it, and give it away at will or for whatever justification may be offered ... We have presented our views and our reasons. The government of His Majesty, Emperor Napoleon III, is great and generous, it is also just, we have entire confidence in it, we will accept with great gratitude and devotion what it pleases to accord us.

It pleased the government to refuse the request, but Petit did not keep his word and a year later submitted a fifty-three-page memoir to accomplish what the four-page petition had not. Here he reviews the education of deaf-mutes and cites Berthier at great length on the merits of sign language and the impossibility of carrying out the express conditions in Itard's will. He quotes Vaïsse on the necessity of using sign in the advanced class. He further reprints extended passages from a book by one of Itard's successors, a Dr. Blanchet, entitled "Means of Universalizing the Education of Deaf-Mutes Without Separating them from Their Families and Speaking People." The purpose of the book was to elaborate on and support a directive from the Ministry of the Interior ordering all the primary schools to accept deaf-mutes, to perfect their speech as far as possible but to use sign as well as oral language. An initial step had already been taken in creating ten nonresidential schools for the deaf and for blind children that were annexed to elementary schools in the several *arrondissements* of Paris. The memoir concludes, then, not only that it was impossible to execute Itard's will because it was impossible to teach without sign but also that there would be almost no one left to take Itard's advanced class in ten years' time since the public schools were becoming the major means for educating the deaf. The government was unmoved by these arguments, and Petit continued to till the Alpine soil by hand. His predictions proved correct, however, in essence if not in detail.

What actually happened was this. Shortly before Itard's death, there was an abortive attempt to make spoken language the sole medium of communication at the Paris institute. This move, backed by Itard's old friend and supporter, De Gérando, who had become a member of the institute's administrative council, was a travesty of Itard's oral method. Itard had written to the administration and published his position quite explicitly:

The language of the deaf-mute is in his hands, as his hearing is in his eyes; to want to give him another language is to act directly counter to the laws of nature, and against the least contested principles of physiology and sound metaphysics. If we are proposing another means of communication it is not at all for this class of [true] deaf-mutes where we believe it applicable, but for another, which is quite distinct and which, strictly speaking, should no more be classed with the deaf than the nearsighted with the blind.

The attempt to suppress sign and to use Itard's methods indiscriminately for all the deaf failed and, in reaction, all teaching of spoken language was abandoned for several years. In 1847, a prominent author visiting the institute found "no serious effort" to teach speech. The articulation class that had grown out of Itard's experiments in the physiological training of the deaf had resumed in 1843, but we are told that it yielded meager results and in practice the partially deaf lost their residual speech at the school and became completely mute. When Clerc visited the class in 1847, he found that it contained twenty students instructed by Vaïsse and that it met four times a week for one hour. He ended his visit "more than ever convinced of the little benefit to be derived from articulation."*

Nine years after Itard's death, the supplementary class was also in session but with only six students, about 5 percent of the institute's enrollment.* Each year two sixth-year students entered the class for a three-year period of instruction. Sign and writing were the primary means of communication. Vaïsse went on to teach the supplementary class and to become director of the institute but he could never overcome the teachers' opposition to oral education. He makes this resistance plain in a letter written in 1871 to a successful oralist, who was invited to demonstrate his methods at the Bordeaux institute (but was later dismissed summarily):

My dear M. Fourcade, you are fully right when you believe in the interest I feel for your labors, whose present success consoles me for the continued ill will of our French instructors in regard to teaching the mute to speak. Without going so far as yourself in the principle of what you call demutization, I approve of your labors even when you oppose them to mine, in which I have unfortunately been betrayed by those whose assistance and sympathy I needed.

Séguin, who calls the institute a "school of mutism," reports that Vaïsse was invited to retire the same year. "Itard's money was taken but his [class] of speech lasted only a few years. M. Vaïsse had become at once useless and compromising." In 1873, Séguin was among a group of visitors to the institute who asked about the language class founded by Itard. They were told that it did indeed exist but was not in proper condition to be visited.

Although the forces of oralism could not hold ground in the bastion of sign, they were able to make inroads elsewhere. The third chief physician for the deaf-mutes, Blanchet, organized a dozen classes in the public schools, which gave oral instruction to the deaf using methods initiated by Itard. The oralist movement was bitterly resisted not only by the professors of the Paris institute but also by Itard's immediate successor, Dr. Ménière, whose dispute with Blanchet was carried to the Academy of Medicine, the same body that had endorsed Itard's original experiments in 1808 and his reports favoring oral instruction of the partially deaf in 1828. After appointing a commission to study the question and devoting no less than ten meetings to discussing its report, the academy concluded that children with residual hearing could benefit from oral instruction and should be placed in separate classes. As for their profoundly deaf peers, "experience has not yet chosen clearly between the French method of education by sign and the German method of education by speech."

Oral instruction also gained ground in the United States. Initially, the Hartford school would have no part of it. In addition to sign language and the manual alphabet, students at the asylum learned to write after they had learned to spell manually, and finally they were taught to read. Articulation was not taught. Braidwood's methods were relegated to parlor tricks "entitled to rank little higher than training starlings or parrots." Gallaudet's successor gave these reasons for rejecting oral methods:

1. Too much time is lost in teaching sound, which is to no benefit in mental culture.
2. Under this system a large number of deaf-mutes must be left without instruction.

3. The intonations of the voice and the distortion of the countenance in teaching and practicing articulation are disagreeable.
4. Success in articulation teaching has come principally to pupils who retained their speech after becoming deaf.
5. The ability to converse in general society is not secured by this method of instruction.
6. More teachers are required, resulting in more expense.
7. Religious instruction must be deferred, and religious worship is almost impossible.
8. In teaching articulation, signs are still indispensable.
9. Lip reading must be taught also.
10. The results of instruction by signs are beyond those attained by articulation.

But in 1843 Samuel Howe, the man who taught the blind and deaf Laura Bridgman and whose Perkins Institution trained Anne Sullivan, Helen Keller's teacher, went abroad with Horace Mann, who later brought about the opening of the first teachers' college in America. The two were greatly impressed by the German schools for the deaf, and Mann published a controversial report favoring the oral method and relating that German teachers "prohibit sign as far as possible." The report drew an acerbic reply from Hartford:

We are persuaded that if we should spend a large portion of the period, scanty at best, allowed to each pupil attempting to teach him to articulate and to read on the lips, the cases of partial failure in the far more essential, yet easier, task of teaching the vocabulary and idioms of language would be much more numerous. Articulation has been excluded from the course of instruction after careful and mature deliberation and, in the New York Institution, after actual and patient experiment; not because the object was considered of little account but because the small degree of success usually attainable was judged to be a very inadequate compensation for that expenditure of time and labor which the teaching of articulation exacts—for the many wearisome hours that must be spent in adjusting and readjusting the positions of the vocal organs, in teaching the "seven sounds of the letter *a*," "the hundreds of elementary sounds," as Mr. Mann says, represented by only twenty–six letters, and the thousand capricious irregularities in the pronunciation of the same letters or combinations of letters.

The author admonishes teachers of the deaf to remember the

disastrous experiment with oralism at the Paris institute and concludes, "We see no present prospect that the teaching of articulation will be introduced into our institutions at all." Nevertheless, just one year after the Mann Report, in 1845, the following resolution was passed by the board of directors of the asylum founded by Gallaudet and Clerc:

> Voted, in view of the facts and results obtained by Mr. Weld, the Principal of the Asylum, during his late visit to various institutions for the education of deaf-mutes in Europe, that the board of directors will take efficient measures to introduce into the course of instruction in the Asylum every improvement to be derived from these foreign institutions; and with regard to teaching deaf-mutes to articulate, and to understand what is said to them orally, that they will give it a full and prolonged trial, and do in this branch of instruction everything that is practically and permanently useful.

Six years later, the same school established a supplementary class of instruction like Itard's; still, sign language was not to be displaced by oral training. The class was the forerunner of the National College for the Deaf, founded by Gallaudet's son, Edward, in 1864. At about the same time, the school took on a special teacher of articulation, and oralism made further gains when Alexander Graham Bell spent time there in 1872 training instructors in his method of teaching the deaf to speak, Visible Speech, based on a phonetic notation developed by his father. The same year, Bell also demonstrated his method at the first oral school for the deaf in the United States, the Clarke School opened in Massachusetts in 1867. It admitted only hard-of-hearing pupils and taught exclusively by lipreading and articulation. By the 1880s there were eleven strictly oral schools in America, thanks in part to Bell's efforts. Not only was he a tireless proselytizer and teacher in the cause of oralism, but he also donated to that cause nearly half a million dollars, about half of the fortune he realized from the invention of the telephone. Most of it went to the Clarke School, the Horace Mann School, and to Bell's own organization, the American Association for the Promotion of the Teaching of Speech to the Deaf, known today by its headquarters, the Volta Bureau.

Back in France, a private school for teaching articulation was incorporated into the imperial institute by ministerial decree in 1855, and a separate institute for oral instruction of the deaf was founded in Paris in 1875 by Pereire's grandson and great-grandson. When the first French Congress on Instruction of Deaf-Mutes was organized three years later, with Vaïsse presiding, the tide began to turn in favor of oralism. A congress at Lyon the following year reinforced the swell, which came thundering in at an international congress in Milan in 1880: "Considering the incontestable superiority of speech over sign for integrating the deaf-mute into society and for giving him better command of language," the congress resolved, "the oral method is preferable to the gestural for the development and instruction of deaf-mutes." Whereas Itard had advocated oral instruction for the hard-of-hearing, the profession now advocated it for all the deaf. And whereas Itard believed that communication in sign was a valuable aid in teaching oral skills, the congress ruled that "since the concurrent use of speech and of signs has the disadvantage of undermining speech, lipreading, and the precision of ideas . . . the pure oral method should be preferred." In the closing moments of the congress, the special French representative cried from the podium, "Vive la parole!"

Reviewing the history of Itard's supplementary class, one of its instructors states that it was only after the Milan congress that the course began to turn out the kind of model student and potential teacher that Itard had envisioned: well read and able to communicate orally. Twenty years later, at the turn of the century, a report to the International Congress of Deaf-Mutes held in Paris could state that the pure oral method was the official method of instruction employed in all schools for deaf-mutes in France.* At the National Institute of Deaf-Mutes, entering pupils were first given imitation training, as Victor was a century earlier, in which they repeated the bodily movements, postures, facial gestures, and, finally, articulatory movements of the instructor. After a few days of these exercises, "to interest the pupil, to give him a taste for speech, to facilitate his communication, and to arrest his development of sign language, he is taught to lipread a few easy short words, without decomposing them into their phonetic elements."

Next came the breathing exercises advocated by Itard and then his graded series of phonetic exercises—in which lipreading, however, replaced auditory training with these profoundly deaf children. As the child gained proficiency, writing and reading were introduced.

Thus, by the time of the Paris congress, oralism had become the medium of instruction at Epée's institute. Nevertheless, Edward Gallaudet was on hand, among many others, to contest strongly the merits of the oralist approach. The supporters of oralism are found among the teachers, he declared, while the supporters of sign are found among the deaf themselves. The very congress itself bore eloquent witness to his claim: as the hearing professors presented paper after paper in support of oralism, the deaf professors, meeting separately, resolved repeatedly in favor of sign.* Gallaudet carried their reiterated demands to meet jointly with the hearing professors to the president and finally to the congress at large, but each time the request was refused. The pretext was that the official language of the congress was French whereas the deaf section communicated in sign. In fact, simultaneous translation would have been possible; many of the deaf had oral skills in any event. Sign might have been a better choice of official language: many of the hearing foreigners frankly admitted that they could not understand the French, and even the French speakers had difficulty with the "barbarisms" perpetrated by the prepared remarks of their guests. That the language problem was indeed a pretext for excluding the deaf, who favored instruction combining sign and speech, was revealed when the president, the third physician to serve the Paris institute after Itard, refused to allow motions passed in the deaf section even to be reported to the hearing section.

Finally, Gallaudet moved that the congress resolve in favor of a mixed method of instruction: to tailor the method to the intellectual and physical aptitudes of the individual pupil, to provide initial oral instruction to all but to continue this mode of instruction only for those who benefit by it. Although Gallaudet was circumspect enough not even to mention the word *sign*, the pendulum had swung full arc since his father's visit to Paris in the days of Sicard, and the congress rejected his motion by more than one hundred to seven. Instead the meeting resolved that "the congress supports the conclusions of the congress of Milan, considering speech incontestably superior to signs." At almost the same moment, the deaf professors were voting the opposite. Therefore Gallaudet moved that the resolution should read that the hearing section, not the congress, considers speech incontestably superior to sign. The motion was defeated.

The Great Sign Controversy continues to this day. In some American schools for the deaf, children receive only a program of oral instruction, with surprisingly much in common with Itard's original methods. In others, signing is tolerated and even employed, as Itard would have had it, in support of oral instruction. In a very few, it is the primary medium of instruction. The scientific and popular press concerned wth the deaf still resounds with the sallies and counterattacks of the warring camps. And the sides are largely drawn up today as Gallaudet saw them in Paris in 1900.

Chapter Ten

Itard's
Legacies

During a career that lasted nearly four decades, from 1800 when he became resident physician at the National Institute for Deaf-Mutes to 1838 when he died in his home in Passy, Itard produced some twenty articles and books of which the most renowned were his two reports on the wild boy of Aveyron and his "Treatise on Diseases of the Ear and Hearing." Writing did not come easily to him, according to his eulogist, Bousquet:

> His thoughts were initially confused and sorted themselves out extremely slowly; and when they seemed arranged, the task of expressing them required another effort as painful as the first . . . It is true that he was not easily satisfied with his work. Wanting to sacrifice nothing of the thoughts to be conveyed, he worked and reworked his sentences, until he found the wording that showed them to best advantage, and he succeeded so well that he made his place among the best writers in medical literature.

Itard's medical publications, especially his two major works, contributed to his international reputation and he enjoyed a thriving practice. He opened a private office in the center of the city and there treated many patients among the nobility. Thus he amassed a considerable fortune in his lifetime, nearly half a million francs. In later years, Itard kept to the deaf-mute institute and treated only its pupils and those patients from the city who came to the Faubourg Saint-Jacques to visit him. Never particularly fond of social life, the aging bachelor devoted himself to his solitary hobbies. He had a cultivated taste in objets d'art, paintings, and furniture, reflected in his will. He had a wood and metal shop installed and spent many hours on woodworking. Most of all, he loved to work in the garden of the institute where Victor, too, had spent many solitary hours regarding nature. There he had a thatched cottage constructed and each day he would spend a few hours reading or in conversation with friends. Itard rented a country home in Passy, now a bustling section of Paris proper, and in the garden he installed a little summer house, as well as a fountain and rows of hedges; he called it "Beauséjour."

With his health failing, his body bent and in considerable pain, Itard became taciturn and brusque. He retired to Beauséjour where he received only a few intimate friends, among them his favorite student and disciple who would establish the education of the mentally handicapped with Itard's techniques, Edouard Séguin. "My first labors were performed in the studio of Itard," Séguin wrote in his article on the *Origin of the Treatment and Training of Idiots,*

> where he bestowed on me the most valuable gift that an old man can offer to a young one—the practical result of his experience. Itard was often sublime during these interviews when, a prey to horrible sufferings, symptoms of his fatal disease, he discussed with me the highest questions. His features would contract and his body writhe in his anguish, but his mind never lost its clearness and precision for a moment. I there learned the secret of his influence over the idiots, as I did that of his weakness in philosophy, till the time when he died at Passy, in 1838.*

Itard's will reveals much about the man: his few family ties, his loyalty to his friends and generosity to worthy causes, his success as a physician, his deep skepticism about the value of surgery and medicine in therapy, his commitment to training instead, which recalls his first teacher's doctrine of "mental medicine":

> I bequeath to my cousins, the children of my Aunt Silbert née Itard, married and died at Volx (Basses-Alpes); to my cousins Joseph and Annette Petit, children of my Aunt Petit née Itard, married and died at Forcalquier, who live at Digne and Forcalquier, respectively*; to my cousin the aforementioned Charles Clément, pharmacist at Oraison; to Joseph Revest, doctor in Marseilles, my equally close relative on my mother's side; to be divided equally among them as follows: (1) the capital and lots that I still own at Oraison; (2) the garden, stable, house, and its furnishings that I have at Riez; (3) a capital of 40,000 francs placed at 4.5 percent interest with M. Margueve, firm of notary Porchet; (4) an entry of 1000 francs annual income at 3 percent in the account book; (5) five of my ten shares in the Bank of France; the total representing more than 100,000 francs, equivalent to what I have received from my family . . .

I bequeath to the Royal Institute of Deaf-Mutes of Paris 8000 francs annual income in perpetuity, comprising the greater part of my placements at 5 percent in the account book; the administrative council shall . . . (1) create in this institute a new class of supplementary instruction [Here Itard spells out the conditions under which the class is to function]; (2) provide my former servant Charby with an annuity of 1000 francs; (3) arrange for a mass to be celebrated in my memory in the chapel of the institute on the anniversary of my death; (4) acquire in perpetuity in the name of the institute a plot in the cemetery of Mont-Parnasse to receive my mortal remains.*

My personal property shall be sold apart from the bequests offered to the following persons who were rightfully dear to me. To M. Rives, the executor of my will, all my silverware, and all my silver plate whether hollow or flatware, and to complete the set 4000 francs. To Dr. Husson, my bedroom clock, said to be in the style of the Middle Ages. [Husson was a pioneer of vaccination, introduced in France in 1800. A student of Corvisart, he taught clinical medicine at the Hôtel Dieu and, as a member of the Academy of Science, prepared their report on Itard's methods of physiological education.] To the Count of Monte-lezun my stickpin of oriental sapphire, trusting that this jewel given me by Emperor Alexander will never leave the family. To deputy Gravier a landscape by Mme. Empis, representing a view of Corsica. [Cathérine Empis was an artist of moderate distinction, the wife of the director of the Comédie Française, and a friend of Itard's.] To M. Frojeot (Faubourg Poissonnière) a solid mahogony table in my dining room in Paris. To Eugène Allibert, former student of the institute, my gold repeater watch and my gold pince-nez. To Dr. Esquirol my clock in Pyrénées marble. [A classmate of Itard's under Pinel, Esquirol was one of the founders of psychiatry. His classic "On Mental Disease" appeared the year of Itard's death.] To Dr. Bousquet all the pictures that decorate the walls of my drawing room and sitting room. [Itard's eulogist, Bousquet, was secretary of the Academy of Medicine of which Itard was a member.] To the oldest and best of my friends, Mme. Charton (Rue Tronchet), the large mirror in my drawing room, mounted in the form of Psyche. To the Marquise of Courtemanche my two carcel lamps with all their accessories and stand. To Mme. Jacquinat Pampelune everything that belongs to me in the gardens and house that I rented at Beauséjour, such as the hermitage, the little Swiss house, the grottoes, fountains, culverts, the table service, etc.; plus the right to continue my lease on the house, which the preceding gifts may make more enjoyable and less costly. To my cousin Paulin Silbert, medical student in Paris, oldest son of my cousin Silbert, doctor in Sisteron, all my books and the pine bookcases that hold them, plus all the furniture in my library and bedroom . . . To

Mme. Empis (Rue Neuve des Mathurins) the clock that is in my office with the two landscapes by Dunoui on either side and the little desk of Brazilian rosewood just beneath. To the widow Lamalle my two silver candelabra with caryatids, which shall be restored to their original condition before being presented to her.

I bequeath to the Royal Academy of Medicine 1000 francs annual income at 5 percent to establish a triennial prize of 1000 crowns [3000 francs] to be awarded to the best book or memoir in clinical medicine or applied therapy, and so that the entries in this contest shall have stood the test of time they must without exception have been published at least two years prior. I bequeath to the same organization the ownership of my "Treatise on Diseases of the Ear and Hearing," which first edition has long been out of print, entrusting them to publish the second with the corrections and additions that may seem suitable to them; for this purpose a commission of members shall be named and they shall be remunerated by the royalties from the edition. To enable the commission to update several major chapters of this work with the improvements made to my instruments and apparatus, I bequeath to the academy the second set of instruments in my country home at Passy, Beauséjour, charging the commission, in order to better understand the use of these devices, to call before it two young doctors who have long served me as aides, Messrs. Berjaud and Rousset.

With all of the bequests distributed, all my remaining property shall be sold, as well as the remainder of my investments, to yield an amount which will probably exceed 40,000 francs including the remainder of my pension, to pay the following expenses and gratuities: (1) A gratuity of 2000 francs to my servant Joseph Millet; 1000 francs to Adèle my housekeeper, recently come to work for me; 1000 francs also to Josephine Doyen, who left because of poor health; leaving also to my servants a bed and bedding with two pairs of sheets; to Joseph, moreover, my servants' uniforms and to Charby all my wardrobe and my wood-and-metal-working tools. (2) The cost of a stone to cover my last resting place and indicate it to my friends (see the design attached); the cost of my procession which I wish to be quite modest; sickness expenses and honoraria generously paid to my colleagues. These expenses covered, I estimate that a rather substantial amount will remain which shall be divided into three parts, one for the welfare service of the twelfth arrondisement [now the fifth, in which the institute is located]; the second for the account of our institute to purchase tools for poor students who leave to practice a technical trade; and the third to be sent to the parish priest of Riez who will distribute it to the ten peasant day-laborers of the town with the largest families in proportion to the number of their children.

I desire my body be returned to the earth intact and unmutilated, being convinced that the ballooning research with cadavers is of little value for the art of healing and will not allow man to escape the sad circumstances of his existence, which are to suffer and to die.

I visited Itard's grave on All Saint's Day, when the French turn out to honor their dead. His plot lay in a section bedecked with flowers and crowded with visitors. Even though it was far in the background, the Montparnasse office building loomed higher than any of the cemetery trees. Some withered flowers lay on the stone, whose design time had almost effaced: an anchor and a cross, his name and the dates 1774–1838, and the inscription *médecin des sourds-muets.*

In the year before his death, 1837, Itard was consulted by the director of the children's hospital of Paris, Guersant: Would Itard accept one of the young idiots in the hospital for his program of demutization and language instruction? "If I were younger, I would undertake his care," Itard replied, "but send me someone suitable and I will direct his efforts." They spoke about young Séguin, then twenty-five years old, a student of Itard and Esquirol, whose father, also a physician, had worked with Itard in his early days at the military hospital, Val-de-Grâce. "If Séguin will accept," Itard concluded, "I will answer for the result." "When Guersant offered me the perilous honor of continuing the unfinished labor of Itard," Séguin wrote a decade later,

I was just recovering from an illness thought at one time to be mortal. However, the desire of sending my name to the ears of one whom I never expected to see again, gave me strength to attempt the enterprise. Itard communicated to me the details of what he had done with his first pupils, and I studied all that had been attempted or performed after him. Gall . . . had called up the question of the cause of idiocy; he thought he had discovered proof of his system of phrenology. The authors who succeeded him: Georget, Esquirol, Lelut, Foville, Calmeil, Leuret, Pritchard, seem to have studied idiocy only to use its phenomena for the destruction of Gall's system, but not for the benefit of the poor idiots, whom they declared incurable.

"Idiots are what they must remain for the rest of their lives,"

Esquirol had written in the authoritative *Dictionnaire des sciences médicales:*

Everything in them betrays a constitution that is imperfect, life-forces misapplied. They are incurable ... There is no way of giving them a larger amount of reason or intelligence, even for a few moments ... In idiocy we come to the final stage of human degradation: here the intellectual and moral faculties are devoid ... the physique of the idiot reflects this total privation of intelligence. Idiots are all debilitated, scrofulous, epileptic, stuporous. Their heads are too large or too small, improperly shaped, flattened on the sides or behind. The facial features are irregular; the forehead is short, narrow, almost pointed; there is a cast in one or both eyes, which move spasmodically; idiots have thick lips and saliva flows out of their half-open mouths; their gums are spongy and their teeth bad ... They are deaf or hard of hearing; they are mute, or articulate with difficulty; they see poorly or are blind. Their taste and smell function no better, for they do not perceive savory or fragrant substances; they eat whatever falls in their laps and reject foods only when they cannot gulp them down ... The sense of touch is no more reliable. The arms and hands of idiots are twisted, maimed, or immobile. They extend their arms and hands irresolutely, grasp bodies awkwardly, cannot hold onto them, and let them fall from their hands. They walk awkwardly and readily fall to the ground. There are those who remain wherever they are placed; others move spontaneously without any purpose and one cannot guess what they are up to.

Thus are the senses of idiots barely constituted. The sensations are weak, the understanding null. There is no sign of intelligence in the idiot because the tools of intelligence are defective. The sensations cannot guide one another since there is no way for training to compensate for so many disadvantages. Incapable of attention, idiots cannot focus their senses; they hear but do not listen; they see but do not observe, etc; deprived of memory, they cannot retain the impressions that may come to them from external objects; they compare nothing; they form no judgments; as a result, they desire nothing; as a further result, they have no need of signs that serve to express things and desires; they do not speak at all. Language is useless to him who does not think. Thus can we judge the degree of intelligence of idiots by their language. They emit a few poorly articulated sounds or cries, or prolonged moans that they interrupt to spread their lips as if they wanted to laugh. If they utter a few words, they attach no sense to them ... The reader certainly anticipates that I have nothing to say about the treatment of a disease which is essentially incurable. To a certain extent one can improve the lot of imbeciles by accustoming them early on to some labor which can provide income for the poor imbecile or distraction for the rich one. But idiots only require attentive and intensive domestic care.

And in the same year that Séguin began the training of the idiot referred by Guersant, the second edition of the Dictionary stated: "It is useless to combat idiocy. In order to establish intellectual activity, it would be necessary to change the conformation of organs which are beyond reach of all modification." Nevertheless Séguin consulted his teacher on the course he should follow: "The desire of knowing if mental medicine had no better remedies than [Itard's] for my first patients induced me to conduct them to Esquirol, to whom we went every week. Esquirol, the oracle of psychological medicine, had nothing to teach me; but he was a man of exquisite tact, and he gave me most excellent counsels upon the application of the processes I suggested to him. His approbation encouraged me in my efforts, while I was maturing in my mind the theory he never knew."

The nascent theory to which Séguin refers was based on the religious and philosophical socialism espoused by Henri Saint-Simon in his *Nouveau Christianisme*. In order to earn a living while beginning his experiments on the treatment of idiocy, Séguin wrote articles on political and economic questions and on art for the principal Paris newspapers. He became associated with a circle of renowned literary figures that included Victor Hugo, all of whom subscribed to the half-mystical, half-practical teachings of Saint-Simon and his successors, Père Enfantin and Olinde Rodrigues. The circle was committed to social reform, and their efforts included revisions in the criminal code and penal practices, civil agitation to improve the lot of the working classes, and work relief for the unemployed, "les misérables." Séguin heard the call and became the "Apostle of the Idiots": "I did not have to look about me very long to find a class of unfortunates . . . a class without standing, a category apart and yet one that has until lately been mixed in with convicts, and remains today confused with the insane and the epileptic; I mean the idiots." Saint-Simonism provided the living springs whence I drew the elements of my initiation into the mysteries of the laws of philosophical medicine. The bases of these laws are these: unity of God, manifested in his three principal attributes; unity of man in his three manifestations of being; the idiot, like other men, a likeness of God, infirm in the modes of expression of his trinity. First, infirm in his mobility and sensibility [in motor and sensory processes]; second, infirm in his perception and his reasoning; third, infirm in his affection and will.

In order to remedy these infirmities, Séguin would apply the methods of Itard, "who was the first, by the education of the savage of Aveyron, to clear the path which I alone took after him."

The idea of Itard came to its most comprehensive realization under trying circumstances. The philosophical school to which he belonged in 1800 had gone to rest before him. In 1830–1840 three schools were disputing the ruling of this century: Divine Rights . . . the Eclectic school, and the Christian school (Saint-Simonism), striving for a social application of the principles of the gospel, for the most rapid elevation of the lowest and poorest by all means and institutions, mostly by free education. The idea of Itard being congenial only to this last school, was nursed in it [and therein] experienced its natural growth and transformation; becoming from individual, social; from proportionate to the relief of special cases, commensurate with the wants of many idiots; and from adapted to this class of sufferers, competent to do the training of mankind.

Itard's last pupil and Séguin's first made considerable progress under their joint tutelage, which Séguin described in his "Summary of What We Have Done for Fourteen Months." Esquirol lent his name to this publication as he did to an affidavit (1839) testifying to the effectiveness of Séguin's methods:

We the undersigned are pleased to affirm that M. Edouard Séguin, born at Clamecy (Nièvre) has begun, with the greatest success, the education of a child almost mute and apparently an idiot—by reason of the limited development of his intellectual and moral faculties. In eighteen months, M. Séguin has taught his pupil to make use of his senses, to remember, to compare, to speak, to write, to count, etc. This training was conducted by M. Séguin following the method of the late Dr. Itard, from whom he received his inspiration. From the character of his mind and the extent of his knowledge, M. Edouard Séguin is capable of giving this system of education all desirable extension.

The same year, Séguin opened a school for idiots, the first ever to be founded. Although Séguin did not know it, the first institutional training of the retarded had begun twenty years earlier, when the American Asylum began to admit a few mute retarded children in company with its deaf pupils. The methods employed originated with Itard's superior, Sicard. Séguin's school for the retarded was remarkably successful and attracted educators from many lands. In a few years, schools for idiots based on Séguin's methods were established in England and several countries on the Continent. The minister of the interior invited Séguin in 1841 to prove his methods on idiot children committed to the asylum for incurables, La Salpêtrière, and a commission was appointed to evaluate the results. The minutes of the meeting of the general council of hospitals on October 12, 1842, report the outcome:

the method of M. Séguin, applied to retarded or almost nonexistent intellects, succeeded in inculcating in these children principles of order, of regularity, of obedience, of discipline, work habits, knowledge of reading, writing, and arithmetic . . . The exercises in which the children engaged have been particularly effective: gymnastics and manual tasks have improved their health and intellectual training has developed faculties that were inactive and limited but nevertheless susceptible to notable improvement. It is consequently desirable to continue this endeavor and to extend it to the greatest possible number of children deprived of reason. M. Séguin could advantageously be charged with applying his method to the numerous idiot children at the Bicêtre Hospital . . . This new trial, carried out for one year, would enable a definite appreciation of the procedures employed by M. Séguin . . . The council has decided: (1) M. Séguin is invited to extend the tryout of his method of education, which he has applied up until now to idiots at the hospital for incurables, to the young idiots at the hospital for the aged [Bicêtre] until the end of 1843; (2) the director of the hospital and the doctors of the insane are charged with following the progress of this education and the effects of the method employed by M. Séguin . . .

The lessons he published in "Theory and Practice of the Education of Idiots" Séguin had given to ten pupils; in the new program he had ninety to contend with. He had this to say about his initial success:

> Whatever interest [the council] has been kind enough to express in my pupils, they cannot make a hospital into a school, they cannot prevent the contact with epileptics from depraving the idiots,* they cannot give me all the wherewithal for instruction and all the necessary freedom of action. If, under conditions as unfavorable as these, I have already been of some service; if my method, truncated as it was by all that the location and the circumstances made impossible, has already produced useful results, then what may I not expect from the hope I have been given of applying the method under more advantageous conditions?

Séguin was given a school at Bicêtre, an assistant, and some supplies. He put into operation a program of physical, intellectual, and moral training that he described in a memoir published in 1843 entitled "The Hygiene and Education of Idiots." A commission of the Royal Academy of Sciences evaluated the program in these terms:

> M. Séguin has in great part surmounted the extreme difficulties [encountered in the education of idiots]. Varied gymnastics have made his pupils stronger and more coordinated. Aided by sensory training, their movements are more accurate and precise. Further, the idiots have learned to subordinate their movements to their minds, which they themselves would never have thought of doing. By methods of teaching which are peculiarly his own ... he has initiated his pupils into a knowledge of letters, of reading, of writing, of drawing, and of elementary arithmetic and geometry. Through the comparison of the different qualities of bodies he has familiarized them with the abstract ideas of form, color, density, weight, and so on ... and with ideas of relations of a higher order, and those ideas which are the highest that the intelligence is able to acquire, for example, ideas of order, authority, obedience, and duty. Also, by applying his pupils to labors of body and mind, he has rendered them wiser and more robust. He has caused a happy change in their ruinous personal habits, and probably will cause the idiots to forget those habits in time, for, with a fixed amount of energy, the more work a person is given, the more it relieves him of bad thoughts. M. Séguin has thus opened up a new career of beneficence. He has given to hygiene, medicine and moral philosophy an example most worthy to be followed.

The Wild Boy of Aveyron   266

In 1846 Séguin published the second of three major works describing his method, *Traitement moral, hygiène et education des idiots*. It quickly became the standard textbook on the training of the retarded and secured its author's international renown. Séguin devoted his efforts at this time to a private school that he opened on Rue Pigalle, having left Bicêtre because of difficulties with the authorities. He supplemented his income by writing and accepted a commission from two fellow Saint-Simonists, Isaac and Eugène Pereire, to write a volume on their grandfather's life and work. It was in this period that George Sumner came to Paris to study Séguin's methods in order to assist Samuel Howe in his plan for establishing a state school for idiots in Massachusetts. Sumner visited the school on Rue Pigalle and studied the training program at Bicêtre, which continued to employ Séguin's methods under the direction of a physician, Félix Voisin, and Séguin's assistant, Vallée. "During the past six months, I have watched . . . nearly one hundred fellow beings," Sumner wrote to Howe in February 1847,

> who were objects of loathing and disgust—many of whom rejected every article of clothing,—others of whom, unable to stand erect, crouched themselves in corners, and gave signs of life only by piteous howls,—others, in whom the faculty of speech had never been developed, —and many, whose voracious and indiscriminate gluttony satisfied itself with whatever they could lay hands upon . . . these . . . I have seen properly clad, standing erect, walking, speaking, eating in an orderly manner at a common table, working quietly as carpenters and farmers, gaining, by their own labor, the means of existence, storing their awakened intelligence by reading one to another; exercising, toward their teachers and among themselves, the generous feelings of man's nature, and singing in unison songs of thanksgiving.

As an immediate result of this account and the complete report which Howe prepared on the conditions and treatment of some 500 idiots in private families and almshouses in Massachusetts, the state legislature appropriated $2500 annually, for three years, to establish an experimental school. James Richards was engaged as its principal and sent to Paris to learn Séguin's methods.

Séguin was too deeply committed on political and social questions not to become involved in the revolutionary upheaval the following year, 1848. Once Charles Louis Napoleon became President of the new Republic, in 1851, he turned on his former allies, assuming the imperial title of Napoleon III a year later. Fearing for his freedom, Séguin emigrated with his wife and child to the United States, where they had friends made on previous visits, and where his work and recent book were well known. The program he had inspired was in progress in Boston; when it was installed in its own quarters as the State School for Idiotic Children (now the Fernald School in Waltham), Séguin organized the classes and introduced his method of training. He also collaborated with Harvey Wilbur whose training program at the Institution for Feeble-minded Youth in Barre, Massachusetts, was patterned after Séguin's at Bicêtre. When Wilbur created an experimental school at Albany, later established permanently at Syracuse, Séguin came to consult and teach. He also assisted James Richards in establishing the Pennsylvania Training School, which he directed for a short time. In 1861 he finished the formal medical training he had begun in France and received an M.D. from the University of the City of New York. He took up practice in the city but often visited Wilbur in Syracuse, where he wrote his third major work, *Idiocy and Its Treatment by the Physiological Method.* In his later years, Séguin conducted research on body temperature; performed an extended investigation of facilities for special and general education in the United States and abroad*; helped to found and served as the first president of an association of superintendents of schools for the retarded, now the American Association on Mental Deficiency; organized a program and trained teachers in the Idiot House of Randall's Island; and published several articles and monographs on the treatment of idiocy. His last major activity was to found, with his second wife, the Séguin Physiological School for Feeble-minded Children, in New York City (later the Séguin School in Orange, New Jersey). The school was just proving a success when he died in 1880. His career started by training one idiot in collaboration with Itard; it ended by influencing—even within his own lifetime—thousands upon thousands of handicapped children throughout Europe and America.

The only medical resources that Séguin could draw on in formulating his program for the training of idiots were the results of Itard's experiments and the various classificatory studies that originated with Pinel. The latter were useless, he complained. The word "observation," shibboleth of *Idéologie*, lost all medical significance when doctors described idiocy "without having followed up this sort of portrait with the recommendation of any treatment, of any improvement obtained by a succession of means attributed to therapy or to moral medicine." "It is necessary to go farther back," Séguin wrote in *Hygiène et education des idiots*, "to find the scientific traces of this work. It is in the Memoirs on the education of the Wild Boy of Aveyron that Dr. Itard set down the true and the only seeds of positive education." Séguin adopted Itard's fundamental approach to education, in which the student is the subject of a kind of medical case study, involving both diagnosis and prescription. He also perpetuated Itard's initiative in education by embracing his teaching techniques in many phases of his program for training the retarded. Séguin's program begins by transforming the living conditions of his pupils, just as Itard did for Victor, applying the precepts of "mental medicine." A favorable environment is arranged, with attention to hygiene, food, clothing, and contact with the out-of-doors. A treatment regimen is established for each student based on a medical profile which gives "a description of his physique and his physiological and psychological state."

The first stage in training is concerned with developing motor control. Séguin found "disorders of coordinated movement . . . among the physiological constants of idiocy." This problem did not confront Itard: Victor could run, climb, leap, and execute skilled movements with his hands. Although Itard had no lessons to offer in this case, his disciple did have the analytical strategy inspired by Condillac; Séguin decomposed complex performances into their motor components and trained these in increasing order of complexity. To develop walking, there were calisthenics with leg flexion and extension followed by exercises on specially modified swings, staircases, and ladders. Climbing a ladder and hanging from its rungs was doubly valuable, for the pupils also learned habits of grasping and manual coordination in which they were particularly deficient. At first, the teacher prompts the pupil's movements by climbing the ladder on the opposite face and, holding the child's fingers against the bars, encourages him to release his foothold. On successive trials the teacher lightens his grasp and the child learns to suspend his own weight. To train more fine manual movements, preparing the child for certain work skills, Séguin took a page from Itard's book and adopted or had built numerous instructional devices: blocks shaped like dominoes were used for superposing and combining; geometric figures were fit into slots of the same dimensions; a nailboard was pierced with holes into which the child fixed and removed nails. Pupils also learned to pick up objects such as beads and pins, to pull ropes and wind up cords, to button and unbutton, lace and unlace, and manipulate bricks, stones, wheelbarrows, dumbbells, files, and so on.

When the superintendent of an insane asylum for the northern counties of England visited Bicêtre in 1847, he was nonplussed at the dexterity of Séguin's pupils:

Three [students] were seated at a small table, partaking of excellent soup. They sat in an orderly and decorous manner, and took their food without scattering it or smearing the person—a circumstance nearly always observable in the neglected idiot. At the request of the intern, who kindly accompanied me, the youngest of the three rose from his seat, and repeated one of Lamartine's fables very distinctly, and with much spirit. During this recitation the others ceased to eat, and appeared to listen with pleasure to the display made by their young friend. Conceiving that this child manifested a precocity and irregularity rather than a deficiency of intellect, I intimated my wish that his cap should be removed, so that I could have the opportunity of examining the shape of his head. He immediately made the attempt to comply, but finding that the strings had become knotted under his chin, he showed some signs of impatience at the obstruction. One of the idiots, seeing his difficulty, rose from his seat, and rendered him the necessary assistance, by carefully untying the knot. I remarked that this youth, who thus noticed the dilemma of his companion, and then immediately relieved him, had all the characteristic appearance of a genuine idiot. I could not observe this simple occurrence without becoming at once sensible that much had been done for these poor creatures, who, born with an imperfect mental organization, have been made capable of exercising the faculties of observation, comprehension, and a power of application, which, a few years ago, it would have been thought impossible to communicate to them.

Itard's legacy to Séguin is nowhere more evident than in the second stage of retardate training, sensory education, which was of course the focus of Itard's education of the wild boy according to the precepts of Condillac. Nevertheless, Séguin arranged the senses in quite a different order. Following Pereire, he considered touch the most fundamental modality, of which all the others were modifications. "The first sense to operate is touch . . . the second is sight (an active sense in the service of the intellect) . . . the third is hearing . . . it is not until much later that taste and smell distinguish . . . flavors and odors. I did not arrange this order that I assign to the awakening of the senses to please myself; I have observed it in young subjects, whether normal or idiotic." His eyes blindfolded, the child receives skin sensations that diminish in contrast; for example, his hand is plunged alternately in hot and cold water, then in warm and cool, then in intermediate temperatures. Similarly, the pupil learns to appreciate contrasts such as light and heavy, rigid and elastic, rough and smooth, large and small, long and short. The sense of hearing is trained in turn. "The sounds, objects of our present studies, are noises, music, and speech. These three classes of sounds speak, respectively, the noises to the wants, the music to the motive powers, the speech to the intellect." Séguin recalls Victor's case: he could hear a nut crack but not a pistol discharge because only the former spoke to his wants. The recognition and differentiation of noises is carried out in silence and isolation. Like Itard before him, Séguin employed a drum and a series of bells that could be struck with a hammer. Music has an important role in the training of idiots first because of its emotional power and second because there is a natural transition from music to speech. As a part of musical training the children learn to accompany the piano by intoning vowels; after articulation training, consonants may be added to these syllables.
Our English visitor describes what these lessons were like:

Forty idiots . . . the majority of them twelve to fourteen years of age . . . were gathered. There were no indications of impatience, no involuntary

271   Itard's Legacies

movements, gesticulations, nor any of those disagreeable moaning whining sounds known to be common among this class of persons. All seemed attentive, and ready to enter upon their exercises . . . I recognized a few with all the characteristics of [congenital idiots] in a marked degree, and most of the others presented similar indications, such as stunted growth, small and peculiarly-shaped head, and singular form and vacant expression of countenance . . .

At the request of [M. Vallée], two of the younger boys advanced from the line in which they were arranged, and stood forward towards the center of the room. Each placed his arm over the shoulder of the other without any degree of awkwardness or unsteadiness, and they remained thus for a short time, standing in an easy and graceful posture. At the sound of excellent music, played on several instruments by three or four old men, they began to dance; first performing a slow movement, and afterwards a quicker step. During the whole dance, each rested his arm embracingly on the shoulder of the other; and it was pleasing to observe the grace and uniformity of their various movements, as well as the accurate time kept by both to the music. They ceased the instant the performers ceased to play, and then retired to the places from which they had advanced. During this time the others remained standing in the same order as at first; there were no signs of restlessness, and many even seemed to regard the dancers with attention and pleasure, whilst only a few retained that vacant expression peculiar to their class . . .

After the completion of this dance, the whole of the boys were desired to sing one of the songs which had been composed for them. It was a very simple air—such as those sung by the classes of Hullah in our own country—and the words were well suited to their feeble comprehension . . . The words were distinctly pronounced . . . the melody was sung with full force, but not over-loud; the time was well-kept; the pauses between each verse distinct; and, as far as I could judge, the tune appeared correct. In short, the whole piece was executed in a style quite equal, if not superior, to what we are in the habit of observing in the junior singing classes of Great Britain.

Séguin devoted even greater attention to visual training. Where there is little control of eye movement, fixation may be trained by placing the pupil in a dark room and projecting a sketch of a favored toy or object on the wall. Little by little, the spot may be displaced on the wall and the child will learn to follow it visually. A game of catch is also an effective means for training this skill. Once the pupil can fixate, he is ready to learn discriminations of color and form. Here Séguin applied many of Itard's techniques and instructional materials, as this passage from his 1843 book makes plain:

> This question stopped us, M. Itard and me, for a considerable time. Lines having been mastered, it was necessary to make the child copy regular figures, beginning, needless to say, with the simplest. In accord with accepted opinion, M. Itard had advised me to begin with the square; I followed that suggestion for three months without succeeding in making myself understood. No direction was exact enough to induce our pupil to bring his second pair of parallel lines to the extremities of the first pair; in vain I marked with my finger the point of intersection of the two lines, pasted a wafer there, used crayons of all colors; four hours a day were consumed in vain at that exercise.

All the hallmarks of Itard's technique are found here: the larger problem is posed and a simple component is set as the first objective; an avenue of approach is taken, and a way sought to prompt the correct response; an impasse occurs and the teacher backtracks. In this case, Séguin revised the assumption that the square was the simplest figure and set his pupil the task of drawing a triangle, which he learned rapidly. Séguin also had his pupils engage in matching-to-sample with patches of color and forms. On the model of Itard's cardboard cutouts, he designed form boards, wooden planks from which circles, squares, and the like had been cut out. These exercises prepared his pupils, as they had Victor, for letter discrimination, which was trained with the aid of metal letter cutouts that were sorted into a chest with twenty-five labeled bins.

We have an eyewitness account of some of the sensorimotor exercises from the same English observer.

> Several pieces of wood, cut in the shape of different geometrical figures, were now brought into the room. These were placed in the hands of different pupils, who named with much readiness the various forms—as round, square, oval, oblong, etc. In order to exercise the sense of touch without the aid of sight, a bandage was placed over the eyes of one or two, and the different pieces were put into their hands; each of them slowly passed his fingers along the edges, and when satisfied with the examination, named the form of the respective portions. In doing this, no error was committed . . .

A large black board was now brought forward and placed on a rest. One or two of the more proficient were desired by M. Vallée to draw upon it first a horizontal, then a perpendicular line, and afterwards to describe a circle, square, and hexagon. Words also were well and readily written in a good round legible hand. The same feebleness and uncertainty of grasp, arising from an imperfect power over the fingers, was again observable, but the writing was fairly executed, and the figures correctly described. They were slowly done, it is true, but still they were well done.

Séguin's speech training proceeded from the sensory training. He used music to develop voice control with vowel sounds, and introduced consonants with the aid of vision and touch, as Periere and Itard had done before him. In these exercises, as in motor training of the legs and hands, Séguin relied heavily on Itard's technique of generalized imitation:

> At the first lesson appointed for the beginning of articulation, the child is made to resume his morning and evening exercises of imitation . . . the movements are mostly concentrated in the hands, the hands brought about the face, the fingers put in and about the mouth. All the parts of the face are moved in correlation with the fingers . . . the mimicry . . . giving the child an analytical survey by the touch, the sight, and the movement of the various parts involved in the act of speech, from without inwards . . . After this, all the organs of speech, the tongue, the lips, and so on, are moved freely in all directions and in every manner; and once, as if by choice, in the middle of the mute, mimical exercises, the lips being well closed, we part them by thrusting out an emission of voice which pronounces *ma* or *pa*.

After the bilabials, less visible constrictions, such as *t* and *k*, are taught, and special attention is given to consonants the child has difficulty in articulating because of some oral or facial deformity. Finally, consonants and vowels are joined in various syllable structures.

Once sensorimotor training is largely completed, Séguin begins the second phase of his three-term program, development of the intellectual functions. Further training in oral and written language introduced this phase. The child learns to copy increasingly complex line drawings, then to discriminate letters by means of matching-to-sample, using a sort of compositor's chest like the one Itard had developed. Next the child is taught the names of everyday objects by placing lettered labels on them, and finally he learns to copy these labels and to read them aloud. All of the steps in this procedure except the reading aloud would have been quite familiar to Victor or, indeed, to Massieu.

Here is what the visitor from England saw:

> The attention of the pupils assembled round a table was now directed to a large sheet of paper, on which was painted every variety of colour. These tints were disposed in a confused manner, so as to prevent the liability which otherwise might arise of mere rote work, or the utterance, from habit, of consecutive words without comprehending their meaning. In this, as in all the other educational arrangements, the attention of the pupil was first directed to the simple and the more striking parts. On this occasion, consequently, the primitive colours were first named, and last the more compound, between which the shades of distinction are less marked. The perfection to which the sense of sight was brought in the power of discriminating nice differences of colour, and of some of the pupils—remembering the uttering of their respective names—was truly surprising.
>
> Several examinations in the names of objects were now undertaken, such as the various articles of dress and pieces of furniture. Following these, the number of days in the week and months in the year were given; then the names of each day and month, as well as the seasons of the year. The replies to these questions relating to names of objects and periods of time were quickly and readily given; and had I not already witnessed so many evidences of the excellent system of training of which these poor fellows have had the advantage, I should have been inclined to doubt whether a proper comprehension of their meaning was attached to the several words they uttered. I had, however, sufficient reason to believe that, to a limited extent at least, they understood what was meant when they gave answers to the questions proposed.

Séguin was highly critical of Itard for failing to train intellectual faculties, for adhering to Condillac's sensualist philosophy; he even states that "the basis of his method and mine are diametrically opposed"; yet he has no specific strategy for developing intelligence. "We can, up to a certain point, oblige the senses to perceive a notion, since the senses are susceptible to environmental control, whereas we do not know how to oblige reasoning to function." In practice, Séguin resorted to two courses of action. First, though employing Itard's exercises for discrimination and concept learning, he put greater emphasis on the student's active involvement and manipulation of objects during training; thus work skills are seen as a part of the student's intellectual and social development. Second, Séguin had recourse to traditional "subject matter" instruction. Number skills are taught with objects and their qualities, and then figures are introduced. The children learn to make purchases with coins. Sentence comprehension is taught beginning with the everyday names the pupil had previously learned and combining them with a few verbs that the child (like Victor) must act out. Adjectives were taught during the study of object qualities; adverbs can now be taught in like fashion. Séguin found the substitution of pronouns for nouns relatively easy to master, as were interjections.

The third facet of Séguin's program, moral education, was implicit in the physical and intellectual training that he provided. Similarly Itard was, for the most part, content to point out this relationship and to look for signs of affection, gratitude, a sense of justice, and so on, in Victor. Séguin was more actively concerned with teaching relationships to other individuals. His goal was to lead the child from his first unwilling movements to independent decisionmaking in a social context. According to Séguin, there are four sorts of will: instinctual, concerned with satisfying the appetites; negative, devoted to maintaining inaction and refusing what is unpleasurable; intellectual, which brings thought to bear on some task; and moral, which guides the individual in his social relationships. The idiot lacks the two higher degrees of will, and the educator's first task is to overcome the two lower forms. To teach obedience, Séguin anticipated a technique explored in recent psychological research: he would command the pupil to carry out actions that he was about to carry out in any event. "To command immediately . . . means to employ the forms of command which can directly touch the child, and take an anticipated direction of his contingent doings." By executing such commands the child learns to obey orders that compete with rather than conform to the responses he is disposed to make. Gradually Séguin withdraws his personal control of the pupil by shifting it to other sources, such as the child's peers. Unlike Itard, Séguin used the group as well as individualized instruction to train motor skills, speech, and social behavior, thus capitalizing on "the invaluable advantages of imitation and rivalry." In collective work such as gardening, the child's activities are no longer directed by his teacher but by natural circumstances and collaboration with fellow pupils.

Our 1847 eyewitness reports:

The first workroom we entered was that of the carpenters. There were in it fifteen idiots, superintended by two journeymen, who both instructed and encouraged them by working with spirit and activity. Although a short time only had elapsed since we quitted the schoolroom, yet some of the youths were already employed, others were looking up their tools or adjusting their aprons preparatory to beginning their work. Near the door stood one who, when I first saw him, struck me as a most deplorable hopeless object, and I accordingly singled him out for especial observation. He began his work by taking up a piece of wood which it was his business to plane. After looking at it a moment or two, he placed it in a vice, screwed it firmly, and commenced turning off the shavings in a workmanlike manner. As if conscious of his merit, he every now and then paused, looked up, and seemed pleased with his own proficiency, and encouraged by the approval awarded to him by his superiors.

This youth is sixteen years of age, and has been in the Bicêtre rather more than three years. When first admitted, he manifested all the characteristics of an inferior animal. His appetite was voracious, and he would devour the most disgusting things. He exhibited, indeed, some traces of a love of approbation, together with signs of an instinctive gaiety, born, as it were, within, and not created by surrounding objects; but he had all the sensuality of a brute, and a vicious propensity to tear and destroy whatever came within his reach. He was, moreover, passionate in the extreme, attacking and biting every one who offered the least opposition to his inordinate and disgusting propensities. Among these was a very singular one—namely, a strong impulse to poke out the eyes of all who came within his reach . . . The voluntary power over his muscles was very imperfect, and he could neither walk nor run properly; he would, however, sometimes spring forward like a wild animal, and at other times he would suddenly start off from his companions, making at the same time a shrill unmeaning cry.

This being, who in 1843 had been in so strange and apparently hopeless a condition, could now read, write, sing, and calculate. I had already noticed in him several manifestations of attachment, and other moral qualities. I now saw him happily engaged, making good use of implements with which, if placed in his hands a few years ago, he would doubtless have inflicted serious injury.

On looking around the room, nearly all the youths were seen to be engaged in sawing, planing, filing, and joining together pieces of wood . . . I was struck with the apparent steadiness of hand with which the various tools were grasped and used, as well as with the judgment which was evidently exercised during the performance of the work . . .

In the [next] department were no less than twelve idiots, who had been instructed in the art of shoemaking. They were superintended by one foreman, who cut out and fixed the work for them. Each little fellow was seated at a separate stall, and beside him were laid the various implements required in his trade. The whole of the boys were working away very busily, boring with the awl, stitching, hammering, and smoothing down in remarkably brisk and workmanlike manner.

The remainder of the youths—those who are not instructed in any handicraft—are employed in agricultural operations . . . The pupils . . . collected their spades in the implement-room, and proceeded in an orderly manner under the care and direction of a farm-labourer . . . A number of husbandmen are engaged to instruct, superintend, and work with the boys; each man having a certain number placed under his charge. He is provided with a list of their names, and before setting out, he calls over the roll, each pupil answering to his name, and stepping forward at the same time with his spade in his hand. Before setting out, they arrange themselves on command in rank and file, shoulder their long, small spades, and march away in military order. On these minor arrangements depends no doubt much of the excellence of the system, both in preserving order, keeping alive attention, and the prevention of the waywardness peculiar to idiots . . .

As no notice had been given of my intention to inspect the institution, I have every reason to believe that what I witnessed was nothing more than the ordinary daily routine.

Séguin stated in 1866 that, in his hands, Itard's program of education was now equal to the task of training large numbers of retarded children and, with adaptation, "competent for the training of mankind." Still it was not until the last year of his life that he published a review of the physiological method in which he spelled out its application to the education of all children, not just the retarded. As it turned out, this wider application of Itard's techniques had to await the turn of the century and the work of Maria Montessori. In her book "The Method of Scientific Pedagogy Applied to Childhood Education,"* which appeared in English translation as *The Montessori Method* in 1912, Montessori acknowledges her great debt to Itard and credits him with founding the education of the mentally deficient. The facts on Victor are a little scrambled, however:

> Itard was the first to attempt a methodical education of the sense of hearing. He made these experiments in the institute for deaf-mutes . . . Later on, having in charge for eight years the idiot boy known as the "wild boy of Aveyron," he extended to the treatment of all the senses those educational methods which had already given such excellent results in the treatment of the sense of hearing. A student of Pinel, Itard was the first educator to practice the observation of the pupil in the way in which the sick are observed in the hospitals, especially those suffering from diseases of the nervous system . . . The pedagogic writings of Itard are most interesting and minute descriptions of educational efforts and experiences, and anyone reading them today must admit that they were practically the first attempts at experimental psychology . . . But the merit of having completed a genuine educational system for deficient children was due to Edward Séguin, first a teacher and then a physician. He took the experiments of Itard as his starting point, applying these methods, modifying and completing them during a period of ten years' experience with children taken from the insane asylums and placed in a little school in the Rue Pigalle in Paris . . . About fifteen years ago . .
> I became interested in idiot children. It was thus . . . that I became conversant with the special method of education devised for these unhappy little ones by Séguin . . . In his *Idiocy and its Treatment by the Physiological Method* . . . Séguin had carefully defined his method of education, calling it the physiological method. He no longer referred in the title to a method for the education of idiots as if the method were special to them . . .

Itard's and Séguin's writings first came to Montessori's attention soon after she graduated from medical school, the first woman in Italy ever to receive a medical degree. Assigned to the psychiatric clinic of the University of Rome, she frequently visited the city's asylums where she found idiot children grouped indiscriminately with the insane. Séguin's 1846 book confirmed her belief "that mental deficiency presented chiefly a pedagogical rather than mainly a medical problem," which she argued persuasively at a pedagogical congress in 1898. As a result, the minister of education commissioned her to give a series of lectures to the teachers of Rome on the education of the mentally handicapped. The course was soon institutionalized as the Normal School of Orthophrenics, and a class of retarded children was annexed to it for Montessori's educational experiments and teacher training. During the two years that she directed this school, from 1898 to 1900, she visited both London and Paris and spent several weeks observing Séguin's program of education in operation at Bicêtre.

> After study of the methods in use throughout Europe, I concluded my experiments upon the deficients of Rome, and taught them through two years. I followed Séguin's book and also derived much help from the remarkable experiments of Itard. Guided by the works of these two men, I manufactured a great deal of didactic material . . . I myself obtained most surprising results through their application . . . Having through actual experience justified my faith in Séguin's method, I withdrew from active work among deficients and began a more thorough study of the works of Itard and Séguin . . . I translated and copied out with my own hand the writings of these men, from beginning to end . . . I chose to do this by hand in order that I might have the time to weigh the sense of each word and to read, in truth, the spirit of the author. I had just finished copying the 600 pages of Séguin's [1846] French volume when I received from New York a copy of the English book published in 1866. The old volume had been found among the books discarded from the private library of a New York physician. I translated it with the help of an English friend. This volume did not add much in the way of new pedagogical experiments but dealt with the philosophy of the experiments described in the first volume. The man who had studied abnormal children for thirty years expressed the idea that the physiological method, which has as its base the individual study of the pupil and which forms its educative methods upon the analysis of physiological and psychological phenomena, must come also to be applied to normal children. This step he believed would show the way to a complete human regeneration. The voice of Séguin seemed to be like the voice of a forerunner crying in the wilderness, and my thoughts were filled with the immensity and importance of a work which should be able to reform the school and education.

The Wild Boy of Aveyron   280

To reinforce her background in pedagogy, Montessori enrolled in the university as a student of philosophy and pursued studies in psychology and anthropology. Then, in 1906, chance gave her the opportunity to apply her methods and studies to the education of normal children. The Roman Association for Good Construction, then planning a number of low-income housing projects, equipped each with a special classroom for educating preschool children. Montessori was asked to organize these "in-house schools," and thus the first Casa dei Bambini was founded, opening in January 1907. Four more were created within a year. The program that Montessori put into practice in these children's houses was based on the parallels she saw between the deficient child, whose development is arrested, and the as yet undeveloped normal child. The latter has not yet acquired muscular coordination and thus lacks many motor and manual skills. His sensory discriminations are not completely developed. His language is primitive. Like the retarded child, he has a brief span of attention.

> Here lies the significance of my pedagogical experiment in the Children's Houses. It represents the result of a series of trials made by me, in the education of young children, with methods already used with deficients. My work has not been made in any way an application, pure and simple, of the methods of Séguin to young children, as anyone who will consult the works of the author will readily see. But it is nonetheless true that, underlying these two years of trial, there is a basis of experiment which goes back to the days of the French Revolution, and which represents the earnest work of the lives of Itard and Séguin. As for me, thirty years after the publication of Séguin's second book, I took up again the ideas and, I may even say, the work of this great man, with the same freshness of spirit with which he received the inheritance of the work and ideas of his master Itard. For ten years I not only made practical experiments according to their methods, but through reverent meditation absorbed the works of those noble and consecrated men, who have left to humanity most vital proof of their obscure heroism.

Maria Montessori directed the children's houses for about four years as knowledge of her method spread throughout Italy and then to Europe and America. In 1909 she gave a series of courses and organized a model school to train teachers coming from all over Europe. The same year the Swiss opened their first children's house, and soon after a national Montessori committee was organized and sponsored courses for students of more than a dozen different nationalities. In 1911, she undertook to revise her materials, until then applied to children aged three through seven, for use in elementary schools, and after some experimentation a second major book appeared, in Italian, "Auto-Education in the Elementary School." A Montessori society was founded in London the following year, and soon Montessori schools opened in England, as well as Italy, Switzerland, Spain, and Holland, fostered by the founder's occasional visits and lectures, and by a spate of articles in popular magazines and the educational literature. Just at the outbreak of World War I, Montessori traveled to America, where she gave courses on her method and organized a demonstration class at the San Francisco Exposition. The period after the war saw the worldwide dissemination of her method; according to the International Montessori Society, twenty-three countries had national societies in 1940. Specialized periodicals appeared notably in Italian, French, English, and Dutch, indicating the countries in which her influence has probably been the greatest. Montessori's subsequent books, which largely expanded on applications of the basic program set forth for preschools in 1909 and elementary schools in 1916, were translated into some eighteen languages. As Mussolini's regime took hold, Montessori went to live in Spain where she remained until the civil war, when the British sent a boat to bring her to England. After a stay in London and then in Amsterdam, she left for Asia, passing the period of World War II in China and India. With the end of the war, Montessori became active again in the national societies that bore her name and in the UNESCO programs devoted to children. She died in Holland in May 1952.

The Montessori method is guided by perhaps a half-dozen major principles of education. The first affirms the biological programming of child development, the child's capacity for self-realization, for "auto-education." The second calls for "scientific pedagogy," a science of childhood based on observation. The third demands a natural environment in which self-development can be expressed and observed. Montessori believed that the school could be made into such an environment, thus becoming a laboratory for scientific pedagogy. This environment should be determined scientifically. "In order to expand, the child, left at liberty to exercise his activities, ought to find in his surroundings something organized in direct relation to his internal organization." All of these principles imply the next, which Montessori calls the "biological concept of liberty in pedagogy": the child must be free to act spontaneously and to interact with the prepared environment. The entire program is concerned with the individual child; the spontaneity, the needs, the observation, the freedom are always those of the individual. Finally, the modus operandi of the method is sensory training.

Reviewing these six principles of the Montessori method, it becomes clear how much it echoes Itard's. It was Itard who first broke with traditional subject-matter instruction and implemented the education of the individual child through interaction with a carefully prepared environment. It was Itard who first called for a scientific pedagogy based on philosophy and medicine, employing the technique of observation with which *Idéologie* had endowed these two disciplines. It was Itard who spent long hours watching for the spontaneous expressions of his pupil in nature as in society, and he who, following the precepts of mental medicine, tailored the child's environment to accommodate and shape his needs. And it was Itard who took Condillac's model of the development of the intellect and first created a program of sensory education.

In practice as in theory, Montessori's methods are, to a large extent, elaborations of those employed with Victor. The greater part of her program is concerned with education of the senses, and most of her considerable array of didactic materials is devoted to this purpose. There are twenty-six sets of apparatus which provide for training all the senses except taste and smell. Many of the devices are based on those originated by Séguin; others come from Itard, such as the drum and bell employed for training hearing or the geometric cutouts for vision. In every case, Itard's method of dwindling contrasts is employed. The program designed to enhance muscular coordination of the limbs and the devices for training manual skills owe much to Séguin. Montessori credits Itard with showing how perceptions and language can be associated, and she quotes at length from his description of these experiments with Victor. In her own method, she follows Séguin's modification of this technique:

First Period.—The association of the sensory perception with the name. For example, we present to the child two colours, red and blue. Presenting the red, we say simply, 'This is red,' and presenting the blue, 'This is blue.' Then, we lay the spools upon the table under the eyes of the child. Second Period.—Recognition of the object corresponding to the name. We say to the child, 'Give me the red' and then, 'Give me the blue.' Third Period.—The remembering of the name corresponding to the object. We ask the child, showing him the object, 'What is this?' and he should respond, 'Red.' Séguin insists strongly upon these three periods and urges that the colours be left for several instants under the eyes of the child. He also advises us never to present the colours singly, but always two at a time, since the contrast helps the chromatic memory.

In teaching writing and reading, Montessori begins by training manual movements, then sets the children to tracing letter cutouts. Lessons based on Séguin's "three periods" help the child to associate the sound of the letters with their sight and feel. Letters are presented singly and also grouped by contrasting or analogous forms. Next the child is presented with a box with four copies of the alphabet arranged in the compartments. The teacher utters a word such as "mama," and the child must select the corresponding letters. When he has laid these out on the table, with more or less prompting, he is urged to say the word aloud, the teacher providing the model. Other words are taught similarly with increasing ease. After each word is composed and spoken, its letters are replaced in the marked compartments. Montessori found that the pupil who has been taught to draw letters and to assemble words from letter cutouts will spontaneously write the first simple words he has learned to assemble and utter. With a child of four this may come about within a month. Reading proper is taught after writing has developed. At first, well-known words that the children have often spoken are written in large script, and the objects they designate are placed nearby. The child knows how to utter the component sounds of the word through his previous exercises in lettering. He is now encouraged to recite these sounds more and more rapidly until he finds himself pronouncing the whole word; at which point it suddenly becomes the familiar name he knows for the nearby object. Numerous words are learned in this way in short order. Most of these techniques trace back through Séguin to Itard. The step of training manual control before writing, the letter cutouts and compositor's chest, the grouping of letters according to contrasts and analogies, the strategy of teaching writing before reading, and of pairing the written names of objects with the objects themselves—all of these were first employed with the wild boy of Aveyron.

"Thus my ten years of work," Montessori wrote in her "Scientific Pedagogy" in 1909,

> may in a sense be considered as a summing up of the forty years of work done by Itard and Séguin. Viewed in this light, fifty years of active work preceded and prepared for this apparently brief trial of only two years [in the Casa dei Bambini], and I feel that I am not wrong in saying that these experiments represent the successive work of three physicians who from Itard to me show in a greater or less degree the first steps along the path of psychiatry.

About a century had passed from Itard to Montessori, from Victor's "classroom" in his teacher's lodgings to children's houses throughout the world. The tributaries of this mainstream in modern education were Condillac, Pinel, Epée, and Sicard: philosophy, medicine, and linguistics converging on two young men in Paris one summer in 1800. Itard had set out to train an *enfant sauvage;* by his journey's end he had become the originator of instructional devices, the inventor of behavior modification, the first speech and hearing specialist, founder of otolaryngology, creator of oral education of the deaf, and father of special education for the mentally and physically handicapped. Sensory education was gaining breadth and momentum as his student Séguin took the helm.

Séguin went on to establish the education of the retarded world-wide and to discern the vast panorama beyond, where the training of the handicapped opened out to the training of all mankind. Montessori, coming later, saw the course she must follow more clearly: extending Itard's program first to the early stages of child development, before formal education, then to revising our conception of education itself, whatever the age of the learner. Montessori died just two decades ago. But our society has so thoroughly absorbed what this evolving system offered that we barely recognize its features, understand why they were sensational discoveries at the time, or appreciate the struggle and the vision of those who rode the stream of history and also changed its course, from Itard to Montessori.

Chronology
Bibliography
Notes
Index

Chronology

Epée born	1712	
Condillac born	1715	
	1735	Linnæus "Systema naturæ"
Sicard born	1742	
Pinel born	1745	
	1746	Condillac "Origin of Human Knowledge"
	1754	Condillac "Treatise on the Sensations"
	1755	Rousseau "Origins of Inequality"
Epée opens school for deaf	1760	
—holds first public demonstration	1771	
Itard born	1774	
	1776	Epée "Instruction of Deaf-Mutes"
Pinel in Paris	1776	
Condillac dies	1780	
	1784	Epée "True Method of Instructing the Deaf"
Victor born (?)	1785	
Sicard director in Bordeaux	1786	
	1788	First U.S. Congress
Epée dies	1789	Constituent Assembly and Estates General
Sicard director INSM	1791	Legislative Assembly
Pinel director Bicêtre asylum	1792	Convention
Sicard imprisoned and released		
Itard health officer	1793	Reign of Terror
INSM installed Rue St. Jacques	1794	
Sicard appointed to Normal School	1795	Directory
Sicard appointed to Institut de France	1796	
Itard appointed to Val-de-Grâce		
Sicard exiled	1797	
Victor seen in Lacaune		
Victor, second sighting	1798	Pinel "Philosophical Nosology"
Victor caught, escapes	1799	Consulate
Victor enters home of Vidal	1800	

Victor: St. Affrique, Rodez, Paris		Pinel "Report to Observers of Man"
Itard resident physician INSM		Sicard returns: "Course of Instruction"
Itard begins training Victor	1801	Itard "Enfant Sauvage," first report
		Pinel "Treatise on Insanity"
	1804	Napoleon Emperor
Itard begins training deaf	1805	
Victor's training ends	1806	Itard "Enfant Sauvage," second report
	1807	Itard "1st Report to Faculty of Medicine"
	1808	Itard "2nd Report to Faculty of Medicine"
Séguin born	1812	
Sicard in London with Massieu, Clerc	1815	Waterloo
Gallaudet and Clerc leave for U.S.	1816	
	1817	First school for deaf in U.S.
	1820	Itard "1st Report to Administration"
	1821	Itard "Diseases of Hearing"
Sicard dies	1822	
	1824	Itard "2nd Report to Administration"
Pinel dies	1826	Itard "3rd Report to Administration"
Victor dies	1828	Academy of Medicine endorses Itard
	1830	Louis Philippe
Itard and Séguin train retardates	1837	
Itard dies	1838	
Séguin first school for retarded	1839	Séguin "Résumé of 14 Months"
Séguin school at La Salpêtrière	1841	
Séguin school at Bicêtre	1842	Séguin "Education of Idiots"
	1843	Séguin "Hygiene and Education of Idiots"
	1846	Séguin "Psychological Treatment of Idiocy"
Sumner studies Séguin's methods	1847	
Séguin emigrates to U.S.	1848	Second Republic; Louis Napoleon
	1852	Napoleon III Emperor
	1861	American Civil War
	1866	Séguin "Idiocy and Its Treatment"
Montessori born	1870	Third Republic
	1878	1st French Congress on Deaf

	1879	2nd French Congress on Deaf
Séguin dies	1880	International Congress on Deaf, Milan
Montessori lectures on idiocy, visits Séguin school	1899	
	1900	International Congress on Deaf, Paris
Montessori first children's house	1907	
Montessori model school	1909	Montessori "Scientific Pedagogy"
	1916	Montessori "Elementary Education"
Montessori dies	1952	

Bibliography

Anon. Trouvé. *Le Censeur des journaux,* May 16, 1797, 237:3 (27 Floréal an 5).

————Enfant sauvage trouvé dans le bois de la Caune. *Le Mois,* 1800, 4(11):182–184 (an 8). (1800a)

————Réflexions sur le sauvage de l'Aveyron et sur ce qu'on appelle en général, par rapport à l'homme, l'état de nature. *Décade Philosophique,* 1800, 7(1):8–18 (an 9). (1800b)

————Sauvage de l'Aveyron. *Gazette de France,* August 8, 1800:1279 (20 Thermidor an 8). (1800c)

————Cause célèbre. Affaire du petit sourd et muet de l'Abbé de l'Epée. *Décade philosophique,* 1800, 23 (3):284–294. (1800d)

————Variétés. *Décade philosophique,* 1800, 33 (4):368–370. (1800e)

———— Sauvage de l'Aveyron. *Journal du commerce, de politique et de Litérature,* August 9, 1800, 321:1283–1284 (21 Thermidor an 8). (1800f)

————[Book review]. "Notice historique sur le sauvage de l'Aveyron," par Bonnaterre. *Journal de Paris,* September 5, 1800, 271:1741–1742 (18 Fructidor an 8). (1800g)

————Bordeaux: Sourds et muets. *Magasin encyclopédique,* 1801, 4:377–378. (1801a)

————Variétés: Aux rédacteurs de la *Décade philosophique. Décade philosophique,* 1801, 32 (4):312–313. (1801b)

————Education of the deaf and dumb. *North American Review,* 1834, 38:307–357.

————Notice sur le sauvage du Tarn. *Société des lettres, sciences et arts de l'Aveyron. Mémoires,* 1842–1843, 4:99–106.

————Seventh Annual Report of the Secretary of the Massachusetts Board of Education. *North American Review,* 1844, 59:329–352.

————Visit to the Bicêtre. *Chambers Edinburgh Journal* (series 2), 1847, 7(158):20–22; (161):71–73; (163):105–107.

————Extract from Dr. Wallis. *American Annals of the Deaf,* 1850, 3:227–233.

————The life and labors of the Reverend T. H. Gallaudet. *North American Review,* 1858, 87:517–532.

————De Gérando. *North American Review,* 1861, 92:391–415.

————Deaf-mute education. *North American Review,* 1867, 104:512–531.

————The Brussels Convention. *American Annals of the Deaf,* 1883, 28:254–262.

————*Notice sur l'Institution nationale des sourds-muets de Paris depuis son origine jusqu'à nos jours* (1760–1896). Paris: Typographie de l'Institution Nationale, 1896.

————Resolutions adopted by the deaf section of the Paris Congress of

1900. *American Annals of the Deaf,* 1901, 46:108–111.

———Troisième Congrès international des sourds-muets tenu à la Sorbonne à Paris les 1ᵉʳ et 2 août 1912. Paris: 35 Rue de Montreuil, 1913.

———Deaf soldiers. *American Annals of the Deaf,* 1917, 62:395–396.

———Le Sauvage de l'Aveyron. *Intermédiaire des chercheurs,* 1924, 87, (864, 948, 996); 1925, 88, (36, 228, 314, 446).

———Le sauvage de l'Aveyron. *Journal de l'Aveyron,* March 29, 1925:1.

———How the deaf mutes were cared for by l'Epée and Sicard. *American Annals of the Deaf,* 1928, 73:366–377, 458–468.

———Célébration, à Luchon, du premier centenaire du docteur Itard. *Gazette des hôpitaux,* 1938, 111:782.

———Itard et le sauvage de l'Aveyron. *Journal français d'otorhinolaryngologie,* 1964, 13:138–148. (1964a)

———L'Abbé de l'Epée et le pseudo-comte de Solar. *Journal français d'otorhinolaryngologie,* 1964, 13:114–124. (1964b)

Adams, M. E. Two schools across the water. *American Annals of the Deaf,* 1896, 41:380–390.

Advielle, V. Lettre à la Société des lettres . . . *Procès verbaux des séances de la Société des lettres, sciences et arts de l'Aveyron,* 1880, 12:137–138.

Affre, H. [Notice sur le sauvage de l'Aveyron.] *Procès verbaux des séances de la Société des lettres, sciences et arts de l'Aveyron,* 1866, 5:70–77.

———*Biographie aveyronnaise.* Rodez: 1881.

Affre, M. Le sauvage du Tarn. *Journal de l'Aveyron,* January 22, 1922.

Aimard, P. *L'Enfant et son langage.* Villurbonne: Simep Editions, 1972.

Amman, J. C. *Surdus loquens* . . . Amsterdam: Wetstenium, 1692. English translation: D. Foot. London: 1694.

———*Dissertatio de Loquella* . . . Amsterdam: J. Wolters, 1700. French translation: Beauvais de Présu. *Dissertation sur la parole.* In: C. F. Deschamps. *Cours eléméntaire d'éducation des sourds et muets.* Paris: Debure, 1779. Pp. 207–362. English translation: C. Baker. London, 1873.

Anastasi, A., and J. P. Foley. *Differential Psychology.* Rev. ed. New York: Macmillan, 1949.

André. Les sauvages de l'Aveyron . . . Proverbe dramatique. (Signé André). *L'Opinion publique,* July 1–3, 1850.

Anglade, J. *Grammaire de l'ancien provençal.* Paris: Klincksieck, 1921.

Association of Medical Officers of American Institutions for Idiotic and Feeble-Minded Persons. In Memory of Edouard Séguin (Being remarks made by some of his friends at the lay funeral service held Oct. 31, 1880). *Proceedings of the Association of Medical Officers of American Institutions for Idiotic and Feeble-Minded Persons.* Philadelphia: Lippincott, 1877.

Astruc, P. J. E. M. Itard. *Progrès médical* (Paris), 1936, suppl., pp. 6–8.

Aubry, J. *La Carence de soins maternels.* Paris: Presses Universitaires de France, 1955.

Baer, D. M., R. F. Peterson, and J. A. Sherman. The development of imitation by reinforcing behavioral similarity to a model. *Journal of the*

Experimental Analysis of Behavior, 1967, 10:405–416.

Baer, D. M., and J. A. Sherman. Reinforcement control of generalized imitation in young children. *Journal of Experimental Child Psychology,* 1964, 1:37–49.

Baillaud-Citeau, H. *Nouvelle contribution à l'étude du cas de "Victor" dit le sauvage de l'Aveyron (Nouveaux Documents historiques).* Thesis, Université Paul Sabatier. Toulouse: Cepadues, 1971.

Baldrian, K. Die Bedeutung Itards für die Entwicklung des Taubstummenbildungswesens; ein Gedenkenblatt zu seinem 150 Geburtstag. *Monatschrift für Ohrenheilkunde und Laryngo-Rhinologie,* 1925, 59:1314–1317.

Ball, T. S. *Itard, Séguin and Kephart: Sensory Education—a Learning Interpretation.* Columbus, Ohio: Merrill, 1971.

Barloy, J. J. Les Enfants-loups. *Sciences et Avenir,* 1969: 273.

Barnard, H. Eulogy. Thomas Hopkins Gallaudet. *American Annals of the Deaf,* 1852, 4:81–136.

Barr, M. W. *Mental Defectives.* Philadelphia: Blakistons, 1910.

Bébian, R. A. *Manuel d'enseignement pratique des sourds-muets.* Paris: Méquignon, 1827.

———*Mimographie ou Essai d'écriture mimique.* Paris: Colas, 1825.

von Békésy, G. *Experiments in Hearing.* New York: McGraw-Hill, 1960.

———The Ear. In: R. Held and W. Richards. *Readings from Scientific American. Perception: Mechanisms and Models.* San Francisco: Freeman, 1972.

Bélanger, A. Le Docteur Itard. *Revue générale de l'enseignement des sourds-muets.* 1904, 6:2–9.

Belhomme, J. E. *Essai sur l'idiotie.* Paris: Germer-Baillère, 1824.

Bell, A. G. Visible speech as a means of communicating articulation to deaf mutes. *American Annals of the Deaf,* 1872, 17:1–21.

———*The Question of Sign Language and the Utility of Signs in the Instruction of the Deaf.* Washington: Sanders, 1898.

———John Braidwood in America. *American Annals of the Deaf,* 1918, 63:459–463.

Bell, A. G., J. C. Gordon, and F. D. Clarke. Report of the Committee on the Hearing of the Deaf. *American Annals of the Deaf,* 1885, 30:59–63.

Bellugi, U., and S. Fischer. A comparison of sign language and spoken language. *Cognitive Psychology,* 1972, 1:173–200.

Bellugi, U., and E. Klima. Aspects of sign language and its structure. In: J. Kavanaugh, ed. *The Role of Speech in Language.* Bethesda: National Institute of Child Health and Human Development, 1974.

Bellugi, U., and P. A. Siple. Remembering with and without words: In: F. Bresson, ed. *Current Problems in Psycholinguistics.* Paris: CNRS, 1974.

Bem, D. J. Self-perception theory. *Advances in Experimental Social Psychology.* Vol. 6. New York: Academic Press, 1972.

Bender, R. E. *The Conquest of Deafness.* Cleveland: Case Western Reserve University Press, 1970.

Bernard, R. Autour du sauvage. de l'Aveyron. *Revue générale de l'enseigne-*

ment des déficients auditifs, 1974, 66:82–89.

Berthier, F. *Notice sur la vie et les ouvrages de Auguste Bébian* . . . Paris: J. Ledoyen, 1839.

———*Les Sourds-Muets avant et depuis l'Abbé de l'Epée* . . . Paris: J. Ledoyen, 1840.

———*Sur l'opinion de feu le Dr. Itard* . . . Paris: Michel Lévy Frères, 1852.

———*L'Abbé de l'Epée* . . . Paris: Michel Lévy Frères, 1852.

———*L'Abbé Sicard* . . . *précis historique sur sa vie, ses travaux et ses succès, suivi de détails biographiques sur ses élèves sourds-muets les plus remarquables, Jean Massieu et Laurent Clerc, et d'un appendice contenant des lettres de l'Abbé Sicard au Bon de Gérando* . . . Paris: C. Douniol, 1873.

Bettelheim, B. *The Empty Fortress: Infantile Autism and the Birth of the Self*. New York: Free Press, 1967.

Bishop, W. H. Impressions of deaf mute instruction in Paris. *American Annals of the Deaf*, 1889, 34:272–285.

Blanchet, A. L. *La Surdi-Mutité*. Paris: Labé, 1850.

———*Moyens d'universaliser l'éducation des sourds-muets sans les séparer de la famille et des parlants*. Paris: Labé, 1856.

Bonaparte, L. (Ministre de l'Intérieur). Lettre du 12 Pluviôse an 8 à l'Administration Centrale du Département de l'Aveyron, à Rodez. Rodez: Archives Départementales de l'Aveyron, L 257.

Bonet, J. P. *Reduction de las letras y arte para enseñar à ablar los mudos*. Madrid: Abarca de Angulo, 1620. English translation: H. N. Dixon. *Simplification of the Letters of the Alphabet and Method of Teaching Deaf Mutes to Speak*. Harrogate: A. Farrar, 1890. French translation: E. Bassouls and A. Boyer. *Réduction des lettres à leurs eléménts primitifs et art d'enseigner à parler aux muets*. Paris: Chez les Traducteurs, 1891.

Bonnaterre, P. J. *Notice historique sur le sauvage de l'Aveyron et sur quelques autres individus qu'on a trouvé dans les forêts à différentes époques*. Paris: Panckoucke, 1800 (an 8). Reprinted in: Anon. *Histoire naturelle de l'homme* . . . 2d ed. Paris: Armand-Aubrée, 1834. Pp. 256–275.

Bonnet-Jalenques, [?]. *Romance du sauvage de l'Aveyron* (Undated). In: H. Brunet, ed. Catalogue of the Société des Lettres, Aveyron, 1917, p. 199.

Bory de Saint Vincent, J. B. Homme. In: J. B. Bory de Saint-Vincent, ed. *Dictionnaire classique d'histoire naturelle*. Vol. 8. Paris: Rey et Gravier, 1825.

Bourneville, D. M., ed. *Raports et mémoires sur le sauvage de l'Aveyron, l'idiotie et la surdi-mutité par Itard, avec une appréciation de ces rapports par delasiauve. Eloge d'Itard par Bousquet*. Paris: F. Alcan, 1894.

Bousquet, J. B. E. Eloge historique, J. M. Itard. *Mémoires de l'académie de Médecine*, 1840, 8:1–18.

Bouteiller, M. La Société des observateurs de l'homme. *Bulletin de la Société d'Anthropologie*, 1956, 7:448–465.

Boyd, W. *From Locke to Montessori*. New York: Henry Holt, 1914.

Brauner, F., and A. Brauner. Le "sauvage" psychotique de l'Aveyron. *La Tribune de l'enfance*, 1969, 7(61):41–50.

Broche, F. Le secret des enfants sauvages. *Miroir de l'histoire*, 1968, 224: 48–55.

Brown, R. *Words and Things*. Glencoe, Ill.: Free Press, 1958.

Buffon, G. L. (Leclerc, Comte de). *Histoire naturelle de l'homme*. Paris: Imprimerie Royale, 1749. Reprinted in: G. L. Buffon. *Oeuvres complètes*. Vol. 5. Paris: Rapet, 1818.

————Discours sur la nature des animaux. In: *Oeuvres complètes de M. le Cte de Buffon*. Vol. 5. Paris: Imprimerie Royale, 1776. Reprinted in: G. L. Buffon. *Histoire naturelle générale et particulière*. Paris: Richard, 1834.

Buisson, S. *Les Sourds-Muets en France . . .* Paris: Guillaumin, 1903.

Burnet, J. *On the Origin and Progress of Language*. Vol. 1. London: Cadell, 1773.

Calmeil, L. F. Idiotisme. In: *Dictionnaire de médecine*. 2d ed. Paris: Béchet, 1837.

Castex, A. Jean Itard: Notes sur sa vie et son oeuvre. *Bulletin d'oto-rhino-laryngologie*, 1919–1920, 18:239–253.

Catford, J. C., and D. B. Pisoni. Auditory vs. articulatory training in exotic sounds. *Modern Language Journal*, 1970, 54:477–481.

Chabbert, P. A propos du sauvage de Lacaune. *Bulletin de la Société des sciences, arts et belles-lettres du Tarn*, 1962, 23:401–402.

Chamberlain, W. Proceedings of the Convention of the New England Gallaudet Association of Deaf-Mutes. Summary of address by L. Clerc. *American Annals of the Deaf*, 1857, 9:67–71.

Champagny, J. B. Lettres du Ministre de l'Intérieur à M. Itard. In: J. M. Itard. *Rapport fait à s. e. le Ministre de l'Intérieur sur les nouveaux développements et l'état actuel du sauvage de l'Aveyron*. Paris: Imprimerie Impériale, 1807.

Chauvin, R. Les enfants sauvages. *Science et vie*, 1949, 378:152–155.

Choris, L. *Voyage pittoresque autour du monde*. Paris, 1822.

Clerc, L. Visits to some of the schools for the deaf and dumb in France and England. *American Annals of the Deaf*, 1848, 1:62–66, 113–120, 170–176.

————Jean Massieu. *American Annals of the Deaf*, 1849, 84–89, 203–217.

————*The Diary of Laurent Clerc's Voyage from France to America in 1816*. West Hartford, Conn.: American School for the Deaf, 1952.

Colona d'Istria, F. Ce que la médecine expérimentale doit à la philosophie —Pinel. *Revue de métaphysique et de morale*, 1904:186–211.

Comenius, J. A. *Orbis sensualis pictus—Hoc est, omnium fundamentalium in mundo rerum et invita actionum pictura et nomenclature. (Die sichtbare Welt, das ist, aller vornehmste Welt-Dinge, und Lebens-Verrichtungen Vorbildung und Benahmung; Noribergae, typis et sumptibus, M. Endteri, 1658)*. English translation: *Orbis pictus: A Facsimile of the First English Edition of 1659*. London: Oxford University Press, 1968.

Condillac, E. B. (Bonnot, Abbé de). *Essai sur l'origine des connaissances humaines.* Amsterdam: Mortier, 1746. Reprinted in: E. B. Condillac. *Oeuvres philosophiques.* Vol. 1. Presses Universitaires de France: Paris, 1947. English translation: T. Nugent. *An Essay on the Origin of Human Knowledge.* London: Nourse, 1756.

————*Traité des sensations.* Paris: Debure, 1754. Reprinted in: E. B. Condillac. *Oeuvres philosophiques.* Vol. 1. Paris: Presses Universitaires de France, 1947. English translation: G. Carr. *Condillac's Treatise on the Sensations.* Los Angeles: University of California, 1930.

————*Cours d'étude pour l'instruction du prince de Parme.* Parme: Imprimerie Royale, 1775. Reprinted in: E. B. Condillac. *Oeuvres philosophiques.* Paris: Presses Universitaires de France, 1947–1948.

————*La Logique.* Paris: l'Esprit et Debure, 1780. Reprinted in: E. B. Condillac. *Oeuvres philosophiques.* Vol. 2. Paris: Presses Universitaires de France, 1948.

Connecticut Asylum for the Education of Deaf and Dumb Persons. *Third Annual Report,* Hartford: Hartford-Hudson, 1819.

Constans, M. Introduction. In: M. Constans, ed. *Notice historique sur le sauvage de l'Aveyron par P.-J. Bonnaterre . . . suivie du rapport de M. Itard au Ministre de l'Intérieur (Septembre 1806) et d'une Comédie Inédite . . . par Vaysse de Villiers.* Rodez: Carrère, [1906].

Constans-Saint-Estève, J. J. Lettre par le Commissaire du gouvernement près le canton de Saint-Sernin au Président de la Commission administrative de l'hospice civil de Saint-Afrique (et suite par un des administrateurs de l'hospice). *Journal des Débats et lois du pouvoir législatif,* January 25, 1800:3 (5 Pluviôse an 8). Reprinted in: *Gazette Nationale,* January 28, 1800 (8 Pluviôse an 8).

Cornié, A. *Etude sur l'Institution nationale des sourdes-muettes de Bordeaux, 1786–1889.* Bordeaux: Coussau, 1889.

Corone, A. Contribution à l'histoire de la sonde d'Itard. *Histoire de la médecine,* 1960, 10:41–42.

Couderc, C. *Bibliographie historique du Rouergue.* Part 1. Paris: Champion, 1918.

Courbon, P. Le Syndrome atavisme ou zoanthropoïdisme mental. In: A. Porot, ed. *Procès verbaux du 22 congrès des médecins aliénistes et neurologistes de France, 1912.* Paris: Masson, 1913.

Culverwell, E. P. *The Montessori Principles and Practice.* London: Bell, 1913.

Davies, S. P. *Social Control of the Mentally Deficient.* New York: Columbia University Press, 1930.

Davis, K. Extreme social isolation of a child. *American Journal of Sociology,* 1940, 45:554–565.

————Final note on a case of extreme social isolation. *American Journal of Sociology,* 1947, 52:432–437.

Dawson, C. A., and W. E. Gettys. *An Introduction to Sociology.* New York: Ronald Press, 1929. Pp. 603–604.

Day, G. E. Report on some schools for the deaf and dumb in Europe: France. *American Annals of the Deaf*, 1861, 13:98–109.

Defoe, D. *The Life and Strange Surprising Adventures of Robinson Crusoe*. London: Taylor, 1719.

Delasiauve, L. J. Education: Le Sauvage de l'Aveyron. *Journal de médecine mentale*, 1865, 5:197–211. Reprinted in D. M. Bourneville. *Rapports et mémoires sur le sauvage de l'Aveyron ...* Paris: F. Alcan, 1894. Pp. xxix–xlvii.

Deleau, N. *Réfutation des assertions de M. Itard sur le traitement des sourds-muets*. Paris: Fournier, 1828.

Demaison, A. *Le Livre des enfants sauvages*. Paris: Editions André Bonne, 1953.

Denis, F., and V. Chauvin. *Les Vrais Robinsons, naufrages, solitudes, voyages*. Paris: Faris, 1863.

Denison, J. The memory of Laurent Clerc. *American Annals of the Deaf*, 1874, 19:238–244.

————Impressions of the Milan Convention. *American Annals of the Deaf*, 1881, 26:41–50.

Dennis, W. The significance of feral man. *American Journal of Psychology*, 1941, 54:425–432.

————A further analysis of reports of wild children. *Child Development*, 1951, 22:153–158.

De Pauw, C. *Recherches philosophiques sur les américains, ou mémoires intéressants pour servir à l'historie de l'espèce humaine*. Berlin: Decker, 1768–1769.

Descartes, R. Lettre à Morus 5/2/1649. In: R. Descartes. *Oeuvres et lettres*. Paris: Gallimard, 1958.

Deschamps, C. F. (Abbé). *Cours élémentaire d'éducation des sourds et muets*. Paris: Debure, 1779.

Destutt de Tracy, A. L. C. *Eléments d'idéologie*. Paris: Courcier, 1817–1818.

Diderot, D. Lettre sur les sourds et muets ... In: D. Diderot. *Oeuvres complètes*. Vol. 1. Paris: Garnier, 1875. Pp. 349–428.

Doctor, P. V. Thirty-second Meeting of the Convention of American Instructors of the Deaf. *American Annals of the Deaf*, 1941, 86:299–349.

Draper, A. G. The Deaf Section of the Paris Congress of 1900. *American Annals of the Deaf*, 1901, 46:218–223.

DuCamp, M. The National Institution for the Deaf and Dumb at Paris. *American Annals of the Deaf*, 1877, 22:1–19.

Dupont, M. *L'Institution nationale des sourds-muets au Congrès de Paris, septembre 1884*. Paris: Imprimerie G. Pelluard, 1885.

————Pages d'histoire. *L'Enseignement de la parole à l'Institution nationale des sourds-muets de Paris*. Paris: Carré, 1897. English translation [extracts]: The Abbé de l'Epée and the teaching of speech. *American Annals of the Deaf*, 1898, 43:316–326.

————*Ministère de l'Intérieur. Institution nationale des sourds-muets de*

Paris. *L'Enseignement auriculaire. Rapports.* Paris: Plon, Nourrit, 1889.

E. D. Nos gravures. *Revue générale de l'enseignement des sourds-muets,* 1911, 13:182–183.

Epée, C. M. (Abbé de l'). *Institution des sourds et muets ou recueil des exercices soutenus par les sourds et muets pendant les années 1771, 1772, 1773, 1774 . . .* Paris: Butard, 1774. Reprinted in: C. M. de L'Epée. *Institution des sourds-muets par la voie des signes méthodiques.* Paris: Nyon, 1776.

———*Institution des sourds-muets par la voie des signes méthodiques.* Paris: Nyon, 1776. English translation: F. Green. Extracts from the "Institution des sourds et muets" of the Abbé de l'Epée. *American Annals of the Deaf,* 1861, 13:8–29. Revised edition: C. M. de l'Epée. *La Véritable Manière d'instruire les sourds-muets . . .* Paris: Nyon, 1784.

———*La Véritable Manière d'instruire les sourds-muets confirmée par une longue expérience.* Paris: Nyon, 1784. Reprinted in: C. M. de l'Epée. *L'Art d'enseigner à parler aux sourds-muets de naissance.* Paris: Dentu, 1820. English translation: F. Green. *The Method of Educating the Deaf and Dumb Confirmed by Long Experience.* London: G. Cooke, 1801. Reprinted in: *American Annals of the Deaf,* 1860, 12:1–132.

———*L'Art d'enseigner à parler aux sourd muets de naissance.* [R. A. Sicard, ed.] Paris: Dentu, 1820.

———*Dictionnaire des sourds-muets, publié d'après le manuscript original et precédé d'une préface par le Dr. J. A. A. Rattel.* Paris: Ballière, 1896.

Esquirol, J. E. Idiotisme. In: *Dictionnaire des sciences médicales.* Vol. 23. Paris: Panckoucke, 1818. Pp. 507–524.

———*Des Maladies mentales . . .* Paris: Baillère, 1838. English translation: E. K. Hunt. *Mental Maladies.* New York: Hafner, 1965.

Esquiros, A. *Paris au XIX siècle.* Vol. 2. Paris: Imprimeurs Unis, 1847.

Evans, B. *The Natural History of Nonsense.* New York: Knopf, 1946.

Fabié, F. Le sauvage de l'Aveyron (vers). *Le Clocher.* Paris: Lemerre, 1887. Pp. 169–173.

Fareng, R. Le sauvage de l'Aveyron. *Revue du Rouergue,* October-December 1959: 402–417.

Fay, E. A. The Braidwood family. *American Annals of the Deaf,* 1878, 23:64–65.

———Contract between Gallaudet and Clerc. *American Annals of the Deaf,* 1879, 24:115–117.

———The Lyons Convention. *American Annals of the Deaf,* 1880, 25: 101–102.

———The Paris Congress of 1900. *American Annals of the Deaf,* 1900, 45:404–416.

———, ed. Letters of Thomas Hopkins Gallaudet and Alice Cogswell. *American Annals of the Deaf,* 1913, 58:227–235.

———The Centennial of the American School at Hartford. *American*

Annals of the Deaf, 1917, 62:370–382.

Ferreri, G. *Il sordomuto e la sua educazione.* Siena: Ancora, 1895–1912.

Feydel, G. Qu'est-ce que le sauvage de l'Aveyron? *Journal de Paris*, September 5, 1800: 18; September 26, 27, 29, 1800: 22–23, 28–29, 40–41 (18 Fructidor an 8; 4, 5, 7 Vendémiaire an 9).

Flanagan, J. L. *Speech Analysis, Synthesis and Perception.* 2d ed. New York: Springer-Verlag, 1972.

Foulquier-Lavergne, P. *Le sauvage de l'Aveyron.* Rodez: Imprimerie de Broca, 1875.

Fox, M. A. La Haute Education des sourds-muets aux Etats Unis d'Amérique. In: H. Gaillard and H. Jeanvoine. *Exposition universelle de 1900. Congrès international pour l'étude des questions d'assistance et d'éducation des sourds-muets. Section des sourds-muets. Compte-rendu des débats et relations diverses.* Paris: Imprimerie d'Ouvriers Sourds-Muets, 1900. Pp. 371–377.

Franck, A. *Rapport au Ministère de l'Intérieur sur le Congrès international réuni à Milan du 6 au 12 septembre [1876] pour l'amélioration du sort des sourds-muets.* Paris: Wittersheim, 1880.

Freeman, F. S. *Individual Differences.* New York: Holt, 1934.

Frishberg, N. From iconicity to arbitrariness. Paper presented at the Linguistic Society of America, San Diego, 1973.

Fromkin, V., S. Krashen, S. Curtiss, D. Rigler, and M. Rigler. The development of language in Genie: A case of language acquisition beyond the critical period. *Brain and Language*, 1974, 1:81–107.

Fusfeld, I. S. The subscription of May 1, 1815. *American Annals of the Deaf*, 1922, 67:92.

Fynne, R. J. *Montessori and Her Inspirers.* New York: Longmans, Green, 1924.

Gaillard, H. *Essai d'histoire de l'enseignement des sourds-muets.* Asnières: P. Scagliola, 1916.

Gaillard, H., and H. Jeanvoine. *Exposition universelle de 1900. Congrès international pour l'étude des questions d'assistance et d'éducation des sourds-muets. Section des sourds-muets. Compte-rendu des débats et relations diverses.* Paris: Imprimerie d'Ouvriers Sourds-Muets, 1900.

Gall, F. J., and G. Spurzheim. *Anatomie et physiologie du système nerveux en général et du cerveau en particulier.* Vol. 2. Paris: F. Schoell, 1812. Pp. 41–44.

Gallaudet, E. M. A day in the Imperial Institution for Deaf-Mutes at Paris. *American Annals of the Deaf*, 1870, 15:129–132.

———Is sign language used to excess in teaching deaf-mutes? *American Annals of the Deaf*, 1871, 16:26–33.

———The Milan Convention. *American Annals of the Deaf*, 1881, 26:1–16.

———History of the education of the deaf in the United States. *American Annals of the Deaf*, 1886, 31:130–147.

———The value of the sign-language to the deaf. *American Annals of the Deaf*, 1887, 32:141–147.

————Life of Thomas Hopkins Gallaudet. New York: Henry Holt, 1888.

————Echoes of the Paris Congress of 1900. *American Annals of the Deaf*, 1900, 45:416–426.

Gallaudet College. *Dictionary Catalogue on Deafness and the Deaf.* Boston: Hall, 1970.

Ganansia, K. Les enfants sauvages. *Le Groupe familial*, 1971, 50:5–11.

Ganière, P. *L'Académie de médecine*. Paris: Maloine, 1964.

Gardner, R. A., and B. T. Gardner. Teaching sign language to an ape. *Science*, 1969, 165:664–672.

Gaynor, J. F. The "failure" of J. M. G. Itard. *Journal of Special Education*, 1973, 7:439–444.

Gayral, L., P. Chabbert, and H. Baillaud-Citeau. Les Premières Observations de l'enfant sauvage de Lacaune. *Annales médico-psychologiques*, 1972, 2:465–490.

de Gérando, J. M. *De l'Education des sourds-muets de naissance*. Paris: Méquignon, 1827.

————Considérations sur le sauvage de l'Aveyron: Ecrit posthume de M. de Gérando. *Annales de l'éducation des sourds-muets et des aveugles*, 1848, 5:110–118.

Gesell, A. L. *Wolf Child and Human Child*. New York: Harper, 1941.

Gonan, [?] (de Montpellier). Lettre à [?] Solier (de Camarès) du 25 Pluviôse an 8. Rodez: Archives Départmentales de l'Aveyron, EI 19.

Gordon, J. C. Deaf mutes and the public schools from 1815 to the present day. *American Annals of the Deaf*, 1885, 30:121–143.

Green, F. *"Vox Oculis Subjecta" A Dissertation on the . . . Art of Imparting Speech . . . to the Naturally Deaf and . . .Dumb; with a particular account of the Academy of Messrs. Braidwood . . . By a parent [Francis Green]*. London: Benjamin White, 1783. F. Green. *A New Edition of "Vox Oculis Subjecta," Part I*. London: 1873. Reprinted Boston: Parents' Education Association for Deaf Children, 1897.

Green, S. The earliest advocate of the education of deaf mutes in America. *American Annals of the Deaf*, 1861, 13:1–8.

Grimal, P., ed. *Dictionnaire des biographies*. Paris: Presses Universitaires de France, 1958.

Groff, M. L. Jean Marc Gaspard Itard. *Psychological Clinic* (Lancaster, Pa.), 1932, 20:246–256.

Guéguen, P. Itard (le Dr) et le Sauvage de l'Aveyron. *Larousse mensuel, illustré*, 1925, 6(216):786–787.

Guiraud, [?]. Correspondance du Commissaire près l'Administration municipale de Saint-Affrique avec le Commissaire central. Rapport du 13 Pluviôse an 8. Rodez: Archives Départmentales de l'Aveyron, L. 493.

Gurlt, E., ed. *Biographisches Lexikon*. Berlin: Urban und Schwarzenberg, 1962.

Haight, G. *Mrs. Sigourney, the Sweet Singer of Hartford*. New Haven: Yale University Press, 1930.

Halle, J. N., and Moreau, [?]. Ecole de médecine. Rapports sur deux mémoires relatifs aux moyens de rendre l'ouïe aux sourds-muets. *Gazette nationale ou Le Moniteur universel*, August 8, 1808, 36 (211): 874–875, 878.

Hamerlynck, L. A., P. O. Davidson, and L. E. Acker, eds. *Behavior Modification and Ideal Mental Health Services*. First Banff International Conference on Behavior Modification. Calgary, Alberta, Canada: University of Calgary, 1969.

Harnois, G. *Les Théories du language en France de 1660 à 1821*. Paris: Les Belles Lettres, 1928.

Hayes, A. *Language Laboratory Facilities*. Washington, D. C.: U. S. Government General Printing Office, 1963.

Hayes, K. J., and C. Hayes. The intellectual development of a home-raised chimpanzee. *Proceedings of the American Philosophical Society*, 1951, 95:105–109.

———*The Ape and the Child*. New York: Hafner, 1967.

Hément, F. *Conférence sur l'enseignement des sourds-muets par la parole (méthode J. R. Pereire)*. Paris: Imprimerie Nationale, 1879.

Von Herder, J. G. *Ideen zur Philosophie der Geschichte der Menschheit*. Riga: Hartknoch, 1785. English translations (abridged): E. Manuel. *Reflections on the Philosophy of the History of Mankind*. Chicago: University of Chicago Press, 1968. T. Churchill. *Outlines of a Philosophy of the History of Man*. London: Johnson, Hansard, 1800. Reprinted New York: Bergman, 1966. French translation: E. Tandel. *Idées pour une philosophie de l'histoire de l'humanité*. Paris: Lacroix, 1874.

Hernández-Peon, R. Reticular mechanisms of sensory control. In: W. Rosenblith, ed. *Sensory Communication*. New York: Wiley, 1961. Pp. 497–520.

Herriot, E. *Madame Récamier et ses amis*. Paris: Gallimard, 1934. English translation: A. Hallard. *Madame Récamier*. New York: Putnam, 1906.

Hervé, G. Le sauvage de l'Aveyron devant les observateurs de l'homme (avec le rapport retrouvé de Philippe Pinel). *Revue d'anthropologie*, 1911, 21:383–398, 441–454.

Hodgson, K. W. *The Deaf and Their Problems*. New York: Philosophical Library, 1954.

Hoefer, F., ed. *Nouvelle Biographie générale*. Paris: Didot Frères, 1861.

Holland, J. G. Human vigilance. *Science*, 1958, 128:61–67.

Holman, H. *Séguin and His Physiological Method of Education*. London: Pitman, 1914.

Houdin, A. *Rapport sur le Congrès international des maîtres des sourds-muets à Milan en 1880*. Paris: Imprimerie Nationale, 1881.

Hunsicker, H. H. Itard. *International Record of Medicine*, 1934, 140:682–684.

Husson, H. M. De l'Education physiologique du sens anditif chez les sourds-muets. *Mémories de l'Académie Royale de médecine*, 1833, 2:178–196. Reprinted in: *Transactions médicales: Journal de médecine*, 1833, 12:249; J. M. G. Itard. *Traité des maladies de l'oreille et de l'audition*. 2d. ed. Paris: Méquignon-Marvis Fils, 1842; D. M.

Bourneville, ed. *Rapports et mémoires sur le sauvage de l'Aveyron, l'idiotie et la surdi-mutité par Itard* . . . Paris: F. Alcan, 1894. Summary in: *Journal général de médecine,* 1828, 103:391–398.

Ireland, W. W. *Affections of Children, Idiocy, Imbecility, and Insanity.* London: Churchill, 1898.

Irzhanskaia, K. N., and R. A. Felberbaum. Effects of stimulus sensitization on ease of conditioning. In: Y. Brackbill and G. Thompson, eds. *Behavior in Infancy and Early Childhood: A Book of Readings.* New York: Free Press, 1967. Pp. 246–249.

Isaacs, W., J. Thomas, and I. Goldiamond. Application of operant conditioning to reinstate verbal behavior in psychotics. *Journal of Speech and Hearing Disorders,* 1960, 25:8–12.

Itard, J. M. G. *De l'Education d'un homme sauvage ou des premiers développements physiques et moraux du jeune sauvage de l'Aveyron.* Paris: Gouyon, 1801. Reprinted in: D. M. Bourneville, ed. *Rapports et mémoires sur le sauvage de l'Aveyron, l'idiotie et la surdi-mutité, par Itard* . . . Paris: F. Alcan, 1894; J. M. G. Itard. *Traité des maladies de l'oreille et de l'audition.* 2d ed. Paris: Méquignon-Marvis Fils, 1842; L. Malson. *Les Enfants sauvages.* Paris: Union Générale d'Éditions, 1964. German translation: S. Krenberger. *Des Wilden von Aveyron.* Vienna: Karl Graeser, 18[??]. English translations: [?] Nogent. *An Historical Account of the Discovery and Education of a Savage Man, or of the First Developments, Physical and Moral, of the Young Savage Caught in the Woods near Aveyron in the year 1798.* London: Phillips, 1802; G. Humphrey and M. Humphrey. *The Wild Boy of Aveyron.* New York: Appleton-Century-Crofts, 1932.

——*Rapport sur la vaccine, fait aux administrateurs de l'Institution nationale des sourds-muets.* Paris: Imprimerie des Sourds-Muets de Naissance, [1801?].

Itard, E. M. [J. M. G.] "Du catarrhe utérin, ou des fleurs blanches," par J. B. Blatin. *Journal général de médecine,* 1802, 14:77–86 (an 10). (1802a)

Itard, J. M. G. Médecine: Réflexions sur l'état actuel de l'enseignement médical . . . *Gazette nationale ou Le Moniteur universel,* March 17, 1802:176 (26 Ventôse an 10). (1802b)

——Notes. In: A. F. Willich. *Hygiène domestique ou l'art de conserver la santé et de prolonger la vie.* Vol. 2. Paris: Ducauroy, 1802 (an 10). Pp. 511–599. (1802c)

——*Dissertation sur le pneumothorax, ou les congestions gazeuses qui se forment dans la poitrine.* Paris, 1803.

——*Rapport fait à s.e. le Ministre de l'Intérieur sur les nouveaux développements et l'état actuel du sauvage de l'Aveyron.* Paris: Imprimerie impériale, 1807. Reprinted in D. M. Bourneville, ed. *Rapports et mémoires sur le sauvage de l'Aveyron, l'idiotie et la surdi-mutité, par Itard* . . . Paris: F. Alcan, 1894; J. M. G. Itard. *Traité des maladies de l'oreille et de l'audition.* 2d ed. Paris: Méquignon-Marvis Fils, 1842; L. Malson. *Les Enfants sauvages.* Paris: Union Générale d'Editions, 1964. German translation: S. Krenberger. *Des Wilden von Aveyron.* Vienna: Karl Graeser, 18[??]. English translation: G. Humphrey and M. Humphrey. *The Wild Boy of Aveyron.* New York: Appleton-Century-Crofts, 1932.

————Extrait de deux mémoires présentés à la Société ... Mémoire sur les moyens de rendre l'ouïe aux sourds-muets ... Mémoire sur les moyens de rendre la parole aux sourds-muets. *Bulletin de l'Ecole de médecine de Paris,* 1808, 1:72–79.

————Mémoire sur les médications immédiates de l'oreille interne, extrait d'un ouvrage inédit sur les lésions de l'oreille et de l'audition. *Journal universel des sciences médicales,* 1816, 3:1–28; 4:1–32.

————Mémoire sur le bégaiement. *Journal universel des sciences médicales,* 1817, 7:129–144.

————Hydropsie. In: *Dictionnaire des sciences médicales.* Vol. 22. Paris: Panckoucke, 1818. Pp. 361–456.

————Rapport fait à MM. les administrateurs de l'Institution des Sourds-Muets, sur ceux d'entre les élèves qui, étant doués de quelque degré d'audition, seraient susceptibles d'apprendre à parler et à entendre. *Journal universel des sciences médicales,* 1821, 22:5–17. (1821a)

————*Traité des maladies de l'oreille et de l'audition.* Paris: Méquignon-Marvis, 1821. (1821b). *Traité des maladies de l'oreille et de l'audition, 2e Ed. [précédée de l'éloge historique de M. Itard, par M. Bousquet], considérablement augmentée et publiée par les soins de l'Académie royale de médecine ...* Paris: Méquignon-Marvis Fils, 1842. German translation: *Die Krankheiten des Ohres und des Gehöres.* In: S. J. Dummler, ed. *Chirurgischen Handbibliothek.* Vol. 4. Weimar: Landes-Industrie-Compt., 1822.

————Deuxième rapport fait en 1824 sur nos sourds-muets incomplets à l'occasion de la jeune Godart. Unpublished manuscript, 12 pp. Paris: Institution Nationale des Sourds-Muets, 1824.

————Rapport de M. Itard ... fait à l'administration le 8 juillet 1825. Unpublished manuscript, 15 pp. Paris: Institution Nationale des Sourds-Muets, 1825.

————*Lettres au rédacteur du "Globe"* [December 7 and 23, 1826] *sur les sourds-muets qui entendent et qui parlent.* Paris: Imprimerie de Lachevardière Fils, [1826].

————Troisiéme rapport contenant un premier aperçu sur la méthode d'instruction à donner à ceux des sourds muets qui sont doués jusqu'à un certain point des facultés auditives et orales (7 juillet 1826). Unpublished manuscript, 10 pp. Paris: Institution Nationale des Sourds-Muets, 1826.

————Expériences propres à constater l'action des ventouses sur l'absorption des virus inoculés. *Journal général de medécine,* 1827, 98:238–239. (1827a)

————*Lettre au rédacteur de "Globe"* [January 11, 1827] *sur les sourds-muets qui entendent et qui parlent.* Paris: Imprimerie de Guiraudet, 1827. (1827b)

————Notes. In: J. C. Hoffbauer. *Médecine légale relative aux aliénés et aux sourds-muets.* [Translated from the German by A. M. Chambeyron.] Paris: Baillière, 1827. Pp. 176–230. (1827c)

————Traitement de la surdité de naissance par les injections dans l'oreille moyenne. *Journal général de médecine,* 1827, 100:222–226, 277–281. (1827d)

————Mémoire sur le mutisme produit par la lésion des fonctions intellectuelles. *Mémoires de l'Académie royale de médecine,* 1828, 1: 1–18. (1828a) Reprinted in: D. M. Bourneville, ed. *Rapports et mémoires sur le sauvage de l'Aveyron, l'idiotie et la surdi-mutité par Itard* . . . Paris: F. Alcan, 1894; J. M. G. Itard. *Traité des maladies de l'oreille et de l'audition.* 2d. ed. Paris: Méquignon-Marvis Fils, 1842.

————Mémoire sur quelques phlegmasies cérébrales (présentées comme cause de fièvres intermittentes pernicieuses.) *Mémoires de l'Académie Royale de Médecine,* 1828, 1:19–31. (1828b)

————Sur l'usage et la forme des cornets acoustiques. *Journal général de médecine,* 1829, 106:284–288.

————Rapport fait à l'Académie de Médecine. In: M. Colombat. *Du Bégaiement et de tous les autres vices de la parole* . . . 2d ed. Paris: Mansut, 1831.

————Rapport général sur les remèdes secrets. *Mémoires de l'Académie Royale de Médecine,* 1833, 2:24–31.

————Sur un mémoire intitulé "Recherches sur la surdité, considérée particulièrement sous le rapport de ses causes et de son traitement" (par Gairal). Mémoires de l'Académie Royale de Médecine, 1836, 5:525–552. English translation: On the surgical treatment of deafness. In: *Dunglison's American Medical Library.* Philadelphia: Waldre, 1838. Pp. 75–92.

————Testament. *Bulletin de l'Académie de Médecine,* 1839, 3:924–926.

Itard, J. M. G., L. J. Thillaye, and I. Bricheteau. *Rapport* [to the Académie de Médecine] *sur le traitement des déviations de l'épine, par la méthode de M. le Docteur* [C. G.] *Pravaz.* Paris, [1828].

Jacobs, J. A. The methodical signs for *and* and the verb *to be. American Annals of the Deaf,* 1856, 8:185–187.

Jakobson, R. *Kindersprache, Aphasie und allgemeine Lautgesetze.* Uppsala: Universitets Arsskrift, 1942, 9:1–83. English translation: A. Keiler. *Child langauge: Aphasia and Phonological Universals.* The Hague: Mouton, 1968.

Jauffret, L. F. Lettre du 9 Pluviôse an 8 aux administrateurs de l'hospice de Saint-Affrique. Reprinted in: H. Baillaud-Citeau. *Nouvelle Contribution à l'étude du cas de "Victor"* . . . Thesis, Université Paul Sabatier. Toulouse: Cepadues, 1971.

Johnson, S. *A Journey to the Western Islands of Scotland.* London: Strahan and Cadell, 1775. Reprinted: *Johnson's Journey to the Western Islands.* Boston: Houghton Mifflin, 1965.

Jolly, P. De l'Imitation considérée dans ses rapports avec la philosophie, la morale et la médecine. *Mémoires de l'Académie Royale de*

Médecine, 1846, 12:581–603.

de Jouy, V. J. *L'Hermite de la Chaussée d'Antin.* Paris: Pillet, 1813–1814. English translation (excerpts): *American Annals of the Deaf*, 1859, 11:78–84.

Kanner, L. Itard, Séguin, Howe—three pioneers in the education of retarded children. *American Journal of Mental Deficiency*, 1960, 65: 2–10.

Kant, I. *Anthropologie en pragmatischer Hinsicht.* Königsberg: F. Nicolovius, 1800. English translation (Part 1, sections 35–43): C. T. Sullivan. *The Classification of Mental Disorders.* Doylestown, Pa.: Doylestown Foundation, 1964. French translation: J. Tissot. *Anthropologie . . .* Paris: Ladrange, 1863.

Keller, F. S., and W. N. Schoenfeld. *Principles of Psychology.* New York: Appleton-Century-Crofts, 1950.

Keller, H. A. *The World I Live In.* New York: Century, 1908.

———*The Story of My Life.* Garden City, N. Y.: Doubleday, 1954.

Kellogg, W. N. Humanizing the ape. *Psychological Review*, 1931, 38: 160–176.

Kellogg, W. N., and L. A. Kellogg. *The Ape and the Child.* New York: McGraw-Hill, 1933.

Kipling, R. *The Jungle Book.* New York: Century, 1894.

Klineberg, O. *Social Psychlogy.* New York: Holt, 1954. French translation: R. Avidgor-Coryell. *La Psychologie sociale.* Paris: Presses Universitaires de France, 1963.

Knapton, E. J. *Revolutionary and Imperial France, 1750–1815.* New York: Scribner, 1972.

Krashen, S., and R. Harshman. Lateralization and the critical period. UCLA Working Papers in Phonetics No. 23. Unpublished report: University of California, Los Angeles, June 1972. Pp. 13–21.

Lallemand, L. *Histoire de la charité.* Vol. 4, Les Temps modernes; part 2, Europe. Paris: Picard, 1912.

La Mettrie, J. O. Traité de l'âme. In: J. O. La Mettrie. *Oeuvres philosophiques.* London: Nourse, 1751.

La Rochelle, E. *Jacob-Rodrigues Pereire, premier instituteur des sourds-muets en France: Sa Vie et ses travaux.* Paris: P. Dupont, 1882.

Larrey, J. D. *Mémoire de chirurgie militaire et campagnes.* Paris: J. Smith, 1812–1817.

Laurent, A. *Mémoire sur l'éducation des sourds-muets, à MM les membres du Conseil d'administration de l'Institution Royale des Sourds-Muets de Paris.* Blois: Dézairs, 1831.

———*La parole rendue aux sourds-muets . . .* Paris: Johanneau, 1831.

Lenneberg, E. *Biological Foundations of Language.* New York: Wiley, 1967.

L'Epée, C. M., *see* Epée, C. M. (Abbé de l').

Lermoyez, M. M. E. Gellé. *Presse médicale*, suppl., July 21, 1923, 58: 1212–1213.

Leroy, J. J. B. *Sur les travaux qui ont rapport à l'exploration de la mâture dans les Pyrénées . . .* Paris: Couturier, 1776.

Lesieux, E. Le "Sauvage de l'Aveyron" chez Madame Récamier. *Revue générale de l'enseignement des sourds-muets*, 1931, 32:95–96.

Lévesque, C. Notice des travaux de la classe des sciences morales et politiques, pendant le premier trimestre de l'an 10. *Magasin Encyclopédique*, 1801, 5:256–257.

Lévi-Strauss, C. *Les Structures élémentaires de la parenté*. Paris: Presses Universitaires de France, 1949.

Locke, J. *An Essay Concerning Human Understanding*. London: T. Basset, 1690. Reprinted in: A. C. Fraser, ed. *An Essay Concerning Human Understanding*. New York: Dover, 1959.

Lovaas, O. I. A program for the establishment of speech in psychotic children. In H. N. Sloane and B. D. MacAulay. *Operant Procedures in Remedial Speech and Language Training*. Boston: Houghton Mifflin, 1968. Pp. 125–154.

————A behavior therapy approach to the treatment of childhood schizophrenia. In: J. D. Hill, ed. *Minnesota Symposium on Child Psychology*. Minneapolis: University of Minnesota Press, 1967. Pp. 108–159.

————J. P. Bereich, B. F. Perloff, and B. Schaeffer. Acquisition of imitative speech by schizophrenic children. *Science*, 1966, 151:705–707.

————L. Freitas, K. Nelson, and C. Whalen. The establishment of imitation and its use for the development of complex behavior in schizophrenic children. *Behavior Research and Therapy*, 1967, 5:171–181.

————B. Schaeffer, and J. Q. Simmons. Building social behavior in autistic children by use of electric shock. *Journal of Experimental Research in Personality*, 1965, 1:99–109.

Maignet, E. *Rapport et projet de décret sur l'origine des établissements pour les sourds-muets indigents*. Paris: Imprimerie Nationale, 1793.

de Maistre, M. Actualités de Jean Itard. *Art et techniques pédagogiques*, 1974, 6:268–281.

Malson, L. Victor sous le regard des sciences humaines. *Le Monde*, March 4, 1970(7819):19.

Mannoni, O. Itard et son sauvage. *Les Temps modernes*, 1965, 233:647–663. Reprinted in: O. Mannoni. *Clefs pour l'imaginaire ou l'autre scène*. Paris: Editions Seuil, 1969.

Manoury, A. L'Enfant sauvage d'après "Mémoire et rapport sur Victor de l'Aveyron." *Aesculape*, 1970, 53 (1):2–63; (2):1–47.

Marks, L., and G. A. Miller. The role of semantic and syntactic constraints in the memorization of English sentences. *Journal of Verbal Learning and Verbal Behavior*, 1964, 3:1–5.

Martha, A. *Exposition universelle de 1900. Congrès international pour l'étude des questions d'éducation et d'assistance des sourds-muets ... Compte-rendu de "L'éducazione dei sordomuti"* [by G. Ferreri] *suivi des procès verbaux sommaires officiels*. Asnières: Institut Départemental des Sourds-Muets, 1901.

Martha, A., and H. Gaillard. *Exposition universelle de 1900. Congrès* international pour l'étude des questions d'éducation et d'assistance des sourds-muets. Procès verbaux sommaires. Paris: Imprimerie Nationale, 1901.

Mason, M. K. Learning to speak after six and one half years of silence. *Journal of Speech Disorders*, 1942, 7:295–304.

Massieu, J., and L. Clerc. *Recueil des définitions et réponses les plus remarquables de Massieu et Clerc*... London: Cox and Bayles, 1815.

Maudit, M. Les sourds-muets et la méthode orale. In: H. Gaillard, and H. Janvoine. *Exposition universelle de 1900. Congrès international pour l'étude des questions d'assistance et d'éducation des sourds-muets. Section des sourds-muets. Compte-rendu des débats.* Paris: Imprimerie d'Ouvriers Sourds-Muets, 1900. Pp. 57–70.

de Maupertuis, P. L. M. Lettre sur le progrès des sciences. In: P. L. M. de Maupertuis. *Oeuvres.* Vol. 2. Lyon: Bruyset, 1768. Pp. 375–431.

Maynard, J. L'Enfant sauvage *Le Rouergat*, January 17, 1969, (1208):8.

Mazars, L. Le sauvage de l'Aveyron. *Miroir de l'histoire.* 1960, 122:198, 200.

Meadows, K. P. Early manual communication in relation to the deaf child's intellectual, social and communicative functioning. *American Annals of the Deaf*, 1968, 113:29–41.

Médici, A. *L'Education nouvelle—ses fondateurs, son évolution.* Paris: Presses Universitaires de France, 1940.

———L'Enfant sauvage. *Education et développement*, 1970, 60:13–21.

Melzack, R., and T. H. Scott. The effects of early experience on the response to pain. *Journal of Comparative and Physiological Psychology*, 1957, 50:155–161.

Ménière, P. *De la Guérison de la surdi-mutité et de l'éducation des sourds-muets.* Paris: Baillière, 1853.

Meyerson, L., N. Kerr, and J. Michael. Behavior modification in rehabilitation. In: S. Bijou, and D. Baer. *Child Development: Readings in Experimental Analyses.* New York: Appleton-Century-Crofts, 1967.

Michaud, J. F., ed. *Biographie universelle. (Nouvelle édition).* Paris: Desplaces, 1858.

Michelet, A. Sur le sauvage de l'Aveyron. *La Tribune de l'enfance*, 1969, 7 (68):16–27.

———*Les Outils de l'enfance.* Vol. 1. Paris: Delachaux et Niestlé, 1972.

Mignet, F. A. *Institut impérial de France. Notice historique sur la vie et les travaux de M. le baron de Gérando*... Paris: Firmin Didot, 1854.

Miller, G. A., and S. Isard. Some perceptual consequences of linguistic rules. *Journal of Verbal Learning and Verbal Behavior*, 1963, 2:217–228.

Mitchell, S. H. The haunting influence of Alexander Graham Bell. *American Annals of the Deaf*, 1971, 116:349–356.

Molinéry, P. Un centenaire à célébrer: Itard (1838–1938). *Paris médical*, 1937, 106:138–140. (1937a)

———Centenaire de la mort d'Itard. *Journal de médecine de Bordeaux,*

1937:791–797. (1937b)

———Le Centenaire d'Itard. *Presse thermale et climatique,* 1938, 79:426–429.

Molinéry, R. and P. Molinéry. La Sonde à cathétérisme de la trompe d'Eustache. *Bulletin de l'Union médicale latine,* 1938, 125:145–167. (1938a)

———Communication du 7 mai 1938 à la Société Française d'Histoire de la Médecine. *Bulletin de la Société Française d'Histoire de la Médecine,* 1938, 32:67–68. (1938b)

Monaci, S. J. M. Itard. In: A. Martinazzoli, and L. Credaro, eds. *Dizionario illustrato di pedagogia.* Vol. 2. Milan: Vallardi, 1896. Pp. 330–332.

Montaigne, (Abbé). *Recherches sur les connaissances intellectuelles des sourds-muets* . . . Paris: Le Clère, 1829.

Montessori, M. *Il metodo della pedagogia scientifica applicato all'educazione infantile delle case dei bambini.* Rome: Maglioni e Strini, 1909. English translation: A. George. *The Montessori Method.* New York: Stokes, 1912.

———*L'autoeducazione nelle scuole elementari.* Rome: Maglione e Strini, 1916. English translation: F. Simmonds and L. Hutchinson. *The Advanced Montessori Method: Scientific Pedagogy as Applied to the Education of Children from Seven to Eleven Years.* London: Heinemann, 1917.

Morel, E. Notice biographique sur le Docteur Itard. *Annales de l'éducation des sourds-muets et des aveugles,* 1845:84–99. English translation: E. Peet. Biographical sketch of Dr. Itard. *American Annals of the Deaf,* 1853, 5:110–124.

Morel, O. *Essai sur la vie et les travaux de Marie-Joseph, baron de Gérando.* Paris: Renouard, 1846.

Neumann, F. *Die Taubstummenanstalt zu Paris im Jahre 1822: eine historisch-pädagogische Skizze als Beitrag zur Kenntnis und Würdigung der Französischen Methoden des Taubstummenunterrichtes* . . . Königsberg: A. W. Unzer, 1827.

Neyer, J. A. *Rodolph ou le sauvage de l'Aveyron.* Paris: Jouanaux, 1800.

Nougairole, S. R. [Lettre sur le sauvage de l'Aveyron.] *Journal des débats et lois du pouvoir législatif,* January 25, 1800: 3 (5 Pluviôse an 8).

Pariset, E. Eloge de J. E. D. Esquirol. In: E. Pariset. *Histoire des membres de l'Académie Royale de Médecine.* Vol. 2. Paris: Baillière, 1850. Pp. 424–482.

Park, R. E., and E. W. Burgess. *Introduction to the Science of Sociology.* Chicago: University of Chicago Press, 1921. Pp. 239–242.

Pays, J. F. *L'Enfant sauvage.* Paris: Editions G. P.—Presses de la Cité, 1970.

Peet, H. Analysis of Bonet's treatise on the art of teaching the dumb to speak. *American Annals of the Deaf,* 1850, 3:200–211.

———,ed. Proceedings of the second convention of American instructors of the deaf and dumb. Discussion, "High school for the deaf and dumb." *American Annals of the Deaf,* 1852, 4:10–18. (1852a)

————Sketch of the life of Baron de Gérando. *American Annals of the Deaf*, 1852, 4:178–187. (1852b)

————Tribute to the memory of the late Thomas Gallaudet. *American Annals of the Deaf*, 1852, 4:65–77. (1852c)

————Necrology [L. Clerc, A. Jacobs, A. Hutton]. *American Annals of the Deaf*, 1870, 15:245–248.

Peet, I. L. The influence of the life and work of the Abbé de l'Epée *American Annals of the Deaf*, 1890, 35:133–150.

Pereire, J. R. *Mémoire que M. J. R. Pereire a lu dans la séance de l'Académie royale des sciences du 11 juin 1749 et dans lequel en présentant à cette compagnie un jeune sourd et muet de naissance, il expose avec quel succès il lui a appris à parler.* Paris, 1749.

————Observations sur les sourds et muets, et sur quelques endroits du Mémoire de M. Ernaud. In: *Mémoires de mathématique et de physique presentés à l'Académie Royale des Sciences par divers savans et lus dans ses assemblées en 1778.* Paris: 1786.

Pestalozzi, J. H. *Wie Gertrud ihre Kinder lehrt . . .* Leipzig: P. Reclam [1801]. English translation: L. E. Holland and F. C. Turner. *How Gertrude Teaches Her Children.* London: Remax House, 1966.

Petit, J. *Mémoire à l'appui d'une demande en concession de terres en Algérie.* Digne: Vial, 1859.

Petit, J., and A. Vial. *Notes sur la demande en concession de terres en Algérie.* Digne: Vial, 1858.

Pinel, P. *Nosographie philosophique, ou la méthode de l'analyse appliquée à la médecine.* Paris: Maradan, 1798 (an 6).

————*Traité médico-philosophique sur l'aliénation mentale ou la manie.* Paris: Richard, 1801 (an 8). English translation: D. D. Davis. *A Treatise on Insanity.* New York: Hafner, 1962.

————*La Médecine clinique rendue plus précise et plus exacte par l'application de l'analyse . . .* Paris: Brosson, Gabon, 1802.

Politzer, A. *Geschichte der Ohrenheilkunde.* Stuttgart: Ferdinand Enke, 1807. Pp. 439–446.

Porcher, A. Itard. *Revue générale de l'énseignement des sourds-muets*, 1938, 39 (9):113–124; 1938, 39 (10):129–132; 1939, 40:1–6.

Porter, S. Bibliographical: Brief notices of the more important publications which have appeared in Great Britain or America having relation to the deaf and dumb. *American Annals of the Deaf*, 1848, 1:33–44, 181–193, 229–237; 1849, 2:39–51, 112–123, 243–250.

————Singular observation of Dr. Itard. *American Annals of the Deaf*, 1856, 8:104–108.

————John Quincy Adams and the Abbé de l'Epée. *American Annals of the Deaf*, 1856, 8:248–249.

————Charles Fox and his deaf mute son. *American Annals of the Deaf*, 1856, 8:249–250.

————Book notices. De Gérando. *American Annals of the Deaf*, 1861, 13:122–125.

Potter, R. K., G. A. Kopp, and H. C. Green. *Visible Speech.* New York:

Van Nostrand, 1947.

Premack, D. Language in the chimpanzee? *Science*, 1971, 172:808–822.

——Teaching language to an ape. *Scientific American*, 1972: 92–99.

Puybonnieux, J. B. *La Parole enseignée aux sourds-muets sans le secours de l'oreille*. Paris: Kugelmann, 1843.

Quérard, J. M. *La France littéraire*. Paris: Didot, 1830. P. 188.

Racine, L. *Eclaircissement sur la fille sauvage dont il est parlé dans l'épître II sur l'homme* [1763]. In: L. Racine. *Oeuvres*. Paris: Le Normant, 1808.

——*Epître II sur l'homme*. Paris: Desaint et Sullant, 1747. Reprinted in: L. Racine. *Oeuvres*. Paris: Le Normant, 1808.

Rae, L. The Abbé de l'Epée. *American Annals of the Deaf*, 1848, 1:69–76.

——The National Institution for the Deaf and Dumb at Paris. *American Annals of the Deaf*, 1852, 4:252–258.

——Dr. Peet's European tour. *American Annals of the Deaf*, 1852, 4:243–252.

——Higher education for the deaf and dumb. *American Annals of the Deaf*, 1852, 4:259–261; 1853, 5:56–59.

Randon, J. P. Lettre du 3 Pluviôse an 8, au commissaire près l'administration municipale du canton de Saint Sernin. Rodez: Archives Départementales de l'Aveyron, L236, 1800. (1800a).

——Lettre du 16 Pluviôse an 8 [au commissaire du gouvernement près l'administration municipale du canton de Saint Sernin]. Rodez: Archives Départementales de l'Aveyron, L236, 1800. (1800b)

——Lettre du 24 Pluviôse an 8 au commissaire du gouvernement près l'administration centrale du département du Tarn. Rodez: Archives Départementales de l'Aveyron, L205, 1800. (1800c).

Rauber, A. *Homo Sapiens Ferus oder die Zustande der Verwilderten und ihre Bedeutung für Wissenschaft, Politik und Schule*. 2d ed. Leipzig: J. Brehfe, 1888.

Reynolds, G. S. *A Primer of Operant Conditioning*. New York: Scott, Foresman, 1968.

Riese, W. *The Legacy of Philippe Pinel: An Inquiry into Thought on Mental Alienation*. New York: Springer, 1969.

Rogers, W. *A Cruising Voyage Around the World*. London: Bell and Lintot, 1712. French translation: *Voyage autour du monde commencé en 1708 et fini en 1711*. Amsterdam: Marret, 1716.

Rogéry, [?]. Lettre du 25 Pluviôse an 8 du secrétaire général de l'administration centrale du Département de l'Aveyron au ministre de l'intérieur. Rodez: Archives Départementales de l'Aveyron, L183, 1800.

Root, G. M., ed. *The Cogswell Letters*. West Hartford, Conn.: American School for the Deaf, 1941[?].

Rosenzweig, M. R. Auditory Localization. In: R. Held and W. Richards. *Readings from Scientific American. Perception: Mechanisms and Models*. San Francisco: Freeman, 1972. Pp. 203–208.

Rousseau, J. J. *Discours sur l'origine et les fondements de l'inégalité parmi les hommes*. Amsterdam: Rey, 1755. English translation: R. D.

Masters. *Jean Jacques Rousseau: The First and Second Discourses*. New York: Saint Martin, 1964.

——*Emile, ou de l'éducation*. La Haye: Néaulme, 1762.

Saboureux de Fontenay, S. Lettre à Mademoiselle xxx. In: J. M. de Gérando. *De l'Education des sourds-muets de naissance*. Vol. 1. Paris: Méquignon, 1827. Pp. 408–430.

Saint-Simon, H. *Oeuvres de Saint-Simon et d'Enfantin*. Paris: Dentu, 1865.

Saint-Yves, I Aperçu historique sur les travaux concernant l'éducation médico-pédagogique. Itard, 1775–1838, Séguin, 1812–1880, Bourneville, 1840–1906. Thesis, Université de Lyon, 1914.

Sarason, S. *Psychological Problems in Mental Deficiency*, 3d ed. New York: Harper, 1959.

Schaffer, H. R., and P. E. Emerson. The effects of experimentally administered stimulation on developmental quotients of infants. *British Journal of Social and Clinical Psychology*, 1968, 7:61–67.

Schröder, H. J. M. G. Itard. *Monatschrift für Ohrenheilkunde*, 1914, 48:358–365.

——J. M. G. Itard zum 150 Geburtstage; Zugleich ein kleiner Beitrag zur Geschichte der Ohrenheilkunde und des Taubstummen-bildungswesens. *Münchener Medizinische Wochenschrift*, 1925, 72:1795.

Séguin, E. *A Monsieur H. . . . Résumé de ce que nous avons fait depuis 14 mois, du 15 février 1838 au 15 avril, 1839 (au sujet de la cure médicale du jeune Adrien H.)* Paris: Porthmann, 1839. (1839a)

——*Conseils à M. O. . . . sur l'éducation de son fils*. Paris: Porthmann, 1839. (1839b)

——*Théorie et pratique de l'éducation des enfants arriérés et idiots. (Leçons aux jeunes idiots de l'Hospice des Incurables.)* Paris: Baillière, 1842.

——*Hygiène et éducation des idiots*. Paris: Baillière, 1843.

——*Traitement moral, Hygiène et éducation des idiots*. Paris: Baillière, 1846.

——*Jacob-Rodrigues Pereire. Notice sur sa vie et ses travaux et analyse raisonnée de sa méthode*. Paris: Baillière, Guyot et Scribe, 1847.

——Origin of the treatment and training of idiots. *American Journal of Education*, 1856, 2:145–152.

——*Idiocy and Its Treatment by the Physiological Method*. New York: William Wood, 1866.

——*New Facts and Remarks Concerning Idiocy*. New York: William Wood, 1870.

——Report on education. In R. H. Thurston, ed. *Reports of the Commissioners of the United States to the International Exhibition held at Vienna, 1873*. Vol. 2, Science, Education. Section K. Washington: U. S. Government Printing Office, 1876. (1876a) French translation: *Rapport et mémoires sur l'éducation des enfants normaux et anormaux*. Bibliothèque d'Education Spéciale III. Paris: Alcan, 1895.

——*Medical Thermometry and Human Temperature*. New York: William Wood, 1876. (1876b)

————Psychophysiological training of an idiotic hand. *Archives of Medicine*, 1879, 2:149.

————Psycho-physiological training of an idiotic eye. *Archives of Medicine*, 1880, 4:217.

Seigel, J. P. The enlightenment and the evolution of a language of signs in France and England. *Journal of the History of Ideas*, 1969, 30:96–115.

Semelaigne, D. *Philippe Pinel (1745–1826)*. Paris: Masson, 1927.

Sherman, J. A. Use of reinforcement and imitation to reinstate verbal behavior in mute psychotics. *Journal of Abnormal Psychology*, 1965, 70:155–164.

Sicard, R. A. (Abbé). Art de la parole. In: *Séances des écoles normales.* Paris: Reynier, 1795. Vol. 1, pp. 115–137, 244–265, 336–358; vol. 3, pp. 138–145; vol. 4, pp. 263–271.

————*Cours d'instruction d'un sourd-muet de naissance.* Paris: Le Clère, 1800 (an 8).

————Relation sur les dangers qu'il a courus les 2 et 3 septembre, 1792. *Annales religieuses*, 1797, 1:13–72. Reprinted in: F. Jourgniac-Saint-Médard. *Relation historique sur les journées des 2 et 3 septembre 1792.* Paris: Bertrand, 1806. A. Serieys. *La Mort de Robespierre.* Paris: 1801. English translation (excerpts): L. Rae. The great peril of Sicard. *American Annals of the Deaf*, 1848, 1:16–24.

————*Théorie des signes pour l'instruction des sourds-muets . . . suivie d'une notice sur l'enfance de Massieu.* Paris: Imprimerie de l'Institution des Sourds-Muets, 1808.

————*Théorie des signes ou introduction à l'étude des langues, où Le Sens des mots au lieu d'être défini est mis en action.* Paris: Michaud, 1814.

Sigourney, L. H. *Letters of Life.* New York: Appleton, 1866.

Silberstein, R. M., and H. Irwin. Jean-Marc-Gaspard Itard and the savage of Aveyron: an unsolved problem in child psychiatry. *Journal of the American Academy of Child Psychiatry*, 1962, 1:314–322.

Singh, J. A. L., and R. M. Zingg. *Wolf Children and Feral Man.* New York: Harper, 1942.

Skinner, B. F. *Verbal Behavior.* New York: Appleton-Century-Crofts, 1957.

Smith, M. Wild children and the principle of reinforcement. *Child Development*, 1954, 25:115–123.

Spitz, R. A. Hospitalism. *Psychoanalytic Study of the Child*, 1945, 1:53–74.

————Anaclitic depression: an inquiry into the genesis of psychiatric conditions in early childhood, II. *Psychoanalytic Study of the Child*, 1946, 2:313–342.

Stevenson, R. S., and D. Guthrie. *A History of Otolaryngology.* Baltimore: Williams and Wilkins, 1949.

Stratton, G. M. Jungle children. *Psychological Bulletin*, 1934, 31:596–597.

Sumner, G. Letter upon the subject of schools for idiots in Paris. Boston: Commonwealth of Massachusetts, House No. 152, 1847. Reprinted in: *Twenty-Eighth Annual Report of the Trustees of the Massachu-setts School for Idiotic and Feebleminded Youth: Report on the School at Bicêtre.* Boston: Wright and Potter, 1876.

Syle, H. W. A summary of the recorded researches and opinions of H. P. Peet. *American Annals of the Deaf,* 1873, 18:133–162, 213–241.

Tafel, J. F. I. *Die Fundamentalphilosophie in genetischer Entwicklung mit besonderer Rücksicht auf die Gesichte jedes einzelnen Problems* . . . Tubingen: Verlags-Expedition, 1848.

Talbot, M. E. *Edouard Séguin: A Study of an Educational Approach to the Treatment of Mentally Defective Children.* New York: Teachers College, Columbia University, 1964.

Taylor, W., and I. Taylor. The education of physically handicapped chil-dren in France. *Exceptional Children,* 1959, 26(2):75–81.

Thiery, F. Les enfants sauvages. *La Tribune de l'Enfance,* 1972, 10(95): 48–52.

Thollon, B. Present condition of the instruction of the deaf in France. *American Annals of the Deaf,* 1912, 57:6–22.

Thouy, L. *Meïchou parmi les Faons.* Aurillac: Editions du Centre, 1961.

Tinland, F. *L'Homme sauvage.* Paris: Payot, 1968.

Tredgold, A. F. *A Textbook of Mental Deficiency.* 3d ed. Baltimore: Wil-liams and Wilkins, 1920.

Turner, W. W. Letter to L. P. Brockett, March 3, 1856. *American Annals of the Deaf,* 1856, 8:250–252.

———Laurent Clerc. *American Annals of the Deaf,* 1870, 15:14–25.

Tyler, E. B. Wild men and beast-children. *Anthropological Review,* 1863, 1:21–32.

Ullman, L., and L. Krasner, eds. *Case Studies in Behavior Modification.* New York: Holt, Rinehart and Winston, 1965.

V. Le Sauvage de l'Aveyron. *Journal des débats,* May 9, 1911. Reprinted in: *Journal de l'Aveyron,* October 1, 1911, 40:1.

Vaïsse, L. *Le Mécanisme de la parole mis à la portée des sourds-muets de naissance.* Paris: Institution Royale, 1838.

———*Des Conditions dans lesquelles s'entreprend et des moyens par lesquels s'accomplit l'instruction des sourds de naissance.* Paris: Hachette, 1848.

———*De la Parole considérée du double point de vue de la physiologie et de la grammaire* . . . Paris: Didot, 1853.

———*De la Pantomime comme langage naturel et moyen d'instruction du sourd-muet.* Paris: Hachette, 1854.

———Saboureux de Fontenay and his instructor Pereire. *American An-nals of the Deaf,* 1878, 23:37–40.

———*Un Document retrouvé et quelques faits rétablis concernant l'his-toire de l'éducation des sourds-muets en France* . . . Rodez: Ratery, 1878. English translation: A document brought to light. *American Annals of the Deaf,* 1879, 24:80–90.

———Jacob Rodrigues Pereire. *American Annals of the Deaf,* 1883, 28: 221–226.

Vaïsse de Villiers, R. J. [Comédie inédite sur le sauvage de l'Aveyron]. In: M. Constans, ed. *Notice historique sur le sauvage de l'Aveyron* ... Rodez: Carrère, [1906].

Valade-Gabel, J. J. *Lettres, notes, rapports relatifs à l'enseignement des sourds-muets*. Grasse: Imbert, 1894.

Van Deusen Fox, J. Cutaneous stimulation: effects on selected tests of perception. *American Journal of Occupational Therapy*, 1964, 18:53–55.

——Improving tactile discrimination of the blind: a neurophysiological approach. *American Journal of Occupational Therapy*, 1965, 19: 5–7.

Varigny, H. Revue des sciences—Les Hommes sauvages du Var et de l'Aveyron. *Journal des débats*, March 6, 1926.

Vernhes, J. "Victor" le jeune aveyronnais le plus célèbre. *Le Rouergue amicaliste*, February 25, 1967, 8:1–2.

Vernon, M., and S. Koh. Early manual communication and deaf children's achievement. *American Annals of the Deaf*, 1970, 115:527–536.

——Effects of oral preschool compared to early manual communication on education and communication in deaf children. *American Annals of the Deaf*, 1971, 116:569–574.

Virey, J. J. *Histoire naturelle du genre humain (avec une dissertation sur le sauvage de l'Aveyron)*. Paris: Dufart, 1800 (an 9).

——Homme. In: *Nouveau dictionnaire d'histoire naturelle* ... Vol. 11. Paris: Déterville, 1803.

——*Recherches médico-philosophiques sur la nature et les facultés de l'homme*. Paris: Panckoucke, 1817.

——Homme, homme des bois, homme sauvage. In: *Nouveau dictionnaire d'histoire naturelle appliquée aux arts* ... *Nouvelle édition*. Vol. 15. Paris: Déterville, 1817. Pp. 1–256, 260–269.

Voison, F. *De l'Idiotie chez les enfants*. Paris: Baillière, 1843.

Wairy, L. C. [Constant]. *Mémoires sur la vie privée de Napoléon, sa famille, et sa cour*. Vol. 3. Paris: Ladvocat, 1830.

Wallis, J. W. ... *Grammatica linguae anglicanae. Cui praefigitur, de loquela sive sonorum formatione. Tractatus grammatico-physicus*. Oxoniae, 1653.

Walther, E. *Geschichte des Taubstummen-Bildungswesens*. Leipzig: Velhagen und Klasing, 1882.

Weld, L. History of the American Asylum. *American Annals of the Deaf*, 1848, 1:7–14, 93–112.

Wheeler, F. R. Growth of American Schools for the Deaf. *American Annals of the Deaf*, 1920, 65:367–378.

Williams, J. A brief history of the American Asylum at Hartford. In: E. A. Fay. *Histories of American Schools for the Deaf (1817–1893)*. Washington: Volta Bureau, 1893. Pp. 1–30.

Wilmot, C. *An Irish Peer on the Continent. 1801–1803. Being a Narrative of the Tour of Stephen, 2nd Earl of Mount Cashell, through France, Italy, etc. ... as related by Catherine Wilmot*. London: Sadler, 1920.

Yebra, M. *Libro llamado refugium infirmorum* . . . Madrid: Luis Sanchez, 1593.

Zaporozhets, A. V. The development of perception in the preschool child. In: P. H. Mussen, ed. *European Research in Cognitive Development.* Monographs of the Society for Research in Child Development, 1965, 30(2):82–101.

Zingg, R. M. Feral man and extreme cases of isolation. *American Journal of Psychology*, 1940, 530:487–517.

Notes

Chapter One. A Wild Boy Is Found

p. 7 "recounts"—Foulquier-Lavergne (1875).

p. 7 "Saint-Sernin"—Itard states that the wild boy "had been seen more than five years before" his arrival at Saint-Sernin (1801, p. 136, 1964 ed.)—that is, in 1795—and he cites the letter in the *Journal des débats,* which says nothing of the sort. Most writers place the first sighting of the boy a year or two before his return to society, but I have found some evidence that bears Itard out and indicates that the boy spent at least three years and probably between five and eight years in the forests. On May 16, 1797, the *Censeur des journaux* published the following announcement: "Found in the outskirts of Figuajet, canton of Salles-Curan, Department of Aveyron, a child apparently ten years old, light hair, large mouth, flat nose, who speaks very little and very poorly; his father, according to his account, is called *Donne à Dieu* [give to God], and his father's cook, Jean. It seems that the child was well cared for in his youth but that he was obliged to flee for safety, as he tells it, at a time when everyone was being killed. He hid in the woods where, from all appearances, he survived for five years on roots and wild fruit. He was almost naked when he was found. The administration of the Department of Aveyron has sent this notice to all municipalities in the district and has published it in several newspapers, in the hope of discovering, if possible, the parents of this unfortunate child" (Anon., 1797). We cannot be sure that this child is indeed the *sauvage de l'Aveyron,* who had a somewhat pointed nose, not a flat one, but most of the other details check: the region in which this child was found, his food preferences, age, and inarticulateness, and even, perhaps, the name *Donne à Dieu;* Itard reports that the first utterance the savage used frequently in Paris was "O Dieu!" If the two children are one and the same, this article shows that the wild boy, like any other normal child, could once communicate in his own language, and it confirms his long sojourn in the forests.

Foulquier-Lavergne (1875) gives 1799 as the date of the first sighting. Baillaud-Citeau (1971) follows his chronology, as do Gayral et al. (1972), except for the first date, which they give as 1798. Malson (1964) also gives 1797 as the first sighting, but the rest of his dating is inconsistent with any other account.

p. 8 "practices"—Constans-Saint-Estève (1800); cited in Bonnaterre (1800), pp. 23–26.

p. 9 "Saint-Sernin"—Biographical data from Foulquier-Lavergne (1875) and Baillaud-Citeau (1971).

p. 9 "[January 10, 1800]"—Most French documents from 1794 to 1807 bear dates corresponding to the Republican calendar, whose year 1 begins with the founding of the Republic on September 22, 1792. A year of 365 days was divided into 12 months of 30 days each, plus 5 or 6 "complementary days" at the end of the year reserved for national holidays. The names of the months were poetically inspired, largely by the climate in France at the corresponding time of year. Fall months had the suffix -*aire*, winter months -*ôse*, spring -*al*, and summer -*or:* Vendémiaire, Brumaire, Frimaire, Nivôse, Pluviôse, Ventôse, Germinal, Floréal, Prairial, Messidor, Thermidor, Fructidor.

p. 10 "[signed] Constans-Saint-Estève"—The complete closing is: "A Saint-Affrique, le 21 nivôse an 8, pour copie conforme à l'original, signé Rainaldis-Nougairoles, administrateur." The accompanying letter to the editor "from one of the administrators of the orphanage" was probably written by Nougairoles, since Bonnaterre (1800) states, "An eyewitness, Cit. Nougairoles, administrator of the orphanage, related to me that when [the wild boy] was pursued across the fields and saw that he was about to be captured, he put his hands on the ground and ran on all fours" (p. 27). The letters appear in the issue of the *Journal des débats et lois du pouvoir législatif* for 5 Pluviôse an 8 (January 25, 1800), page 3, and are surely the referent of Bonnaterre's footnote 7: "Lettre du citoyen N . . . insérée dans le *Journal des débats*, 5 pluviôse an 8" (p. 22). Itard (1801) later gives the same citation. Humphrey and Humphrey (1932) appear to have their dates and names confused, therefore, when they write: "In 1799, the year seven by the new calendar, there was published in the Journal des Débats a letter by one Citizen Bonaterre [*sic*], describing a wild boy taken in the woods" (p. vi). Going by his account, Bonnaterre (1800, p. 28) apparently had not heard of the boy until 3 Pluviôse an 8 (January 23, 1800), two weeks after his capture and twelve days after the date of the letter from Constans-Saint-Estève. The gist of Nougairoles' report also appears in an unsigned article in *Le Mois* (Anon., 1800a).

p. 11 "commissioner"—Guiraud, cited in Bonnaterre (1800).

p. 12 "(May 16, 1796)"—Biographical data from Baillaud-Citeau (1971).

p. 13 "delay"—Randon (1800a).

p. 13 "peoples"—Bouteiller (1956), p. 452.

p. 14 "immediately"—Jauffret (1800).

p. 14 "forthwith"—Bonaparte (1800).

p. 14 "Rodez"—Variously spelled Rhodez, Rhodès, Rodez. Saint-Affrique is spelled Saint-Afrique in some documents. The modern spellings have been used everywhere.

p. 14 "11th"—That is, January 31. This letter is quoted at length in Bonnaterre (1800), but the original has not been found.

p. 14 "rustic child you had sent him"—The letter written by the government commissioner for the district of Saint-Affrique on 13 Pluviôse an 8 (February 2, 1800) has not been found; it is paraphrased in Bonnaterre (1800), pp. 26–27.

p. 15—"identity"—Randon (1800b). The same day Randon wrote to the commissioner at Saint-Affrique: "Nothing will be overlooked to compensate the boy for the discomfort he seems to be experiencing in his new way of life, and should the observations to be made on his account add something to those you have already made, it will truly be my pleasure to let you know . . . Please rest assured that I will do everything to ensure that this poor child has a happy existence; it will be some time before he can be made to feel that his new way of life is better than the freedom to which he had become accustomed." The original letter has not been found, but this excerpt is cited in Affre (1866), p. 73.

p. 15 "in his behalf"—Cited in Affre (1866), p. 72. The original letter has not been found.

p. 16 "literally"—The letter appealing for information (Randon, 1800c) read as follows:

"24 pluviôse an 8 [February 13, 1800]
"To the government commissioner to the central administration of the Department of Tarn
"I turn to you, Citizen colleague, to obtain some definitive information concerning a young child of about 12, who was apprehended in the district of Saint-Sernin, from which he was sent by the government commissioner to the orphanage at Saint-Affrique, and who was brought on the 15th [pluviôse] to the central administration of Aveyron, in accord with my instructions. This young child is mute; he even appears deaf; his behavior, his tastes, everything indicates that he was isolated from society for a long time and completely abandoned on his own.
"It would indeed be interesting to learn his origins and above all to know what events could have reduced him to an existence that so strongly resembles that of a savage. All the steps I have taken to gather facts that are certain leave me still in incertainty, given the variety of accounts I have received. Word has it that some time ago he was apprehended and brought before the central administration to which you are affiliated and from which, it is added, he escaped.
"I have also been told that two or three years ago some hunters spotted him in the Lacaune woods, but the solid information that I would like to provide on his account cannot be based on 'word-has-it.' He is currently in the hands of Citizen Bonnaterre, Professor of Natural History, and the Minister of the Interior has just written two letters to the central administration of Aveyron demanding the boy urgently.
"Everything that has been said so far concerning this child is a bit fabulous and especially exaggerated. Before sending him off to Paris, I would like to have some positive information concerning his origin, the places where he lived—in a word, everything that would enable me to communicate only what is sure and plausible. I believed that in turning to you it would be possible to arrive at a satisfactory result, and I await with impatience everything that I can learn in this matter."
p. 17 "Combes"—Rogéry et al. (1800)
p. 17 "circulate"—Neyer (1800), Foulquier-Lavergne (1875).

p. 17 "throat"—Cited in Affre (1866), p. 75. Letter dated 25 Messidor an 8 (July 14, 1800).

p. 19 "readers"—Anon. (1800c). A similar article appeared the next day in the *Journal du commerce* (Anon., 1800e). Several newspapers urged their readers to make a calmer and more critical appraisal (A., 1800; Feydl 1800). The public might be taken in by a fraud (Bernard, 1974) just as Epée was by the pseudo-count of Solar. This fascinating tale, in which the abbé encounters a deaf-mute street urchin and becomes convinced that he belongs to the noble family of Solar, was recounted twice in the courts, once in an appeal to Parliament and again in a play by Bouilly that had great popularity at the time (Anon., 1964b). The play contributed to public awareness of efforts in behalf of deaf-mutes and thus to freeing Epée's imprisoned successor, Abbé Sicard.

p. 19 "Rousseau"—The following discussion owes much to Tinland's masterful book (1968).

p. 19 "monkeys"—Cited in Bory de Saint-Vincent (1822), vol. 8, p. 270.

p. 20 "object?"—Buffon (1776), vol. 10, p. 115, 1834 ed.

p. 20 "Europe"—Maupertuius (1768), 382.

p. 20 "nine cases"—In the twelfth edition of his work (1766).

p. 20 "Hanover (1724)"—Rousseau (1775), pp. 183–186, n. 3, 1964 trans. by Masters.

p. 21 "the arts"—Constitution of 5 Fructidor an 3, art. 298.

p. 21 "races"—Bouteiller (1956), p. 451.

p. 21 "he would prove"—Locke (1690), book 3, chap. 6, sec. 26 (vol. 2, p. 77, Dover 1959 ed.). Locke attributes the passage to Giles Menage.

p. 22 "Plant?"—Bory de Saint-Vincent (1822), vol. 8, pp. 270–271.

p. 23 "problem"—Herder (1785), book 9, chap. 2, p. 233, 1800 trans. by Churchill.

p. 23 "beast"—Descartes (1649), pp. 1319–1320, 1958 ed.

p. 24 "language of the deaf"—Gardner and Gardner (1969).

p. 24 "speak"—Virey (1817), p. 211.

p. 24 "twentieth century"—Kellogg and Kellogg (1933); Hayes and Hayes (1951, 1967). Also see Premack (1971, 1972).

p. 24 "learn from deaf-mutes"—In general, I have retained the term "deaf-mute" rather than the more modern term "deaf," and "idiot" rather than "retardate," in keeping with the period in which the story takes place.

p. 25 "is doubtful"—Singh and Zingg (1966), pp. 252–258.

p. 25 "reason comes from heaven"—Racine (1763), vol. 6, p. 575, 1808 ed.

p. 25 "instilled"—La Mettrie (1751), p. 207.

p. 25 "idiot"—Condillac (1746), part 1, sec. 4 (vol. 1, p. 43, 1947 ed.).

p. 26 "animals"—Itard (1801), p. 125, 1964 ed.

p. 26 "education"—Ibid., p. 128.

p. 26 "possesses"—Herder (1785), chap. 6, book 3 (p. 67, 1800 trans. by Churchill).

p. 27 "predators"—Kant (1800).

p. 27 "child"—Racine (1747), vol. 2, p. 125.

p. 27 "environment"—Buffon (1749), vol. 3, p. 364.

p. 27 "one at a time"—Condillac (1754).

p. 28 "francs"—To judge the corresponding amount of money today, the *Annuaire statistique de la France* reports that the index of wholesale prices was 130 in 1820; in 1973 it was 27.5. By this criterion there has been approximately a fivefold reduction in the purchasing power of the franc. If we use an exchange rate of five francs to the dollar, the franc amounts cited in the text correspond conveniently to the same amounts in dollars today. This equivalence is only very approximate; for one thing, the commodities we consume today barely overlap with those consumed in 1820.

I want to acknowledge the helpful comments of Professor C. P. Kindelberger of Massachusetts Institute of Technology and Professor David Landes of Harvard University; they are, of course, not responsible for my interpretation.

p. 28 "communicate with him"—Anon. (1800d), pp. 368–369.

p. 28 "offices of pity"—Shakespeare, *The Winter's Tale,* II.iii. 184–189.

p. 29 "magazines"—Wilmot (1920), p. 71.

p. 29 "present"—The novels are: Neyer (1800), Demaison (1953), Thouy (1961). The poems: Bonnet-Jalenques (1917), Fabié (1887). The plays: Vaïsse de Villiers (1906), André (1850), Foulquier-Lavergne (1875). The film: *L'Enfant sauvage* (Truffaut, 1970; also see Pays, 1970).

Chapter Two. The Savage Described

p. 33 "ideas"—Bonnaterre (1800), p. 45.

p. 33 "exposed to the sun"—Virey (1800), p. 302.

p. 34 "fairly narrow"—Ibid., p. 305.

p. 34 "lifeless in our wild boy"—Ibid., p. 304.

p. 34 "hastens their growth"—Ibid., p. 310.

p. 35 "a little inward"—Virey (1800), pp. 306–310.

p. 36 "joy, desire, and distress"—Ibid., pp. 320–321.

p. 37 "all these metals"—Ibid., p. 336.

p. 37 "pleasant laugh"—Ibid., p. 310.

p. 38 "articulate language"—Ibid., pp. 322–325.

p. 39 "appeared to me"—Ibid., pp. 337–338.

p. 39 "care about it at all"—Ibid., p. 324.

p. 39 "green walnuts"—Ibid., pp. 328–331. Virey continues:

"Our young boy scrapes and digs up earth readily with his long fingernails to retrieve potatoes and other roots, etc.; he likes particularly broad beans, cabbage, peas, chestnuts, hazelnuts, beechnuts, walnuts, acorns, kidney beans, potatoes, and so forth; he does not seem to have much taste for wheat and the other cereals. He mainly goes after wild fruits and the natural foods that can be found on the ground in the forest. He has been seen to eat fresh sawdust by the handful. Some claim that he even did not reject bark, that they saw him eat some. He likes bread less than fruit, and he consistently refuses white bread; but he has become accustomed to rye bread and he ordinarily eats two and a half pounds of it a day, which does not count his other nourishment. What is rather curious is that he refuses apples, pears, cherries, currants, plums, and the like . . . Sugar and the foods that contain it are refused like these. Seasonings, salt, pepper, and so on, and all the spices that seem to us agreeable and tasty are as displeasing to his palate as his bitter fruits are to ours. Those that have a hard shell he cracks with a rock, a skill that he learned from men, for previously he used his teeth. He knows quite well how to shell, using his long fingernails, the walnuts, beans, and so on, that he eats; he shows a lot of dexterity in doing it, but he is unconcerned with cleanliness and his clothes are not spared.

His only beverage is pure water and in large quantities. To drink, he dipped his mouth into the rivers or springs; but he now knows how to use a vessel. He systematically refuses wine, beer, spirits, and the like; he finds these beverages very distasteful; and if he is led unsuspectingly to drink some from a closed vessel, he rejects it at once, making signs of disgust. He has become somewhat accustomed to milk, which he refused because he didn't know it, as with many other things.

"When eating things that pleased him, this child of nature rocked slightly from side to side while muttering continuously, which showed his satisfaction: he takes care to stack his fruits in a pile as he eats them; he lays them out quite adroitly. It is a pleasure to watch him put peas or other nourishment in his mouth with his little fingers (for he never uses any utensil); he does it with so much skill that he never lets a single piece fall; he gets everything into his mouth in one flick of the fingers, and does not chew for long. He is greedy and impatient when he sees some food; he wants to swallow it immediately; he is after quantity rather than quality" (pp. 331–333).

p. 41   "hidden stockpiles"—Ibid., p. 332.
p. 42   "expects nothing"—Ibid., p. 304.
p. 42   "the mind of the boy"—Ibid., p. 297.
p. 42   "anything of the sort"—Ibid., p. 341–342.
p. 42   "cries out"—Ibid., p. 302.
p. 42   "where he wandered"—Ibid., p. 316.
p. 43   "favorite amusement"—Ibid., pp. 319–320.
p. 43   "a pretty girl etc."—Ibid., pp. 332–334.
p. 43   "children ordinarily are"—Ibid., p. 346.
p. 44   "girl from Chalôns"—This is the same wild girl from Sogny, Mlle. LeBlanc. The village of Sogny, in the Champagne region of France, is a few miles from Chalôns, where she was raised in a convent.
p. 44   "to warm up"—Virey (1800), p. 311.
p. 45   "well-behaved"—Ibid., pp. 315–316.
p. 45   "wetness"—Ibid., pp. 312–313.

p. 46 "first caught"—Ibid., p. 304.

p. 46 "inches rapidly"—Ibid., p. 301.

p. 46 "normal rate"—Ibid., pp. 302–303.

p. 46 "outside for that"—Ibid., pp. 313–315.

p. 47 "Mathieu"—Well-known deaf-mutes from the institute at Paris.

p. 48 "Nature"—Virey (1800), pp. 347–350.

Chapter Three.   A Dispute over Diagnosis

p. 51 "indifferent to everything"—Itard (1801), p. 131, 1964 ed.

p. 51 "studies in science"—The best biographies are by Porcher (1938), Morel (1845), and Castex (1920). Some additional details are found in Bousquet (1839), Bélanger (1904), Molinéry (1937a, b), and Hunsicker (1934). Derivative profiles are in Hoeffer (1861), Michaud (1858), Quérard (1830), and Grimal (1958). Hoeffer, Michaud, and Bousquet give erroneous birthdates. J.-M.-G. Itard sometimes used the initials E.-M. before his surname.

p. 53 "his earlier life"—Itard (1801), pp. 130–131, 1964 ed.

p. 53 "diagnosis"—Hervé (1911), p. 397, n. 1. Also see Séguin (1856).

p. 53 "different circumstances"—De Gérando (1848), p. 111. The manuscript probably dates from 1803 and may be the text of an address to the French Institute on this topic which the author is claimed to have given (Varigny, 1926).

p. 54 "other men"—Condillac (1746), part 1, sec. 4, chap. 2 (vol. 1, p. 44, 1947 ed.).

p. 54 "occupy us"—Condillac (1754), part 4, chap. 7, sec. 3 (p. 225, 1930 trans. by Carr). Itard cites this passage on the cover of his 1801 report on the wild boy.

p. 55 "intellectual state"—Itard (1801), p. 134, 1964 ed.

p. 55 "bodily movement"—For biographies see Michaud (1858), Semelaigne (1927), Riese (1969).

p. 56 "no treatment"—Lallemand (1912).

p. 56 "heavy and mechanical"—Pinel (1800), p. 165, 1806 trans. by Davis.

p. 69 "continued instruction?"—Translated from Hervé (1911). Humphrey and Humphrey (1932) state: "By an unfortunate trick of fate, Pinel's report is not available today ... Diligent search has failed to unearth the report. (Such search was made by the editor of the reprinted edition of Itard's reports; the present writer also searched in the libraries of Paris without result. Apart from Itard's own account there are singularly few contemporary records of this popular sensation of the years 1799 and 1800 —fn.) Thus there is lacking today a most important source of first-hand information on the state of the boy when he was found" (p. vii). The first trace of Pinel's manuscript appears, by a trick of fate, in the Proceedings of the Society of Letters, Science, and the Arts of Aveyron, where a letter from a member states that he has received all of the papers of the Société des Observateurs de l'Homme including the Pinel report, twenty pages, in quarto, handwritten (Advielle, 1880). The abridged version in the text omits these passages from part 2 of the report: Concerning the fourth male: "A fourth child, ten years old, has all the characteristics of an albino: delicate white skin, hair and eyebrows as white as snow, eyes of a pale pink color, and very light-sensitive; both eyeballs protrude and are in continual motion. This child has the other sensory functions, and his ideas are limited to objects of basic necessity." Concerning the second and third females:

"We can put more or less in the same line of idiocy another girl, ten years old, delicate constitution, a face with color in it, an alert and a lively look. She has had convulsive seizures since birth, and she has always been incapable of locomotion. Every day she has convulsive accesses of about a quarter of an hour, and she executes such singular movements of the trunk and limbs that the best comparison is to a dancing puppet. She is as insensitive to threats as caresses, identifies no one, opposes nothing, and gives no indication of reluctance when we pretend to take away her food; from time to time, without provocation, she gives vent to uncontrollable bursts of laughter, momentary transports of delirious gaiety; she cannot articulate any sound or pronounce any syllable although her tongue has ordinary dimensions and mobility; she makes only some vague sound occasionally, but whatever gestures we employ, whatever objects we present, she gives no sign of sensitivity or intelligence, and everything indicates a total absence of ideas.

"A third young girl, eleven years old, can also be placed at the level of the two preceding. Her behavior was normal up to seven years of age, and she seemed to have all the earmarks of understanding that can be expected from this period of life. The second dentition led to convulsions not long after, and since that time she has lost the use of speech and the liberal exercise of her intellectual functions. Attacks of epilepsy, which continue to this time, have brought about the most remarkable changes; she has an air of astonishment and her eyes are almost always directed at random; reduced to a kind of torpor, she remains crouching in her bed, the vertebral column slightly bent and her limbs in the state of flexion. When she is vexed, she lets out a sharp cry and makes an automatic movement with her arm, striking the air at random and without any direct intention. She does not seem, for that matter, to have any memories, and the nebulous feeling of vengeance stops with that of pain. She seems to hear sound, but she cannot pronounce any syllables and she is completely deprived of the use of speech."

Chapter Four.   From Condillac to Itard

p. 73   "outsider"—De Gérando (1848), pp. 112–113.
p. 74   "intellectual development"—Itard (1801), p. 128, 1964 ed.
p. 74   "excesses"—Colona d'Istria (1904).
p. 75   "Pinel's banner"—Bousquet (1840).

p. 75 "at the same time"—Condillac (1780), part 1, chap. 2 (vol. 2, p. 375, 1948 ed.).

p. 75 "sensory impressions"—Pinel (1802), pp. 6–7, 1804 ed.

p. 76 "Bicêtre"—Pinel (1801), cited in Riese (1969), p. 5.

p. 76 "way of life"—Pinel (1802), p. 456.

p. 76 "psychotherapy"—The proper translation is problematical. The *Dictionnaire de l'Académie Française*, the authority in such matters even to this day, gave the following illustration of the use of the word *moral* in its 1825 edition: "Le physique influe beaucoup sur le moral, et le moral sur le physique" (the body strongly influences the mind, and the mind, the body).

p. 77 "particular patient"—Itard (1801), p. 137, 1964 ed.

p. 78 "embrace"—Itard (1802), vol. 2, pp. 530–533, n. 6.

p. 78 "written characters"—Epée (1784), p. 64, 1820 ed. (Sicard, ed.).

p. 79 "such an idea"—Locke (1690), book 3, chap. 2, sec. 1 (vol. 2, p. 8, Dover 1959 ed.).

p. 79 "have no other instructors"—Epée (1784), p. 85, 1801 trans. by Green.

p. 79 "all of Europe"—Sicard (1795), vol. 3, p. 139.

p. 80 "possible or necessary"—Epée (1784), p. 60, 1801 trans. by Green. Another example of the controversial methodical signs: In a public demonstration, Epée was asked to dictate in sign the word *inintelligibilité* (unintelligibility). It was immediately transcribed correctly by the deaf pupils. "I needed only five signs performed in an instant, as you have seen", the abbé said to his guest. "The first announced an internal activity; the second represented the activity of someone who reads internally, that is, who understands what is said to him; the third declared that this arrangement was possible. Doesn't that give the work *intelligible?* But with a fourth sign, transforming this adjective into an abstract quality, isn't *intelligibilité* the result? Finally, by a fifth sign, adding negation, do we not have the entire word *inintelligibilité!*" (Berthier, 1840, pp. 76–77).

p. 80 "lady's bonnet"—Esquiros (1847), p. 419.

p. 80 "dictation by signs"—Sicard (1800), p. xxxvi, 1803 ed.

p. 81 "of this feat"—"I imagined, then, that by causing my pupils to perform a public exercise in four languages . . . the result would evidently be that the Deaf and Dumb are capable of education like other children: consequently, I flattered myself that perhaps there would be found some Potentate, State, or Sovereign, that would be desirous of forming an establishment for them within their dominions. From thence forward there would be someone after me (it matters not in what country) who would continue this work; and sooner or later, other Powers or States would recognize the advantage of it. Is this illusion or error on my part?" Epée (1776).

p. 81 "Condillac"—Michaud (1858), Anon. (1896). The programs of these public demonstrations are printed in Epée (1774).

p. 81 "the human mind"—Condillac (1775), part 1, chap. 1, (vol. 1, pp. 428–429, 1947 ed.).

p. 81   "not by speech"—Sicard (1800), p. xlix, 1803 ed.

p. 82   "about his method"—Condillac (1775), part 1, chap. 1 (vol. 1, pp. 429–430, n. 1, 1947 ed.).

p. 82   "Louis XVI"—Decrees of November 21, 1778, and November 27, 1785. Reprinted in Blanchet (1850), vol. 2, pp. 235–237. A portion of the funds confiscated from the Celestine convent was allocated to Epée's school, as was a part of the convent itself. It was not until September 1790 that Epée's successor could get the 1785 decree implemented and move in to the new quarters which were, in any case, in very bad condition. The school's treasurer advanced his own resources to finance the repairs; he was never repaid, but the school remained at this location for three and a half years.

p. 82   "easily the best"—Cornié (1889). By other accounts, Sicard was the only person to present his candidacy (Anon., 1896). Abbé Masse, a disciple of Epée's, served as acting director until Sicard was installed in office, April 1, 1790.

p. 83   "make us happy"—Sicard (1792). My narrative is based on this source.

p. 86   "education of deaf-mutes"—Maignet (1793).

p. 86   "founded in 1791"—Decree of July 21, 1791. Reprinted in Blanchet (1850), vol. 2, pp. 237–240.

p. 86   "teach the wild boy"—Decrees of 8 Germinal an 2 (March 28, 1794) and 16 Nivôse an 3 (January 5, 1795).

p. 86   "methods of instruction"—Sicard (1795).

p. 86   "never existed"—Michaud (1858), p. 286. For a biography of Sicard, see Berthier (1873).

p. 87   "enough for me"—Sicard (1800), p. xli, 1803 ed.

p. 87   "in that language"—Ibid., p. 483.

p. 87   "perfectly well"—Ibid., p. 484.

p. 87   "make the agreement"—Massieu and Clerc (1815), pp. x–xi.

p. 88   "a belief in Him"—Sicard (1795), vol. 3, pp. 144–145.

p. 89   "abstract values"—Sicard (1800), pp. 18–19, 1803 ed.

p. 90   "Abbé Sicard"—The institution for deaf-mutes was founded at Bordeaux in 1786 and directed by Sicard after he had studied under Epée.

p. 90   "a great deal"—Berthier (1873), pp. 146–154.

p. 90   "of their qualities"—Sicard (1795), vol. 1, pp. 255–265.

p. 91   "un corps vivant"—Sicard (1795), p. 266. The errors in the original French are represented by similar ones in English.

p. 92   "current metaphysics"—Séguin (1843), p. 4.

p. 92   "on the student"—See Médici (1940).

p. 93   "Comenius"—Comenius (1658).

p. 93   "Rousseau"—Rousseau (1762).

p. 93   "Pestalozzi"—Pestalozzi (1801).

p. 93   "plan of this essay"—Condillac (1746), vol. 1, pp. 4–5, 1947 ed.

p. 94   "how to think"—Ibid., p. 115.

p. 95   "pupil!"—Ibid., pp. 43–44.

p. 95   "childish play"—Itard (1801), p. 157, 1964 ed.

p. 95   "played with him"—Condillac (1775).

p. 95   "devices in education"—Michelet (1972).

p. 95   "Education Nouvelle"—Médici (1940).

p. 95   "behavior modification"—See, for example, Ball (1971); Ullman and Krasner (1965).

Chapter Five.   The Return to Society

p. 99   "applauds this effort"—Hervé (1911), p. 389.

p. 99   "objects of instruction"—Itard (1801), pp. 137–138, 1964 ed.

p. 100   "builder's rubbish"—Ibid., p. 139.

p. 100   "enlightened teacher"—Ibid., p. 140.

p. 101   "incredible eagerness"—Ibid., pp. 140–141.

p. 101   "little sound"—Ibid., pp. 141–142.

p. 101   "his education"—Ibid., p. 128.

p. 102   "mental processes arise"—Condillac (1746), vol. 1, pp. 10–14, 1947 ed.

p. 102   "keener impressions"—Itard (1801), p. 145, 1964 ed.

p. 102   "an early age"—Condillac (1775), introduction, vol. 1, p. 406, 1947 ed.

p. 102   "sufficiently exercised"—Condillac (1746), vol. 1, p. 18, 1947 ed.

p. 102   "all the senses"—Itard (1801), p. 148, 1964 ed.

p. 102   "even more marked"—Ibid., p. 149.

p. 103   "physiologists"—Ibid., pp. 149–150.

p. 103   "his detractors contend"—E.g., Mannoni (1969).

p. 103   "safe side of the compartment"—Melzack and Scott (1957).

p. 103   "at the anise"—Irzhanskaia and Felberbaum (1967).

p. 103   "filled with peppermint scent"—Van Deusen Fox (1964, 1965).

p. 103   "then tested"—Schaffer and Emerson (1968).

p. 104   "from any of the senses"—Hernández-Peon (1961).

p. 104   "on the other"—Itard (1801), p. 149, 1964 ed.

p. 104   "sore throats"—Itard (1802), vol. 2, pp. 513–514.

p. 104   "encouragement and instruction"—Itard (1801), p. 153, 1964 ed.

p. 105   "ideas relative to his wants"—Ibid., p. 133.

p. 105   "his bonfire"—Ibid., pp. 151–152.

p. 105   "searches toward them"—Ibid., p. 152.

p. 106   "in his gaze"—Ibid., p. 153.

p. 106   "secondary reinforcer"—Holland (1958).

p. 107   "in the country"—Itard (1801), pp. 153–155, 1964 ed.

p. 107   "valet de chambre"—Wairy (1830), pp. 34 ff.

p. 108   "the philanthropist"—Herriot (1904), pp. 95–96, 1906 trans. by Hallard.

p. 109   "recount their dispute"—Wairy (1830), pp. 48–51.

p. 110   "childish play"—Itard (1801), pp. 156–157, 1964 ed.

p. 111   "things that surround him"—Ibid., pp. 159; 160, n. 1.

p. 112   "his little exercises"—Ibid., pp. 161–162.

p. 112   "for their functions"—Ibid., p. 163.

p. 112   "for language acquisition"—Lenneberg (1967); Krashen and Harshman (1972).

p. 113   "articulating any sound"—Itard (1801), p. 164, 1964 ed.

p. 113   "propensity to imitation"—Ibid., p. 163.

p. 113   "subjects was undertaken"—Baer, Peterson, and Sherman (1967), pp. 407–408.

p. 113   "almost immediately"—Itard (1801), p. 165, 1964 ed.

p. 113   "echoic behavior"—Skinner (1957).

p. 114   "trained to do this"—Lovaas (1967).

p. 114   "like *d* and *l*"—Jakobson (1942).

p. 115   "foreseen at first"—Condillac (1746), vol. 1, pp. 61–62, 1947 ed.

p. 115   "shut behind them"—Itard (1801), p. 169, 1964 ed.

p. 116   "expressing them"—Ibid., p. 168.

p. 116   "received the charge"—Ibid., pp. 146–147.

p. 117   "at the same time"—Ibid., p. 174.

p. 118   "the same result"—Ibid., pp. 174–175.

p. 118   "brightest hope"—Ibid., p. 175.

p. 119   "fruit of comparison"—Ibid., pp. 176–177.

p. 120   "lack of attention"—Ibid., p. 177.

p. 120   "some days' practice"—Ibid., p. 177.

p. 120   "their intensity"—Ibid., pp. 177–178.

p. 120   "disobedient and uncooperative"—Cited in Keller and Schoenfeld (1950), pp. 139–140.

p. 121   "clear cause"—Itard (1801), pp. 178–179, 1964 ed.

p. 121   "he shed tears"—Ibid., pp. 179–180.

p. 122   "responsiveness also appeared"—Lovaas, Schaeffer, and Simmons (1965).

p. 122   "Orléans"—Deschamps (1779).

p. 122   "without any mistake"—Itard (1801), p. 181, 1964 ed.

p. 123   "discrimination became infallible"—Ibid., pp. 181–183.

p. 123   "the word and the thing"—Ibid., p. 183.

p. 124   "word *lait*"—Ibid., p. 184.

p. 125   "was the object"—Itard (1807), pp. 208–209, 1964 ed.

p. 125   "future achievement"—Itard (1801), p. 184, 1964 ed.

p. 125   "with more time"—Ibid., pp. 184–185.

p. 125   "he was an idiot"—Cited in Hervé (1911), p. 397.

p. 125   "talk a little"—Virey (1803), p. 331.

p. 126   "Joseph-Marie de Gérando"—Often spelled, Dégérando. For biographies see Morel (1846), Peet (1852), Porter (1861), Anon. (1861).

p. 126   "authoritative"—De Gérando (1827).

p. 127   "otherwise cared for"—Lévesque (1801), pp. 256–257.

p. 127   "produced so much"—De Gérando (1848).

p. 129   "he is being given"—Anon. (1801), pp. 312–313.

p. 130   "expect from him"—Itard (1801), pp. 185–187, 1964 ed.

Chapter Six. A Report to His Excellency

p. 133　"lung tissue"—Itard (1803).

p. 133　"Champagny"—Champagny (1806). Cited in Itard (1807), pp. A1–A2.

p. 134　"Sauvage de l'Aveyron"—Itard (1807).

p. 134　"receipt of the documents"—Champagny (1806). Cited in Itard (1807).

p. 134　"mechanical trade"—Champagny (1806). Cited in Itard (1807), pp. A5–A6.

p. 134　"communicating ideas"—Itard (1807), pp. 207–208, 1964 ed.

p. 134　"than a savage"—Séguin (1866), p. 18.

p. 135　"the French alphabet"—A = [a] = pâte; E = [ ] = premier; I = [i] = si; O = [o] = mot; U = [y] = lu.

p. 136　"happy life"—Itard (1807), p. 198, 1964 ed.

p. 136　"outward expression"—Ibid., p. 199.

p. 137　"I might give to it"—Ibid., p. 201.

p. 137　"without having learned"—Condillac (1775), introduction, vol. 1, p. 406, 1947 ed.

p. 137　"teach us to judge"—Buffon (1749), vol. 5, p. 194, 1818 ed.

p. 137　"preschool children"—Zaporozhets (1965).

p. 138　"sense of smell"—Itard (1807), p. 204, 1964 ed.

p. 138　"plan of instruction"—Ibid., pp. 203–204.

p. 139　"to alleviate it"—Ibid., pp. 204–205.

p. 139　"matching-to-sample"—Reynolds (1968).

p. 140　"at hand"—Itard (1807), pp. 210–211, 1964 ed.

p. 140　"the forgotten one"—Ibid., pp. 211–212.

p. 141　"of his errand"—Ibid., p. 212.

p. 141　"classes or categories"—Brown (1958), p. 7.

p. 142　"names in succession"—Itard (1807), pp. 213–214, 1964 ed. (italics added).

p. 142　"boredom at Bicêtre"—Ibid., pp. 214–215.

p. 143　"a glowing look"—Ibid., pp. 215–216.

p. 143　"to their similarities"—Ibid., p. 217.

p. 144　"properties in common"—Ibid., pp. 217–218.

p. 145　"species of trees"—Condillac (1780), part 1, chap. 4 (vol. 2, 1947 ed.).

p. 145　"what happened"—Itard (1807), pp. 218–219, 1964 ed.

p. 145　"of a plate"—Ibid., p. 219.

p. 146　"automatic habits"—Ibid., pp. 219–221.

p. 148　"and ate it"—Ibid., pp. 224–225.

p. 149　"exactly parallel"—Ibid., pp. 225–226.

p. 149　"lever pressing"—Baer and Sherman (1964).

p. 149　"with retarded"—Baer, Peterson, and Sherman (1967).

p. 149　"or schizophrenic"—Lovaas (1966, 1968).

p. 150　"the will of others"—Itard (1807), p. 226, 1964 ed.

p. 150　"the eighteenth century"—La Rochelle (1882).

p. 150   *"Natural History"*—Buffon (1749), p. 182, 1818 ed.

p. 150   "Pereire's life and work"—Séguin (1847).

p. 150   "Gascony accent"—Séguin (1866), p. 18.

p. 151   "Bonet's manual alphabet"—Bonet (1620).

p. 151   "fifteen months"—Séguin (1876), pp. 54–55.

p. 151   "pupils to speak"—In another interview she stated that Pereire placed the main emphasis "on pronunciation, then writing. He also used the two other methods [gestures and the manual alphabet] . . . He made us pronounce first the five vowels, then syllables, from the easiest to the more difficult . . . He employed an eartrumpet whose horn could be rotated depending on whether one wanted to speak to the student or he wanted to speak to himself . . . As his students became stronger in pronunciation, he prescribed gestural language which he used as a means of explanation and which he set aside as soon as he could teach without it . . . [Signed] M. M. Marois, former mute" (Valade-Gabel, 1894, pp. 162–163).

p. 151   "this process"—Cited in Séguin (1876), pp. 53–54.

p. 151   "sense of touch"—Ibid., p. 54.

p. 152   "of the language"—La Rochelle (1882), p. 50.

p. 152   "a teacher and essayist"—Vaïsse (1878, 1883).

p. 152   *"Emile"*—Rousseau (1762).

p. 153   "my first experiments"—Itard (1807), p. 229, 1964 ed.

p. 154   "an accelerating pace"—Lovaas (1966, 1967, 1968).

p. 155   "given him life"—Itard (1807), pp. 232–233, 1964 ed.

p. 155   "or punishment"—Ibid., pp. 234–235.

p. 156   "muscular strength"—Ibid., p. 235.

p. 157   "his attributes"—Ibid., pp. 238–240.

p. 158   "passing fancy"—Ibid., pp. 241–242.

p. 158   "hemorrhage is abundant"—Ibid., pp. 242–243.

p. 159   "further observations"—Itard (1801), pp. 187–188, 1964 ed.

p. 159   "unforeseen obstacle"—Itard (1807), p. 244, 1964 ed.

p. 159   "fruit of education"—Ibid., p. 245.

p. 160   "his outbursts"—Ibid., p. 246.

p. 160   "private education"—Ibid., p. 190.

Chapter Seven.   Interpreting the Legend

p. 164   "lost or abandoned"—Esquirol (1838), pp. 374–375.

p. 165   "teaching reading"—Fareng (1959).

p. 166   "household objects"—See Michelet (1972).

p. 167   "unfortunate young man"—Dacier (1806), pp. 7–9 in Itard (1807).

p. 167   "efforts that were made"—Virey (1817), p. 269.

p. 167   "the year 1828"—Malson (1964), p. 97; Hervé (1911), p. 398.

p. 167   "he had accepted"—Séguin (1843), p. 5.

p. 167   "consequently, of independence"—Séguin (1856), p. 146.

p. 167   "beyond notions"—Séguin (1846), pp. 9–10; (1843), pp. 5–6.

p. 168 "voice this criticism"—Séguin (1846), Delasiauve (1865), Ball (1971).

p. 168 "intellectual faculties"—Halle and Moreau (1808), p. 875.

p. 168 "organized instruction"—Mannoni (1965).

p. 171 "become one too"—Bory de Saint-Vincent (1822), vol. 8, pp. 271–272.

p. 171 "at their will"—Gall and Spurzheim (1812), vol. 2, pp. 41–42.

p. 171 "ever be obtained"—Ibid., pp. 42–43.

p. 172 "elongated backwards"—Larrey (1817), pp. 17–18. Also cited in Singh and Zingg (1966) and in Rauber (1888), who points out that the Lithuanian man may have been quite normal and that, in any event, a misshapen skull is not proof of idiocy.

p. 172 "contend, its result"—Lévi-Strauss (1949), pp. 3–4.

p. 172 "Lévi-Strauss"—Montessori (1912), Gesell (1941), Dennis (1941, 1951), Tyler (1863).

p. 172 "born retarded"—Destutt de Tracy (1817), vol. 1, pp. 291–292.

p. 172 "physiological means"—Séguin (1866), pp. 17, 21.

p. 173 "he does not understand"—Anon. (1800b), p. 9.

p. 174 "Zingg"—Zingg (1940), Singh and Zingg (1942).

p. 175 "urges, like hunger"—Zingg (1940), p. 510.

p. 175 "can many idiots"—The quote is from Dennis (1941), who cites Tredgold (1920).

p. 176 "is satisfactory"—Delasiauve (1865), p. xlv, 1894 ed. Dennis (1941), p. 431, Anastasi and Foley (1949), Brauner and Brauner (1969), Davis (1940), Freeman (1934), Klineberg (1954), Kellogg (1931), and Michelet (1969) all give this objection to the hypothesis of congenital retardation in wild children.

p. 176 "child psychiatry"—Bettelheim (1967), Brauner and Brauner (1969), Silberstein and Irwin (1962); also Klineberg (1954).

p. 176 "Victor, we are told"—Brauner and Brauner (1969); Bettelheim (1967), pp. 371–372.

p. 177 "blazing embers"—Itard (1801), p. 178, 1964 ed.

p. 177 "the forgotten one"—Itard (1807), pp. 211–212, 1964 ed.

p. 178 "wild boy of Aveyron"—Itard (1801), p. 134, 1964 ed.

p. 179 "to recover speech"—See Tinland (1968), pp. 65–66, 82; Leroy (1776), pp. 8–9.

p. 179 "Robinson Crusoe"—Defoe (1719).

p. 179 "according to his diary"—Rogers (1717).

p. 179 "ability to speak"—Rogers (1717), pp. 192–200. Also see De Pauw (1772), part 3, sec. 2, pp. 352–353.

p. 179. "how to speak"—Malson (1964). See Itard (1807), p. 65, 1964 ed.

p. 179 "diverse environmentalists"—Tafel (1848), Zingg (1940), Anastasi and Foley (1949), Malson (1964, 1970), Singh and Zingg (1966), Tinland (1968), Michelet (1969).

p. 179 "the following challenge"—Dennis (1941, 1951). Delasiauve (1865) expressed a similar opinion.

p. 180 "air of civilization"—Bousquet (1840), p. 6.

p. 180 "physical endowment"—Gall and Spurzheim (1812), p. 44.

p. 180 "as Rauber does"—Rauber (1885). Tredgold's term is *isolation amentia* (1920).

p. 180 "his asocial habits"—Freeman (1934), Kellog (1931), Smith (1954).

p. 180 "period for language learning"—Sargent (1950), Davis (1940, 1947).

p. 180 "least gifted of infants"—Itard (1801), p. 163, 1964 ed. Other diagnoses include hearing defect (Brown, 1958), mixed aphasia (Anon., 1964a), hereditary mental atavism (Courbon, 1913), and fraud (Feydl, 1900; Anon., 1800d; Anon. 1964b; A., 1800; Barnard (1974).

p. 181 "most favorably"—Itard (1821), pp. 361–362, 1842 ed.

p. 181 "speech by imitation"—Ibid.

p. 181 "note of it here"—Itard (1828), p. 113, 1894 ed.

p. 181 "annihilated in their case"—Itard (1827), p. 183. Bousquet (1840) and Séguin (1866) took the preceding quotation out of context and claimed incorrectly that it shows that Itard finally realized Victor was congenitally retarded.

p. 181 "California girl"—Fromkin et al. (1974).

p. 182 "Itard's tutelage"—See Michelet (1969), p. 24, and Brauner and Brauner (1969), p. 47; Dacier (1806); Itard (1807); but Sarason (1959) considers the progress slight.

Chapter Eight. Victor's Legacy to the Deaf

p. 185 "post-mortem dissections"—In Itard's day, otology was largely restricted to procedures affecting the middle ear, principally perforation of the eardrum and catheterism of the Eustachian tube. Itard practiced these techniques and was an authority on both (1836). However, he believed that their only merit was to allow the physician to douche the middle ear and apply medicines to it directly. For this purpose he perfected a metallic tube, the *sonde d'Itard,* still in use in otology today (Molinéry and Molinéry, 1938a, b).

p. 185 "more easily overcome"—Itard (1825), pp. 3–4.

p. 185 "half a century earlier"—Pereire (1749).

p. 185 "have been reconstructed"—Séguin (1876), La Rochelle (1882).

p. 185 "during their lifetime"—Talbot (1964), pp. 18–19.

p. 186 "November 26, 1807"—Itard (1807). The traditions of this august body go at least as far back as 1675, when the Faculty of Medicine in Paris began formal monthly deliberations called Prima Mensis. In 1731, the Royal Society of Medicine was founded and, with the coming of the Revolution, the two fiercely competitive groups were dissolved by decree. The postrevolutionary period of reconstruction saw the birth not only of the French Institute with its three "classes," and of the Society of Observers of Man, but also of the Société Libre de Santé de Paris, founded privately on February 17, 1796, which changed its name to Société de Médecine de Paris on February 15, 1797. The government ordered the

Society of Medicine to meet bi-weekly at the School of Medicine in Paris, created during the Revolution. The group took the name of Société de la Faculté de Médecine in 1806. (A list of the society's periodical publications under various names appears in the introduction to the *Bulletin de la Société de Médecine de Paris* for 1866.) Meanwhile, an Academy of Medicine was formed privately in 1804 and officially recognized in 1805 (Ganière, 1964). Thus had history carefully reconstructed the old rivalry, if in an attenuated and somewhat more constructive form.

p. 186 "requested us to present"—Halle and Moreau (1808), p. 874.

p. 186 "methods of teaching speech"—*Bulletin de l'Ecole de Médecine de Paris (et de la Société établie dans son sein)*, 1808, p. 54 (published with the *Journal de Médecine . . .*, 1808, vol. 15); meeting of April 14, 1808.

p. 186 "their various exercises"—Ibid., meeting of May 12, 1808.

p. 187 "simple hardness of hearing"—D'Olivet (1811), p. 248, 1927 trans.

p. 187 "to each of them"—Itard (1821), pp. 355–356, 1842 ed.

p. 188 "one of its Bulletins"—The record is in Itard (1808), the quote from Itard (1825), pp. 6–7.

p. 188 "profoundly deaf"—Itard estimates that more than half of the institute's pupils were profoundly deaf, according to his "Treatise on Diseases of the Ear and Hearing" (1821); he gives the figure of two-thirds in a later unpublished memorandum (Itard, 1824).

p. 188 "from this instruction"—Itard (1821), pp. 356–357, n. 1, 1842 ed.

p. 188 "Diseases of the Ear and Hearing"—Itard (1821).

p. 188 "dated 1824"—Itard (1824).

p. 188 "all the vowels"—With the exception of the contrasts d'où–do and et–eux (/u/ – /o/, /e/ – /ø/) according to Husson (1833).

p. 189 "he presented them"—Von Békésy (1960) describes modern techniques for measuring absolute and differential thresholds. For a discussion of auditory localization see Rosenzweig (1972).

p. 191 "the first syllable"—Itard (1821), p. 365, 1842 ed.

p. 191 "voice print machine"—Potter, Kopp, and Green (1947).

p. 191 "synthesized speech"—Flanagan (1972).

p. 192 "null for them"—Itard (1821), p. 369, 1842 ed.

p. 193 "lost for him"—Ibid., p. 304, 1822 ed.

p. 193 "the first place"—Miller and Isard (1963), Marks and Miller (1964).

p. 194 "listen and observe"—Itard (1821), pp. 362–363, 1842 ed.

p. 195 "during their development"—Ibid., p. 369.

p. 195 "Teaching Deaf-Mutes to Speak"—Bonet (1620), Peet (1850).

p. 196 "whole day's conversation"—Digby (1645).

p. 196 "foreigners and the deaf"—Wallis (1653), Anon. (1850).

p. 196 "published in 1692"—Amman (1692, 1700).

p. 198 "I may be wrong"—Epée (1776), pp. 9, 57; 24, part 2. Although Epée believed that the only means of returning the deaf to society "is to teach them to comprehend by eye and to express themselves orally" (1776, p. 155), he sent three letters in defense of sign to Samuel Heinicke, who founded German education of the deaf in 1778, based on oral instruction to the exclusion of sign. The controversy was aired before the Academy of Science at Zurich, which gave the day to the French School.

p. 198   "Thouron"—Sicard (1795), vol. 1, p. 252; vol. 3, p. 266.

p. 198   "as the mouth"—The eight simple vowels, indicated by these key words: *acte* (the *a* is intermediate between those in *father* and *act*), *et* (as in *ate*), *eux* (German, *öffen*), *premier* (*believe*), *ile* (*eel*), *haut* (*owe*), *outré* (*boot*), *une* (German, *über*). He taught pronunciation of the vowels in the order indicated, [a, e, ø, ə, i, o, u, y] in phonetic notation. Reasonably enough, Itard omitted the vowels in *elle, heure,* and *homme* [ɛ, œ, ɔ], which are similar to those in *et, eux,* and *haut,* [e, ɛ, o], respectively. The former do not occur at the ends of words, so the pupil does not run the risk of being misunderstood if he makes one vowel serve the place of two, as many Frenchmen do. Similarly, Itard left the vowel in *âme* (intermediate between those in *father* and *law*), [ɑ] to one side; it is very similar to the one in *acte,* [a], and it is quite infrequent, although a few contrasts survive: *tache/tâche,* (stain/task), *patte/pâte* (paw/paste). The nasal vowels were those in *anse, onze, Inde,* and *humble,* which correspond roughly to the vowels in *âme, homme, elle,* and *heure.*

p. 199   "*chateau*"—Likewise *c* would do the duty of *k, c,* and *q,* while *h* is never pronounced. This left seventeen consonants to teach; postponing the nasal consonant in *pagne* for the end of training (it is perhaps the most difficult and the least frequent), Itard wrote the rest as follows: Pa/Ba, Ta/Da/, Fa/Va, Sa/Za, Cha/Ja, Ca/Ga, Ra/La, Ma/Na. (*J* is one sound, as in Engl. *azure,* Fr. *Jean.*) In phonetic notation [p/b, t/d, f/v, s/z, ʃ/ʒ, k/g, r/l, m/n].

p. 199   "respectively"—Also one that does not occur in English (or Spanish or German or even often in French for that matter), the initial sound in *huit.* The semivowels were practiced first in SV syllables, then in CSV syllables (*Louis, lui, Dieu*), including those with a nasal vowel (*loin, chien*).

p. 200   "head-long rush"—Itard (1821), p. 377, 1842 ed.

p. 200   "along the way"—von Békésy (1960).

p. 200   "to about half"—von Békésy (1960).

p. 200   "language laboratory"—Hayes (1963).

p. 201   "correcting it"—Itard (1821), p. 379, 1842 ed.

p. 202   "desired result"—Perhaps Itard was trying to teach the educated pronunciation [b i l j a r], which his pupils rendered like the common people [b i j a r]. This distinction was common in the sixteenth century, and by the nineteenth the latter pronunciation was standard.

p. 202   "confused by ear"—Itard (1821) p. 383, 1842 ed.

p. 203   "aural counterparts"—Catford and Pisoni (1970).

p. 203   "the foreign tongue"—Itard (1821), p. 388, 1842 ed.

p. 203   "down in writing"—Ibid., p. 389.

p. 204   "deaf-mute forever"—Itard (1802), vol. 2, pp. 554–555, n. 6.

p. 204   "sign language"—Halle and Moreau (1808), p. 878.

p. 207 "learned a sign"—Morel (1845), p. 92.

p. 207 "a foreign language"—Itard (1808), p. 78.

p. 207 "these reports"—The "first report" was published in the *Journal universel des sciences médicales* (Itard, 1821). The manuscript of the "second report" erroneously states that the first appeared in volume 22 of the *Journal général de médecine* (Itard, 1824). The manuscript of the "third report" is dated July 7 (Itard, 1826). Also found was a manuscript on the same topic, "Rapport de M. Itard . . . fait à l'administration le 8 juillet 1825" (Itard, 1825).

p. 207 "Itard's original reports"—The Commission of the Academy of Medicine gave its evaluation at a meeting of the Academy on May 6, 1828. The report, prepared by Husson, is summarized in the *Journal général de médecine* (1828, vol. 103, pp. 391–398) and in *Transactions médicales, Journal de médecine* (1833, vol. 12, p. 249). The full report is given by Husson (1883), and reprinted in the second edition of Itard's *Traité* (1842) and in Bourneville (1894).

p. 208 "everything from nothing"—Itard (1821), pp. 325–326, 1842 ed.

p. 209 "I just described"—Ibid., p. 326.

p. 209 "verbs, and tenses"—Itard (1827), pp. 192–193.

p. 210 "flashes of brilliance"—Itard (1821), pp. 327–329, 1842 ed.

p. 210 "trust of the mind"—De Jouy (1813).

p. 211 "seek his fortune"—Itard (1821), pp. 327–329, 1842 ed. A pupil of Massieu and Clerc, F. Berthier, wrote: "[Clerc's] progress was so rapid in all phases of instruction that in 1807 the renowned director wanted him to serve as teaching assistant to Massieu, whom Clerc soon left very far behind" (1873, p. 182). Clerc (1849) gives some charming reminiscences of his friendship with Massieu and the latter's unworldly ways.

p. 211 "age of eighteen"—Peet (1852), Anon. (1858), Humphrey (1857).

p. 212 "deaf and dumb persons"—Weld (1848), Barnard (1852).

p. 212 "school in Paris"—The following excerpt from the *Edinburgh Encyclopedia* published two years earlier shows clearly what instructors in the citadel of oralism thought of Epée's manual methods and school: "Although he still continues to trammel his pupils with the system of Methodical Signs, he has so far improved upon the method of his predecessor, that he instructs them fully and correctly in the meaning of words, and teaches them to compare for themselves. Many of them, we have understood, are extremely intelligent; but why he does not teach them Speech, we know not. If, however, the method which he pursued in instructing Massieu at Bordeaux, and the detail of which constitutes his work, we must say, that this system is one of the most tedious, intricate, and metaphysical, that it is possible to conceive. They who have profited by the simplicity and good sense of Wallis and Watson, will not be readily prevailed upon to work through many pages of the declamation and useless subtlety of Sicard" (Anon., *Edinburgh Encyclopedia*, 1813, vol. 8, p. 13).

p. 212   "hear with the eye"—Johnson (1775).

p. 212   "Francis Green"—F. Green (1783), S. Green (1861).

p. 213   "Bell recounts"—Bell (1918), Fay (1878).

p. 213   "make no comment"—Gallaudet (1888), p. 66.

p. 213   "received no reply"—Root (1924), pp. 66–67.

p. 214   "can determine this"—Ibid., p. 80.

p. 214   "authority and power"—Massieu and Clerc (1815).

p. 216   "so in Connecticut"—Fay (1913), pp. 230–231.

p. 216   "means of communication"—Root (1924).

p. 216   "Alice's schoolmates"—A more detailed description of Alice's instruction through the medium of sign and pantomime appears in Mrs. Sigourney's *Letters of Life.* The account is particularly interesting because the events took place during the first year the school was open, 1814 (Haight, 1930)—two years before Gallaudet and Clerc returned from France with the sign language used there—yet rather extensive manual communication was clearly in use in Mrs. Sigourney's classroom: "Then also, my dear little silent disciple, Alice Cogswell, the loved of all, had her pleasant privilege of examination. Coming ever to my side, if she saw me a moment disengaged, with her sweet supplication, 'Please, teach Alice something,' the words, or historical facts thus explained by signs, were alphabetically arranged in a small manuscript book, for her to recapitulate and familiarize. Great was her delight when called forth to take her part. Descriptions in animated gesture she was fond of intermingling with a few articulate sounds, unshaped by the ear's criticism. In alluding to the death of Henry II of England from a surfeit of lamprey-eels, she invariably uttered, in strong, guttural intonation, the word 'fool!' adding, by signs, her contempt of eating too much, and a scornful imitation of the squirming creature who had thus prostrated a mighty king. Fragments from the annals of all nations, with the significance of a multitude of words, had been taught by little and little, until her lexicon had become comprehensive; and as her companions, from love, had possessed themselves of the manual alphabet and much of the sign-language, they affectionately proposed that the examinations should be of themselves, and that she might be permitted to conduct it. Here was a new pleasure, the result of their thoughtful kindness. Eminently happy was she made, while each in rotation answered with the lips her question given by the hand, I alternately officiating as interpreter to her, or critic to them, if an explanation chanced to be erroneous. Never can I forget the varied expressions of intelligence, *naïveté*, irony, or love that would radiate from her beautiful hazel eyes on these occasions" (Sigourney, 1866, pp. 221–222).

p. 216   "right way Alice trust"—Root (1924) p. 72.

p. 217   "J. C. Hottinguer"—Fay (1879).

p. 217   "fifty-two days"—See Clerc's diary (1952).

p. 217   "there were thirty-three"—Williams (1893).

p. 218   "sign language from Clerc"—Turner (1870).

p. 218   "in the 1760s"—Vaïsse (1878). The dates given by various authors for the beginning of Epée's school range from 1755 to 1770.

Notes   338

p. 218 "neighbors understood us"—Sicard (1808); cited in Berthier (1852), pp. 37–38.

p. 219 "Dictionary of Signs"—Epée (1896).

p. 219 "Sicard was still compiling"—According to Petit (1859), p. 13.

p. 219 "Theory of Signs"—Sicard (1808).

p. 219 "I please to dictate"—Epée (1784), p. 86, 1801 trans.

p. 220 "danger of loss"—Cited in Turner (1870), p. 18. The New York School for the Deaf was established soon after the one in Hartford. After an unsuccessful experiment with oralist methods, students of Clerc were called in to reorganize the instruction: H. Peet was appointed principal and Barnard and Bartlett instructors. L. Vaïsse, professor at the Paris school on leave in New York, joined the group. Guided by Bébian's "Practical Manual of Instruction for Deaf Mutes" (1827) and De Gérando's two-volume compendium on the education of deaf-mutes (1827), the school taught colloquial sign language without the use of methodical sign and in its natural word order. Further reflecting recent developments in Paris, largely at Itard's instigation, courses in articulation were offered. See Syle (1873), pp. 146–162. The Kentucky Institution for the Deaf and Dumb, the first west of the Alleghenies, was also founded by one of Clerc's pupils, J. J. Jacobs. Clerc also helped to found the Pennsylvania Institution, which was directed for over a half century by his pupils, L. Weld and A. Hutton, as well as institutions in Ohio, Virginia, and Quebec.

p. 220 "language for the idea"—Williams (1893), pp. 22–23.

p. 220 "disuse and oblivion"—Rae (1852), p. 246.

p. 220 "A Refuge for the Infirm"—Yebra (1593).

p. 221 "Bonet's book on him"—According to Séguin (1876), p. 57.

p. 221 "later in 1869"—Clerc (1848).

p. 222 "the medium of signs"—Itard (1824), pp. 9–11.

p. 223 "[devinement]"—Husson (1833).

p. 223 "reciprocal agreement"—Itard (1827), pp. 202–203.

p. 223 "successful results"—Morel (1845), pp. 92–93.

p. 224 "indispensable"—Itard (1826), pp. 6–8.

p. 224 "oral instruction"—Séguin (1866), p. 19.

p. 224 "more fluently"—Sicard (1795), pp. 268–269.

p. 225 "than by voice"—Ibid.

p. 225 "1825 report"—Itard (1825), p. 13.

p. 225 "less complete"—Itard (1821), p. 391, 1842 ed.

p. 225 "degree of deafness"—Itard (1827), p. 181.

p. 225 *American Annals of the Deaf*—Vernon and Koh (1970, 1971).

p. 226 "fewer passed them"—These findings would have given pause to Alexander Graham Bell, founder of the Volta Bureau and advocate of the pure oral method of deaf instruction. In an 1898 pamphlet questioning the "Utility of Signs" he wrote: "Mr. Jenkins expresses the opinion that the graduates of schools that employ the sign-language are better educated than those of oral schools. This of course would be an argument if it were established by facts, but Mr. Jenkins offers no evidence in its support" (p. 8).

p. 226   "the other child"—Husson (1828), p. 138, 1894 ed.

p. 226   "same conclusion"—Listed in the previously cited studies.

p. 228   "to water garden you"—"Voulez-vous que nous arrosions ce soir votre jardin?" "Nous, ce soir arroser jardin toi."

p. 228   "vaguely in sign"—Itard (1826), pp. 3–6.

p. 228   "himself by reading"—Itard (1827), pp. 193–195.

p. 229   "former just one"—Bellugi and Siple (1974).

p. 230   "American Sign Language"—Stokoe, Casterline, and Croneberg (1965) list nineteen handshapes; a twentieth found with children learning Ameslan has been added to the top row, third from the left.

p. 232   "hand are used"—Bellugi and Fischer (1972).

p. 232   "their components"—Itard (1827), pp. 195–196.

p. 233   "in Ameslan and in English"—Bellugi and Fischer (1972).

p. 234   "nouns and adjectives"—Houdin (1881).

p. 235   "imposed on Ameslan"—Esquiros (1847), pp. 424–425.

p. 235   "for *cook, explain*"—Bellugi and Klima (1974).

p. 235–236   "become more encoded"—Frishberg (1973).

p. 237   "deaf-mutes to speak"—Husson (1828), pp. 138–140, 1894 ed.

p. 237   "Meeting in 1824"—The Imperial Academy of Medicine became the Royal Academy with Napoleon's downfall and the Bourbon Restoration. Its first meeting was on May 6, 1824. Itard's "Report on Mutism Produced by Lesions of Intellectual Functioning" appeared in the Academy's first volume of annals (Itard, 1828).

p. 237   "materials for comprehension"—Itard (1824), p. 107, 1894 ed.

p. 238   "the complete sentence"—Ibid., p. 114.

p. 238   "retained in memory"—Ibid., pp. 114–115.

p. 238   "negroes in our colonies"—Ibid., p. 115.

p. 241   "speaking teacher"—This portion of the will appears in Bélanger (1904), Berthier (1852), and Morel (1845). The entire will is reprinted in Petit (1859).

p. 241   "complete his education"—Itard (1827), pp. 189–190.

p. 241   "through reading"—Ibid., p. 195.

p. 242   "the foreign language"—Itard (1821), p. 388, 1842 ed.

p. 242   "of their apprenticeship"—Morel (1845), pp. 95–96.

p. 243   "society at large"—Berthier (1852), p. 87.

p. 243   "linked to each other"—Condillac (1746), introduction, vol. 1, p. 4, 1947 ed.

p. 243   "would be destroyed"—Reported in Berthier (1852), p. 38.

p. 243   "exists before language"—Ibid., p. 89.

p. 244   "images of signs"—Ibid., pp. 89–90.

p. 244   "American asylum"—Clerc (1848).

p. 244   "sign was used extensively"—Esquiros (1847).

p. 244   "cover the child's eyes"—Vaïsse (1854); cited in Petit (1859), pp. 29–30.

p. 247   "accord us"—Petit and Vial (1858), pp. 2, 4.

p. 247   "memoir"—Petit (1859).

p. 247   "Speaking People"—Blanchet (1856).

p. 248   "with the blind"—Itard (1821), p. 12.

p. 248   "to teach speech"—Esquiros (1847), p. 452ff.

p. 248   "derived from articulation"—Clerc (1848), pp. 116–117. Also see Rae (1852), p. 247. Day (1861) gives a scathing account of the inadequacies of oral training observed during a visit to the Paris Institute in 1861.

p. 248   "institute's enrollment"—According to Esquiros, there were twenty-four students originally; the convention increased the enrollment to sixty in 1793. By 1847, there were one hundred fourteen students.

p. 248   "sympathy I needed"—Quoted in Séguin (1876), p. 62.

p. 249   "useless and compromising"—Ibid., p. 61.

p. 249   "condition to be visited"—Séguin (1876), p. 106, 1895 French trans.

p. 249   "education by speech"—Ménière (1853), p. 352.

p. 249   "starlings or parrots"—Connecticut Asylum (1819), pp. 6–8.

p. 250   "attained by articulation"—Wheeler (1920), p. 372.

p. 250   "controversial report"—Mann (1844).

p. 250   "combinations of letters"—Anon. (1844), p. 333.

p. 251   "permanently useful"—Williams (1893), p. 24.

p. 251   "Edward in 1864"—Rae (1853), Fox (1900).

p. 252   "congress at Lyon"—Fay (1880).

p. 252   "instruction of deaf-mutes"—Houdin (1881), p. 27. Also see Gallaudet (1881), Denison (1881).

p. 252   "should be preferred"—Houdin (1881), p. 28.

p. 252   "Vive la parole!"—Ibid., p. 41.

p. 252   "communicate orally"—Bélanger (1904).

p. 252   "deaf-mutes in France"—Maudit (1900). On the history of oral instruction in France, also see Dupont (1889, 1897) and Blanchet (1850).

p. 252   "phonetic elements"—Anon. (1896), p. 42. A visitor to the Institute in 1896 wrote, "It seemed strange to us that, in a school where so much honor was paid to the [Abbé de l'Epée], there should not be one class taught by the method which in America we always associate with his name" (Adams, 1896, p. 385). However, the pupils used signs among themselves; see Bishop (1889).

p. 253   "favor of sign"—Anon. (1901), Gaillard and Janvoine (1900), Draper (1901), Gallaudet (1900), Fay (1900). Between the so-called International Congresses of Milan (1880) and Paris (1900), there was one at Brussels (1883) of lesser importance (Anon., 1883).

p. 254   "superior to signs"—Martha and Gaillard (1900).

Chapter Ten.   Itard's Legacies

p. 257   "medical literature"—Bousquet (1840), p. 18.

p. 258   "Passy, in 1838"—Séguin (1856), p. 148. Séguin's English naturally reflects the fact that he had left his native France only eight years earlier.

p. 258   "Digne and Forcalquier respectively"—Actually his half-nephew and half-niece, not his cousins. Itard's father, Joseph, was married twice, to Jeanne Baptiste and to Itard's mother, Anne Breissan; each had daughters by an earlier marriage. Itard's half-sister, Anne, married Ange-Honoré Petit and they had three children, Joseph, Annette, and Honoré (Petit, 1859).

p. 259   "mortal remains"—The plot is located in the third division, twelfth line, 1 East, Cimetière Parisien du Sud-Montparnasse, Concession 390, cadastre 113 3e, No 3606.

p. 261   "suffer and to die"—The will is quoted in Petit (1859), pp. 5–9.

p. 261   "for the result"—Cited in Séguin (1856), pp. 146–147.

p. 261   "declared incurable"—Ibid., p. 147.

p. 263   "intensive domestic care"—Esquirol (1818), pp. 508, 514–515, 523.

p. 263   "all modification"—Calmeil (1837), p. 225.

p. 263   "he never knew"—Séguin (1856), p. 148.

p. 263   "Olinde Rodrigues"—Saint-Simon (1865).

p. 263   "I mean the idiots"—Séguin (1843), p. 2.

p. 264   "affection and will"—Séguin (1856), p. 148.

p. 264   "took after him"—Séguin (1846), p. 4.

p. 264   "training of mankind"—Séguin (1866), p. 23.

p. 264   "Fourteen Months"—Séguin (1839).

p. 265   "desirable extension"—Quoted in Séguin (1846), p. 14. Also appears in the 1895 French translation (1876a).

p. 265   "its deaf pupils"—Turner (1856).

p. 265   "employed by M. Séguin"—Quoted in Séguin (1843), pp. 108–109. Also appears in the 1895 French translation (1876a).

p. 265   "Education of Idiots"—Séguin (1842).

p. 266   "depraving the idiots"—It was the practice at this time to place idiots with epileptics in special sections of insane asylums. In 1837, there were 5960 patients at La Salpêtrière and Bicêtre, including 143 idiots, or a ratio of about one in forty. Itard stated that one out of every four children examined at the Institute for Deaf Mutes suffered from idiocy (Calmeil, 1837).

p. 266   "advantageous conditions?"—Séguin (1843), p. 108.

p. 266   "worthy to be followed"—Published February 6, 1843. *Comptes-rendus des séances de l'Académie Royale des Sciences*, 1843, pp. 1295–1299. Quoted in Holman (1914), pp. 29–30.

p. 267   "Félix Voisin"—Voisin (1843).

p. 267   "songs of Thanksgiving"—Sumner (1876), p. 62.

p. 268   "Harvey Wilbur"—Remarks in memory of E. Séguin by H. Wilbur. In: Association of Medical Officers (1880).

p. 268   *"Physiological Method"*—Séguin (1866). This book was a revision of one written in French in 1864 and translated by Dr. L. P. Brocket of Albany.

p. 268   "body temperature"—Séguin (1876b).

p. 268   "U.S. and abroad"—For the Vienna International Exhibition of 1873, see Séguin (1876). He made another survey trip in 1877 and published a second edition of the report (Séguin, 1880).

p. 268   "treatment of idiocy"—Séguin (1870, 1879, 1880).

p. 269   "moral medicine"—Séguin (1846), p. 70.

p. 269   "positive education"—Séguin (1843), p. 4.

p. 269   "psychological state"—Séguin (1846), pp. 217–223.

p. 269   "constants of idiocy"—Ibid., p. 138.

p. 271   "communicate to them"—Anon. (1847), p. 20.

p. 271   "normal or idiotic"—Séguin (1843), p. 25.

p. 271   "to the intellect"—Séguin (1866), p. 103.

p. 272   "Great Britain"—Anon. (1847), p. 21.

p. 273   "that exercise"—Séguin (1843), p. 59. The passage is discussed in Talbot (1964).

p. 274   "were well done"—Anon. (1847), p. 71.

p. 274   "pronounces *ma* or *pa*"—Séguin (1866), p. 108, 1907 ed.

p. 275   "questions proposed"—Anon. (1847), p. 72.

p. 275   "diametrically opposed"—Séguin (1846), p. 10.

p. 276   "reasoning to function"—Ibid., p. 460.

p. 276   "psychological research"—Bem (1972).

p. 276   "contingent doings"—Séguin (1866), p. 159, 1907 ed.

p. 277   "imitation and rivalry"—Séguin (1842), p. 2.

p. 278   "ordinary daily routine"—Anon. (1847), pp. 105–107.

p. 278   "training of mankind"—Séguin (1866), p. 23.

p. 279   "not just the retarded"—Séguin (1876); see esp. 1880 ed.

p. 279   "Childhood Education"—Four excellent educational appraisals of the work of Séguin and Montessori are: Médici (1940), Fynne (1924), Boyd (1914), and Ball (1971). Concerning Séguin, also see Holman (1914) and Talbot's comprehensive and scholarly monograph (1964).

p. 279   "special to them"—Montessori (1909), pp. 33–34, 1912 trans.

p. 280   "medical problem"—Ibid., p. 31.

p. 280   "school and education"—Ibid., pp. 41–42.

p. 281   "obscure heroism"—Ibid., pp. 45–46.

p. 282   "Elementary School"—Montessori (1916).

p. 283   "internal organization"—Montessori (1917), p. 70.

p. 283   "to this purpose"—A comprehensive list appears in Michelet (1972).

p. 284   "chromatic memory"—Montessori (1909), pp. 178–179, 1912 trans.

p. 285   "path of psychiatry"—Ibid., p. 46.

Index

Academy of Medicine, 5, 207, 237, 241, 243, 249, 259, 260; report on deaf-mutes, 226; conclusions on Itard's three reports, 236–237; endorses sign, 236–237

Academy of Sciences, 54, 56, 150, 151, 259; endorses Séguin's methods, 266

Acquired ideas. *See* Ideas, acquired

Adjectives, 146–147, 276

Affective functions, 134, 135

Alembert, Jean Le Rond d', 12

Alexander, Emperor, 259

Allibert, Eugène, 242–244, 259

Alphabet: cutouts, 122; manual, 195

American Association for the Promotion of the Teaching of Speech to the Deaf, 251

American Sign Language (Ameslan), 208, 220, 225; introduced in U.S., 211–221; origins, 218–220; spoken language contrasted, 229–236; combination of elements, 232; economy of, 232–234

Ameslan. *See* American Sign Language

Amman, J. C., 195, 196

Anatomical studies, 22

Aristotle, 22, 23, 79

Arousal, 103–104

Articulation, 112–114, 151, 152, 198–203, 248–252. *See also* Oralism

Audio active language laboratory, 200–201

Auditory training, 253, 271–272

Autism, in wild boy, 176–178

Aversive stimulation, 121

Avoidance conditioning, 62

Azy d'Etavigny, 150

Beauséjour, 257, 259, 260

Bébian, R. A., 220, 234

Behavior modification, 165, 182

Bicêtre, 5, 6, 55, 173; Séguin's programs, 265–266; visitor's account, 270–275, 277–278

Békésy, Georg von, 200

Bell, Alexander Graham, 212–213, 251

Bellugi, Ursula, 233

Berthier, Ferdinand, 243, 247

Blanchet, A. L., 247, 249

Body location in sign language, 229, 232

Bonaparte, Lucien, 4, 14, 15, 126

Bonaventura, Saint, 220

Bonet, Juan Pablo, 151, 195, 196, 197, 220, 221

Bonnaterre, Pierre-Joseph (Abbé), 11–17, 58, 68, 87, 170, 172, 177; report on wild boy, 33–48

Bordeaux Institute, 86

Bory de Saint-Vincent, J. B., 171

Bousquet, Dr. (Itard's eulogist), 179, 257, 259

Braidwood, John, 212, 213

Braidwood, Thomas, 212, 213, 249

Breathing exercises, 199–200, 252

Breissan, Anne (Itard's half-sister), 245

Bridgman, Laura, 250

Brown, Roger, 141

Buffon, Georges-Louis Leclerc, Comte de, 20, 27, 137, 151

Casa dei Bambini, 281–282, 285

Category learning, 141–144

Celestine Cloister, 83, 86

Chalkholder, 145–146

Champagny, Jean-Baptiste, de Nompère de, Duke of Cadore, 133, 134

Cheneau, Yves, 179

Children's houses, 281–282, 285

Clarke School, 251

Clerc, Laurent, 220, 221, 235, 237, 243, 244, 248, 251; compared with Massieu, 210–211; agrees to bring sign language to United States, 216–217; goes to Hartford, 217–218

Cogswell, Alice, 211, 214–216, 217

Cogswell, Dr., 211, 213
Collective work, 277–278
Commands, learning to follow, 276–277
Comenius, 93, 95
Compositor's bench, 122–123, 129
Condillac, Etienne Bonnot de, 21, 25, 26, 54; statue, 27, 92; knowledge, and theory, 73–74; Itard, influence on, 73, 78; chateau analogy, 75; sensory experience, 75–76; the mute, denied memory and reasoning, 79; Epée's sign language, opinion of, 81–82; Sicard, influence on, 86; analytic method, 91; theory of mind, tested by Itard, 92–95; education, idea of strict progression, 93; intellectual development in children, 94; education, knowledge of pupil's needs, 95; perception and attention, 101–102
Consonants: confusion by hearing handicapped, 186–187; discrimination, 190–192; progression, Itard's, 198–199, 201–203
Constans-Saint-Estève, J.-J., 7–10, 12, 14, 83
Coordination training, 269–270
Corvisart, Jean, 74, 259
Creativity, 145–146
Cuvier, Georges, Baron, 56

Daubenton, Louis, 19
Deaf: sign vs. spoken language, 207; sign language, 208–209; disadvantages, Itard's reasons, 209; development of intellect with sign, 225–226; German schools, 250. See also Deaf-mutes
Deaf, education of: compared to teaching orangutans, 23; projects for reform, 86; and Condillac, 91; begins in U.S., 211–221; advantages of sign, 220–226; reading as complement to sign, 225
Deaf, oral education of, 150, 152, 185–193, 195–196, 222–226, 240–241, 249–254; instructional devices, 186; discrimination training, 189–193; breathing exercises, 199–200; imitation training, 200–201; Itard's, 207, 238–239; opposition to, 249–250. See also Oralism

Deaf-mutes: boy from Chartres, 54; instruction, influence on Itard, 78; medical treatment of, 186; writing and reading, Itard's concern with, 241
Décade philosophique: report on wild boy, 127–129; describes proper examination, 173
Decroly, Ovide, 95
Defoe, Daniel, 29, 197
De Gérando. See Gérando
Dalgarno, George, 197
De l'Epée. See Epée
Dennis, Wayne, 172, 175, 176
Descartes, Réné, 19, 23, 74
Deschamps (teacher of deaf), 122
Destutt de Tracy, Antoine, 172
Dictation, by sign, 82, 86, 87
Digby, Sir Kenelm, 196
Diderot, Denis, 12, 27
Discrimination: difficulties, 120, 121; of letters, 122; of consonants, 190–192
Discrimination training, 120, 121, 135, 136; for hearing-handicapped, 187–193
Disease, influence of socialization, 104

Echoic behavior, 113
Ecole Normale Supérieure, 86
Economy of sign language, 232–234
Education: and the mentally retarded, 77–78, 237–239; of wild boy, philosophical bases, 92; shift of focus from materials to learners, 94–95; of American deaf, beginnings, 211–221; in morality, 276–278; of senses, 271–274. See also Deaf, education of
Education Nouvelle, 95
Empiricism, 5
Emotional development, 154–157
Encoding of signs, 235–236
Enfantin, Barthélemy Prosper (Père Enfantin), 263
English, contrasted to Ameslan, 229–236
Enlightenment, 19, 26, 53
Epée, Charles-Michel (Abbé de l'), 74, 150, 154, 197, 207, 211, 212, 218, 219, 220, 221, 226, 234, 235, 236, 244, 285; begins deaf-mute instruction, 78; influence of Locke, 78; advocate of sign, 79, 197; development and method of sign, 79–82; influence of Condillac, 81;

Index   350